FIRE IN THE WIND

THE LIFE OF DICKEY CHAPELLE

FIRE IN THE WIND

THE LIFE OF
DICKEY
CHAPELLE

Roberta Ostroff

BALLANTINE BOOKS
NEW YORK

Grateful acknowledgment is made to Macmillan Publishing
Company for permission to reprint "I Have a Rendezvous
with Death" from *Poems* by Alan Seeger
(New York: Charles Scribner's Sons, 1916).

Library of Congress Cataloging-in-Publication Data
Ostroff, Roberta.
Fire in the wind : the life of Dickey Chapelle / Roberta Ostroff.—1st ed.
p.   cm.
Includes bibliographical references and index.
ISBN 0-345-36274-8
1. Chapelle, Dickey, 1919–1965.   2. War correspondents—United
States—Biography.   3. News photographers—United States—Biography.
I. Title.
PN4878.C44O84   1992
070.4'333'092—dc20
[B]   91-92146
CIP

Text design by Debby Jay

Manufactured in the United States of America

First Edition: March 1992

10 9 8 7 6 5 4 3 2 1

This book is for my mother and father,
for keeping the faith.

CONTENTS

III. AGAINST ALL ODDS

ACKNOWLEDGMENTS

I WOULD LIKE to acknowledge the people who helped me in the journey of this book, some spiritually and creatively, others in practical ways that I found to be equally important: Brook Simons; Lorraine Tilden; my agent, Madeleine Morel; Susan McRae, for her loyal attention to the first gnarly draft; my editors at Ballantine, Betsy Lerner, Joëlle Delbourgo, and the ever-perceptive Ashton Applewhite; Stevie Blick; Kay Chapelle; Floyd A. Rappaport; Jerry Chamales; Richard Benson; Alex Abella for transcribing Tony Questa's manuscript; Dickey's brother, Robert P. Meyer, and his wife, Marian Meyer; Dickey's niece, Betsy Meyer, for her enthusiasm and detective work; Charlotte Woellager, for hunting down Dickey's childhood friends; Stan Malick and Kathy Wentworth, Golda Meir Library, University of Wisconsin, Milwaukee; Harold L. Miller, reference archivist, Myrna Williamson, Andy Kraushaak, Christine Schelshorn Iconographic Collections, the State Historical Society of Wisconsin; the erudite former American counsel in Budapest, Richard Selby; Colonel Philip J. Fehlen; Mary Jane and Sergeant Robert Morrisey for their personal reminiscences of Dickey; Nancy Palmer, Dickey's photo agent, for squirreling away all that stuff and letting me at it; Bob Poos; Marty Casey, for getting me to the Cuban exile community; the late Louise Meyer; Harold Haas, historian, Lighthouse Squadron Association, Milwaukee. And to my husband, Jón Páll Bjarnason, who was always there.

INTRODUCTION

I FIRST HEARD about Dickey Chapelle seventeen years ago, as a free-lance journalist and fellow at the American Film Institute. Along with other literate sorts, I was part of a desperate search by the faculty to find the perfect fellow and keep the funding coming in. A year before, a whole flock of visual artists was chosen. The year of my appearance, journalists were going strong. Another fellow, a former correspondent for a news weekly, held Dickey up to me as the romantic ideal of his youth, the definitive woman combat reporter. He had met her while a graduate student at the University of Missouri in 1963, where Dickey had come to accept first prize in the Magazine Picture Story category of the twentieth annual "Pictures of the Year" competition, co-sponsored by the National Press Photographers Association, the University of Missouri School of Journalism, and the *World Book Encyclopedia*. The prize was for her ground-breaking picture story "Helicopter War in South Viet Nam" in the November 1962 issue of *National Geographic* magazine, the first time a combat-ready American was photographed in Vietnam. My friend, an egotistical young man whose taste in women ran toward willowy blondes, found himself smitten by the tiny, nearsighted, middle-aged woman with the voice of a marine drill instructor, whose reputation for "eyeballing" had made her a legend. He claimed that for the next several years he searched for a willowy blonde with the heroic guts of Dickey Chapelle.

In 1986 I was hired to write a screenplay based on the life of Dickey

Chapelle. By the time the first draft was finished, so was the film company. I accepted this not uncommon event with the ho-hum cynicism of a true Hollywood veteran but I could not as readily dismiss its subject, whom I'd come to admire, and who, I was certain, would return to obscurity.

Regardless of her astounding life, or quite possibly because of it, Dickey Chapelle is not discussed in the few books about important women journalists, nor in any detail by professors of journalism. She is mentioned only in passing, in studies of the press in Vietnam.

Her life was so obviously different from my own, yet I sensed a connection—and not only because we were both free-lancers, independent, strong women. Uh-uh. The search for the connection has fueled this biography. Her life was spent seeking danger, and it didn't stop when she turned forty—indeed that's when she hit her stride. She learned to parachute with the special forces and began to reap hard-earned journalistic rewards. The only combat I covered was on the streets of Los Angeles, only once hearing the sound of sniper fire. There was nothing seductive about it, though it did get the adrenaline pumping, as I cowered with my male photographer on the floor of a squad car. But there was no siren song accompanying this experience, no feeling of being part of something bigger than myself, the feeling that made combat Dickey's compulsion.

Dickey was a woman who'd gone full bore out, pulled out all the stops, driven by her own demons, conviction, and intent on taking charge of her destiny. Weighed down by the America of the Depression, the Second World War, and the repressive fifties, she knew that in order to do what she wanted, she'd have to outfox the boy's club mentality of the world of foreign correspondents. So she created a public persona that gave her freedom. But it also ensnared her.

The conflict was apparent in the descriptions that survive her: freak, adrenaline junkie, flaming crusader for truth, crazed commie hater, hero, military groupie, sex-crazed broad, phony. Was all this said of her simply because she was a hell of a determined woman whose ambition steam-rolled those who got in her way? Or was she, as some of her actions demonstrate, a useful innocent, a naive tool of the CIA, the right-wing *Reader's Digest,* and other assorted opportunists? She was all of these. She was also as dedicated as any religious convert to the truth as she saw it. But she did not fare well in issues falling outside her midwestern morality of black and white, good guy against bad, and toward the end of her life, the indistinguishable grays the world had become sent her searching harder, further, for the moral certainty of her youth. She looked for it in causes and commitments, ever more desperate forays. Her career suffered and lost professional objectivity as she strove after her elusive truth, becoming increasingly caught up in stories that put her up against the mushrooming government censorship of her time, receiving little support from her colleagues. Her way of life, a series of searches for absolutes, became incompatible with the times in which she lived. Combat, with all its uncertainty, became the only accountable activity with a logical end point. But by 1962 even this certainty was vanishing as combat became an impersonal, push-button proposition.

"Here and now in the missile age I fear that I can die not because I am less worthy to live than someone of another creed committed against mine," she wrote that year from Vietnam, "but just because one of the two missile installations, neither of which I have ever seen, has a mechanical malfunction. . . . Even the human will is lost in that kind of shuffle of machinery." Four years later she would die in that country as she went marching after her truth. She paid it no lip service but pursued it in combat from World War II to Vietnam with a deliberateness that constantly enraged government news censors and won begrudging admiration from her bemused colleagues. She sloughed through mud, jumped from planes, and endured the intense discomforts of jungle and desert, apparently never losing her sense of humor, all in the name of "eyeballing" her story.

On a scroll presented by the Women's National Press Club in Washington to the Overseas Press Club in New York at memorial services for Dickey, she was lauded as "the kind of reporter all women in journalism openly or secretly aspire to be. She was always where the action was. . . ." Dickey Chapelle inspired. Her memory was further honored by the marines, who named a hospital in Vietnam for her; by the 82nd Airborne, who named a drop zone for her; and by a Dickey Chapelle transcontinental train carrying gifts to Vietnamese children.

After my initial amazement about her larger-than-life heroics subsided, I became obsessed with uncovering the woman behind the legend, and "finding" Dickey demanded diligent tenacity. She was, like Kris Kristofferson's lyrics, "a walking contradiction, partly truth and partly fiction," created by Georgette Louise Meyer, a pudgy, ebullient girl from Milwaukee, Wisconsin, whose lust for adventure placed her in a man's world from the time she could form complete sentences. She became, alternately, Dickey Chapelle, sex kitten; Dickey Chapelle, honorary marine; Dickey Chapelle, tough professional; and always Dickey Chapelle, a sentimental dame who led with her heart. This conflict was manifested by her varied appearances. Descriptions and photographs range from a scrupulously dressed woman who favored tailored suits to an unkempt creature who had lived too long among the troops. She was intermittently "sexy" or "masculine," "feminine," and a "paper doll"; she was "asexual," "fat," and "dumpy"; she was "slender" and "blond." Her stepson described her as "better than pretty: she was interesting!" All these roles produced some bewildering contradictions, not only in her personal relationships but in her disconcerting idealism, pushing her into bizarre political alliances, rushing her headlong into some of history's bitter wars and lost causes, such as the exiled "Cuban Freedom Fighters" raids against Fidel Castro. And, once in a losing game, her temperament was such that she was unwilling to extricate herself until the bitter end. This same reeling romanticism gave her the fortitude at forty-one to jump out of airplanes to cover foot soldiers, and to embody the inspiring belief that if you want it badly enough, whatever it is, you can get it. No doubt the highest tribute to this persona was the inclusion of Dickey Chapelle in the gung ho comic strip of the 1950s and 1960s, Steve Canyon. But even this accolade was flawed: it spelled her name wrong.

Trying to discover the real person behind a myth is a little like setting out down a lonely country road in the face of a blizzard warning. You trust you'll make it, but as your windshield snows up, you're not too certain. Beyond the constant retelling of Dickey's heroics, her bravery and her grit, there was precious little knowledge of the woman.

Had Dickey Chapelle not been a pack rat, this biography would never have been written. Fortunately Dickey lived before the era of the inexpensive long-distance phone call, so she wrote letters. She made copies of all of them, which she saved, along with shopping lists and receipts from the telephone company. She left clues in her reporter's notebooks.

Dickey Chapelle had few intimates. The people who knew her best, her mother, Aunt George, and Tony Chapelle, were dead. It was apparent that Chapelle set up this screen, allowing her acquaintances—and everyone she knew was an acquaintance—to know only what serviced the myth, usually limiting their familiarity to a specific role in her life. Ten minutes into an interview with one of her so-called friends, it became obvious they knew less about her than I. Few knew if she was married, divorced, a mother; few knew where she called home. Larry Hughes, the editor of her autobiography, remarked that "she left no trail" and was relieved to find a living relative to whom to send a small royalty check after holding on to it for decades.

Hence, the marines knew her as a good marine; the CIA's Ed Lansdale saluted her as a compatriot and "good girl guerrilla"; childhood friends thought of her as "weird." As most were married, her lovers preferred anonymity, though all felt affection for her. One described her as giving him the best loving when gunfire went down.

The more I gleaned, the clearer it became that these contradictions and inconsistencies were for her a necessity. For example, Dickey's 1962 autobiography, *What's a Woman Doing Here?*, was fascinating—for what she chose to delete. She was scrupulous in omitting events that would debunk her carefully crafted image and, from her point of view, threaten her livelihood. Nearly one-third of the book is devoted to heavily self-edited travails in Hungary, where she was imprisoned for fifty-three days during the 1956 revolution, ostensibly for entering the country without a visa on a mercy mission. Investigation makes clear that her story was a cover. I conjecture that her real motivation was a lot more interesting, if less of a 1950s-style fairy tale: she was involved in espionage, and it backfired. In her autobiography she devotes little more than a few lines to her family, her aunts and mother, while her voluminous correspondence with them revealed an uncommonly close and influential relationship. She barely mentioned her husband of fifteen years, her mentor-cum-tormentor, Tony Chapelle. She wrote her autobiography in the narrow confines of her times, the stifling hothouse of 1961, when the greatest sin of all was nonconformity.

Though Dickey did not consciously set out to be a nonconformist, the life she chose to live demanded it. To succeed, she had to disregard her gender and become an adventure girl. This persona provided her with the protection she needed to realize her destiny, but like all disguises, it exacted a price. She was in constant conflict. And that is where I connected with Dickey. Is there any woman whose pursuit of an independent destiny in our society has not involved conflict, even deceit? And who, in consequence, has not paid some price? Dickey took it to the furthest extreme; she paid stiff fines. She was a woman intent to be the best, to go as far as she could—on her own.

Dickey was bright—indeed, so brilliant in mathematics that she earned a full scholarship to the Michigan Institute of Technology in 1935. The immediacy of her photos had tremendous power. Though not the photographic equal of Margaret Bourke-White, she was a committed journeyman photographer who would spend months on assignments other photographers would have given a few days or none at all. Bill Garrett, her editor at *National Geographic,* said, "She was a reporter who didn't kid herself that she was great." She was no Margaret Bourke-White, nor would she compare to contemporary woman photographers like Susan Meisielas, Eve Arnold, or Mary Ellen Mark. The value of her photos was their authenticity, which meant the world to her. They were quality snapshots of events she eyewitnessed, events few photographers had the courage to seek out. The frames did not yield poetry, but reality. They were I think her way of seeing and then proving to disbelieving editors that she indeed was there. Her writing for publication had the same utilitarian quality. The value of what she wrote was where it originated, in the eye of the storm. Always needing to prove herself, she ventured where few other correspondents dared. Some of her best and most moving writing is in the immediacy of her notebooks from Vietnam in 1960–61, which I quote from in the text.

Dickey's correspondence, along with boxes of her mostly unprocessed photographic work, unpublished versions of her autobiography, miscellaneous drafts of at least one other book, articles, news clippings, ninetynine reporter's notebooks—spanning thirty-five years of her life—take up eighteen boxes and ninty nine reporter's notebooks at the archives of the Wisconsin Historical Society at the University of Wisconsin at Madison. This material contains the parts of Dickey she scrupulously omitted from her public image yet went to elaborate lengths to preserve, entrusting it to be archived before leaving for her last fateful trip to Vietnam, which of course raises another question. Did she in fact know that she wouldn't be coming back? I believe it entered her mind every time she set out on a patrol, and that she'd made her peace with its inevitability, in charge of her destiny to the very end, dying exactly where she wanted to, on a disputed piece of earth following a marine point.

Except for interviews I conducted, I have drawn exclusively on the Chapelle archives and the bibliography listed at the end of the book.

Amazing as it may seem, Dickey Chapelle saw and lived all the events that follow.

If ever there were a conflict when the issue of press access was front and center, it was the recent Persian Gulf war. Knowing how she despised any government control of the press, I cannot help wondering what Dickey would have done. I'd like to think that she would have beaten the pack—as she always did—by parachuting into Kuwait City.

R.O.

Altadena, California
March 1, 1991

I have a rendezvous with Death
At some disputed barricade—
When Spring comes back with rustling
And apple blossoms fill the air.
I have a rendezvous with Death
When Spring brings back blue days and fair.
It may be he shall take my hand
And lead me into his dark land
And close my eyes and quench my breath—
It may be I shall pass him still.
I have a rendezvous with Death
On some scarred slope of battered hill
When Spring comes round again this year
And the first meadow flowers appear.
God knows 'twere better to be deep
Pillowed on silk and scented down—
Where love throbs out in blissful sleep
Pulse nigh to pulse and breath to breath
Where hushed awakenings are dear.
But I've a rendezvous with Death
At mid-night in some flaming town
When Spring trips north again this year—
And I to my pledged word am true—
I shall not fail that rendezvous.

> "I Have a Rendezvous with Death"
> by Alan Seeger

Found among Dickey Chapelle's personal papers.

FIRE IN THE WIND

THE LIFE OF DICKEY CHAPELLE

Prologue

November 2, 1965—
On the front near Chu Lai, South Vietnam

CAPTAIN Philip J. Fehlen hung up the field telephone and winced. Whenever Fehlen's outfit, B Company, First Battalion, Seventh Marines, was going on an operation, Major Mike Stiles at the Third Amphibious Marines seemed to herd the press over in droves.

This particular telephone call from the public information officer in Da Nang announced the arrival of five reporters due in that evening, the night before D-Day of Operation Black Ferret. The hook was that one of them was a woman.

Fehlen was struck by a disquieting thought. What if it were Marguerite Higgins? The sexy, blond syndicated journalist who'd been in the area a month earlier was legendary. During the Korean War she'd reportedly said that if she had to fuck every general to get the Pulitzer Prize, she would—and she'd gotten it. Whether or not she'd fucked them all, he didn't need the aging siren around his horny nineteen-year-old troops the night before an operation.

"What next?" wondered Fehlen, looking at his notebook, sweat-stained courtesy of the jungle's one-hundred-degree-plus temperature. When the hawk-nosed twenty-seven-year-old, former Stanford University track captain stood up, his nearly seven-foot height caused him to stoop slightly as he leaned outside the tent. The wide Song Tra Bong, a river he had come to know well, glistened at the edge of the encamp-

3

ment. The California-born surfer would watch the primitive fishing boats floating down the river on their way to the South China Sea. Evenings were the river's active time, when dragons woke and echoed back the sounds of war.

The ripe, mild November air wasn't oppressive compared with last August when Fehlen had first arrived in Chu Lai. Even the mosquitoes dive-bombed with less intensity now. The leeches, too, seemed somewhat satiated. In just four months he had adapted so well to these crawling creatures that only a pricking suck would wake him, and then only for the time it took to break an iodine stick over its rubbery hide.

The fertile river bottomland that extended nearly to the dunes, bordering the big American airfield at Chu Lai four miles away, was strung with hamlets. The mostly level ground was dense with rice paddies, lush coconut palms, and banyan trees. In the afternoon haze, the peasants and lumbering water buffalo seemed to drift under the clouds. This was Fehlen's zone of assignment, the southern sector position north of the village of Binh Son and the Song Tra Bong. Like all marine positions in the area, Fehlen's was set up to guard the airfield at Chu Lai.

Beyond the river more rice paddies ended at the country's only highway, named Highway One. Built by the French during their ascendancy, the north-south road ran the entire length of the country. A railroad followed the paved artery, but the enemy, called Viet Cong, had shut it down. The highway paralleled the rugged coast, reminding Fehlen of the treacherous roads of Baja California in the way it snaked along the harsh jungly Annam Mountains, past the Viet Cong sanctuaries. The next day's search-and-clear operation, Black Ferret, was designed to push the Viet Cong southward toward the river, where they would be cut off from the hamlets that supplied food and recruits.

Fehlen watched a peasant woman in black pajamas, her head covered by a cone-shaped hat woven of bamboo. She moved slowly through the paddies, her back curved under the weight of a basket on carrying poles of bamboo balanced on her shoulders. There were no wheelbarrows for a peasant woman's burdens, be they rice, chickens, or pigs; and when the monsoons flooded the trails along the paddies, the women would scurry back and forth across the flooded land with their back-bending loads.

He wondered if the woman ever thought about the war or what kind of weapon might kill her. Did she panic when an airplane circled overhead or when an artillery shell crumped nearby? Maybe her meaningless death would come during a lull in the afternoon at the hands of a terrorist who had already assassinated her leader and burned her village.

Later that afternoon, Albert A. Allen, the gunnery sergeant, arrived with a list of the reporters. Fehlen relaxed. The woman was not Higgins (then at Walter Reed Army Medical Center dying of a rare parasitic disease possibly contracted in Vietnam), but someone he'd never heard of, Mrs. Dickey Chapelle. She was covering the operation for the weekly Dow Jones newspaper, the *National Observer,* and WOR radio in New York. The list also included an NBC cameraman, a couple of marine combat reporters, and a free-lance journalist he knew from an earlier operation. "When it rains it really snows," commented the gunnery sergeant.

Fehlen ordered Allen to toss Communications Officer Livermore out of his tent and make it feminine for the lady. "Check her out when she arrives," ordered Fehlen. "She could still be a screwball." He trusted Allen.

In truth, Fehlen always looked forward to visits from the press, despite their annoying habits when it came time for filing deadlines and making headlines. In these first days of American combat troops in Vietnam, most reporters covering the war were professionals seasoned by battles from World War II through Algeria and Korea, places Fehlen had only read about. And even though they tended to exaggerate, particularly when lubricated by alcohol, Fehlen admired them. One of them would invariably offer to contact his folks when they got stateside, and he appreciated the gesture.

The press corps arrived as Fehlen was inside his tent, planning the next day's "walk in the sun." Fehlen disliked the Pentagon-ordered search-and-clear missions, the tactical operations that this war seemed to consist of. Even the operation names like tomorrow's Black Ferret were rumored to be cooked up by some guy sitting in a Capitol Hill office, unlike such infamous World War II operations as Operation Bread Basket, whose names had meaning. If once in a while they found evidence of the enemy, they inevitably lost a couple of troops to booby traps or sniper fire in the process. Maybe that was why it was beginning to feel like a long war.

Allen, the gunnery sergeant, popped his head into the tent. "She's no Higgins," he said, adding, "she's been here before." Then he disappeared.

Well, that was good news, thought Fehlen. Although he had much to do before dawn, Fehlen broke out the Scotch and invited the press into what he laughingly referred to as his "spacious tent."

"Captain Fehlen?" A low, smoky voice cut through the tent. He looked up. No mistaking that silhouette for Higgins's curves, he thought.

"Dickey Chapelle," she announced, sweeping into the tent, trailing mud and smelling of tobacco and a French perfume called Nuit de Longchamps. She was a small, birdlike woman wearing a rumpled pair of custom-tailored fatigues. Her feet were encased in crud-covered jungle boots, her fatigues covered with military patches. The captain recognized the parachute wings of the 101st Airborne's First Special Forces on her left breast pocket flap. Her right pocket flap sported the paratrooper wings of the South Vietnamese airborne.

She was wearing an Australian bush hat, the left brim snapped up in the rakish manner of the U.S. Special Forces and its center pierced with a well-worn Marine Corps insignia. Also sewn to her hat was the lightning-bolt-and-sword emblem of the elite U.S. Special Forces, the Green Berets. On her shoulder was the bamboo-and-swallow patch of the crack South Vietnamese irregulars, the Fighting Sea Swallows, former scourge of the Viet Cong. A microphone was stuck on her hat, with a wire running down to a tape recorder attached to a web belt. She looked like a cross between Queen for a Day and an Eagle Scout.

Under this assemblage, a high, shiny forehead collided with oversize black, harlequin-framed glasses that flared out from her small nose like bat wings. A pair of incongruously delicate pearl earrings flashed from her earlobes, her one concession to femininity. She wore them, Dickey had told a friend, so that despite her masculine voice and stride, she would not be mistaken for a lesbian or a marine.

She moved to Fehlen's cluttered table with big, confident strides, head high, arms swinging forward, and shook his hand, angling her small, pointed chin directly over his military maps. As she moved, two battered Leica cameras, one under each arm held by crossed neck straps, bumped against her body. Film cartridges, fastened on the straps with wide, green duct tape, rumbled above her waist.

Bending forward, she studied the map as though it were a familiar photograph, patting it with her hand. Her wrist and fingers were swollen with ugly, infected mosquito bites. One particularly nasty sore oozed from her right trigger finger.

She bent down, reaching into the top of her boot, and in true marine style pulled a pack of Pall Mall cigarettes from her sock. She plucked a gold Dunhill lighter from one of her utility pockets and lowered the cigarette to the flame. In the light of the fire, her face looked sun-baked and leathery. Fehlen figured her for fifty. She snapped the lighter shut, dropped it back into her pocket, and exhaled. Then, backing away from the map, she fixed Fehlen with an engaging smile and said: "Something about setting out on a mission early in the morning starts the whole day off with a bang. Don't you agree, Captain?"

The booming voice reminded Fehlen of any number of drill instructors. It seemed out of place coming from the tiny woman.

"Well, we still have a couple of hours left," quipped one of the correspondents, pushing a bottle in her direction, "so relax." She ignored the offer, pacing with her big steps around the tent.

"I haven't had such cushy quarters since Iwo, when the navy gave me the sick wardroom," she said. The comment brought forth a series of groans from her colleagues, but Fehlen leaned forward. "Iwo?" he asked, impressed.

"Chapelle's been on every front since World War Two," offered one of the men.

"Yeah," said another, yawning. "She even landed with the marines on Okinawa, right, Dickey?" Actually she hadn't, but she wasn't one to deflate her own legend.

Despite their lack of enthusiasm, the reporters knew all about her achievements, the same way they knew how many runs were scored by Willie Mays, the champion San Francisco Giants outfielder. "Not bad for an old broad," she said, winking at Fehlen with a grin. "I just wanted to introduce myself. You have a lot of work to do. I hope your radio man isn't put out."

Fehlen waved his hand dismissively. "Ah, Livermore, he doesn't mind a bit."

"But seriously," she went on, inhaling the cigarette smoke deeply, "I would much prefer to sleep with the troops." She paused for a well-measured beat to see her colleagues' reactions, adding, "In a foxhole."

"Hey, Dickey," one of the reporters shouted, taking a slug of Scotch. "Where'd you get the paratrooper wings? In a box of Cracker Jacks?"

Over the laughter, she cocked her head in his direction. He was very young. In his spanking-new combat outfit, she thought he looked like a magazine advertisement.

"I earned them," she answered matter-of-factly. She lowered her head, looking at her wing-covered pocket flaps. "I swear to God I don't know where I'd put a third pair." She looked straight at the young man. "You know, I bet when I was dodging bullets in Hungary, you were still in journalism school." Then she smiled at her colleagues and, turning to leave, bade them good night.

The tent grew quiet. One reporter sighed, like most of his colleagues happy to see her go. He had run into Dickey earlier in the year on an unbelievably hot afternoon in the Mekong Delta, one hundred miles south of Saigon, when she was jeeping off on some dangerous errand. Chapelle didn't wear well, tending to laugh too long and telling the same old war stories over and over. He didn't know whether she was an exceedingly brave woman or just panicked about growing old. "Good riddance," he uttered inside the tent. "The only time that woman shuts up is when she's lighting a cigarette."

THE NEXT MORNING was D-Day for Operation Black Ferret. The company was transported by trucks to the highway. Dickey hooked up with Lieutenant Mauriski's third platoon out on the right flank, which proceeded up the high cane valley along the Song Tra Bong. Dickey marched in step. When snipers opened fire, she hit the dirt like an axed tree, a straight-knee belly flop. Impressed, Mauriski noted in his log, "She's a veteran."

By late afternoon, with muggy rain clouds filling the sky, Fehlen secured the only high ground in the area. It was a small, cane-covered hill, the obvious place for the night's bivouac, so the lanky captain was not surprised by the elaborate welcome. The hill was crawling with enemy *punji* traps—foul iron spikes coated with human excrement and planted in camouflaged holes. There were also, he estimated, hundreds of *punji* stakes—eighteen inches of sharp, excrement-covered bamboo staves concealed in high grass at an angle. They sliced feet like razors.

Fehlen looked up. Above him, lumbering through the afternoon sky, was the chopper carrying the battalion commander, Lt. Col. Paul V. Kelly. As the rotors began kicking up the earth below and the big metal bird went into its squat, snipers from one of the hamlets below the hill started firing. One of the machine gunners opened up and chopped a Charlie out of a tree. Running full bore, Mauriski's platoon pursued the other sniper into the hamlet, losing him in the cane brake. Dickey trotted along with the platoon, her recorder running as she whispered, "The enemy is so close, I can see his feet."

Fehlen set off to canvass the area, accompanied by his bodyguard, an unruly sergeant in need of constant supervision, and the radio engineer. Fehlen's swagger stick tripped the matted cover of a burrow known as a "spider's hole." The sergeant lowered his rifle at the two Vietnamese peasants crouched inside. Under interrogation, one of them informed the translator that a battalion of Viet Cong were in front of them, planning to attack the company that night.

"Great, that's great, Fehlen," chirped Dickey, pacing back and forth inside his tent later that afternoon. Her hands were tucked behind her back, and she moved forward with the bouncing motion of a gleeful child. "Your company'll be excellent bait."

Fehlen nodded, trying to scratch out a defense in his notebook. "I just hope the reinforcements get here before they attack."

"No," she gasped, whipping off her glasses. "Don't you see?" she demanded as if he were mentally impaired. "This is your chance to be a hero. You'll get the Navy Cross for sure. Why, they might even want to make you commandant." Her blue eyes lit up her plain face at the prospect. "I can't wait." She stopped her pacing only long enough to fix him with an eager smile. She didn't look old anymore. She glowed like a schoolgirl.

"Dickey," Fehlen responded evenly, "this whole thing is making me kind of nervous. I don't have that many guys. I just want to get us out of this alive."

She shook her head so fast that her cap flipped off. A few strands of not particularly pretty blond hair fell loose from a prim bun adorned with an old-fashioned green velvet bow. She hurriedly pushed the cap back down.

"Look," she said with authority, "you'll destroy these guys." She crouched on the ground, her kneecaps cracking. "The Oriental has always underestimated the marines in defensive positions. It's been going on since the Second World War, Fehlen. They'll come running in. You'll gun them down." She spoke as if she were a three-star general. "You got some reserve?" Fehlen nodded. "Okay," she continued, leaping up. "Maybe they'll penetrate a little, but they'll sweep by." Fehlen could see that the woman was definitely looking forward to the prospect. "You'll be a hero," she stated smugly.

Even though she spoke as an insider, with as much authority as one of his military strategy manuals, Fehlen couldn't quite reconcile himself with her heroic vision. A hero to him was John Wayne in *The Sands of Iwo Jima,* walking into the water and smoking his cigarette all the way to the end. Real cool. Fehlen was not cool. He was nervous as hell waiting on the reinforcements. But he decided to prepare for the attack, and he did it much the way Dickey had suggested.

Fehlen put his boys in real tight against the hamlet. Even with his officers and noncommissioned men, it was impossible to remove the mass of *punji* stakes that covered the hill. In the twilight, he feared somebody would detonate a VC booby trap by tripping its nylon fishing wire. Miraculously, only one injury occurred, when the third platoon radio man put a stake through his instep and was out of the operation.

At sunset, Delta Company arrived along with General Lewis W. Walt, the junior major general in the corps and commanding general of the Third Marine Amphibious Force. The reinforcements brought four 81-mm mortars and two 106 recoilless rifles. Dickey looked disappointed. "There goes your Navy Cross," she said, sighing. "They'll never attack now."

At dinner with General Walt, Dickey brightened. At fifty-two the strapping, big-headed Walt, with his marine-regulation haircut, was a three-star general and the holder of two Navy Crosses. He had been hand-picked by Marine Commandant Wallace M. "Wally" Greene, Jr., to lead the marines of the I Corps in the northern area of South Vietnam.

Although Walt had not known Dickey during World War II, he met her shortly after the war ended. Then, as now, she seemed to him to be more energy than woman. Seated at his table, she was a blur of activity, a cigarette in one hand, a forkful of food in the other, eating, talking, and drinking simultaneously. When Walt asked her about the worn marine insignia pinned to the center of her hat, she spluttered, "Commandant Greene gave it to me. I was poleaxed!"

Later that night on the *punji*-staked hill, some of the noncommissioned officers and a few reporters stood around the company command post trading jokes and talking war. Dickey stood off by herself, swinging at the needle-nosed mosquitoes strafing her from all sides. She had long stopped hoping for acceptance. She didn't go drinking with them to prove she was one of the boys, although with her gruff, loud voice and penchant for wearing fatigues, she had often been mistaken for one. She knew that her friend Bill Garrett, the *National Geographic* photo editor, liked to tell about the time he was with her in Ladakh, India, when she'd gotten kicked out of the woman's toilet. That same night he'd sat dumbstruck when she'd met him for dinner in a tight-fitting navy-blue knit dress. It wasn't any easier for women to figure her out. Perhaps to dispel rumors that she was a lesbian, maybe to satisfy her constant craving for attention, she liked to pass around her wallet with pictures of young marines, referring to them as her "admirers." One American woman living in Vietnam who met Dickey recalled that "you never knew what was going to come out of her mouth. She would be sitting there eating dinner, talking about some military maneuver she had just been out on, and suddenly blurt out, 'And then we had sex.' "

Despite her fame for covering combat—she had been touted on lecture series as *the* bayonet border reporter—she seemed to friends and colleagues driven by a need to prove herself better, tougher, than the far better known journalist Marguerite Higgins and photographer Margaret Bourke-White, always making it a point in her letters to her editors that she was once again either "the first woman" or had "stayed the longest and gone further forward than any reporter, man or woman."

Dickey had only one concern: keeping up. A marine information officer in Crete in 1958 had laid out the ground rules for her career covering the troops: "Just keep up with them and don't remind them of what they're missing back home." She lived her life by those words and was haunted by the specter of failure to keep up. She did not stay in the safety of the rear battalion, as many reporters did when covering conflicts, but kept up with the foot soldier or jumped with the parachut- ists. Besides, she preferred staying with the troops twenty-four hours a day, sleeping in a foxhole. Unlike the correspondents, who didn't know what to make of her, the marines accepted her as she was. She traveled with enough supplies in her small combat pack for three weeks in the field.

Friends back in New York worried about her. Her apartment building across the street from Bellevue Hospital, where she rented a one-room studio, was described by one visitor as a "tenement." She seemed always short of cash and hustled constantly for assignments. She chain-smoked, had a hacking smoker's cough, and lived on strong black coffee. The constant risks she took to cover stories had not rewarded her with plum assignments. If anything, the hard-earned assignments often backfired, resulting in imprisonment, censure from her colleagues, even injury.

But she continued. The war, battle, combat, made sense to her. It was black and white. You fucked up, you died. Nothing could be simpler, purer, more effective than that bit of knowledge. It took care of anything that could have bothered and confused her, as so much did lately. The clarity of a battleground—though it too was becoming hollow and remote with all the new technology—still reassured her.

She had to stop showing off in front of the troops. Another fall like the one she'd demonstrated with Mauriski's platoon, and they'd have to send her back to the States. Her kneecaps were throbbing; the recent surgery seemed to have made them more sensitive, not, as she had hoped, stronger.

Right before leaving New York, she had stopped by the offices of *Argosy*, the bristlingly macho magazine that had hired her despite its longtime prejudice against women contributors. She hoped to pick up an assignment in Vietnam, but *Argosy* was sending its managing editor, Milt Machlin. Machlin was, like her, in his forties. It would be his first time covering this war. She advised him to visit the Delta and to stay away from the mountains. "There's no sense killing yourself running after those kids up and down mountainsides," she said. "It's tough enough keeping up with them as it is."

Looking at the jungly, sheer mountains, she was now wondering ruefully if she shouldn't have followed her own advice. But as tough it was, no amount of pain would keep her away. In 1961, when she'd first arrived in Vietnam and it was being played down as a brushfire war with less than a dozen Western reporters covering it, she had spent seven months patrolling and parachuting with the U.S. Special Forces and the Vietnamese irregulars, marines, army, paratroopers. From then on she had taken a notably proprietary interest, determined to make Vietnam hers, the same way Korea had belonged to Marguerite Higgins and World War II to Margaret Bourke-White. Now that American ground troops had been committed, she had heard there were four hundred reporters, nearly all of them younger than she, knocking around. Fortunately for her, most of them stayed in Saigon, getting the daily battle updates as handouts from U.S. government press information officers.

Besides her distrust of all official handouts, she was a photojournalist— and there was no way she could do her job, which was covering combat, sitting in a bar and rewriting the official accounts. Others did, but she prided herself on not writing up anything she could not personally see and verify. "About as authentic as patent medicine," she'd grumble. She personally counted the critically wounded and the dead on operations she covered. She called it "eyeballing."

For two thousand years, between civil wars and foreign invasions, Vietnam had been warring. In 1954, when the French left the country after being defeated at Dien Bien Phu by the Vietminh, Vietnam became divided into a communist north and a noncommunist south. At that point the United States, in an effort to stem communist China's advance, threw its weight behind South Vietnam, sending in two hundred military advisers whose job, according to official policy and newspaper accounts, was *not* to fight, but to lead and advise the South Vietnamese troops.

Dickey quickly discovered that what she saw and what the public read about Vietnam were worlds apart. She had tried desperately to tell the real story of the military advisers whom she had personally seen die in this country since 1961, alongside the Vietnamese soldiers. She believed that American support would have been forthcoming if the truth were known. But like so much of what she was seeing lately, it went against American policy and her accounts were censored. It horrified her that handouts and news briefings were replacing eyewitness accounts. Despite her identification with the American military, she knew they were the least objective people around. Let the reporters back in Saigon file their stories off the handouts; she wanted to be free to exercise her right as a journalist to observe, report, and criticize—and see it in print. The war she had watched American boys die in four years earlier was still undeclared. She was still pushing her way onto military choppers. Only now she pushed harder. The government now was forbidden by law to provide her or any other correspondent covering the war with transportation, food, and housing. It was disconcerting to be made to feel unwelcome by her own people when all she wanted was to do her job, standing in a foxhole with mud up to her ass, waiting to be attacked.

She smelled rain. November was the country's dry season, meaning the rain came in gentle torrents instead of monsoon buckets. The moon was already arched in the sky, moving in and out of focus through the heavy clouds.

She was tired, wired, lonely, and nervous about tomorrow's operation.

She had a twelve-week contract with the *National Observer,* and she had spent nearly three weeks looking and hoping for a good action story. Although her heart was willing, she doubted if her body and her spent lungs would carry her through another war. The only other search-and-clear operation she'd gone out on, about ten days earlier, called Red Snapper, had turned up cold trails, empty tunnels, and invisible sniper fire. Yes, she was disappointed that the reinforcements of Delta Company had arrived. It would have been a front-page story if the Viet Cong had attacked, and this old broad needed a front-page story. A gentle, steady rain began.

Looking around at those apple-cheeked marines, she wondered whether they were as tough as the enemy. For years she had been harassing the military about toughening up their training. She often wondered if the American brass understood what they were up against. From her four years of observing the Viet Cong, she knew they were well-disciplined, highly motivated guerrilla fighters. They could march fifty miles a day with fifty-pound packs on their backs through the crushing heat of this slippery green hell, nourished by a ball of rice. She hoped these boys digging in around her were up to the challenge.

A marine trudged up the muddy hill, his rifle nudging a Vietnamese peasant dressed in a black shirt and floppy white trousers, captured running from a village. Under interrogation, he denied being a Viet Cong or a sympathizer. He said some sixty Viet Cong had been to his village earlier, heavily armed with mortars and moving in their direction.

There was no way to tell if this peasant was the enemy. He was probably running to save his life. He may have been running from the marines because of Viet Cong propaganda posted on the village bulletin board warning him of American torture. He may have been running because if the Viet Cong sympathizers in his village saw him talking to the marines, they would inform on him and he would be killed. Regardless of the prisoner's information, it was decided to dig in. Dickey grabbed a shovel. "I'm calling this the Hilltop Hilton," she cracked.

The young reporter she had seen the night before in Fehlen's tent walked over to her. His combat clothes still looked brand new. "I got to ask you," he said, moving closer as she shoveled, oblivious. "Are you the woman reporter who said that she'd never met a man she liked as much as war?"

"Wasn't me," she snapped. *Liking war wasn't her problem.* "What about you?" She turned to face him. "Were you the reporter who sent the wire to Saigon that read 'Arrive ten tomorrow morning. Please arrange battle'?"

He smiled, shaking his head. "Touché." He looked down at the dirt.

Well, she thought, at least he's not demonstrating against the war.

"Don't you think the front's a pretty weird place for a woman?" he asked quietly.

"Weird?" she asked above the clunking sounds of the entrenching tools. "You bet." Dickey looked up at him, pausing to whip a vagrant strand of hair back under her wet cap. "Like I've been saying for years, it's no place for a man, either. But if we're going to have wars where our men are being killed, nobody except a woman can tell the story to other women."

He asked her about being arrested in Hungary during the 1956 revolution, and she insisted fiercely that she had been "captured by soldiers." Then she told him not to take it personally, but there was a real difference between the two. He asked her about her time in the mountains of Cuba with Castro, then shook his head and wondered how she could have gotten mixed up with those ragtag anti-Castro Cubans in Florida.

"They are called action groups," she noted brusquely, "trying to reclaim their country from tyranny." She searched his face. He wasn't buying it. He was too clean and too young to know about people willing to die for what they believed in. *It wasn't that she liked war. It was no longer a question of choice.* As he walked away, she wondered if he would also one day become caught up in chasing the high—the feeling she'd once felt that kept bringing her back to war, only to elude her. Which is why, despite knowing guerrillas only shot the leader of a patrol, that's the position she chose, right behind the point. She believed if it were to be found, it would be up front. The risk was worth it.

She coughed, lighting another cigarette. Out to the west, a flare dropped by an air force plane illuminated a piece of the night. When it hit the ground, the four-foot canister turned night into day. "I guess the air force hasn't decided whose side they're on yet," Dickey chortled, loud enough for the entire encampment to hear.

She didn't know what bothered her more, the rats, bats, mosquitoes, leeches, flares, or being alone in the foxhole. She always felt better when she had somebody holding her when the fireworks started. It didn't matter how many times she'd triumphed over her rising panic, she still got scared. The fear, too, kept bringing her back.

Dickey yawned. She unlaced the jungle boots stolen from the public information office in Saigon. Even though they weren't allowed to help her, nothing said she couldn't help herself. She pulled off her muddy socks to inspect blisters the size of grapes on both feet. She would have to drain and wrap them. Her knee was swelling like a black eye. There was no getting away from it, her body was a disaster area.

She unhooked the microphone from her Australian bush hat, which had been given to her four years earlier, in Laos at Ban Hat Bay on the Nam Seine River, by a former lover, wire service photographer Clancy Stone. He had taken it off his head and placed it squarely on hers, saying, "It'll keep the sun out of your eyes and protect your face." She missed Clancy tonight with the enemy so close. Clancy loved fireworks. But after his wife had a baby, he started taking fewer chances. "When you start being too cautious," he told her, "it's time to get the hell out." So he had.

The rain slackened. The wind moving under the clouds carried the smell of the country to her, the warm, sweet, sour-mash odor of the rice paddies rising in the wet steam. When she had first humped with the Vietnamese patrols in Tay Ninh four years before, she'd been haunted by that smell and the sound the soldiers' boots made when they sloshed through the water.

"Tonight we are together, tomorrow we must part. . . ." The words to the South Vietnamese marine song floated into her fuzzy brain. She had first heard it, she recalled, on that patrol near Tay Ninh that horrible, hot July afternoon. The Vietnamese marines of the Fourth Company of the First Marine Battalion had been singing it as they set out that dawn from their barracks.

Each young man tied a two-pound ball of rice onto his web belt behind his bayonet. They expected to walk about twenty kilometers through the rice fields and the jungle before dark.

The weapons and ammo they carried were American made and heavy, having been designed for men at least a third larger. Only the point, Private First Class Ngo Sy Lien, was not heavily burdened. The thirty-one-year-old Vietnamese, a soldier for ten years, was to be married in five days. Agile and skilled, Lien had marched point so many times he simply assumed the position.

They were driven in shiny blue U.S. military aid trucks from Tay Ninh, an enemy stronghold close to the Cambodian border, to a crossroads with the cratered road to the border of Cambodia. The wreath-and-oak-leaf symbol of the military district was painted on the doors of the truck with the shield showing the red, white, and blue and clasped hands of the U.S. military aid on the tailgates.

The battalion commander, a cocky captain who had been trained at Quantico, Virginia, as a Vietnamese exchange student, was waiting for the platoons. He spoke fairly good English and thought their mission was "crummy." Instead of a swagger stick as a badge of office, he used a very short, underdecorated sword. He liked to emphasize his final commands with a downward slash of the sword across the nearest vegetation. He did this gaily as his men set out, whacking at a a bunch of red flowers, which fluttered onto the crushed blue rock of the roadway and landed at his boots.

Some ten thousand yards down the road, systematically gouged by the enemy so that no vehicle could pass, lay the objective, the village of Xom Hihn. It sat seven thousand yards from the border of Cambodia and was fired on daily by the enemy. It was deserted, except for some embattled civil guards inside its wooden garrison. Their presence was the only obstacle to the enemy's reinforcement attempts in South Vietnam.

Four platoons of South Vietnamese marines were escorting forty hired peasants, carrying ammo, through rice fields and jungle to the garrison at Xom Hihn. It was not a particularly dangerous operation, Dickey had noted on leaving the barracks at Tay Ninh. It would never be written up in a communiqué.

For the first hour they kept their file straight, a tactic that Dickey thought unfitting for such an unconventional war, where the guerrillas killed only the man in front. They progressed steadily forward, walking on the gray earth half walls that kept the water standing in the rice fields. In the lead, Lien kept his rifle at the ready, while he leapt in his tennis shoes from one wall to the next.

An old man, two young women, and a little girl were walking on the road toward Tay Ninh, carrying reed baskets. The captain's swarthy orderly stopped them by raising his hand, asked for their ID cards, then reached for their bundles. His well-muscled hands moved slowly over the bread, the clothing, and the rice in the reed baskets. The old man's face was impassive, the women were demure, and the little girl was open-eyed with curiosity. Allowed to continue, they moved through the ranks of the rear company.

Out on the point of the far flank, Private First Class Lien picked up the pace again, as did his fellow points, toward the road, inexorably forward. Dickey marched behind Lien. On the far, heat-bent horizon, she saw waves of flat fields, low earth walls, and suspicious clumps of trees, but no motion. The clouds were scudding on the blue sky, and the marines were grateful. They provided moments of shade and brought gusts of cooler air in little passing breezes. The marines lifted their sweaty faces to the clouds.

After three hours, Dickey, moving in Lien's platoon, looked down at her jungle boots. They were covered with paddy dust, but her stomach was filled with rice dipped in the salted fish sauce called *nuoc mam.* She plucked an orange jungle orchid and set it in her hair.

The going was slower now. Nobody spoke much. The breathing was harder, but that was to be expected. Lien, screened by trees, could not see his captain's sword and its gestures. All the patrol had to rely on was a marine with a radio on his back barking forward the static-filled orders from the company commander. Over the radio came word that the last five earth huts they passed had been empty, but that warm food was seen on the smoking fires. The people had been frightened out—by the marines? The enemy? Nobody knew.

Three spaced shots broke the early morning quiet about a second between each lonely pop of the enemy's MA-36 rifles. Dickey knew that the shots, because of their meticulous timing, were meant not to hit, but to signal the marines' whereabouts.

Private First Class Lien, his head circled by two large yellow butterflies, kept moving. When very young he had been trained by the French as a commando against the communist Vietminh, and watching him, Dickey thought he'd learned well the commitment *"Vous fatigué, marchez; vous blessé, marchez; vous mort, marchez."* Enemy signal or no enemy signal, she knew Lien would keep walking. She wanted to scream out the story, the tiny jungle patrol of men marching inexorably forward. . . .

There were supposed to be four Viet Cong companies in the vicinity, but they were scattered. The four marine double platoons made a solid block, so the odds were they would hit only one enemy company at a time.

The swaggering captain, whose orders she felt inferior to the training of his men, dropped his air of cool, waving the black sword blade so that it cut the sunlight, his young, impatient voice snapping out. Two mortar crews ran off the road, dropping the heavy base plate and standard and tube and cylinder of ammunition into the grass. They took their entrenchment tools off their packs and began to hack the ground, hurriedly turning out two emplacements for the 81-mm mortars.

As they worked, a dozen deep bursts of automatic fire rattled Private First Class Lien's platoon. The bursts came steadily, with barely a pause, punctuated by high-pitched angle shots.

Then it was very quiet. The two yellow butterflies that had been circling over Lien flew away.

One of the marines shouted, "We've had an accident," and ran toward Lien's platoon. Dickey had been inches in front of Lien when he'd gone down in the translucent shade of a jungle patch. She watched while the corpsmen injected him with morphine and attempted to remove the bullet from his neck, but the pain was still too intense.

When Lien got control of his voice, he uttered his last words: "In the name of Buddha." He did not send a message to his parents in North Vietnam or to the girl waiting to marry him in Saigon. The men placed him on a stretcher and wrapped him in a poncho.

Dickey wrote that the heat grew terrifying, as it often did in the Indo-Chinese afternoon, that Lien did not live long enough to know or care whether the mission on which he had gone on that purple dawn had been successful. The marines neither saw nor pursued the guerrillas. Not the lack of bravery, but the inefficiency she saw at the command level and the awareness that modern soldiering was now a push-button, long-distance game, rather than one based on personal prowess, disturbed her. She filled two notebooks trying unsuccessfully to fit the mission into an acceptable context, wryly noting that she no longer understood its "ethos." She wrote that although she understood war's morality, even enjoying the simple rigidity of its "God is on our side, good and right are *forward*, evil and wrong are *back*," its logic now escaped her; the logic that created its philosophy in the days of the sword and club, "the terrible intimacy of combat where interpreting a breath or pressure of another person can mean life or death," no longer held currency. Death by modern soldiering, she regretfully conceded, was incomplete.

"A soldier makes a pact with self and country to keep going when his every nerve cries out against it," she wrote, "to risk himself to pure chance when there is a lot of hostilely flung lead in the air. But his survival is rarely a matter of his effort or even his soldierliness."

Private First Class Lien did not die "because some man is faster in perception or harder in hitting or sturdier in the face of pain." He died because of a "bubble in an oil line or a tremor on a hand sight," because of his commander's poor orders. Its pointlessness disconcerted her. Dying didn't scare her. Indeed, one friend recalled that "she held death as lightly as a flower."

"It doesn't hurt to get killed," she wrote, pondering Lien's death. "I've been knocked unconscious often enough to be pretty sure about this." But she could not understand it in terms of modern soldiering, "since killing became something you do with a finger to a target you have to be taught to seek and see only as a flicker of a uniform or worse, a mark on a map. I suspect—I think there is a cosmic irony here some-where—that in my time may come that consummation most devoutly to be desired—the decline and fall of violence as a desirable way of life. The logic is drained out of its ethos and it just may not be any fun any more."

Control was all that remained important, control of your nerves, of your fear . . . and as for "good" and "right" and even "freedom," they were just words, just journalist's words that saluted the human need for a conviction of virtue, but she didn't see them having any content she could see or feel or touch outside her paycheck. Lien's death symbolized all that was wrong with this war. War. For her it was still the only game, but what a grubby game.

A leech had fastened itself to her arm. Realizing she was out of iodine sticks, she held the Dunhill's flame on it instead. It had stopped raining. The night sky was lit up with more air force flares, clunking onto the earth like errant floodlit meteors.

"Just hope one of them doesn't hit you on the head," somebody whispered to her. It was Fehlen, stooping over her. "I have some extra flak vests. I thought you might want one for tomorrow."

"Thanks, Fehlen. That's all I need, an extra seven pounds," she answered in a hoarse, raggedy voice. "I'm having a hard enough time keeping up." Dickey had been turning down flak jackets since the com-mander of a transport ship in Okinawa had offered her one in 1945. She explained then that the weight of the jacket combined with the eight-pound speed graphic camera made shooting action pictures too difficult. In the next twenty years her cameras had gotten lighter, but the protective garments still got in her way.

Fehlen had yet to meet a journalist who accepted his offer. He wondered if they believed they had some kind of holy dispensation. But his sense of chivalry, born of his movie heroes—the Duke, Richard Widmark, Van Heflin—pressed him to continue offering the bulky vests. After a day's patrol in broiling heat, he would unzip the vest with the appreciation of a woman kicking off her girdle. But regardless of their discomfort, he insisted his lads wear them zipped to the neck.

"I know to keep my head down," she said.

He stood up. "Okay," he answered, "I'll see you in the morning." He later mentioned he didn't know why, but even sitting there in the mud, the woman had a lot of class. "I know you're disappointed about the assault," he said, "but the game's not over yet." She watched the young captain lope away effortlessly and envied his well-oiled joints.

The clouds skirted under the moon as the heavens opened. She huddled beneath the poncho, head down. After some cold instant coffee from her canteen, she reached into her knapsack for the pint of Jack Daniel's she'd bought at the press center in Da Nang, where she had stayed up all night schmoozing with the reporter from California. She took a swig, shuddered at its burning taste, wiped her mouth with her hand, and glanced at her watch.

By the light of the Dunhill on her gold Cartier tank watch, one more extravagant gift from her ex-husband, Tony, it was two o'clock in the morning.

In the distance, the sounds of automatic fire echoed like a promise. Man, the enemy was close; she could feel their heat. It gave her goose bumps. A man would have calmed her down tonight. She could feel herself rushing too fast. Well, there would be time enough for a social life when she got back to Saigon and the civilized bar of the Hotel Majestic.

She stretched to touch the stars, and a bolt of pain shot up from her knees. She closed her eyes tightly. She would will it away. Looking around at the young marines sleeping like babies in the rain, she knew if she had to crawl to eyewitness tomorrow's mission, she would. A week earlier she had crawled during Operation Red Snapper. But she hadn't felt ashamed. The men understood she was less sure of foot. They had extended a hand, and she'd only fallen once.

She punched on the Sony tape recorder. Barry Farber, the talk show personality at radio station WOR in New York, had been enthusiastic about her offer to record the daily sounds of combat she'd be encountering on patrol as well as interviews with the grunts. Though he wasn't paying her, he'd furnished her with the bulky reel-to-reel battery-run tape recorder and offered to broadcast her reports, time allowing. As usual, any opportunity to get her story out was more important than the money involved. Farber told her not to worry about being heard, reminding her she had the *only* voice he knew of that *could* be heard above machine-gun fire. She couldn't argue that, but speaking into a tape recorder made her nervous. She didn't trust this newfangled voice-activated business, so she'd rigged her own setup for her field work. She pinned the microphone to her cap and just let the tape roll, and when something was happening she'd bend her head and the microphone would pick it up. "War, as some wise man put it," she began, having detached the microphone from her hat, holding it tightly in her hand, "is only a choice of hazards. Will the night be shattered with the firecracker noises, the pinpoints of light, the death and mutilation, that mark an ambush?"

"Hey, what the hell are you doing?"

She looked up. One of the marines crawled toward her. "Working," she announced. Then she whispered, "How come you're not sleeping?" His scrubbed face looked so young, she wondered if he shaved.

"Can I bum a butt?" he asked. When she lit it, it trembled in his mouth.

"Better get some sleep," she said in a husky whisper. "You're going to need it tomorrow." Silently he hunkered down beside her.

"Not tired?" asked Dickey. He shook his head and cupped the cigarette against the rain. She swept her hand toward the invisible line of mountains.

"Listen, the only reason they didn't attack tonight was because the reinforcements came," she whispered. For a second she thought she should take the kid's hand and squeeze it. It might make the both of them feel better. Instead she reached into the dirt, grabbed some, and moved it between her fingers. "The enemy knows where we are, but with men curled up on either side of me, I feel very safe," she said into the microphone. "I feel like I can touch the stars."

The marine nodded his head, listening to her. She was not the kind of woman a man would fool with if he knew what was good for him. She definitely knew what she was talking about into that microphone, with her bugle-clear teacher's voice. Yes, he thought. They know we are here, and we know they are here, and sometimes I feel like they're living inside my brain.

Dickey was going to say something else, but her voice was shot, which always happened when she talked too much and was tired. "This is Dickey Chapelle in Vietnam," she said, signing off.

The young marine clambered into the foxhole, moving close to her. She removed her glasses. He moved closer, spreading his poncho over her and bringing her next to him. "This is good," she decided. She did not want to be alone tonight. She was happy. She was home.

The morning cracked open with a rainbow over the hill. Helicopters were landing and trucks were waiting on the highway. By seven-thirty the men of Company B were ready to move out. Fehlen walked over to tell Dickey the platoon she was scheduled to go with had canceled its patrol, so she'd have to find another. She was telling a joke to one of the men, and Fehlen waited until he'd finished laughing.

"Dickey, what's your pleasure this morning?" he asked in his courtly, mannered way. Her eyes skirted the encampment.

"Wherever the action is," she replied.

"Well, I think the second platoon is going to see something today because they have more hamlets to clear," he suggested.

Dickey shook her head. "Too many reporters. How about letting me go on out with the same platoon I was on yesterday? Is that okay with you?"

"Sure," said the tall marine. "Mauriski is one of the best platoons I've got. Go to it, Dickey." Mauriski's platoon was lining up to move down the hill, around the same positions Fehlen had worked around the night before. Mauriski was the point, and Dickey fell in right behind him.

"Say, Phil, I understand Dickey Chapelle is here."

It was the voice of Fehlen's favorite priest, Father John McNamara. The chaplain, trim and athletic, was in fatigues, his sleeves rolled up, a cap on his head. He walked over to Fehlen. "I sure would like to meet her," the priest said. The troops were moving out now, the trucks on the highway glittering under the sun. "Tell me," McNamara pressed, "what kind of woman is she?"

Fehlen moved his head slightly to read his watch. It was seven fifty-eight. "She's right over there with Mauriski's platoon."

As the two men turned to look, the earth shattered. The force of an exploding booby trap sent the captain and the priest flying backward.

"Somebody's got it with a mortar round," shouted Fehlen, running toward the rocketing bodies and the smoke.

Mauriski, walking the point, had tripped a nylon fish wire attached to an M-26 hand grenade underneath an 81-mm mortar round. He was not seriously wounded. Platoon Sergeant Albert P. Milville, twenty yards from the explosion, was knocked flat. Four other marines, including one of the corpsmen, caught shrapnel pieces in their arms but because of the flak jackets received only minor lacerations. Dickey, right behind Mauriski, was lifted twenty-one feet up and laid back down. She was covered with blood. Her throat, slit open by a shrapnel shard, throbbed in a crimson flood. Fragments of the grenade and mortar shell shimmered from the back of her head, her arms, her legs.

McNamara bent over her. Henri Huet, the Associated Press photographer, shot the photo that ran worldwide of McNamara delivering the last rites to Dickey. The day before, she'd lost a bet with Huet that her unit would be fired on before his. Reportedly she'd told him, "Okay, tomorrow I'll have my chance."

Fehlen knew she was dead, even though her mouth was moving and her eyes fluttered. Dickey's aunt Lutie was told the last words her forty-six-year-old niece gasped before her lips stopped moving were "I guess it was bound to happen."

At 8:22 A.M., the med-evac chopper carrying Dickey, two of the more seriously wounded marines, and the reporters took off for Da Nang, the headquarters for marine forces in Vietnam. Fehlen gathered up Dickey's belongings, the battered Leicas, her tape recorder, her hat, her notebooks. He watched the steel dragonfly rise, rotors *thrump*ing, kicking out dust. She was killed so fast, he thought. She would have been one of the correspondents who would have contacted his folks stateside. A real trooper, he thought as the chopper socked the air and hammered out. He turned away to take care of the living. He and the company moved out.

The press never returned to Operation Black Ferret. The story was with Dickey in Da Nang.

PART ONE

OPEN SESAME

1

Love at First Sight

MARY HOLGATE and Florence
Ballencourt stood inside the sixth-grade classroom, their noses pressed
against the window. Marching up and down on the snowy rear yard of
the Atwater Grammar School in Shorewood, Wisconsin, was their classmate, Georgette Louise Meyer, called Georgie Lou for short. On this
bitter winter morning in 1929, the chunky ten-year-old was bareheaded
and coatless.

One month earlier the New York stock market had crashed, sending
many a ruined speculator off a Manhattan skyscraper to his death. The
decade would be known as the Great Depression, but all that Georgie
Lou had on her mind that winter morning in that Milwaukee suburb was
screaming triumph. Her hero, Commander Richard Evelyn Byrd, was
at that very moment planting the American flag at the South Pole. She
tromped in soldierly cadence, her glasses sliding down her nose, her chest
out, head high, knees snapping out with purpose.

The petite blond-haired Flo lived across the street from Georgie Lou.
Every morning the two girls would walk to school together. And every
morning Georgie Lou would stop at the flagpole in front of the Shorewood Village Hall and salute. Flo, who considered herself as patriotic as
any other inhabitant of the conservative midwestern community,
thought her friend's behavior excessive and did not share the morning
ritual.

27

Nor did Flo or Mary share Georgie Lou's tomboyish habits of scaling neighborhood fences or shinning up trees, where she would dangle over the limbs, the hem of her skirt ripped and wafting in the breeze. The two friends thought that Georgie Lou's big, loping farmboy strides were hysterically funny.

As far as her classmates were concerned, nothing about the loud, box-shaped Georgie Lou fit. Her unfashionable dark blue and gray dresses and formless corduroy skirts, homemade by Georgie Lou and her mother, were always askew. Her blouses hung sloppily over her waistband. The snow boots she wore religiously made her feet look as big as gunboats. Even the bow on her straggly brownish blond hair was forever slipping onto her collar. Georgie Lou, who had skipped a grade, bored everybody with her constant chatter about Commander Byrd and aeronautics. Her prowess in arithmetic and reading impressed nobody except the teachers. But although no one was overly fond of her, more than fifty years later former classmates well remembered Georgie Lou.

Face flushed, glasses misty as she marched, Georgie Lou looked over at Mary and Flo and waved for them to join her, shouting, "C'mon outside, the cold weather is exhilarating. The commander said so himself." Mary and Flo shook their heads vehemently.

Georgie Lou turned away. Through her frosted glasses the world had become a white blur, a swirling vista that she imagined looked in many ways like the Antarctic. That was where she longed to be, not in this dull middle-class suburb practicing her penmanship and being ostracized.

Her boots crunched against the frozen ground. Although she knew the commander did not believe in girl adventurers, she could prove the exception if given half a chance. She could read a compass. Thanks to her mother's constant prodding, she could recite Shakespeare. She was rarely bested by other students. When she was, her competitive nature exploded. One former classmate who had bettered Georgie Lou on a math quiz said she would never forget the look of rage on Georgie Lou's face. To another classmate Georgie Lou confided she was memorizing the dictionary and had gone as far as the letter *D*. The classmate remembered the incident decades later, wondering whom she was trying to impress.

Mary and Flo recalled that the other students were not kind to the odd, hefty girl whom Mary could not recall ever playing with dolls or being invited to after-school parties. She was often called "high pockets" or "smarty pants," frequently pushed and shoved on account of her strangeness. So the lonely girl solved her circumstances by reinventing herself; a method she'd rely on throughout her life when reality became too painful. She finessed it so well that her younger brother, Robert, spent his early years invisible beside her, convinced that his sister was a Shorewood big shot, popular in school, with many boyfriends.

Georgie Lou created her own universe, leaving the stifling community of Shorewood far behind for an exciting world where only daring, courage, and steadfastness mattered. She was the center of that universe, its action-packed heroine. In that amazing place, free of the snubs of her classmates, unhampered by her chubbiness and nearsightedness, Georgie Lou Meyer became part of history, flying through all its great pageants in a biplane, goggles wrapped around her face, a silk scarf whipping in the breeze of the open cockpit. The rattling whir of the engine obliterated all other sounds as the wind blew through her hair. She roared above the earth with Byrd in his Ford trimotor. Unlike the rigid confines of her mother's house, where the dirty habits of pets were not tolerated, in her world Georgie Lou cuddled Byrd's trusty companion, the fox terrier Igloo, in her lap.

When she was not spending time with Byrd, she would be a scout for the North during the Civil War, manning the underground railroad for runaway slaves. Or she might be riding gunner with Captain Eddie Rickenbacker, America's World War I flying ace, leading the Ninety-fourth Aero Pursuit Squadron over the fields of France.

Or she might find herself on horseback charging up Cuba's San Juan Hill with the flamboyant nineteenth-century war correspondent Richard Harding Davis. There, accompanying Teddy Roosevelt and his bully Rough Riders, she, too, would file news dispatches on the progress of the 1898 Spanish-American War. Sometimes she would be Betsy Ross, maker of the first American flag; or Florence Nightingale, swooping in a winged ambulance over the fields where the war wounded lay. Georgie Lou could not bear to see suffering in others.

Thinking about all this adventure sent her twirling in the snow, faster and faster, she and the world blurring together. From inside the classroom, Mary and Flo watched their classmate's whirling-dervish dance with amusement until the door opened to reveal Edna Meyer, Georgie's mother, standing commandingly in the doorway, her rubber galoshes dripping melted snow.

In the big woman's hands were her daughter's drab, sensible winter garments: a hand-knitted cap, a gray wool coat, and a maroon-and-yellow argyle scarf hand-knitted by Edna. Dangling from the collar of the coat was a military-looking medal from a cereal giveaway promotion.

The stern, pop-eyed Edna came so often to school on some real or imagined errand for her daughter that she was a fixture. Mary Holgate felt sorry for Georgie Lou. Something about the woman, her erect carriage, her intensity, sent a real chill up the backs of Mary and the rest of the students. Years later Mary would shake her head and grit her teeth in remembrance of Edna. "Maybe she was so protective of Georgie Lou because she knew she was different from the other kids."

Outside, Georgie Lou still twirled in the snow, shouting Byrd's motto: "The only certainty is uncertainty." She closed her eyes, spread her hands into wings, and ran forward. A pair of hands swooped onto her wrists, shaking her to earth. Georgie Lou opened her eyes; she would have known her mother's grasp blindfolded. Edna was shaking her like a rug.

When she was eleven years old, Georgie Lou wrote that she thought her mother was one of the smartest people alive, and in later years she would describe her family as a living rendition of a Norman Rockwell illustration, a big, happy, permissive family against whom she could never rebel. But by all accounts the family was anything but sublime, ruled as it was by Edna's emotions, a roller coaster of such highs and lows that Robert Meyer described them, in midwestern understatement, as "worrisome." He said the family was concerned that his mother would one day go off on an emotional spree from which she wouldn't return. More often than not it was the rebellious, headstrong Georgie Lou who would set off the fireworks. The demanding, strong-willed Edna would collapse into hysterics at the mention of her daughter's dreams of adventure. Edna's emotional tirades had a real impact upon the high-strung Georgie Lou. They terrified the young girl, so much so that she sought to control her own, and as a youngster would be described by her acquaintances as "aloof" and "serious." It would be a lifelong fight to harness her emotions, and there were occasions as an adult when she succeeded; after her release from an Iron Curtain prison she became famous for the phrase "Courage is not the absence of fear but the control of fear."

Edna's hysterics did not diminish with time, either. As an adult in New York, struggling to make her mark, Georgie Lou was the recipient of Edna's constant nagging. As long as Edna was alive, Georgie Lou shouldered the blame for her mother's outbursts, guiltily asking as a thirty-six-year-old, "Though I write seven long pages on a busy day, thereby implying how important what you say and think is to me, have I done anything *loving*? or have I just pushed you further along in one of your tendencies that seems somehow to be a *hurtful* one, the emotional binge?"

Perhaps it was Edna's disappointed youth that created the phobic, controlling woman and mother. She seemed to have no other desire than to mold Georgie Lou's destiny, as if doing so would make up for her own short-changed experience, even out the score. As a young woman attending Milwaukee's Downer College, where she majored in cooking and minored in sewing, she'd contracted tuberculosis, at the time a life-threatening illness requiring a long convalescence. She survived the disease and graduated from college with a degree in domestic science. At the age of twenty-three, the only time Edna ventured from Old Milwaukee, tragedy struck. She had married an Illinois-born orchardist and minister and moved with him to Idaho, where she taught the basics of home design to the hearty women of Boise. A short time later her husband was killed in a flood. Edna returned home, by family accounts "devastated." Edna never traveled very far from home after that; leaving the world tours to her two sisters, she later wrote that for her, "true happiness can only be found in a well-ordered home." As a witness to World War I, she was a firm isolationist and had a violent distrust of the military. She was also terrified of airplanes, the other thing Georgie Lou and her father adored. Mary Holgate recalled that when Georgie Lou was thirteen, she announced to her mother that she intended to follow in the footsteps of her hero, Richard E. Byrd, by becoming a pilot. Mary Holgate watched a horrified Edna grab Georgie Lou and make her promise she would never fly.

Although Georgie Lou's life would become for the most part a successful rebellion against her mother's control, Edna's influence remained constant. In the years to come, when the grown-up Georgie Lou became the world-famous combat photojournalist Dickey Chapelle, she had friends believing she had left Shorewood and Edna far behind; she never did. A monkey puppet named Oscar, given to her by Edna when she was a ten-year-old in bed with a childhood illness, became ragged and torn, but she kept it with her her entire life.

Standing on the snowy ground, Edna plunked the coat over Georgie Lou's shoulders, pushed the cap onto her head, and wrapped the scarf tightly around her neck. Then, fixing her daughter with her steely blue eyes, she dragged her out of the school yard.

A local wag had once remarked that one could fire a cannon down Milwaukee's main drag, Wisconsin Avenue, at midnight and not hit a soul. The same could be said about its suburb, Shorewood, at high noon. In the driveways of the affluent community's big, brick family homes, Milwaukee businessmen were brushing snow off the hoods of factory-new Oldsmobiles and Buicks. German maids in black shirtwaist dresses were sweeping front porches or chasing neighbors' dogs off the wide, snow-covered front lawns. Smoke drifted out from brick chimneys, forming clouds in the frosty air.

If the Depression was hurtling the country to hell in a hand basket, nobody in this protected community of Protestant German-American and English families had seen it. Set against the high bluffs and sandy beaches of Lake Michigan's north shore, Shorewood streets rang with the sounds of children playing, not the cries of the destitute and downtrodden. Nobody in the little village of two thousand souls was selling apples or standing in soup lines.

Edna, her two sisters, and a brother (who apparently died young) had grown up in Milwaukee inside a large Victorian house built by their father, George Engelhardt, a prosperous tobacco importer and Milwaukee native. The big house with its parquet floors always smelled of tobacco, mostly the Cuban leaf that George hand-selected on his buying trips to that island. The girls' mother, Martha, had been born in Munich, Germany. Before she had come to America, Georgie Lou's grandmother had ambitions of becoming a circus performer, working on the trapeze or as a bareback rider. She was described as a tiny, lively woman who wrote poetry, tutored Georgie Lou in German, and taught her granddaughter how to use a treadle sewing machine.

In 1916 Edna's sophisticated older sister, Louise, nicknamed Lutie, married Hans Meyer, a successful, self-taught electrical engineer whose skills would take him and Lutie periodically to China and Japan. Six months later, three years after her first marriage, Edna married Hans's younger brother, Paul Gerhard.

The four Meyer boys, second-generation German-Americans, lost their father when they were quite young. When Paul, the youngest of the boys, was ten years old, he was forced to leave school to support his widowed mother. He married Edna when he was thirty-four. On their marriage license, he listed his vocation as "clerk." The couple moved in with Edna's parents.

The midwestern prairie town of Old Milwaukee was known as the Deutsch Athens of America. For more than a hundred years a steady population of German immigrants had been settling on the banks of the Milwaukee River and re-creating it to resemble their homeland on the Rhine. The beer barons Pabst and Schlitz had erected Flemish-Renaissance-style mansions. On every street corner were beer taverns and beer gardens, now shuttered down by Prohibition. There were German-language newspapers and restaurants serving up Wiener schnitzel and liver dumplings.

Paul and Edna had been attracted to the new suburb of Shorewood because of its modern feeling and its distance, if only a few miles north, from the old world German downtown. When they moved to Shorewood in 1928, Paul was a traveling salesman for a steel company, doing well enough working on commission to support his wife and children in comfort. He became active in the local Republican party and drove a new Ford. Edna retired from her teaching career and hired a German maid, who arrived dressed in a long black skirt and apron and who, along with Grandma Engelhardt, taught the children German.

The Meyer house on Shorewood Boulevard was a square, gray, eight-room, two-story house with red-painted trim on the windows. The house faced north, in the direction of the older community of Whitefish Bay, across a plateau of white oak and sugar maple, the former hunting grounds of the Souk and Algonquian Indian tribes.

In this setting of middle-class comfort, Georgie Lou regularly wrote and starred in plays for Edna, Mary Holgate, and Flo Ballencourt, as well as for her aunts, Lutie and Georgette, nicknamed George. The two childless women, constant visitors to the big house, doted on Georgie Lou, spoiling her rotten. They would gush over her portrayal of Betsy Ross or Florence Nightingale, and when Edna was out of earshot, they would encourage Georgie's wilder ideas on aeronautics and exploration.

On one or two occasions Georgie Lou's brother, Robert, five years younger, found himself dragged into his sister's theatrics. But for the most part, as with everything in the house, it was his sister's show. As her kid brother, Robert both idolized and despised Georgie Lou, once telling her adoringly, "You can do anything," yet burning with envy that she had his parents' complete and uninterrupted attention. In later years the resentment would erupt into loud arguments between the two. But as a youngster, Robert Paul decided it would do no good to compete. "It would have been like competing with a monster," he commented sharply years later. "I couldn't win."

Aunt George, the youngest of the three Engelhardt girls, was her father's favorite, a divorcée and career woman living in New York, a tomboy and Georgie Lou's favorite, too. Aunt George, who came often to visit her sisters, had miraculously retained her childish sense of wonder and, recalled Robert, "always knew what kids were thinking. Especially little boys. She would always give the perfect gift." It was no doubt George, while scrunched with Georgie Lou and Robert under the sink brewing root beer, who handed her niece the book that would change her life—an edition of Richard Harding Davis's experiences as a combat reporter, bound in red.

All of this playing went on unbeknownst to Edna, sitting on a mohair couch chain-smoking and contemplating her daughter's future. Edna had already decided that Georgie Lou would be a writer, no doubt in the mold of Louisa May Alcott, from whose widely read *Little Women* Edna had chosen the appellation "Marmee." As a self-described "interior decorator," Edna considered herself an arbiter of taste. Her son recalled that his mother was given to putting on airs, ordering shopgirls around. "Going into a store with her was a whirlwind experience," he recalled, also mentioning that when accompanied by Georgie Lou, a nonstop talker, it became impossible to be heard over the voices of the "two peas in a pod."

Mary and Flo, frequent guests at the Meyer house, rarely summoned up the nerve to speak with Edna. But they were very fond of Georgie's father, whom they recalled as a patient, quiet man who could be depended upon to chauffeur and chaperone his daughter and her friends to sports events, which he seemed to enjoy as much as they did.

The neat, short, balding man, like his wife, was embarrassed by outward displays of affection and rigidly refused to use hyperbole in his sales spiels. He had very definite ideas on how to raise his children, all of which clashed with his wife's. Edna was determined to protect Georgie Lou to the point of suffocation, an approach her husband, despite his reticent exterior, strongly opposed. He was described by his daughter as a dedicated baseball fan, a man who moved deliberately and spoke firmly, a loyal reader of the weekly *Literary Digest* and the *Milwaukee Journal.* He strove to build his children's confidence, encouraging independence and physical prowess despite his wife's objections. It was Paul who first introduced Georgie Lou and Robert to the great adventurers of the day, to the lectures and films of challenge and conquest that had become so popular as to be a national pastime: the flights of Charles Lindbergh and Amelia Earhart; the great exploits of the naval pilot and explorer Commander Richard E. Byrd. Despite Edna's predictable hysterics and the bitter accusations that Paul was betraying her by nurturing Georgie Lou's rebelliousness, he ignored her, as would his children as they matured and toughened. He would often take Georgie Lou and Robert with him to construction sites. Georgie Lou wanted to please her father, and she wrote that although he would not praise her verbally, she could tell when she had pleased him. One occasion stood out. He invited his daughter in his quiet voice to follow him as he walked fearlessly across the high metal beams of an unfinished building, assuring her she wouldn't fall if she looked ahead, not down.

"I was always frightened, but I never could bring myself to admit it," she once wrote. "So I did as he told me." She didn't know then that her father's advice would inform her lifelong quest to be where the action was.

Mary Holgate remembered Georgie Lou's recitation of Brutus's famous speech from Shakespeare's *Julius Caesar* in the fifth grade—the last straw for the girl's less brilliant classmates. On the way home for lunch some of the kids pushed Georgie Lou into the ice for showing off. "I guess if it had been the fifties or sixties," said another former classmate, "she'd have been called a nerd."

Later that day Edna Meyer arrived in class with a peace offering of homemade fudge, which she left on the teacher's desk. "I don't know why it stands out in my mind so vividly," said Mary Holgate. "But I remember she said she wanted everyone in the class to have a piece of the fudge, and the children who pushed Georgie Lou to have the biggest piece. I thought it was terrible. After all, Georgie Lou was nearly ten years old. Her mother should have let her work her problems out by herself."

Although Shorewood had once been cut off from downtown Milwaukee because of poor and outdated trolley lines, by the time Georgie

Lou was a teenager the main street was a short bus ride away. Its cosmopolitan air, its Chinese restaurants and movie theaters, became a favorite weekend haunt for Shorewood's teens. But Edna refused to let her impressionable daughter go anywhere without adult supervision. In 1933, when Georgie Lou was fourteen years old, Prohibition ended, the beer gardens opened, and the breweries churned. As far as Edna was concerned, there was far too much going on in Milwaukee's streets.

But it wasn't the fear of alcohol that terrified Edna, it was the budding world of aviation. In spite of the hard times of the Depression years, the public, particularly young people, had become caught up in the excitement of flight. Every day records of speed and distance were being broken. Itinerant pilots were taking paying customers for five-minute hops in the skies over Milwaukee. Although Georgie Lou had promised Edna she would never set foot inside an airplane, Edna rightly feared the promise would not last long amid the airplanes for hire in downtown Milwaukee. Edna, whose idea of a night on the town was going to an "eat club"—which was nothing more than couples gathering to eat at each other's houses—did not intend to lose her daughter to some whirling piece of metal.

While Mary and Flo journeyed to the wilds of Milwaukee and another classmate turned Georgie Lou green with envy with a firsthand description of how it felt to go flying—"it was noisy and cold"—Georgie Lou was detained in Shorewood. But, being a resourceful girl, she found other amusements. She stood on the corner of East Capitol Drive and Oakland Avenue in a crowd of spectators at the National Guard Armory's polo grounds, watching the famous horse soldiers of the 105th, First Wisconsin Cavalry, strut their stuff.

Despite the sun streaming down and the flies buzzing around the platoon, the brave cavalry did not stir. They sat, erect as toy soldiers, on their McClellan saddles, their shiny boots stuck into the nickel-plated metal stirrups, waiting for their clear-eyed, mustached captain to give his call. The captain would raise his arm to twelve o'clock and shout, "Troops, column of troopers, follow me, gallop! . . ." The bright-yellow-and-scarlet coat of arms with the ringed horse's head above the left chevron glowed . . . the hoofs thundered, and the dust rose into clouds. . . .

At night, with her head nestled in soft down pillows and her book, *Yancey's Aerial Navigation and Meteorology,* fourth edition, falling from her hands to the floor, Georgie Lou would snuggle with Oscar, her furry monkey, and gaze up at pictures of flying ships she had tacked to the walls.

Edna may have forbidden her to fly, but she could not control her daughter's dreams. They were of pugnacious, high-nosed World War I–vintage birds of prey, built of spruce with Irish linen–wrapped bodies: Count Ferdinand von Zeppelin's lighter-than-air great ship, the *Zeppelin, Z-1;* the tough French World War I Morane Saulnier monoplane, fitted with machine guns that could be fired through the propeller; the German Fokker D-7 biplane, constructed for maneuverability with a 220-horsepower liquid-cooled Mercedes engine; the famous *Sopwith Camel,* the Allies' World War I all-around fighter biplane; the underpowered, ungainly biplane Curtiss Jenny; and more.

Cluttering her desk were framed glass photographs of men she dubbed "exponents of the deed, not the word": Commander Richard Evelyn Byrd and Germany's blond Baron Manfred von Richthofen, known as the Red Baron. With their silk neck scarves flowing, their leather flight jackets creased and lined, their goggles and helmets crowning their heads, they seemed so alive, so ready for action. Any minute she expected them to crack the glass.

"I wonder, I have wondered, more than once, just what it is that makes us want to fly," Georgie Lou wrote, using her pen name, G. L. Meyer.

Georgie Lou's first published piece, titled "Why We Want to Fly" (By One of Us Age Fourteen), evolved from a letter she typed, having learned that skill at the advice of Aunt George, to *United States Air Service* magazine, a bimonthly publication featuring stories on the military and commercial aeronautics industry. The article was printed in the September 1933 issue and paid seven and a half dollars, three dollars of which Georgie immediately pledged toward a year's subscription to *USAS,* which she believed was the most important magazine printed in America at the time.

By this time a decision about Georgie Lou's future had been reached, as were all decisions in the family, by the entire clan. Lutie's successful, worldly engineer husband, Hans, who often took his niece to the Milwaukee water towers to explain hydraulics to her, had shown real aplomb in finding an occupation that would calm his nervous sister-in-law while satisfying Georgie Lou's love for flight. She would become an aeronautical engineer. She could design and write about planes without ever stepping inside one.

Edna was already delighted that her daughter had begun her first brilliant step toward a writing career by publishing in a national magazine, even though it was an aeronautics publication. But had Edna read the article carefully, she might not have been so sanguine. Her daughter's dreams of flying were obsessive.

Georgie Lou wrote that her love for flying was "identical to 1,000,000 other boys—and girls—in this country who *want to fly*. The phrase in our minds is an Open Sesame to heaven. . . ." She believed that the world of aviation, "because it is unexplored by most of us, seems to be a place where dreams come true overnight, courage is tried and proved, heroes plentifully abound, and there is no dearth of Glory—capitalized in our minds. That attitude is quite deplorable, you will say, but it has one redeeming feature; this Glory idea has stimulated our initial interest. It was a case of love at first sight."

She went on to write that aviation appealed to two kinds of people— engineers-to-be, like herself, and another class, "which our parents refer to as daredevils, who want action—and plenty of it. They have no desire to work so that others can fly—they want to sit behind the stick themselves. They want to make their mark with the ship and in the air." She might have added that this latter group was the one she identified with. She had already written rather presciently that although she found engineering "to be the greatest and most fascinating field . . . few of us, it is true, will succeed. Aviation will remain only an avocation to the majority of us—a large majority." The article was dedicated to "all the parents who wonder why" and stated that "as much as some parents . . . regard flying as the most popular means of suicide . . . far be it from me to try to convince them . . . differently."

The magazine's editor, Earl N. Findley, a kindly seventy-seven-year-old aircraft industry pioneer, began corresponding with Georgie Lou— and became the lonely girl's confidant, after he reprimanded her for having put one over on him—her signature, G. L. Meyer, had convinced him she was a boy (to which she explained that using G. L. Meyer was a matter of expediency since "Georgie Lou is a horticultural curiosity"). For the next five years she would write him copious, ebullient letters about aeronautics as well as teenage angst. Even though she had written she wanted to become an engineer, did he think women would make good scientists? She trusted him. He was, after all, "the only person I know who knows the difference between an elevator and an aileron."

Findley agreed with Edna. "You will make your own opening somewhere in the field ruled by the written word," he declared in a letter dated November 24, 1933. "It is a fascinating though precarious existence to put one little word after another until you have told your story. But a person with your facility in expression will not be happy doing anything else but."

"You have got me all wrong, sir," she wrote to Findley in January 1934. "I *don't* want to be a writer at all—and be chained to a typewriter all my life. I want to be an aeronautical engineer." Nevertheless she applied to *USAS* for a job as a staff reporter, informing him that "whatever a boy could do, she, a girl, could match it and hoped he would not be thinking, 'Now if she were only a boy.' "

Findley could not offer her a job at the time, but he offered to help her "to some position in aeronautics along the lines you most desire; it would be a fine feather in my helmet."

FLO BALLENCOURT LIKED GEORGIE LOU for the very reason that most of the kids ignored her—because she was different. For instance, Flo knew no other Shorewood girl who would so willingly awaken before the crack of dawn to join her for a long walk to the local bird estuary at Estes Park. It was on one of these expeditions into the wilds that Georgie Lou stated, "I know I'm different from the other girls in Shorewood, and I don't care," adding that she hoped to marry a prizefighter. Flo would say much later that she always knew from then on that Georgie Lou would grow up to be somebody special.

Sitting on one of Edna's painstakingly re-covered morris chairs, playing bridge, Georgie Lou would blurt out the strange aviation lingo she'd picked up hanging around the local airfield and eavesdropping on the pilots. She had nagged her father into taking her on three trips to the local airdromes.

"Boy, wouldn't it be crackerjack," she wrote to her good friend editor Findley on May 30, 1934, "if the local drome could get itself one of those Boeing 247s or a new Douglas?—man, it would send my lift-drag ratio with regard to my spirits into somersaults.

"But I still get a big kick in being close enough to touch any old ship, although I haven't done it much. . . ." she added wistfully.

In the late summer of 1934, as Edna sat in her living room smoking a cigarette and reading Freud, the placid Milwaukee heavens outside were growing dark and noisy with metal birds. Curtiss Jennys and British-built de Havilland biplanes were swooping low over the city, waking up the rubes to glory and death. The promised death-defying thrills were waiting on the outskirts of town, at the local airfield, one hundred acres owned by the Curtiss Wright Airplane Company.

There was no better place in Depression America for stomach-churning cheap thrills than the local air circus. The inexpensive admission provided hours of entertainment that horrified and exhilarated spectators. Aerial stunt fliers, wing walkers, and parachutists performed their death-defying maneuvers all through the nation's heartland, where its endless cow pastures served as ready-made landing fields.

But despite the advertised hype for acts called "Bullet Drops" and "Death Drops," the performers were amazingly competent, the accidents few. The costumes were strictly military; it was a fact that the women in the audience went crazy for medals and stripes. And at fifteen, five feet tall and weighing one hundred fifty-three pounds, Georgie Lou was no exception.

The only way that Georgie Lou could go to air shows was by cajoling her hardworking father into such a weekend afternoon. They would evade Edna's nagging questions with some vague, acceptable answer and hurry out to the local airfield. Once there, Georgie Lou would hold her father's hand, standing in the wood bleachers near the airfield hangar in view of the pump house.

Some of the country's finest stunt pilots would zoom their planes above the wood bleachers, while the crowds squinted, craning to follow the aircraft as it nosed upward, trembling to climb into a "loop." Like the other spectators, Georgie Lou's mouth would dry up as the announcer terrorized her with the pronouncement that certain death loomed if the plane could not gain the necessary altitude, which miraculously it did, inching its shiny beak upward and over to complete the circular stunt. Her stomach mush, her mouth cotton, Georgie Lou had never seen such beauty of form and function in her life. She could have watched that smooth magic until her neck froze.

No doubt Georgie Lou would have preferred an American Airlines Air Travel Discount Card for Christmas 1934. But the gifts she received, in light of the Meyers' dire financial condition—her father, like sixteen million other Americans, was now out of work—brought forth shrieks of glee. She recounted her haul to Mr. Findley in a 1935 New Year's letter. There was a Neuffel & Esser poliface slide rule and her own copy of *Simple Aerodynamics* by Carter, fourth edition. There was an eight-inch, detailed metal globe and a supplement to *Yancey's Aerial Navigation and Meteorology,* which she had been reading eagerly for two years.

By then her parents had rented out their big house and moved the family in with friends. From there they moved again to an apartment on Oakland Avenue next door to the peripatetic Lutie and Hans.

Georgie Lou entered her senior year at Shorewood High School at the age of fifteen, having skipped one full year. Other than playing fullback on the girls' soccer team, which she enjoyed, Georgie Lou—wearing boys' shirts over her corduroy skirts and tromping through the neighborhood in her snow boots—confided to Findley that she couldn't wait to get out of Shorewood, that her desires ran "MIT-ward, since for confounded reasons I can't join the Navy and attend Annapolis"—Richard E. Byrd's alma mater, the Naval Academy at Annapolis. The only way to college was by scholarship.

Findley suggested that Georgie Lou write to MIT, minus her usual exuberance, "in a business-like dignified manner, your burning desire to be the greatest lady designer of airplanes." His previous offer to help her in aeronautics was sincere. He would write a letter recommending Georgie Lou for a scholarship to Purdue and the Massachusetts Institute of Technology.

Georgie Lou Meyer's photograph for the Shorewood High class of 1935 reveals a serious young woman, steady eyes gazing out of a round, smooth, blemish-free face. Her special interests were noted under the photo as the Radio Club and the School Security Patrol. About this time she wrote a letter to Findley, bragging to him of leading an otherwise all-boy campaign on increasing underclass participation in the Student Council. Georgie Lou's unnerdlike interest in politics came naturally, not only from her father, who would discuss the ideal of representative government with his daughter, but from her grandparents. As the great-granddaughter of German immigrants, she'd listened to the often told tales of how her ancestors had fled Germany a century earlier, its repressions and wars, for the freedoms guaranteed by the American Constitution. This, she was told, was her cherished birthright, which needed to be safeguarded; and to illustrate, she would hear about the fierce anti-

German sentiment that swept the country during World War I. The Meyers' patriotism was deadly earnest, and the idealistic Georgie Lou never took her birthright for granted. How attractive to right an alleged injustice to her fellow students. Here in staid Shorewood High the seeds were sown for a lifetime's participation in causes. Her patriotism, sometimes grown rabid, fueled by her inextinguishable idealism, would find her battling her tyrants wherever they arose, even to defending anti-American policies. She proudly reported to her pen pal Earl Findley that her tireless involvement in the student body resulted in "the most successful of Shorewood High's political campaigns." She was also a member of the editorial staff of the high school newspaper, *The Ripples.*

Bob Shaw, the seventeen-year-old editor of *The Ripples* and the paper's gossip columnist, was a wealthy Shorewood High bon vivant and owner of a 1935 two-tone green Oldsmobile convertible. On what he remembers vaguely as "some kind of dare," he asked Georgie Lou out. "I remember that she had her hair cut short like a boy's, and I had never dated a girl with a crew cut."

It took young Shaw some time to work up the courage. "She was not the kind of girl I would normally have been attracted to." She was smart, homely, overweight, and at the Friday afternoon sock hops she could always be seen leading some young boy across the dance floor. "She looked like Gertrude Stein. It wasn't that I thought she was sexually odd, as much as I didn't think of her sexually at all." Bob remembered her not from *The Ripples,* but from their history class, where she argued repeatedly with the instructor and was usually right. At last he summoned up the courage and asked her out. She accepted.

When he came to pick her up, Georgie Lou came bounding out of the door, ignoring the corsage he offered. She went over to his car, banged the front fender, and asked, "How fast does this baby go?" Bob was speechless. Georgie Lou then quoted him arcane information on the inner workings of RPM. He was impressed, but not enough to ask her out again. Bob Shaw never saw Georgie Lou again. Unaware that she'd become a world-famous combat reporter, he always thought she would end up designing automobiles.

About that time Georgie Lou began calling herself Dick. It was prompted by an actual meeting with her hero, Admiral Richard E. Byrd, at the Milwaukee Auditorium, sometime prior to his 1936 Antarctic expedition. Byrd had been feted for his first aerial crossing of the South

Pole in 1930 with a ticker-tape parade down New York's Fifth Avenue. He was made a rear admiral by the navy and further immortalized with a congressional medal. But he was finding it difficult to raise funds for his second expedition to Antarctica. In the bone-dry Depression, the expense of exploration was considered frivolous.

The aristocratic admiral's Antarctic project, against all odds, was the kind of mission G. L. "Dick" Meyer understood so well. In her eyes it contained every stubborn belief necessary to be defined as heroic. The admiral was truly an "exponent of the deed." He cared little for what the world thought about his dreams, pursuing them against all obstacles. His bold single-mindedness of purpose appealed to her sense of idealism, inspired her own struggling individuality. If a man as great as Byrd could narrow life down to one immediate goal, letting nothing get in its way—and fulfill it—so could she. The only catch was, she later wrote, "being a girl, I'd have to try harder."

Dickey's brother remembered that while his dad waited in the auditorium—"he would never go backstage"—Georgie Lou and Robert found the great man. Robert watched Byrd and his sister shake hands and recalled that Dickey was "uncustomarily impressed and moved." She did not wash her hands for a week.

Dickey was barely sixteen years old when she graduated from Shorewood High in the summer of 1935. The bright, immature girl continued to upset her classmates, this time Bob Shaw, when out of the blue she, rather than Shaw, was named valedictorian. Thanks to her outstanding marks and Findley's sponsorship, she had been accepted on scholarship to Purdue and MIT. She chose the Massachusetts Institute of Technology at Cambridge because, unlike Purdue, it offered her a full scholarship for her freshman year. She immediately began calling herself a "Tech woman."

Edna handled her daughter's flight from the nest without the anticipated tantrum. Georgie would be leaving home, but she would be leaving to live among the brightest people of her generation. Edna hoped she would abandon her unladylike passions by finding some nice young man to marry and bless Edna with grandchildren. At the very worst she would follow in her aunt George's footsteps as a career woman until she found a nice young man.

Dickey spent the summer stacking children's books at the local library and dreaming of fame and fortune as a glamorous airplane designer. She also wrote her first manuscript. Titled *The Airplane Book*, it was a comprehensive primer on modern aviation for young readers. She described scout planes and flying hotel planes and a future rocket ship that would be shot like a bullet into space. Each time the manuscript came back rejected from one of New York's publishing houses, Dickey put it into a fresh envelope and sent it back. "Maybe somebody will mistake it for another manuscript and publish it," she confided to Mr. Findley.

2

Young Savage

O N THE EARLY fall day that Dickey Meyer left Milwaukee on a bus bound for Cambridge, Massachusetts, she could barely contain her excitement—not about her continuing education, but about her freedom. The promised land lay before her. Even though well-chaperoned living arrangements had been made—she was to be nanny to the children of a navy lieutenant pilot in Cambridge in exchange for her room and board—she would, for the first time in her life, be on her own.

As the squat, working-class skyline of downtown Milwaukee retreated, Dickey turned to the infinitely more promising open highway. It was like her life, this empty, uncluttered straightaway, moving past the flat, open wheat fields of the prairie, past the silos with American flags rippling on their roofs, past the grazing dairy cattle that stared dumbly at the bus as it roared by . . . and away from the stifling mentality of Shorewood and Edna's chokehold. Against the afternoon's purpling sky, a herd of geese was silhouetted. Taking a cigarette from behind her ear, Dickey recalled the letter she had written to Earl Findley right before leaving. Not only had she promised to design a transpacific transport that would make the newest commercial airliners, the Douglas DC-1 and the Boeing 247, "look like box kites," but she also confided that she was going to be the "first woman in the Meyer clan to upset the quiet of Cambridge."

Dickey was one of seven women admitted to MIT's freshman class of 1935. As soon as she arrived she made good on one of those promises.

For sixteen years the curious, immature adventure girl had been under her mother's thumb. Now she intended to see, feel, and taste everything. She devoured Cambridge, then moved on to Boston. Having outshone her classmates at Shorewood without even trying, she was confident her future at "Tech" would prove as easily conquered and rarely attended class.

Her hair was kept as short as a boy's. She dressed in trousers, a man's shirt and tie, and a battered blue raincoat. If her mannish dress and hair brought curious looks, they were deliberate. Although MIT was by nature a conservative school, the times were not. The great honking noise of the 1920s and its flaming youth were very much present on the college campuses, even intensified against the uncertainty of the Depression. It was a perfect time for an overprotected girl to bust loose, to shock, to rebel, to be seen, as she wrote of herself, "living in the manner of a young savage."

Instead of attending classes, she went to watch airplanes. Her idea of living wickedly was camping out at the Boston airport, the Boston Navy Yard, and the neighboring Coast Guard base. At the Navy Yard she felt a surge of great excitement and privilege when she was allowed to handle the men's tools to fit a blade into a ship's turbine.

She was so impressed by the sophisticated tracking system she observed at the Coast Guard base that she sold an article about it to the *Boston Traveler* newspaper as a feature story for the going rate, eight dollars.

Despite her earlier declaration to bring the aviation world to its knees with her radical designs, she could barely sit through classes in freshman engineering and beginning chemistry. Too much was going on around her. By her second semester she was barely passing her freshman classes, realizing much to her chagrin that her classmates were as bright as, if not brighter than, she, and far more serious about their education. But it mattered little, because she had latched on to something infinitely more exciting than calculus, writing to Earl Findley on July 1, 1936, that "for the past semester I have made expenses by acting as a flying girl reporter for the *Boston Traveler*."

On the day a flood cut off food and mail to the city of Worcester, necessitating that airplanes drop-zone supplies to the imperiled city,

Dickey cut school to go to the airport. This was to avoid taking a chemistry exam for which she had not studied—and if she could prove she was gainfully employed during the time the test was being given, she would be able to reschedule the exam. Years later she told a group of Worcester women she had cut the class because she was failing it and it was just as well. "I would not have made a good engineer." She also described it as the first time she'd "eyeballed" a story.

Upon arriving at the airport, she conned her way into a maroon Bellanca, at the time the biggest plane in the world, which was being loaded with bread for the hungry populace of Worcester. In her autobiography Dickey wrote that her promise to her mother *never* to set foot in an airplane froze her temporarily. But an impatient baker trying to load more bread told her she was standing in his way and should make up her mind. She rationalized that Edna would forgive her—if she ever found out—because of the plane's mercy mission.

By this time the college coed had learned how to handle her mother, in a method not unlike that used by her father. Since Edna would worry about her no matter what she did, Dickey told her nothing and went ahead and did exactly what she pleased. Years later after Dickey's autobiography was published and one of her relatives commented that she had been a very selfish, inconsiderate child, Dickey told her aunt Lutie that the comment was justified. She wrote that as an adult, she understood that Edna's worry was a manifestation of her "love," but that she "with childish insensitivity" put her interests before "Mother and Dad." She continued, "I used to feel that no matter what I did my mother still would worry about me; hence the only solution I could think of was to remove myself first and then at a distance to indulge myself in what I wanted to do, reporting as little of it as I dared."

Looking out the window of the Bellanca at the perfect checkerboard world below, she felt triumph and elation. She had always dreamed of flying—now she was doing it. As much as she respected her mother's vast intelligence, Dickey now knew with some authority that there were certain things Edna was ignorant about. Like flying. It wasn't, as Edna believed, suicide. It was what Dickey had always believed it to be—"an Open Sesame to heaven."

THERE WAS ONLY ONE uncharted field left. Dickey Meyer, a self-described savage, discovered "sex energy." Dickey had come to understand the lopsided morality of college life. Despite the nominal tolerance of women, granting them access to the hallowed halls of male-dominated institutions such as MIT, the philosophy was circumscribed, conservative. Apparently there were two kinds of college women: the ones who were respected and the other kind, whose sole purpose was to be necked with. She understood that boys cared only about the girls they held in regard. This type of woman was called an OAO (one and only).

Dickey was soon the OAO of a senior engineering student named Herbert Weiss. In an ancient photograph he appears skinny, bespectacled, and intense. A Harvard pal of Dickey's, a former Shorewood High classmate and fellow nerd named Stuart Hoyt, dismissed "Herb" as a "lovesick mush" and "mental cripple." But Dickey's pose in the fading photograph seems romantic and attached. She is beside him in a tight-fitting dress that reveals every inch of her robust bosom. For the first time in her life, she was aware of herself as a sexual creature, describing herself as "beautiful." Herb's intentions with Dickey were strictly honorable. He wanted to marry her and spent a great deal of time helping her pass her classes. She felt like a spinning top, torn by a sense of obligation—he was obviously her first lover, she was intensely loyal—and the urgency of being an avowed "adventure girl."

Stuart Hoyt, Dickey's Harvard friend, her lone male confidant in matters of the heart, was privy to her confusion and counseled her to dump Herb because he was a "jerk" and she was a "doer." Nevertheless, the hopelessly loyal Dickey and her lover planned to marry, much to Hoyt's consternation. The two, she wrote, scandalized the department, staying up all night to record his wind tunnel experiments. She relished their wild reputation. Her enthusiasm for necking seemed to have peaked about this time. Found among her personal papers is a rhapsodic, mercifully unpublished article entitled "In Defense of Necking, by a Coed Who Has Done It, Aged 16."

Describing herself as an "average American co-ed, whose greatest ambition is to be an airplane designer," she explained she came by her knowledge of necking as a harmless method of burning up "sex energy" through actual experience and "bull sessions" with the boys in her department. She noted that one of the advantages of being a female in the engineering department, unlike her "sisters" in the liberal arts, was the opportunity to see the problem of necking "through the eyes of boys."

As far as Dickey was concerned, now that she knew what boys were thinking, she could honestly state she knew more about sex than her mother did; and necking was "a direct blow to loose life and conducive to a good marriage." If girls got into trouble, Dickey believed it was their parents' fault for not being candid with them: "My mother told me what not to do, but she didn't tell me how to handle a situation I just might find myself involved in."

About this time, Dickey's well-chaperoned living arrangements were interfering with her newfound sexual adventures. Feeling hemmed in, she took another step toward independence. She quit her job as a nanny, and with ten dollars sent by Edna and the eight dollars from the *Boston Traveler* article, she rented one-half of an attic room on Pinckney Street in Boston for $2.50 a week. The rooming house was around the corner from Admiral Byrd's house. She had come upon it circling his house during a snowstorm.

Each night when the plane for New York flew over her rooming house, she would dash out and across a bridge into Herb's arms. They recited German poetry to each other: *"In deinen Armen war es so schön, warum musste ich dich verlassen?"* ("In your arms it was so beautiful, why did I have to leave you?")

When the now worldly Dickey Meyer returned to Shorewood for Christmas 1935, she shocked her former high school friends. At the annual Christmas tea at Flo Ballencourt's house, Mary Holgate, still a senior at Shorewood High, stood stunned as Dickey, in high heels and smoking a cigarette, strutted up to the high school counselor, Miss Doerflinger, and brazenly announced, "The boys at Tech prefer black lingerie." Mary recalled that Miss Doerflinger "smiled amusedly."

Mary and Flo saw Georgie Lou once more after that, years later in the 1960s when she returned to Shorewood as a popular lecturer to visit her aunt Lutie. Georgie Lou (neither Flo nor Mary could ever call her Dickey) had become a slender blond New Yorker, they recalled. She was dressed in an expensive tailored suit and high-heeled shoes. Flo made an overture of friendship when she ran into Georgie Lou in the local market but felt "she had already turned her back on the past."

By the end of her first year at MIT, Dickey's grades were so poor she'd lost her scholarship and had barely passed her freshman courses. The competition at MIT was fierce, and as she had written in the article Earl Findley had published in 1933, "Few of us, it is true, will succeed."

When Dickey returned home in the summer of 1936, her parents, having ridden out the worst of the Depression, were once again ensconced in their big house on Shorewood Avenue. Paul Meyer, fifty-two, had stayed off the relief roll by working for President Franklin Delano Roosevelt's vast Works Projects Administration, the New Deal agency that built roads, schools, post offices, and airports.

Contrary to Dickey's autobiography, the Meyers did not make light of her failure. True, they did not toss her into the street, and there was no doubt they still loved her—but she had disappointed them profoundly. "It was a big deal," her brother recalled. Dickey, always the favorite, reeled from the unfamiliar lash of parental displeasure. She would have to take time off from college, get a job, and save up the necessary tuition funds to return. On July 1, 1936, she wrote Earl Findley that "the past seventeen years of my life have been one long struggle to be original—I even play unheard-of systems of bridge and have new ideas about which side of the road to drive upon. . . . This letter marks the funeral oration of that system in my personal history." Once again she asked Findley for a job, explaining that she could not return to MIT until the spring of the following year, about the time it would take her to "solve some of my financial difficulties." She added rather urgently that she had "no particular obligations here at home, and can and have travelled alone."

Unable to convince Findley to hire her, Dickey spent the summer and fall of 1936 working as a typist in the accounting section of the *Milwaukee Journal* and saving money for spring tuition at MIT. She traveled to Chicago, seventy-five miles south of Milwaukee, where, according to a letter from Stuart Hoyt, she had an affair with a married man, probably a pilot, whom Hoyt was convinced "you didn't particularly enjoy . . . from any but the intellectually curious point of view." The affair was a welcome diversion from her confused mental state. She was torn between pleasing her family—particularly her father, whose opinion meant so much to her and whom she knew she had already disappointed— which meant returning to MIT—and continuing in her dull job, where she was not making use of any of her reporting skills but where she could make up to her parents by handing over three-quarters of her salary. She was confused about Herb. She shared her anxiousness with Hoyt, who reiterated her dilemma: "The question is now not one of when, but rather if at all you will be coming back to Tech." He went on to berate her "12-year-old sense of idealism" for taking up the "cause" of repaying her family. "Georgie, you've amply repaid all you have to for the childhood support given you, and for God's sake it's your life that counts, not a retired WPA inspector's or a gushing mother who missed youth and youth's joys herself. . . ." And then he asked her to send him a box of Sheik condoms, because he couldn't find them in Cambridge.

Although letters from Stuart Hoyt insisted she "return to Tech and become the aeronautical engineer just like you said," mentioning that he never thought of her as "the adventure girl type," all that summer and into the fall Dickey knew her heart was not in designing planes and never had been. The idea of being a famous designer appealed to her, but the classes were boring. She was at her core a "daredevil type, who wanted action—and plenty of it." How could she reconcile that with her parents' expectations? Or with the brilliant Herb who arrived to resolve their estrangement? In what he later described as a "miserable experience" the two broke their engagement. Dickey put his picture inside a box of childhood papers. Only Stuart Hoyt seemed pleased, since he'd always believed she had better things to do than "bring a few kids into the world."

In a last-ditch effort to please her father, Dickey returned to MIT in the spring of 1937. A marginal sophomore, she was soon failing her classes, and at last the dean sent for her. "It didn't take the calculus I hadn't mastered," she later wrote, "to predict what was going to happen." She did not cry until she was on the bus for home. "I'd left home with all my family's hopes as class valedictorian. Now, two years later, I was coming back having flunked out of college."

EDNA'S DREAMS OF MATERNAL PRIDE in her daughter's college career were shattered. The disappointed woman retreated to her backyard with a kind of weary resignation. Her well-known green thumb brought forth spectacular blossoms that, unlike her two rebellious children, bent or spread as she demanded. While she pruned the rambler roses, lily of the valley, columbine, and currant bushes, Robert, now calling himself "Slug," and his pals were busy setting off cherry bombs in the doorways of unsuspecting neighbors. Dickey, meanwhile, was tempting fate.

Dickey had struck a deal with Elmer Francke, the chunky, red-haired pilot and flight instructor who ran the local air circus. She offered to be his private secretary in exchange for flying lessons. He hired her on for the summer.

ACCORDING TO MILWAUKEE OLD-TIMERS, the Curtiss Wright airfield attracted all sorts of strange characters, not only gypsy pilots, but physical misfits and drifters; it was the midwestern equivalent of a carnival midway. The airfield drew the confused Dickey Meyer like a magnet. On the bus home from MIT, she had cried, shamed by her academic failure; but such indulgences as shame did not exist in the airfield society, with its avowed disregard of conventional morals. These spirited outsiders had devised their own set of values, embodying for the dispirited Dickey a world she had long been seeking: men of action, exponents of the deed. Nobody in this ragged cast of characters cared if she got an A in chemistry. None of the pilots seemed to mind that she was a confused, smart, and mouthy kid, that she preferred trousers to skirts, and that she jumped uninvited into their conversations. They would tease her, tell her she looked more like a boy than a girl. But she knew it was because they appreciated her. She knew it because whenever she would pick up a broom and start sweeping out the hangar, one of the pilots would grab the broom and tell her she didn't have to do that.

Elmer Francke might bark at her all day and slam his office door in her face, but then he would amble out and sheepishly shout, "Oil up your typewriter, toots, and get in here pronto! I got some letters for you to type and you can sign 'em yourself. And for Chrissake, get 'em right this time."

It gave her a rich, warm feeling when Francke talked to her like that—as though she were one of the gang. She, Dickey Meyer, the only girl in the place, had found another bull session to crash—far more forbidden and dangerous than the boys' dorm at Tech.

It is doubtful that Edna was any more aware of the deal her daughter had struck with Francke than she had been of the flight over Worcester. But even if she had known, there was little she could do. Her daughter was now eighteen years old and had already expressed a will as strong and unbending as hers. Edna continued to worry, probably more than ever, as she watched her now aimless Georgie Lou take on the airs and slang of the rowdy pilots; but Edna's disappointment and the vagaries of the family's finances had taken the wind out of the woman's sails, causing her to slacken the reins she had held so tightly for so long. About this time she returned to teaching night school classes in interior design, where her class notes were organized in concrete terms of "order," whether it had to do with the color coordinates of a kitchen or the placement of a vase of flowers. Paul Meyer, however, had not yet given up on his daughter. It would take more than her flunking out of college to shake his faith. As if to emphasize this, Paul and Slug often went flying with her.

"She was a terrible pilot," offered Robert, recalling one incident when she'd nearly killed all of them while flying blindly through a sudden storm. Yet their faith was stronger than their fear, and they continued to go up with Dickey. Eventually she also realized the truth. She was, she later wrote, "the least-promising flight student who ever near-crashed a trainer on each circuit of the field." Her lousy vision, unbridled enthusiasm, and endless shrieks of joy at each takeoff—and grateful landing—made for a near hysterical pilot. Slug became the beneficiary of the remaining flight lessons.

Every weekday morning Dickey stood in front of the downtown Milwaukee Swedish bakery, her chubby fingers clutching a bag of fresh-baked, still warm rolls and a bottle of tomato juice, waiting for Elmer Francke to pick her up in his blue sedan. By 1937 the squat, stockily built Francke, like most of the remaining gypsy fliers and small-time flight operators, was fighting to survive in the face of a fickle public and stiff government safety regulations. When the red-eyed Elmer arrived, Dickey plopped onto the seat and slammed the door shut, greeting him with a cheerful "Hi, chief." He responded with the stony quiet of a vicious hangover. Wordlessly she handed him a can of tomato juice and a roll.

"I hired you to be a secretary, not a nurse," he growled, pushing away her offerings with disgust. Unruffled, she munched on the warm roll, enjoying the first sight of the Curtiss Wright airfield as Elmer screeched to a stop in front of the brick airplane hangar. The airfield's wire-fenced one hundred acres, its orange wind sock rippling like a fish on a hook, was the most exotic stretch of land she had ever set eyes upon. Even Francke's daily black mood, his unshaven mug, his hung-over eyes, couldn't dampen the thrill of just sitting in the hangar, inhaling airplane exhaust while banging out letters to bill collectors.

The stunt pilots would wink at her and call her "toots" or "sugar" as they ambled into the brick hangar. Dickey loved the smell and creak of their frayed leather jackets as they strolled past. They always seemed to be doing something so important. It wasn't only their dashing outfits—the high tan riding boots, khaki breeches, leather jerkins, and long silk scarves—and their faces covered with dust and airplane oil that drove her crazy. It was their whole attitude, men of deeds who didn't give a damn what anyone thought of them.

She gladly lied to their wives and their girlfriends when asked to. She didn't bat an eye when one of their girlfriends, still wearing last night's dress, would come wheeling out of the hangar into the morning air. She didn't mind that the pilots had bad teeth and hangovers. "I got a weakness for airplanes, too," she muttered as they breezed past her to their planes. "I know what it's like," she would say.

And on top of that, they took her up into the sky. They swept her high, spun her, descended in stomach-lurching swoops, skimmed their lightweight planes over the tops of the countryside silos. They buzzed over the heads of cows and over the highways. They touched the clouds and winged out and over the water towers fronting the Milwaukee River. The terror was thrilling.

These rough-talking pilots were not like Admiral Byrd. They were always trying to grab her by the waist in the corner of the hangar, and she was always telling them to quit it. But they knew how to fly. Once she saw one take up a plane with a faulty landing gear. By the time the teenage boys in the hangar realized it, it was too late to warn him.

A crowd gathered, and Dickey came running out. The plane seemed to be floating over the hangar. There was no parachute inside the plane, and she had no heart to watch the inevitable crash. But like the silent crowd, she could not look away. Her stomach was churning; she felt like throwing up. She put her hands over her eyes with the horror of what was sure to come, then spread her fingers. She could not look away. Suddenly the bird began to rise, higher above the landscape. She watched mutely, waiting now for the certain crash. Instead, somehow—a miracle—the landing gear thrust out. The plane caressed the field and settled down like a hen on a basket of eggs. The crowd shuddered in relief, and the pilot clambered out of the cockpit.

"That damn wheel didn't want to come out," he told Dickey. This time she let him put his arm around her as they walked to the hangar. "For a while, I thought it was all over. But I decided to just keep trying. I didn't have nothing to lose."

She wrote that after what she had seen she believed "miracles could happen. If you believed in them and kept your head."

At noon she would leave the hangar and walk the five hundred yards across the cement-scarred field to Ma and Pa's Diner, a small wood-frame shack painted green. As soon as she pulled open the fly-specked screen door, she was hit by the radio blasting the latest horse race out of Belmont.

Ma and Pa, the ex-carney couple who ran the little diner, rarely won at the races but never stopped trying. They regaled her with tales about the old days when they'd lived high on the hog and how all they needed now was to get themselves a stake. Dickey, whose only memory of gambling was playing dice with Grandpa Engelhardt, lapped up their stories along with the cold potatoes and sausage. In an early unpublished story, she wrote that she believed Ma and Pa to be the most real people she had met; they were not afraid to dream big. When they told her about the good old days of diamonds and big cars, something inside her got quivery and full of fire. She had added some new role models to her heroic pantheon; right up there with Richard E. Byrd were the gypsy pilots and the carney loser-dreamers—heady, dangerous company.

Summer was ending and with it her job with Elmer Francke. Dickey returned to the *Milwaukee Journal* and the dead-end, routine position of typist in its accounting department. She most certainly tried selling free-lance pieces to the paper on aviation, meeting with little success despite, or perhaps because of, her steady badgering of the editor at the city desk. But whatever disappointment she may have felt disappeared when she went to the airfield—which she did every weekend. At eighteen years old, aware that Elmer Francke's propellers were cutting not pieces of silver ribbon, but rolls of toilet paper to open the Sunday air circus, she still loved it. If anything, she thrilled more to the dangers knowing that all the parachutists earned for their split-second bravery before pulling the ripcord was five dollars; that the wing walkers, moving so casually on the flimsy wings or jumping from one plane to the other, received only two dollars and fifty cents for defying death.

However, it was the aerial displays, precision flying, and spellbinding loops of pilot Mike Murphy that really kept her enthralled. Sometimes he would really get the crowd churning by performing outside loops. Unlike the regular loops, which began only after the plane had climbed into a high altitude, the outside loops began in level flight, with the plane inverted as it made its circles, moving into stunning half rolls back to level flight.

The danger was beautiful. The demands of the outside loop put stress not only on the plane, but on the pilot as well. The plane had to be light, with a good lift and a powerful engine, in case the pilot needed sudden power to lift up and out. Mike told her that sometimes the outside loop gave him terrible headaches and bloodshot eyes; often pilots went temporarily blind doing loops.

By now Dickey couldn't keep everything from her high-strung mother. It did not take a clairvoyant to divine that her daughter's youthful adoration of pilots had grown into a major addiction. Edna was more than repulsed by the pilots. They were irresponsible and shiftless, and their rattletrap planes were terrifying. She had nightmares about her Georgie Lou running off with one of those seedy characters.

In a letter to Earl Findley dated January 6, 1938, Dickey unconvincingly wrote him that "I still am fired by a not utterly inexplicable desire to design airplanes. When I was fourteen, I knew precisely why 'we want to fly'; at eighteen, I have learned to accept the fact, ask no questions, and be as happy as possible about the whole thing, even if the only explanations that I can think of are distinctly unflattering."

She went on to discuss her interest in writing. "I would like to try turning some of what I have seen into black on white. I have had some rather interesting if not thoroughly conventional experiences reporting which might be used in fiction, like getting arrested on 'Suspicion of Lunacy' once in Salem, and getting knocked out for being mistaken for someone else at an airport which will remain nameless for obvious reasons." These youthful incidents would remain unmentionable family skeletons. When asked about them years later, Dickey's brother waved his hands and refused to answer. His sister didn't seem to have a problem with them, however. Writing in the same letter to Findley, she commented, "My parents have, however, a strange aversion to the use of such incidents in connection with my personal little 'By Line,' which you may understand even if I don't." This was the last letter she wrote to Mr. Findley. Her desire was to leave Shorewood, particularly now that her behavior was proving embarrassing for her staid family. Even Paul Meyer, her most loyal supporter, had grown anxious about her future. She applied for a job as a secretary with American Airlines in Chicago and was turned down. Lonely and frustrated, she continued to hang out at the Milwaukee and Chicago airfields, befriending itinerant skywriting pilots who worked for oil companies. Only the fraternity of shiftless barnstormers made any sense to her.

About six months after Dickey wrote Earl Findley about being slugged by a pilot, her parents, united for the first time, fearful for their daughter's future, packed her off to Coral Cables, Florida, where Edna's parents were retiring. Exactly what precipitated the move is unknown, but it most certainly involved some incident with a pilot. Dickey wrote only that "when Grandpa and Grandma moved into their retirement home in Coral Gables, Florida, they took me along to stay with them. My folks knew of no stunt pilot's little airport close to Miami and I couldn't find one either." No doubt the ever-frantic Edna believed that in this swank Miami suburb, where mango trees sprouted on manicured lawns and red-tiled roofs topped houses built like Chinese pagodas, her Georgie Lou would be safe from such riffraff.

Little did Edna know that the country's most popular air show extravaganza, the decade-old All American Air Maneuvers, was held a few miles from her parents' grapefruit tree-lined street. When Dickey saw the signs advertising the upcoming event, she hunted down the show's publicist, Bob Quinn. The tall, red-haired Irishman was harried, tough-talking, and desperate for an assistant. His small office was stacked with five years' worth of unfiled correspondence. He needed somebody to write up press releases, make hotel reservations for the world's top aviation reporters who would be arriving in droves, and chaperone the six beauty contestants who would be competing for the crown of Miss Aviation.

Enthusiastic and eager, Dickey seemed well suited for the job. She knew all about air circuses; she wore glasses and looked smart. She bragged to him about her newspaper experience at the *Boston Traveler*, and she looked old enough to chaperone the young lovelies. Quinn hired her as his "city editor" at the princely wage of fifteen dollars per week, which was not bad at all in the last year of the Depression. Dickey's grandfather was suspicious about her prospective job, but after he paid the irascible Quinn a visit, the elderly guardian of his granddaughter's virtue was satisfied that a job actually existed and that his high-spirited Georgie Lou would not be taken advantage of.

The three-day-long Eleventh Annual All American Air Maneuvers was held at the Miami airport beginning on January 5, 1939. It featured an air race from New York to Miami, aerobatics, a beauty contest, cash prizes, trophies, and what *The New York Times* called "the largest mass tour of civilian planes ever held in the world." This flying extravaganza, which attracted the top stunt pilots and racers, also brought army and navy planes. There were rigged mock battles, complete with re-creations of miniature towns and ammo dumps, and an air opera that included the use of bombers, dirigibles, fighter planes, and antiaircraft batteries.

The winter spa of Miami became a carnival town. Restaurants and bars jumped with well-heeled tourists. Pink-and-turquoise deco-modern hotels lining Miami Beach's Ocean Avenue were packed with party-going out-of-towners who lay on the palm tree–dotted white sand beaches under gaily colored, rented umbrellas. Pleasure yachts from New York and the Bahamas zipped around the sheltered mansions on Miami Beach's Bay Harbor Islands.

Dickey Meyer saw little of the snazzy action; she was far too busy cranking out press releases and making hotel reservations for the visiting aviation reporters. Even a sudden tropical downpour did not quench the excitement. As the excited crowd watched the unveiling of a bronze plaque in memory of Amelia Earhart, the sun broke through the rain. Two Miss Aviations—there had been a tie—were crowned to the cheers of four thousand spectators.

Away from the crowd ogling the Miss Aviations, Dickey was whooping it up as two small detachments of fighting craft from the United States Naval Air Reserve Base at Opa-Locka, Florida, flew over the field. They were B-17 bombers, part of what the army called its "Flying Fortresses." As she stood next to one of those huge four-engine defenders, wondering how a ride in that baby would feel, her boss came running up to her, waving his arms.

He was about to give her the assignment that could make her career in aviation public relations: to accompany the beauty contestants to Havana for the Cuban air show, a replay of the Miami show designed to showcase the talents of the Cuban air force. Her orders were to keep her eagle eyes on the girls, making sure they got off the boat in Havana and back onto it to Miami.

She had been regaling Quinn with her experiences as Boston's flying girl reporter. Now he was going to let her prove herself on this, her first foreign assignment. She was to file as many stories as possible to the Havana bureaus of the Associated Press and *The New York Times*.

Dickey was giddy with anticipation. Not only had she landed her first foreign assignment, but also she had bought her first silk dress, and, theoretically, was working for *The New York Times.* Life had not looked so good since she'd set out to conquer Cambridge almost four years earlier.

She was nineteen, on her own in Havana, and with her silk stockings clinging to her plump legs, she was ready for anything. A limousine whisked her and the beauty queens to the famed white sands of posh Veradero Beach and the swank Cabaña Club, then to a dinner party at the Havana Country Club, where she sat next to her favorite stunt flier, Mike Murphy, and drank champagne—lots of champagne.

The guests spent a good part of the evening toasting the country's new ruler, some guy named Batista. A young, flashy Cuban air force captain, Manuel Orta, led the toasts. He was mustached and charming, his uniform a field of dazzling medals. Dickey was promptly smitten.

Orta was a great admirer of all things American. He especially admired Mike Murphy's flying and declared he would attempt to duplicate his hero's aerobatics with an outside loop the next morning in one of his newly acquired American planes, a Curtiss Hawk. Dickey thought the captain extremely bold. Unlike the lightweight acrobatic planes used by American stunt fliers, designed especially to withstand the stress of acrobatic flying, the Hawks were considered far too heavy. If one ran into trouble in a climb, its monstrous engines, designed to carry heavy payloads like bomb racks and huge quantities of gasoline, would not react quickly enough for the pilot to bail out. In addition, the plane's ground visibility was notoriously poor. What if the fearless Orta became temporarily blinded, as often happened during the outside loop?

The following morning, the sun seemed uncommonly bright and irritating to Dickey. Each time she looked straight ahead, counting the crowd at the Rancho Boyeros Airport, she winced and renewed a vow to drink less champagne in the future. But, as miserable as she felt this morning, the night before had certainly been worth it. She could definitely get used to the exciting, glamorous life of a reporter.

The place was crawling with Cuban spectators and American press. Back in Miami Dickey had sharpened pencils and made hotel reservations for some of them, but here in Cuba they'd have to sharpen their own pencils, because technically she was working for *The New York Times.* She perched herself on the fender of a gleaming fire truck, her notebook open on her lap and a pencil stuck behind her ear.

The flamboyant Captain Orta waved to his wife and children and climbed into the heavy-framed Curtiss Hawk. The announcer's voice pierced the murmur of the crowd. As the stunt was explained, the excited crowd became silent. Dickey squirmed uneasily, considering the odds, unsure whether she was nervous from her hangover or some creeping premonition. She lit a cigarette.

Orta took the plane up one thousand feet, climbing over the crowd and getting ready to dive down into the loop. "With the greatest precision, the Hawk held course until it whipped past the far end of the crowd," Dickey wrote later. "It rocked four times. . . . This brought it passing straight and level, but upside down directly in front of the audience.

"Orta began to execute the most difficult part of the most difficult maneuver, the recovery from the outside loop. At first the nose did rise. Then it was not rising anymore. The whole plane was trembling in the sky. . . ."

But Dickey had seen such impossible situations before, hadn't she? Back at Curtiss Wright she had witnessed a miracle, hadn't she? She had seen stunt fliers like Mike Murphy spin planes like tops and emerge unscathed—why not Orta, with his flashing dark eyes? He was so brave. He simply had to survive—if he could see. Maybe he had lost his vision, the way Mike had described it. . . .

For a few cruel seconds the plane seemed to continue rising. Then there was an empty space in the sky where the big plane had shuddered. It did not tumble to earth. Its heavy body dropped, and the crash sent an echo through the field as the ground splattered with thunder and metal. Dickey froze as people ran past her. She did not want to report this. She did not—repeat, did not—want to look at death.

When she finally got to what remained of the plane, she was stopped by a soldier's rifle. She was still holding her cigarette, and there was gasoline sprayed all over the ground from the shattered tank. She smashed out her cigarette, shouted, "¡Prensa!"—"Press!"—and stepped closer to the wreckage. A deafening stillness had descended. Orta's proud, flashing eyes and cocky, reckless swagger had been stopped by a propeller blade thrust through his chest.

"The sight was almost empty of horror at first because the destruction had been nearly complete," Dickey wrote. "There was no sound, nor any reminder of suffering."

So this is how it is, she thought numbly. The bright, blinding sun cracked black over the wreckage. No breeze rustled any piece of the disaster. The footsteps of the retreating crowd did not echo. Only eerie silence prevailed, as if the crash had swallowed up all the noise on earth.

She thought about the captain's wife and children, part of the audience he had so wanted to impress. She thought of the dispassionate news story she was going to have to file, reducing a man, his life, vitality, and persistence, to the mere facts of his death: his age, how many people were present, what time it occurred. As if drugged, she slowly became aware that it was her job. That was what reporters did. They reported. Whether they wanted to write about the horrors they witnessed had nothing to do with the job. Her job was to get to a phone, and she started running.

By the time Dickey found a telephone, everyone else had already filed. Only one newsman was left, yelling into the phone—the reporter for the Hearst-owned International News Service, a wire service that would feed the grim information to the daily newspapers it serviced. In only minutes *The New York Times* would have the story, even if she didn't call in. Dickey scrambled wildly through her handbag, unable to find the phone number of the Havana bureau of the paper. Watching her frantic search, the reporter started to laugh and at last connected her with the Havana bureau.

"He told me that he wouldn't have connected me with the competition so quickly, except that he'd already scooped me," she wrote. "He told me not to depend on other reporters to put me in communication with my office. Which is how I learned a first principle about reporting."

After blurting out the story to the bureau, she wandered to a stretch of lawn, still badly shaken. She sat down, hiked up the hem of her silk dress, and lit another cigarette, unable to get Orta's dancing eyes out of her mind. She also was aware that if she was going to write about the glory of flying, she had better be prepared for the cruel reality of its failures. It was the part nobody liked to talk about. She didn't know how to reconcile this ugly reality with the thrill and beauty of flying, but she knew if she kept at this reporter's game, she was going to see her share of both.

The INS reporter, having found Dickey's clumsy amateur reporting amusing, could not wait to tell her story to his colleagues. Besides, after the morning's tragedy they needed a good laugh. It so happened that one of the reporters milling about as he shared his tale was United Press's aviation editor, Theon Wright. He had just become the public relations director for the New York office of Transcontinental and Western Air, later to be known as Trans World Airlines. In her autobiography Dickey wrote that Theon "inexplicably found something in the tale to my credit and hired me as his assistant."

Actually Theon hired Dickey as his secretary, a far less glamorous job. Yet however boring the job must have looked to this girl so hungry for action, it served several important purposes. For one thing, it got her easily away from her loving if overly vigilant grandparents and into the high-stakes world of New York. And since the job was with a large, well-known company, its legitimacy would satisfy Edna.

3

"Seven Miles a Minute"

ALTHOUGH there is no correspon-
dence between Edna and Dickey during this period, letters in the years
to come would reveal, not surprisingly, that Edna was opposed to her
daughter's decision to move to New York, job or no job. What was the
point of having children, Edna would demand, of maintaining a lovely
home, if your children weren't there to enjoy it with you?

But Dickey Meyer was having too good a time to let her mother's
chronic nagging bother her. She might have been adrift on a sea of
indecision, her future unfocused, but she sensed a place for herself in
Manhattan. The island, described in guidebooks of the time as a "melt-
ing pot" of 1,867,312 multicultured souls compressed into an area twelve
and a half miles long and two and a half miles wide, excited her. It gave
her confidence in its endless possibilities. Its rush was her tempo. Everywhere she looked—and she did a lot of looking when she first arrived—
people were bustling. Under her feet, subway trains ran the length of the
metropolis in endless, pounding circuits. If the world of Milwaukee
never understood her, the hum of Manhattan embraced her immediately, speeding her along in its constant forward motion. It was a city
of faces, all of whom she wanted to know. The fact was she didn't know

anybody except her girlish aunt George, who lived alone in a tiny apartment on noisy Fourth Street in Greenwich Village, its winding streets bright with cafes and bars, home to the city's bohemian artists and writers. Dickey rented an apartment the size of a prison cell at the Hotel Pierrepont, across the East River in Brooklyn Heights. She was there only to sleep and change clothes, spending most of her time discovering the island, sometimes in tandem with the gregarious George, who knew where to buy Greek goat cheese, Italian sausages, Jewish delicatessen, and Chinese joss sticks. Dickey was never lonely walking by herself, because she was traveling around the world. When the din, the screeching peddlers and their pushcarts, the traffic, and the old world peasant women keening in the streets threatened her equilibrium on the jarring streets of the Lower East Side, she would run up Allen and onto Pike to the upward thrust of the Brooklyn Bridge, on which she crossed the East River.

From her windowed cubicle in the fifty-three-story Lincoln Building on Forty-second Street, she could gape at the Chrysler Building, which seemed dizzyingly to pierce the sky, or she could look down at the endless crowds entering and leaving Grand Central Station. Even if the job of typing out press releases to the city's photo and aviation editors was achingly boring, the city's myriad possibilities never failed to thrill her. Besides, the job had its perks. She took part in the opening festivities of La Guardia Airport, driving over Pulaski Skyway in a flag-bedecked airline limousine to watch Mayor Fiorello La Guardia cut the ribbon. She flew out to California and back for free. Some weekends she'd find herself at Brooklyn's Floyd Bennett Field, where three dollars would buy her fifteen minutes in an airplane over the glamorous island.

She attended the 1939 World's Fair at Flushing Meadow in Queens, visiting the marine transportation exhibit several times. Standing with thousands, she watched the nightly fireworks display at the Lagoon of Nations. She kept returning to see the General Motors Futurama exhibit, where she sat on an armchair on a conveyor belt and was carried over the world's largest animated model of what the world would be like in 1960.

Whenever Dickey wanted to know what was going on in the world, she would take the short walk up Broadway, "the Great White Way," to Times Square and the *New York Times* Building. On a belt circling the exterior, electric bulbs spelled out spot news in moving letters visible blocks away. All the news was about Hitler. The Nazis were signing a nonaggression pact with the Soviets. The United States Congress wanted to enforce the Neutrality Act. Standing in the crowd, she could smell the war coming across the Atlantic. It haunted her.

She remembered growing up, how her grandfather, Limburger cheese ripe on his breath, would recount his father's hasty departure from Germany in 1848 because he opposed the draft laws of the duke of Württemberg. She later wrote that "pacifism" was a "fact" of her family tradition, although her brother disputed that. "I had been well-taught that violence in any form was unthinkable," she wrote. "It was so unthinkable that it became as attractive a mystery to me as sex seemed to be to other teen-agers."

Some Sundays she would walk through the deserted city, letting the sun dance over her in the splendor of Central Park. But most weekends she traveled by bus or commuter train to air shows, now writing stories about them that she occasionally sold to the *New York Times* Aviation Section. At one of these shows, at the Long Island Aviation Country Club, she talked her way into a navy fighter biplane—the Grumman F3, then one of the world's fastest planes—by asking its owner, Le Roy Grumman, if he had ever known a reporter who had given a first-person account of the sensations of a terminal-velocity power drive. He said "no." Although the F3 was built as a single-seater, the plane Dickey was looking at had a second cockpit, constructed for prospective buyers. Impressed by her eagerness and knowledge of aviation, he invited her to take a ride and experience the brutal force of nine G's.

Antigravity suits had not yet been invented, so Dickey was counting on her three-dollar-and-ninety-eight-cent girdle to keep her body from flying apart. The pilot tossed her a parachute, telling her, "Don't forget to scream." He continued, "When your eyes black out, it'll be from the G. Give your gut a break. Scream, so it'll tighten up." He told her that should the plane go into a spin, she should quickly jump out of the plane. He explained, "I'm not waiting for any damn dame, is that clear?" Mr. Grumman personally hooked her up to the parachute.

She wrote about the experience in an unpublished article entitled "How It Feels to Go Seven Miles a Minute": "We go up to 10,000 feet. I want to yell, 'This is it! Now we'll find out if a girl can dive seven miles a minute—and live.' I hold my breath. The engine roars. We dive for a huge circle in the airport's sod. I tense myself for the expected pull-out."

Later she wrote that the stabbing roar of the wind and the engine was the loudest sound she had ever heard, and the most painful. She had nothing to stuff into her ears but her fingers. She figured the speed, when she could, by the size and shape of the earth, how the airport had first appeared as they went into the dive, small as a postage stamp, stabbing into a handkerchief, forming into a tabletop, a lawn, a flying field, all the universe. . . .

Visions of Captain Orta were churning in grisly display through her mind as the pilot pressed ahead. "But I wasn't dead! Ahead of us came a flash of light from the horizon, not only the darkness of earth. Then, as the pressure drove the blood from my eyes, it all turned black and I could feel the other effects of the terrifying G. The flesh on my cheeks pulled into dewlaps, my calves were stretched like rubber toward my heels, I could not move a muscle of my arms and legs. Finally I remembered to scream, but what I screamed or if I made a sound I could not tell.

"At seventy miles an hour we float in to a landing," she continued. "Shakily, I get out, still in one piece. Everybody is amazed. Maybe I have traveled faster than any other woman. I have proved, I think, that girls could become combat pilots."

When Dickey stumbled out of the plane, named the *Scarlet Woman*, she was too weak to talk. It took her four days to recover, and her girdle never did.

Right before her death, Dickey's octogenarian aunt Lutie recalled that love of aviation brought her niece and Tony Chapelle together. Dickey wrote that Tony, a World War I navy photographer, directed TWA's publicity pictures and shared her love of aviation. He was a pilot and a photography teacher. Shortly after her thrilling ride in the *Scarlet Woman*, Dickey signed up as one of Tony's students. The class met on Saturdays. She was uncharacteristically awestruck around him, though not by his physical appearance: he was short and chunky, with lots of brown hair, a dark mustache, and laughing brown eyes. It was his deep melodious voice that impressed her, and an inexplicable sense of danger, that drew her like a magnet. She noted that he was one of the most cheerful people she'd ever met, except when he'd been crossed, when he would explode in a frightening "Homeric wrath." He was the first man she'd ever encountered who seemed to pulsate with confidence, especially when he was teaching photography. He taught it as a guru, introducing his unknowing students to a special, mysterious world. He moved quickly and corrected like a drill instructor. It was in his teaching that she sensed what for her had always separated the men from the boys, his single-mindedness of purpose. When he told her he held only one thing sacred, photography, her fate was sealed. He discounted writing, except for captioning photographs.

As Dickey's Prince Charming, Tony introduced her to a group of New York women aviators who were forming a nonprofit, all-volunteer woman's flying organization called the Women Fliers of America. Dickey became the group's volunteer public relations director in the summer of 1940. The WFA, which swelled to a membership of one thousand New York–area women by the end of that year, offered discount flying lessons and, when World War II was declared, would take over the domestic duties of flying the mails, delivering planes from factories to air bases, and performing ground duties. Dickey once again took flight lessons, but there is no indication that she received her pilot's license.

Unquestionably the most impressive part of being a WFA member was the uniform, a sleek adaptation of the United States Army's flying suit. Worn with a white helmet, the royal-blue corduroy outfit also featured sleeves that could be buttoned back or worn full length and closed at the wrist. Pictures of WFA members in their summer and winter flying suits appeared frequently in the women's pages of *The New York Times.* The photos were taken gratis by Tony, who would later explain—when the WFA objected to Dickey's inclusion of the photos without the group's permission in one of her U.S. government fluff books—that he had volunteered only because of his friendship with Dickey.

The impact Tony Chapelle had on the naive, farm girl–plain Dickey Meyer was evident in a publicity photograph of her in her WFA uniform. The man's artistry wasn't purely technical; he also had masterful powers of persuasion. By this time he had convinced her she was beautiful. The photo ran in the *Milwaukee Journal* sometime in the summer of 1940. A former Shorewood High classmate remembered how stunned she was when she opened the newspaper. Scanning the caption in disbelief, she thought at first that the editor had made a mistake. This couldn't possibly be her weird, dowdy dumpling former schoolmate.

Under the heading READY TO DEFEND HER COUNTRY appeared a Hollywood version of Dickey Meyer, lipsticked and nostrils flaring, her hands clenched around the harness straps of a parachute. A white aviator's helmet covered her head. Her eyes looked heavenward, eager and inspired, as if they'd finally glimpsed their starry future. (Unseen, on her bra strap, dangled a silver leg on a pair of wings, a gift from the photographer.) In the clichéd Hollywood pose, Tony had caught all of Dickey Meyer's romantic yearnings. His photographic illusion had given bodily form to her lifelong fantasies. The street-smart Svengali had breathed life into her youthful dreams.

There is probably nothing quite so appealing to a jaded appetite as a fresh canvas. Tony, more than twenty years older than Dickey, a skirt chaser and hustler, eyed that unformed girl as though she were a yard of newly stretched muslin on an easel. The attraction was mutual. Tony looked like the prizefighter that Georgie Lou Meyer had confided to Florence Ballencourt she wanted one day to marry. He was, like Dickey's father, a short, authoritative man who appeared to have great faith in her youthful idealism. Blind to his weaknesses, dismissing the advice of well-meaning friends like her boss, Theon, she saw in him a man of action who cared only for his craft. What's more, no matter how many stunt pilots Dickey may have slept with, none of them could compare with the sophisticated, mysterious Tony. Certainly none were as passionate a lover as the man with the camera.

Tony Chapelle was an imposter who, like Dickey, was continually reinventing himself. According to naval records, he was born Anthony Capelli on December 20, 1898, in New York. He was one of four children born to Anthony and Caroline Capelli, both of whom were deaf-mutes. "When I die I want to go just like my old man: with a bottle in one hand and a blonde in the other," one acquaintance recalled Tony saying. In fact, according to relatives, Tony's father was killed when he drunkenly stepped in front of a passing streetcar. A nephew recalled that the Italian family struggled to make ends meet. When Tony was eighteen, he joined the navy and saw the world. About the time that he met Dickey, he began going by the name Chapelle. His nephew quipped that he probably did it because "it sounded classier than Capelli," but he may have been doing it for more pragmatic reasons, such as avoiding past encumbrances. He told Dickey he had been married once before and was divorced. He told her he had learned photography as an aerial "spotter" during World War I. Conrad "Ron" Chapelle, Tony's son by the woman believed to be his second wife, claimed his dad's plane was shot down, he was injured, and he subsequently received several medals for his bravery. But a check of his military records reveals a decidedly dull naval career. He signed on as a yeoman third class with no record of wounds or awards. Ron Chapelle's heroic story is the wishful fantasy of a boy who was abandoned by his parents at the age of two to a series of foster homes. When flush Tony would send Ron money. He would rarely visit. When he did he would show up in an expensive car, dressed snappily. Ron recalled his father as charming and superficial, but he also believed that if Tony had ever loved anybody, it was Dickey. "He cried real tears when she died and seemed genuinely upset."

Like Dickey, Tony left hardly a trail, despite his many affairs, marriages, and, according to Ron, his reported offspring. He was, in the words of one wife, "a real mystery man." The difference between them, Ron recalled, was that Dickey took a real interest in him. As a concerned stepmother, she spent many a Saturday riding the New York Central to Pawling in upstate New York, where Ron was attending Pawling Trinity Prep School, financed by Tony, to drill the teenager in grammar. "She believed," Ron said, "that if I was going to use the language, I'd better damn well know how to use it. I guess you can say that she also taught my dad where to dot the *i,* and he taught her how to use a light meter." When Dickey and Tony broke up, they met Ron at Grand Central Station. Although their explanation was logical, professional needs having gotten in the way of their marriage, Ron was devastated. They were the closest he'd ever come to having a family.

Tony would often rent a plane to fly Dickey, his most promising photography student, over the George Washington Bridge. At Tony's urging, Dickey learned photography. He convinced her it would enhance her writing career. She wrote that Tony believed photos were "your reason for being," telling her, "it doesn't matter what you've seen with your eyes. If you can't prove it happened with a picture, it didn't happen."

While she hung over the side shooting with his four- by five-inch, eight-pound Speed Graphic camera, he'd yell over the noisy engine for her to think about what she was photographing. Fearing that she would bring forth his terrible temper if she messed up, she focused carefully and shot. Dickey proved a brilliant student.

Dickey credited Tony with teaching her everything she knew about photography. It was later recommended by both her photo agent and another lover that she forget everything Tony had taught her, but at the age of twenty Dickey considered Tony her guru, her great lover, and the man who unlocked the key to her destiny. "You have taught me to love loving," she told him.

All her life she had been looking for direction for her boundless energy and insatiable curiosity. Now, this confident, worldly man, with his dimples and tattoo of a monkey on his right forearm, who had seen war and lived life, was spoon-feeding it to her. Tony would later write that he wanted to help her "realize her childhood dreams," although it is doubtful he took seriously her desire to emulate Richard Harding Davis and Richard E. Byrd. What he really wanted was to freeze that naive, blindly smitten disciple in time. It was not an unrealistic desire. Dickey absorbed his image of her like a sponge. Although when they filled out their marriage license they listed two different addresses, it is most likely that by this time they were living together in Tony's East Thirty-first Street Manhattan apartment. Dickey's transformation was far too profound to have been effected without constant supervision, and Tony could not tolerate living alone. He stepped into Dickey's life with vitality and decision. He tossed out her formless clothes and dressed her in tailored, sexy silks and velvets and peek-a-boo French lingerie. She opened charge accounts at some of New York's finest department stores, Saks and Lord & Taylor. He gave her a maharajah's feast of what he called "golden baubles." There was a moonstone brooch and one in jade, lapis lazuli, and coral; a gold Mido watch; a gold Cartier watch; a gold Dunhill cigarette lighter; pearl earrings; and gold-and-emerald cuff links. The gold Dunhill lighter was a mate to one Tony carried. When he handed it to her, she gasped with delight and told him it made her heart throb. She didn't wear her glasses often, but when she did they didn't look like Coke-bottle bottoms anymore. Instead they were harlequin-shaped, outrageously big, and dramatic. She wore lipstick, and she colored her hair a golden blond that had a way of picking up the sun. Her once pudgy body disappeared. She was now running at slender, high-speed efficiency, a light one hundred pounds. Dickey Meyer emerged a lustrous young woman.

Years later Tony liked to tell the story of his marriage proposal. He presented Dickey with a velvet-boxed diamond engagement ring. She accepted the proposal but refused the gift. She wanted not another piece of jewelry, she told him, but her own camera. He bought Dickey a Graflex Speed Graphic camera.

In her autobiography she wrote hardly anything about Tony, though next to her bond with her mother, whom she also declined to write about, theirs was the most enduring relationship of her life. The reason for this reticence was one of enlightened self-interest: disclosure would soil the myth she had spun so elaborately, the adventure girl who for career reasons had no sex or past, particularly one as filled with scandal as her life with Tony would become. Beyond this instinct for keeping her celebrity pure, she was also protecting herself from Tony's "Homeric wrath," which she had come to know all too well. Yet despite their tempestuous moments, they remained close, and Dickey was steadfast. She remained loyal to his masterful ability with the camera. His lessons were learned "bone deep as quickly as I could. And I don't think I've ever forgotten any of them."

"If you were a real photographer," Tony told the attentive Dickey, "you'd be on the spot where things happened before they happened." He told her a photographer did not walk to plane crashes, as she had in Cuba. "You're sitting on the fire truck before the airplane hits and nobody takes time to throw you off, so you get out there ahead of the police. Ahead." He further instructed her always to be the "first" on the scene, not to hang back, no matter how insecure she might feel.

Tony was five feet seven and weighed upward of two hundred pounds. But he had a gift that served him far better than physical charms: his voice. It was what drama teachers call an instrument, like the voice of an evangelist or radio actor, a voice that conveyed majestic forbearance. It had such charisma that when Dickey's 107-year-old aunt Lutie was asked how her niece first met Tony, she declared that Dickey had met him over the telephone. "She fell in love with his voice." There is a certain unanimity among his former wives as well as female acquaintances that the short, walrus-shaped ex-sailor could, in the words of his last wife, "charm the tits off a brass monkey."

Lutie stated that Dickey was happy with Tony for "fifteen wonderful years." She also recalled that Tony would always call her, even after the two split up. "I guess he was on his—how many wives did Tony have? Anyway, he would call me, tell me, 'Lutie, I'll always love Dickey.' "

OCTOBER 2, 1940, was one of those wonderful Indian summer days in Shorewood. Folks in shirtsleeves were raking the leaves from their front lawns. Although the war in Europe was mushrooming, America was firmly maintaining its head-in-the sand, isolationist attitude. One month earlier President Franklin Delano Roosevelt had inaugurated the draft, calling up eight hundred thousand men. For now, only embattled Britain stood between America and Hitler's growing European fortress.

But inside Edna Meyer's house, on this rare warm day, there was little thought about the war. While the minister, Roscoe Graham, cleared his throat and thought about the solemnity of the afternoon wedding between Edna's daughter and this New York fellow, the nervous, excited mother of the bride bustled around filling one crystal vase after another with her abundant floral harvest. The bridal mainstay, lily of the valley, looked particularly beguiling. The silver Chantilly place settings sparkled.

Fifteen-year-old Slug, tall as a pole and socially awkward, stood dumbstruck on the front porch of the Meyer house as the sleek black 1938 Buick convertible with its New York plates came purring down the street. The car's white sidewall tires didn't so much kiss the curb as whisper against it. For a few seconds Slug stared disbelievingly at the good-looking young woman sliding out from the passenger side. His sister looked like an ad for Pabst Blue Ribbon beer. She was wearing a light blue summer dress, and her hair looked blond and wonderful. She was even wearing jewelry, pearl earrings tastefully appointed and a thin gold watch glimmering on her wrist.

The driver of the car was short and stocky and walked with a fighter's easy, loping gait. He was wearing a dark suit and a black fedora hat, just what Slug expected a New York gangster to wear at his wedding. Slug had never seen a man as manly as Tony. The boy liked his swaggering future brother-in-law right away.

Tony took Slug's hand and shook it with real gusto, looking the young boy straight in the eye while grabbing Dickey's waist like a ball player catching a pop fly. Slug was so impressed that he overlooked the man's painfully embarrassing behavior with his sister. The Meyers did not go in for public displays of affection. Edna and Paul stood outside clearing their throats uncomfortably while Tony and Dickey embraced. Years later, Slug's wife, Marian, spoke with envy about Tony and Dickey's spontaneous affection, hoping that it would rub off on her reticent husband. "It was never embarrassing," she said of their kissing and hugging. "It seemed very natural."

In the bright afternoon light, Tony's face looked to Slug as it had to his sister, a fighter's face, scarred and weather-beaten, the face of somebody who could take care of himself and Georgie Lou. But what impressed Slug the most about Tony was that the guy knew his sister inside out and, amazingly, still loved her.

The only information the Meyer family had about the man who was marrying their daughter that afternoon in Edna's garden was what he had told Georgie Lou. They knew he was divorced, a New Yorker, a professional photographer, and a World War I navy veteran. They thanked their lucky stars he wasn't a stunt pilot. Edna and Paul and the rest of the family were worried about his age, which he'd listed as forty-three on the marriage license. He was so much older than their twenty-one-year-old child, but he didn't seem middle-aged at all. He moved around the family like a beam of radiant light, seeming bigger and younger than he was. He had them spellbound with the tales of adventure his rich orator's voice kept spinning.

The ceremony was small. The aunts could not attend. Georgie Lou called her old friends, Mary Holgate and Flo Ballencourt, but they were away at college. However, Mary's parents did attend. Mrs. Holgate, like most women who met Tony Chapelle, was so taken by him that she told her daughter he was one of the most charming men she had ever met. It seemed he had been everywhere. He knew sheiks and counts, had visited the Taj Mahal, and had slept in castles and Bedouin tents. The solid, unsophisticated Meyers never doubted him, because they couldn't imagine anyone making up such amazing stories.

"Tony taught our family a lot," recalled Slug, now Robert P. Meyer, a professor of geophysics at the University of Wisconsin's Madison campus. "He taught us that if you are going to do something, do it right and do it first class." Robert remarked that Tony delivered this advice in a voice that sounded halfway between God's and Humphrey Bogart's.

Edna liked the intent way he listened to her every word. It was just as well that she didn't know what he was thinking. He had sized up his midwestern mother-in-law in a hot tick, believing her to be one of the most manipulative women he had met. Later he would write, "She only thinks of men in terms of how they can service her." But on that warming afternoon, Tony listened to Edna as if she were the only person in the world. From Edna's point of view, Tony was to act as her surrogate; it was understood without much discussion that he would watch over and guide Georgie Lou, keeping her out of harm's way. From that day Edna would refer to Tony as Georgie Lou's "bulldog."

The Meyers were so impressed by their son-in-law that even if they had known that the afternoon's wedding ceremony was not legal—Tony was still married to Carmel, the mother of his son, Ron, who would not get around to divorcing him for six more years on grounds of desertion— they'd still have liked him. Nothing like Tony Chapelle—certainly no one as charming or as warm—had ever entered their world.

4

Baptism by Fire

Less than three weeks after Dickey and Tony were married, they were on their honeymoon in Canada, a nation already at war with Germany. The newlyweds were working on a story about American pilots who had signed up for service with the Royal Canadian Air Force. Tony was shooting the story for the Scripps-Howard newspaper chain. Dickey's byline would appear later that month in *The New York Times* Aviation Section.

Dickey had by now managed to sell a few pictures to daily newspapers and, emboldened by Tony's encouragement, readily quit her job as Theon's secretary to pursue free-lancing full time. Dickey's decision was influenced by her husband's current financial state, which changed like the phases of the moon. He was experiencing a windfall from his free-lance photo assignments, his photo-printing business, his photography classes, and one or two side hustles, enough to support a wife who wanted to become a reporter/photographer.

The article in *The New York Times,* datelined October 27, 1940, was prefaced in italics by the note that Dickey Meyer, as she was then known professionally, was the first woman newspaper correspondent to be permitted access to Canadian air force bases. Dickey reported that American fliers, anxious to get "into the show," as one of them told her, were entering Canada at the rate of sixty-five a week to volunteer in the Royal Canadian Air Force.

With the same guileless ease with which she had taken to calling herself a "Tech woman," Dickey now considered herself a "dedicated" photographer. However, her initial attempts at selling to *Life,* America's prestigious picture magazine, were met with curt rejection. *Life* had made a great star of photographer Margaret Bourke-White, personally picked by its publisher, Henry Luce, to shoot the magazine's debut cover, but her fame opened no doors for other, less well-connected women photojournalists. There were women in journalism at the time, as there were women in sports, hors d'oeuvres at a cocktail party. The world of print journalism, when Dickey set out to conquer it as a photog-rapher-cum-reporter, was a closed society of white, mostly upper-class men, driven by the boys' club mentality. Any outsider wanting in, particularly one not favored like Bourke-White by brilliance and the sponsorship of a publishing czar, had to push hard, ask no favors, and, unlike her male counterparts, prove herself time and again. In truth, Dickey's photographs were not in the same league as those of Bourke-White, whose haunting pictures from the front lines goaded Dickey from the pages of *Life.* But the one area in which she did equal and possibly excel Bourke-White was determination and ambition.

As would prove typical, Tony's financial state changed daily, although his actual cash flow rarely made a difference in his life-style, which for the most part was always comfortable. He claimed this "never mattered to me and Dickey." And he was right. Dickey's needs for expensive clothes and jewels fluctuated. They were more a fling than a necessity. At this particular time Tony was experiencing a dwindling cash flow from his apartment-based photo-printing business, and despite the break in their rent—they managed their Riverside Drive apartment building in exchange for free rent—Dickey was soon out pounding the pavement for a job as well as hustling her photos, making an occasional sale to a newspaper or one of the picture magazines. She also cranked out two government fluff books, *Needed: Women in Government Service* and *Needed: Women in Aviation.* She wrote to her former boss, Theon Wright, now at the company's headquarters in Kansas City, Missouri, asking for a reference.

"You can certainly call on me for any recommendation you want," Theon wrote her on January 25, 1941. "As a matter of fact, I could conscientiously recommend you as a young lady who was too good (no sarcasm intended) for her job. If anybody wants a red-hot promoter who looks better in a pilot's uniform than she does at a secretary's desk, tell them to drop me a note. . . ." He went on to add that he trusted her marriage was "as happy as can be expected—and that's a general statement, not a personal insult." He followed it up with an interesting postscript: "I might have advised you to keep your feet on the ground, but I know how you like to fly."

Despite being turned down by *Life* and *Look* and nearly every other picture magazine, Dickey continued to go out every day and take pictures. She credited Tony with stoking the fires, encouraging her to do picture stories on spec, which they would process together. Her tenacity paid off. In the spring of 1941 she sold a "spec" picture story to *Look* magazine—a six-page spread lovingly processed by Tony "until it was perfect" about a woman in Brewster, New Jersey, who was working in an aircraft plant on the wings of RAF fighter planes on their way to the Battle of Britain.

Dickey's publication in *Look* failed to set any fires under magazine photo editors. But having finally cracked one of the "biggies," as she would refer to *Look,* she continued trying—and eventually made two more sales to the magazine.

On the afternoon of December 7, 1941, Dickey and Tony left their brownstone apartment with its view of the Hudson for a relaxing drive to upstate New York. On the radio, Helen Forrest was singing the hit tune "Green Eyes" with the Tommy Dorsey orchestra, when a bulletin came on.

Tony and Dickey pulled over to the side of the road as the radio broadcaster announced that six great American battleships had been sunk or paralyzed, brutally stopping American striking power in the Pacific. Like the rest of the American public, they were stunned.

The following day, after President Roosevelt called December 7 "a date which will live in infamy," all but one member of the Senate voted for war against the Axis powers. Three days later Germany and Italy declared war on the United States, and Congress passed a joint resolution accepting the state of war, "which has been thrust upon the United States."

The attitude across the country was one of dramatic and swift cohesion. Political differences were subordinated. America mobilized. The patriotism that sprang from the attack on Pearl Harbor was so overpowering that the isolationists and the interventionists quickly came together in the common cause of fighting against an enemy so rapacious and evil. Even among the Anglophobic, isolationist, pacifist, and anti-Semitic groups such as the America First Committee, supported by individuals as diverse and powerful as aviator Charles Lindbergh and Colonel Robert McCormick, the publisher of the *Chicago Tribune,* there came an awareness that it was time for America to take its head out of the sand and "lick hell out of them." Two weeks after war was declared, *Life* magazine ran a black-and-white cover of the flag, waving in the breeze. The same piece of cloth had aroused the country in the Spanish-American War and the First World War, but it had never wrapped around the country as it did in this media blitz. And when it flew from the top of an ugly volcano on the Pacific island of Iwo Jima, it would become the most famous war picture ever.

Tony immediately volunteered to teach sailors aerial photography. He was assigned as chief petty officer to the Coco Solo Naval Air Station in the Canal Zone, Panama, and sailed out of New York Harbor on a chilly January morning.

Despite newspaper advertisements advising its patriotic women read-ers that the best way of saying "We won't be beaten" was a weekly visit to the local beauty salon, Dickey had her own ideas. First she sat down and poured out her feelings in a thinly disguised fictional story that she dedicated to "the hundreds of thousands of women who are making, with their own hands, the might of America's air power." In her story the heroine, a young girl named Nikki, manufactures a part for her lover's plane—a pilot named Ty who is headed for action overseas. In the story Nikki conceals her grief, happy that Ty is going off to fight "to preserve the American way." About this time, Dickey's book *Needed: Women in Aviation* was released, dedicated to her husband, Tony. She told an interviewer from a local newspaper that she hoped her book would help American women who felt they wanted to do something "which ties in directly with the war, something to better the chances of the men they love." The reporter described Tony as having flown over France, deep into enemy territory during World War I, recording with his camera where railroads had been hit. When the reporter asked Dickey where her husband was, she answered, "I don't know, thousands of miles from here, I think." In fact, Dickey had determined to join Tony and launch her career as a combat photographer. Unfortunately the navy did not allow a wife to accompany her husband, unless of course she happened to be an accredited war correspondent.

Having learned something about hustling from her masterful husband, Dickey parlayed her three sales to *Look* magazine into a trip to the Canal Zone with two firm assignments: one on the gun crews working on freighters running the blockade, the other on an American worker in Panama. It was understood she would have both pieces, which she'd begun working on in New York, finished within two weeks of her arrival in Panama. But before she could leave on the assignment, she needed wartime accreditation, and that meant approval by the War Department.

The young wife made her first trip to Washington, D.C., on a hot, sticky May morning. On the bus ride, crowded with enlisted men, Dickey tried to keep crisp in the steamy humidity while she rehearsed all the questions she believed the army's public relations officer, a Colonel Dupuy, might ask. "It developed that he had only one question," wrote Dickey. " 'I presume you realize, Mrs. Chapelle,' began the colonel, 'that troops in the field have no facilities for women?'

"The classic military semantics—the I-presume-you-realize wording—was never more just. I'd not only failed to realize it, I'd never given it a minute's thought. I had no answer ready and stood dumb. Frantically my mind went to what I knew of the—what was it again—Fourteenth Infantry?

" 'Colonel,' I said earnestly, 'I'm sure the Fourteenth Infantry has solved much tougher problems than that, and they'll probably think of a way to lick this one, too.' The colonel regarded me impassively, then picked up a sheaf of papers in a bent clip and began writing his name near the bottom. They were my papers. Even upside down I could see that.

"Out of panic had come the right answer! It probably was the only right one. And one which I was to make to the same kind of question most of my life to armies on five continents."

One month later the twenty-three-year-old blonde left New Orleans at dawn on a United Fruit freighter for Panama. She purchased a ticket with $250 of the $300 advanced by the magazine, three-fourths of the fare to be reimbursed by United Fruit when she reached her destination. She sent Tony a cable, "No more mail," a code they had worked out to alert each other of their actions. She must have sent it with great joy and excitement, but her husband received it with trepidation. Although he had been the catalyst and encouraged Dickey to become a professional photographer, he'd never taken seriously her youthful mooning over high-risk adventure. No doubt he was confident that his impressionable child bride would cast aside those idealistic dreams for the prevailing values of wifely duties. As proud as he must have been over her having bagged an overseas assignment with a national magazine, he felt threatened. As much as he missed her admiring presence, she had stepped onto his turf. Tony, described by all who knew him as a philanderer, probably had an affair going in Panama, a diversion now upset by his wife's dramatic message. Another real concern was the fact that his wife was young, pretty, and blond and would be surrounded by uniformed men half his age—if she ever got past the blockade. For the first time he was beginning to sense the depth of Dickey's will and lack of prudence. The implications were disturbing.

The initial euphoria that had swept the country was fading by June 1942 when Dickey set off to see war close up. Regardless of hit songs like "Good-bye, Mama, I'm off to Yokohama" and "You're a Sap, Mr. Jap," U.S. and British forces were being routed in the Pacific. Guam had fallen, and, like dominoes, so had Manila, Singapore, Bataan, and Corregidor. Nazi U-boats preyed up and down the East Coast, from Canada to the Gulf of Mexico and into the Caribbean. By May 1942 eighty-seven ships had been sunk in American waters.

Dickey's editor at *Look*, Daniel Mich, wanted her to get pictures of the freighter's gun crews and its convoy. But the SS *Marta*, chosen for Dickey by the navy, carried no guns or convoy escort as it churned through waters infested with German U-boats. The ship, which Dickey described as squat with unlovely lines, carried some naval officers, a dozen construction workers whom she was photographing for her *Look* assignment on American workers in Panama, and one fare-paying passenger: correspondent Dickey Chapelle.

A few hours prior to the ship's departure from New Orleans, a weary travel agent told the passengers that if they were on the deck when one of the U-boat's torpedoes hit—not if, but *when*—to take cover until the metal stopped flying. He further instructed that since the holds of the *Marta* were sealed by refrigeration, the boat would not sink fast. In fact, he said reassuringly, they would probably have plenty of time to get to their lifeboats with their luggage.

With this as her bon voyage, Dickey clattered around the main deck setting up her tripod and her bulky Speed Graphic camera, clicking off frames while standing on the ship's anchor chain. She was attempting to follow Tony's instructions: "You have to plan the picture in your mind's eye and move to the vantage point from which to shoot before you raise the camera," he had told her over and over about the heavy, clumsy camera.

As the ship chugged past the Louisiana bayous on its two-week voyage, Dickey casually tossed the wrappings from her film pack over the side while a man in rumpled pink pajamas jumped up and down on the deck beneath her, shouting something she could not hear.

None too gently the purser took her aside. He informed her that the man jumping up and down was the captain of the ship and wanted her off the main deck until they reached open seas. He further instructed her that if she did not get off the anchor chain, she would find her legs amputated when the line was let go and would probably fall into the hatch and break her neck to boot; and that if she did not stop tossing pieces of paper over the side, the U-boats would be around them like sharks.

She spent her days in her cabin hammering out copy about the men of the freighter, hoping *Look* would like it, describing it to her editor as "how they live and what they fear most and why they stick at it—in these times." Personally she would have welcomed a torpedo; at least then she'd have a story. When not in her cabin she could be seen careening around the deck, stumbling over lines or hanging over the side, watching navy patrol planes overhead. The planes, she would later learn, were there because of Tony. Her "coded" wire alerting him of her arrival had set his bulldog heart on edge. Dickey was traveling on an unarmed freighter about to run a blockade that had seen the sinking of thirteen ships in ten days, so at his insistence and often with him on board, navy patrol planes had been escorting the freighter.

On the fourth day out, the crew spotted the periscope of a U-boat moving alongside. But for some reason—either the presence of the navy patrol planes flying over earlier that day or the sad shape of the SS *Marta*—the ship did not attack. "In the end, everyone concluded that the *Marta* had been paid the ultimate insult," wrote Dickey. "Some U-boat skipper, after a leisurely look, didn't think she was worth the expending of a torpedo."

When the *Marta,* guided by navy patrols overhead, finally docked at

Colón in the Canal Zone on June 25, 1942, Dickey was promptly arrested by naval intelligence. A lieutenant approached her, waving her "No more mail" wire to Tony and upbraiding her for what had become a naval military matter—her husband's worry had ceased to be a personal affair when the entire patrol wing of the navy began flying volunteer extra missions to ensure the safe passage of a banana boat.

Dickey was released within an hour. Whatever excitement she may have first felt about being reunited with Tony was replaced by rage and humiliation. Her husband's interference degraded her new status as an accredited war correspondent. She was indignant that in the midst of a bitter war, navy patrol planes had been expended to watch over her. It was like being back at Atwater Grammar School with Edna. The tension between the two was obvious by the fact that during her first two weeks in Panama, Dickey did not stay with Tony in Coco Solo, but resided at the Hotel Washington in Colón. Her unpleasant welcome aside, she had other concerns. She dashed off a letter to her editor, updating him on her lack of progress and lack of funds.

"This is to let you know that I've arrived safely with one completed, one half-finished, and two prospective pieces in my camera bag," she wrote on June 27, 1942. The freighter piece she had hoped to have for him was still in the censor's hands. This was a condition for accreditation during the war. Every correspondent agreed to submit copy and film for censorship by the army's section staffs. Then both film and copy traveled to Washington to be censored again, by either the navy or army. After this ordeal (which could take weeks and render a story out of date), the material would be released to the publisher.

It was her plan, she wrote *Look,* to cover the Bushmasters, the Fourteenth Infantry Regiment being trained in the Panamanian jungles. She pleaded for more time. "This outfit," she informed Mich in the same letter, "hasn't so far seen a correspondent, much less a photographer, so what I get will be exclusive." She added, "These boys are the original jungle unit and are now complete with a snake expert and an all-male hula-hula chorus." From there she planned to attach herself to the naval air station at Coco Solo "to do a yarn on chief petty officers."

What Dickey did experience with the Bushmasters was the wet, steamy misery of the Panamanian jungle; it had been chosen for training because of its heavy vegetation and heavy rainfall, in the belief that any Pacific island would be easy to conquer after this. Her pale fine skin and long blond hair not only attracted appreciative male stares, but proved irresistible to the mosquitoes; as she waded in the jungly pools, her slender ankles were attacked by carnivorous fish. All this would have been worth it if she could have gotten some decent shots. But the camera's fabric shutter curtain and leather bellows were attacked by fungus, and its bulk—twenty pounds including leather shoulder case— left it vulnerable to damage. The slow-speed film never picked up enough light through the thick jungle vegetation for a decent print. And, to cap it all off, Dickey went broke purchasing film and bulbs.

Dickey was to photograph the Bushmasters for nearly a year, her whole stay in Panama. She had them strip to the waist and slough through the jungle; she shot them on night exercises. She stood next to the muzzle of a field piece so she could photograph the gun as it was being fired; the blast knocked her flat. She wasted a precious amount of government ammo trying to shoot night-firing practice. And on top of that, she lost the film.

"It's called being Pearl Harborized," she explained jauntily in a July 9, 1942, letter to Daniel Mich, blaming the army censors for losing forty-eight frames. She suggested she might have better luck pursuing a story on a rubber plantation in Costa Rica, and once again pitched her idea on chief petty officers at the naval air station at Coco Solo, "a heck of a good Navy yarn which we can have with no other picture mag competition."

By then Dickey was living with Tony in Coco Solo in a tiny pink-painted bungalow with a high, red-tile, wide-eaved roof, its windows barred with black ornamental wrought iron. She frequently appealed to *Look* for money. "None of these projects is going to be possible to do unless I cease being flat broke, which is what I am now."

By September *Look* sent her some money, though it was not in payment for either of her two finally completed and filed "assigned" pieces. She had also sent off a third, on her Bushmasters, and was anxious to have the magazine's reaction. Dickey informed Mich she planned to stay an additional sixty days. She wanted the magazine to send her Super XX film because there was none to be found on the isthmus. And she wanted to know why she'd had no response to her six letters. She was finding it progressively harder to convince the army to cooperate with her when she couldn't get any word from her office. "They're beginning to think the whole thing a little queer."

Dickey would later describe herself on arrival in Panama as a "pretty cocky girl," and on this, her first major assignment, she behaved more like a competitive dilettante than a committed photographer on a two-week shoot for a national magazine. She soon realized that the *only* story out of Panama was the one the censors wouldn't let her tell, "the terrible struggle against Nazi U-boats." Dickey was determined to make as big a splash with the Bushmasters as Margaret Bourke-White had on the European front. Still smarting from her embarrassing arrival, she became almost obsessed with the need to succeed, as was clear in her letters to Mich. "If you-all have been reading Margaret Bourke-White's publicity recently," she wrote him in December, "you might like to know that *Look*'s girl Friday was in uniform before 'Peggy' [Bourke-White's nickname] was and that they're letting me shoot something besides castles these days."

Dickey had mentioned in another letter to editor Mich that magazines were arriving two months late, which explained her uninformed letter. She had no way of knowing that Bourke-White's other assignment in England was riding with and photographing the B-17 Flying Fortress in England. As to her comment about being in uniform before her nemesis, she must have meant she was the first accredited woman photographing a unit of fighting men in the jungle. Certainly she was aware that Bourke-White was the first woman correspondent accredited to the army and that this had required the design of a new uniform. She served as its consultant and model. The uniform was approved by the Army War College and tailored for her by the tony outfitters Abercrombie & Fitch.

Dickey was having problems not only with her assignment, but with her husband. Instead of giving her the unstinting support she had come to expect of her mentor, Tony seemed to want their relationship to fall back into its old student-teacher pattern, she being a "Joanie-come-lately" to his class of twenty-seven sailors training to become aerial cameramen. Moreover, she had begun to sense his faithlessness. Their home served as the classroom's off-duty base, not only for the sailors, but for lively nurses and any other Americans who found their way there. Dickey, a product of the traditional Midwest, was still naive enough to believe that she was somehow responsible for Tony's weaknesses, an attitude Tony fostered. She accepted the guilt, as most women did, reasoning she must try harder to be a better wife. (In later years she would refuse jobs that paid more than her husband earned because accepting them would have been an act of disloyalty.) Thus she endeavored to please Tony, not only by sitting at her master's feet, but by keeping watch over a constantly simmering pot of spaghetti sauce.

Whatever money Tony was making as chief petty officer was not enough to support his wife's shooting budget, though he'd quickly have spent it on a ticket back to New York for her. He may have indulged his kittenish bride at home, but in Panama things were not that simple. Her needs were becoming demands in the face of his primary obligation, training men for missions that would see three dead and seven wounded.

By Christmas the first glamour of being a war correspondent was being replaced by a real sense of failure. Dickey wrote her editor that she wanted to do a story on the Caribbean Defense Command's jungle school. She wanted to shoot a "mass commando maneuver"—a *Look* exclusive. She had already shot some of it; should she continue? "I have every confidence that the long delay in getting squared away with the red tape down here needn't interfere in any way with good material from Panama," she wanted Mich to know. She would be checking the cables to see that "*Look* makes good the investment it already has in this area. . . ."

On January 7, 1943, Mich responded. "I have your several letters written in December." He had written her agent, Gertrude Algaze, upon receipt of the first letter, "and [they] assured me they would write you directly, that since we had not been able to use the three stories already sent us, we do not feel we can authorize you to go ahead with any more." He apologized that she'd had to wait so long "to hear."

No longer attached to *Look,* chastened by her failure, and once again dependent upon her preoccupied husband, Dickey was determined to pull her budding career out of the fire before returning to New York. Her pride demanded she prove to Tony that she had the grit to call herself a professional. Hadn't he always encouraged her before with the words "Try again"? Nobody ever said being a professional photographer would be easy. Besides, she didn't want to leave him. Despite the tension inside the little house, they still had their good moments, their great lovemaking. She spent her days scouring the Canal Zone for stories she could sell for five dollars to the *Panama-American.* She spent her nights in the clubby atmosphere of Tony's classes, swallowing her pride as she performed the functions of a teaching assistant, helping students mount their photos or standing over a two-burner kerosene stove, cooking spaghetti dinners for Tony and his students. And before too long, it seemed to pay off with, of all outfits, naval intelligence. Willing to let bygones be bygones, they assigned her to take a photograph of Frank Knox, the bluff former newspaper publisher and secretary of the navy in that spring of 1943.

As she crouched against an officers' club room full of sailors, Secret Service men, and some of Tony's students, Knox eyed her, the lone woman, with interest. Her camera steady on its tripod, the flashbulbs exploded like pistol shots. The room grew silent as the Secret Service men reached for their guns. Dickey wrote that into the silence "I said in the smallest possible voice, 'I'm sorry, sir.' " She later wrote that Knox was not upset; in fact, he found the situation fairly amusing. But the rest of the navy didn't. On the following day, a pissed-off Tony was heaped with more abuse. After being raked over the coals about his obstreperous wife, he was ordered to send her home. She was, after all, a navy wife in a war theater, and all navy wives had long since been sent home. Smarting with embarrassment, Tony promptly informed his commanding officer that his wife took orders not from her husband, but from the War Department, so the commanding officer did the next best thing. On the following day, when Dickey returned from another exhausting afternoon shooting the Bushmasters, the house was strangely quiet. Tony was gone. He'd been ordered back to New York. Within days, Dickey, broke and somewhat dispirited, was lured back to New York by Tony's wires, promising tender loving care and gallons of fresh milk.

FOR THE NEXT TWO YEARS Dickey's war corresponding desires were tempered not only by her disastrous experience in Panama, but by the fact that her husband had been assigned stateside. He was working for the Office of War Information at the Army Pictorial Center on Long Island, preparing to set up photographic centers in Asia for propaganda purposes. By 1943 restrictions on showing the real-life casualties of war were lifted. The Signal Corps and Office of War Information had set up outlets for wartime pictures throughout Europe and the Far East. Dickey was concentrating on being a wife, while banging out six more books on aviation. She noted she typed two thousand words a day and that she despised it so heartily that years later, whenever she hesitated about going on patrol or jumping from an airplane, she would steel herself by recalling those days: "Well, it's better than writing two thousand words a day, isn't it?" She was also finding the time to ply her picture stories to a spate of women's magazines, thus building a reputation as a free-lancer.

At this time the editorial policy of the women's magazines—despite the growing number of women working in the nation's defense industry—was summed up in a letter from *Life Story* magazine, a popular woman's monthly, to potential contributors. The editors were certain that their women readers wanted articles "as much about the sugar coating as the pill . . . chiefly for entertainment and inspiration, rather than for self-improvement."

In 1944 *Life Story* was expanding its features section and asked Dickey if she was interested in writing about the "ordinary doings and problems of women's lives, personal readjustments, love and marriage, homemaking, charm and beauty, careers and recreation, child care, budget, and so on." The magazine's editor believed their audience was "one you know well, since it is not very different from that of other publications in which your work has appeared." They hoped she would find *Life Story* "a new and profitable market for the kind of writing you do so successfully."

On February 19, 1945, as the U.S. Marines were landing on Iwo Jima beach to fight the bloodiest battle of the Second World War in the Pacific, Dickey was flying to Honolulu with fourteen navy flight nurses as *Life Story*'s "own photographer-correspondent overseas."

Less than a month earlier she had badgered her editor at *Life Story*, Ralph Daigh, to send her to the Pacific. Once again her catalyst was Tony, who was being transferred by the Office of War Information to Southwest China's wartime capital, Chungking. He had his uniform and was waiting for his travel orders when Dickey felt the old itch for action return with a vengeance. There was no way she was going to spend the time waiting for Tony to return, typing two thousand words a day, and looking out at the Hudson. So she hit on the idea to get an assignment in the adjoining theater. She viewed it as a perfect opportunity to be "in the war" without actually "being" in combat. If she did well in the Pacific, *Life* itself might finally be interested in her. And perhaps it would mend the breach with *Look*. If she screwed up, at least Tony wouldn't be within earshot.

Dickey had been accredited to the U.S. Navy's Pacific Fleet shortly before this flight, while covering navy flight nurse training in Oakland. It was part of a *Life Story* series she had begun a month earlier on nurses at the country's naval installations. When she arrived in Oakland, her credentials had come through, allowing her to follow the nurses to the Pacific. When the navy's public relations officer asked how she wanted her credentials to read, she said, "Reporter/photographer." That would not be possible, he replied. She must be one or the other. Ever mindful of the competition, she asked how many women reporters were in the Pacific. Learning there were several reporters but no photographers, she made her decision to become accredited as a photographer.

In order to cover combat, a correspondent needed accreditation. The War Department, from which every correspondent agreed to take orders in exchange for credentials, had rules prohibiting women from witnessing combat. In addition, the navy, to which Dickey was accredited, had on its books certain rules governing the conduct of correspondents. For purposes of billeting and mess hall privilege, each correspondent was given an "assimilated" rank, a designated status. Dickey was henceforth ranked, if only technically, a lieutenant commander—which meant she would be taking her orders directly from Admiral Harold Miller, the public relations officer for the entire Pacific fleet.

The public relations officer who assigned her to the Pacific never asked her what she would do about the lack of facilities in the field, because she would never go there. She wrote that she got a real kick out of asking to be sent "forward" every time she ran into a naval public relations officer because she loved the way it sounded. And she knew it was a big joke; they'd never let her near the front. No woman correspondent was allowed to spend the night with the troops, unless navy nurses were already there. If she went against these orders, scrupulously drawn to prevent women from covering combat, she would lose her accreditation. This was in the form of a folding leather-backed card; a glassine-enclosed insert said she was permitted to use a camera on shipboard in battle. Official status was also conferred by two uniforms, which she wore only to pose for the photographs that were filed with a draft of her navy obituary.

When Ralph Daigh, Dickey's editor at *Life Story* (later called *Today's Woman*), applied to navy public relations for her credentials, he told them that Dickey would be photographing women at war "anywhere west of the mainland." But Daigh believed his readers would be better "entertained" if Dickey could get him an exclusive. In fact, he whispered a more concise order into her ear: "I want you to be sure you'll be the first woman somewhere . . . any of those islands will do." And even if Daigh had not uttered the words, Dickey would have chanted them to herself.

Winging her way to Honolulu, navy accreditation clenched tight in her fist, she thought about Tony. Although he had received his orders months before her brainstorm to go off to war, he was still waiting for his departure date in New York, while she had received her accreditation within forty-eight hours. The reason was pure utility: the navy had quickly granted editor Daigh's proposal because they had recently discovered the value of public relations.

In her autobiography, Dickey wrote she felt "guilty as the dickens" when Tony faced the awkward business of seeing his wife off to war on an overcast winter's day; but a letter to one of her friends told another story. Her brother, not Tony, had seen her off that January when she began her assignment. Perhaps his ego was bruised at being left behind; perhaps he was understandably apprehensive about her second stab at war corresponding. After all, her poor showing in Panama had reflected on him, and he didn't want a repeat in China. Last but not least, there was the promise he'd made to Edna—and there wasn't much he could do to look after her little girl with oceans between them.

From subsequent correspondence between the two, it can be seen that the warm, wonderful bear of a hubby who had applauded Dickey's youthful ideas of adventure had grown sour after Panama, while Dickey had only been waiting for another opportunity. He had definite ideas about how his wife should behave. As much as he had worked to instill her with confidence in her photography, he never planned on her operating far from his guiding control. One friend explained that he wanted her always "within the sound of his voice, so that she could do things for him." The Pacific hardly qualified.

So Slug saw her off on the first leg of her assignment, leaving Monmouth, New Jersey, where he was now stationed with the army, at two in the morning. He had written, "Sir, I request permission to go to New York. I want to say good-bye to my sister. She's leaving for the front." Dickey told him that he should be ashamed of such brotherly overstatement. As far as she knew that icy dawn, standing in front of a piano showroom on Fifth Avenue, she was simply junketing by plane to various naval installations to cover the training of navy flight nurses. Slug gave her a light kiss while an impatient naval driver waited in a nearby station wagon to take her to Floyd Bennett Field in Brooklyn.

During the flight to Honolulu, Dickey and the nurses sat on canvas sling seats surrounded by hospital gear and stacks of mail en route to American fighting men in the Pacific. The plane, a navy transport called the *Martin Mars,* was the world's largest at the time and on its return flight would evacuate the wounded.

Twenty years later Dickey recalled the flight with uncharacteristic nostalgia, reflecting that she was never again to feel so special and privileged. She was the first woman photographer and, at twenty-five, the youngest of all women correspondents accredited to the Pacific fleet.

She identified with the nurses sitting beside her, girls who, like herself, were not content to be "lookers-on." With the sudden equality allowed women during the war, they were being allowed to participate in specific ways—with the tacit understanding that they would return to the kitchen when the war ended and the men came home.

Thus empowered, Dickey could handle her mother. When Edna asked where she was going, she replied, "Honolulu," carefully neglecting to mention Pearl Harbor. When Edna worried about the soldiers, her daughter assured her that these were "professional men" with families who would pose no "threat" to her well-being.

As it had for her fellow passengers on the flight, the war brought direction to Dickey's life. Patriotism bonded them all, just as it had brought the entire country together. To hell with the life they had been leading, they all said, the war was too important. But neither Dickey nor her story subjects, the navy nurses around her, had a clue about what really happened in a war.

Despite the weeks of training that Dickey had gone through with them, none of them knew a forward area from a forward pass or how an exploding mortar shell created grotesque forms that were no longer human. The closest they had come was newsreels. Neither she nor any of the nurses wondered about clean sheets, warm food, or sleepless nights. They didn't think about dead young men with innocent, clear-cut faces who looked like they were asleep or those who had no faces left. Instead they talked about the availability of bobby pins in the South Pacific and rated the looks of the officers on board. None of the women, many of whom would never make it back, considered the real danger of war; they thought only of their own roles, heavily influenced by Hollywood fantasies in which suave captains moved confidently through the officers' clubs.

As it had when she left for Panama, Dickey's success again beckoned brightly. Besides her assignment with *Life Story,* she also had a contract with the McBride Publishing Company. The book was to be a photo-and-interview collection of the officers of the Pacific fleet, their ships, and their men and was tentatively titled *I Cover the Pacific Command.* It was her third manuscript for McBride, and she hoped it would sell more copies than her two previous efforts, *Needed: Women in Government Service* and *Needed: Women in Aviation.* She had every reason to believe that this time she would make Tony proud.

As Dickey and one of the nurses worried aloud about finding lipstick in Honolulu, the copilot interrupted, shouting over the engine noise that the marines had just landed somewhere. One of the nurses asked him to spell it out: "I-w-o J-i-m-a." He added, "The landing is not going well. It's worse than Tarawa."

Twenty years later Dickey recalled the way the announcement had made her stomach lurch. What, she wondered, could be *worse* than Tarawa? The lumbering plane had turned eerily silent.

On November 20, 1943, a few hours on Tarawa, a coral-strewn atoll in the center of the Gilbert Islands, had cost the marines more men than they had ever lost before—990 dead and 2,311 wounded. Moreover, the racked and battered, coral-sheltered inlet of Tarawa had held no strategic importance in the South Pacific. On the other hand, occupation of the narrow, heavily fortified pear-shaped island of Iwo Jima was critical. The eight-square-mile, volcanic rock island was less than seven hundred miles from Japan, the closest American troops had come to Tokyo.

Iwo Jima was being used by the Japanese as a radar warning station. Its three Japanese-built airfields provided bases for its fighter interceptors. By capturing Iwo Jima's airfields, American B-29 bombers and their P-51 fighter escorts would gain critical advance bases, as well as emergency landing fields for disabled B-29s en route to Tokyo. It was the last fortress barring American forces from mainland Japan. The sight of the island was enough to fill anyone, even the gallant marines, with dread. The dead volcano Suribachi, commanding the south end of the island, loomed 556 feet from its ashy surface. No sea birds flew over it; only typhus-carrying mites were carried along in its wind of ash. Just before the first wave of marines landed on its beach, one of them allegedly saw bursts of fire rolling out of dead Suribachi.

When the *Martin Mars* landed in Honolulu, all the enlisted men had the same request: "Stand still." They gaped at the disembarking women as though they were movie stars. Dickey and the nurses obeyed.

Servicemen had achieved a rarefied heroic status after the Japanese attack on Pearl Harbor. It was said that one thousand marriages a day were performed between enlisted men and stateside women. The romance was perfunctory; nobody expected to be coming back from the enemy beaches. Marines, sailors, and soldiers seemed to know, down to the second, how long it had been since they had last seen an American woman. Dickey never saw so many eyes so wide and adoring in her entire life. It swept her right up.

But standing in the navy's press communications room in Honolulu, Dickey soon forgot her initial thrill about the war. The dispatches clattering in from the front lines at Iwo Jima were chilling. The body count after the first day's landing was twelve hundred. The usually cynical, wisecracking wire service rewrite men groped wordlessly through the dispatches. Walking, sliding, dropping, and crawling on their bellies over the sliding sands, the waves of marines were being decimated throughout the island by twenty thousand superbly trained and committed Japanese. A barrage of enemy shells, hurled from mortars the size of metal trash cans, burst upon the marines from nearly a thousand gun emplacements secreted all over the torturous island. The wounded, pinned down by incessant enemy fire, lay helpless under the shellstorm. Corpsmen rarely got through the frenzied barrage. Bodies, blown apart, lay like discarded puppets.

For a day and a night, inside the pressroom in Honolulu, Dickey read the gruesome dispatches of ships being sunk or land units being wiped out, until she was too weary to read any more. It was too terrible to believe. The United States was losing.

Her assurances to Tony and Edna that she would go no farther than Honolulu vanished in light of the dispatches. (She doubted she had fooled Tony in any case.) She itched to be in the thick of it; only a fool would feel otherwise. She wanted to see it and photograph it, and not only for the glory and fame. Looking around the eerily quiet room, she felt a sudden release, a clarity of purpose. When the public relations officer asked where she wanted to go, she wiped away her tears and replied, "As far forward as you'll let me," and for the first time she meant it.

Dickey was taken aboard a C-47 to Guam. The thirty-eight-hundred-mile flight took the propeller-driven plane twenty hours. An exhausted Dickey realized the marines were extending her the highest courtesy when they let her sleep on top of the mailbags.

When she awoke, she was looking into the face of a young, gap-toothed marine from Brooklyn. "You know something?" he said to her. "I don't know what day it is. I don't know what time it is. You want to know something else, sister? I don't know where we are, and I don't give a shit."

On the recently won island of Guam, the pressroom was linked directly to the USS *Eldorado*, the Iwo Jima–anchored communications ship of the assault fleet. War correspondents who had landed with the marines would make daily runs from the bloody beach to the *Eldorado* to file their dispatches, then hit the beach again.

Unable to sleep, Dickey focused blurred eyes to read that the marines, under cover of air and sea support, were burning and blasting their way up Suribachi's almost vertical cone. As enemy fire rained down, the wounded were being lowered over the sharp cliffs on ropes and stretchers. Four days after landing, using flamethrowers and grenades, forty marines scrambled up the crater to plant the wind-whipped American flag on Suribachi's peak. Finally a part of the impregnable island had been secured, but at a terrible price.

When news of the flag planting reached the morbidly quiet Guam pressroom, along with news that the marines had killed 717 of the enemy clinging to the crater of the volcano, the room exploded into cheers. Dickey sobbed into her cotton handkerchief and blew her nose.

Thirty-six hours later she went to see Admiral Harold Miller, the public relations officer for the entire Pacific fleet and her commanding officer. He was seated behind one of the widest polished oak desks she had ever seen. When she requested permission to go forward, Admiral Miller, looking annoyed, shook his head. "The front," he told her, "is no place for a woman."

"Yes, sir," agreed Dickey, who had no problem finding the right words for the occasion. "The only other group of people for whom it is no place is men. And as soon as there aren't any men with wives and mothers who have to be sent there, my editor won't be expecting me to go there, either. Because as long as our men must kill and be killed—then no one except a woman can tell the story to other women."

The admiral set his hands firmly on his desk. "Permission denied," he answered, fixing her with eyes cold enough to send a chill up her back. "Look here, my dear girl," he intoned, "the only reason we don't want women correspondents going in at once is this. Men, my girl, are very gallant. They will always risk their lives to save yours. I hope," he said, eyeing her evenly, "you understand the probable consequences. That is all."

She definitely understood them, but she sure as hell didn't want to blow her assignment, either. "I'm going to keep on asking."

"And I'll keep saying no," answered the admiral with a tight smile.

Dickey wanted to ask him if he was sure about all that gallantry stuff, but she was afraid the humorless man might think she was being mouthy. She didn't want to provide him with any excuse to yank her credentials. Difficult as it was, she buttoned up her mouth, determined nevertheless to figure out a way to get to the front.

Miller ordered her to accompany the USS *Samaritan,* a block-long hospital ship that was being dispatched to pick up the critically wounded from Iwo Jima. Her job was to photograph the wounded and document the use of whole blood in their treatment. The hospital ships were anchored a few miles from the embattled beaches, not as far forward as she wanted, but in the right direction. The words of her editor, "be the first somewhere," and her own need to do it goaded her.

It was a five-day ocean run from Guam to Iwo. The mood on board the noncombatant USS *Samaritan* was cheerful. On the second day out Dickey was awakened by the ship's shrill alarm klaxon. The four-deck-high hospital ship, with four huge red crosses painted on its white sides, was under enemy attack.

Dickey wrote in her autobiography that her first impulse was to stay below. "Behind me, a seaman's voice rang young and clear in the stillness. 'Photographers are crazy.' That was what it took. As long as one person thought I was a photographer, I was willing to take the next step toward being one."

She stood alone on the deck under a bright sun, watching in mute, paralyzed terror as a Jap zeke plane unleashed its bomb over her head. But it splashed into the ocean a few hundred yards from where she stood, arms limp at her sides. When the plane circled and rose once more, she had mustered her courage and was determined to get a picture. Racing to a prearranged security station, up three ladders to the ship's flying bridge, she squeezed under the mount of the ship's searchlight. As the public address system blared its instructions to take cover, the zeke came into focus in her viewfinder. Crushed under the platform, her hands trembling, she attempted to focus on the second enemy run.

Later she wrote, "No bomb came. Instead I saw an orange lance in the sky and then a ceaseless stream of them arc toward the plane. A navy destroyer was opening up with all her anti-aircraft guns as she charged across the water toward us. . . . She . . . jinked . . . climbed up and, without loosing another bomb, turned tail and fled."

Dickey noted that everyone aboard celebrated loudly the escape but that she joined in only with a great sense of shame. She had forgotten her telephoto lens. The 50-millimeter lens on the camera was unable to record an image of anything she had witnessed. *Why* was she always screwing up? Thousands of miles from Tony, she could hear him berating her alibi. "I hadn't shot even the flyspeck-in-the-sky kind of picture I should have made," she wrote. "In short, I'd fluffed the coverage of my own baptism of fire. . . ."

5

Looking for the Front

Tʜᴇ ɴɪɢʜᴛ before the *Samaritan*
reached Iwo Jima, Dickey watched a movie in the company of the ship's
three hundred men. With her new sense of purpose, it struck her as very
odd to be sitting and laughing at Bob Hope cavorting in some silly film
called *Louisiana Purchase* while only a few hours from their rendezvous
with casualties from one of the most bitter battles in amphibious warfare
history.

Dickey wandered over to the welldeck. The ship moved along, her
aseptic whiteness floodlit. Under a full moon Dickey watched young
corpsmen chin themselves on the deck's rigging; she thought about
tomorrow—payoff day, as she saw it. "I know I'm taking the whole thing
too damn seriously and someday I'll view my own behavior a little wryly,"
she wrote Tony that night about her increasing identification with the
men on board, "but I can't escape the obvious comparison with any
other green kid out here the night before finding out how much he really
has learned."

"Well, baby," she could imagine him replying, the insinuation syrupy
in his voice, "what did you expect?" He was still waiting to leave New
York, the rumors now being that the job in Chungking might not

materialize. She felt the familiar pang as she pictured him alone in New York, where he'd probably already found comfort in the arms of another woman. "Tony was so charming," recalled Marian, Dickey's sister-in-law. "But as soon as the mouse was away the cat would play."

Standing on the *Samaritan*'s deck, Dickey realized that being in the Pacific was a risk, not only professionally, but to her marriage. Tony disapproved, and his approval, like her dad's, meant the world to her; but ever since Panama she had been riddled with doubt, wondering if she weren't simply kidding herself about making it as a war correspondent and trying to come to terms with her increasingly odd marriage. More and more she wondered how she could reconcile her love for the man who had awakened her sexually and declared his undying love, yet who was a blatant philanderer. She was finding it harder and harder to pretend to ignore it; indeed, she'd begun to throw ugly fits, something she didn't think she was capable of. She hated those scenes; they made her feel dragged out and hadn't changed anything.

Had he taught her photography so she could have a career, or because he needed an able-bodied unpaid assistant? Certainly if he wanted her to succeed, as he so often said, why would he place such harsh limits on her striving? He knew that for her a life on the sidelines was unthinkable, rendered so by her inviolate stubborn will, fed by her childhood heroes, nurtured by her father. So she hoped he would understand that she could not leave until she had made good her mission, her editor's instruction to be where the action was before anyone else. Judging by her encounter with the Jap zeke, she wryly figured it might well take the duration. And added to her uncertainty, her guy had started bribing her into hurrying home with promises of "honest chow": pork chops, mashed potatoes, real butter, and "all the cold milk you can drink."

Nine days after the marines had first landed, when the "White Angel"—Dickey's name for the ship "because it means mercy still exists"—nudged into its anchorage two miles from the Iwo beach, plenty of blood was still being spilled on the north end of the island. Three divisions of marines were engaged in combat, in which four marines went down for every yard gained, battles aptly titled "Death Valley" and "Meat Grinder." Twenty-seven Medals of Honor would be earned on this island. Yet even as the battles raged, the Seabees were clearing the wreckage from the beach with their mighty cranes. Field hospitals were operating. At Iwo's biggest airfield, Motoyama, now held by the marines, a fifteen-hundred-foot-long airstrip was in operation.

Five hundred and fifty-two casualties boarded the *Samaritan* that first day. A few walked onto the deck, some stumbling between the shoulders of the corpsmen; most of them were carried on stretchers. Sometimes the trip from the beach to the ship took hours; waves hurled the beetle-shaped Higgins boats about, the stretchers strapped to their landing ramps. Four corpsmen would board each landing craft and hoist the wounded to corpsmen waiting on the lower platform of the *Samaritan*'s gangway.

Until then Dickey had never considered the corpsmen as heroic. That day she watched them risk their lives passing hundreds of wounded and dying men, from one careful quartet to the next, over the shifting area of open water between the bouncing boats and ship's gangway. "These are brave men," she wrote Tony. "They went in unarmed where others fully armed hesitated. The wounded may curse the ship's conspicuous-ness, but when they come aboard they are grateful."

From the flying bridge, she could see the island enveloped in smoke and fire. American planes streaked across the sky while battleships fired toward the lee of Mount Suribachi, now pierced by the Stars and Stripes. The knobby spindle of the volcano was lit by the fire of exploding shells and skittering grenades. The sunburned young men being lifted aboard on stretchers, impish faces covered with volcanic ash, looked as if they were only sleeping. Other boys looked like nothing that had ever been human, reduced to blood and mashed faces, stumps where limbs had been.

A week after D-Day Dickey was following Admiral Miller's orders to document the use of whole blood by photographing the wrecked human cargo coming off the beach and onto the deck of the hospital ship. She was painfully aware that any ten-year-old boy back in the States, after a single fight in the schoolyard, knew more about human violence than did she or most other American women. And though the newsmagazines had been running graphic pictures of the wounded to keep the folks back home committed to the sacrifice demanded by the war, she doubted such honesty would be welcomed by the readers at *Life Story*. Already several of her male colleagues had refused to shoot certain grim pictures because they didn't want their wives to see them. But although her editor wanted her to be "first somewhere," which meant on the beach where the action was, she was fearful of the consequences that would come from countermanding Admiral Miller's orders. She rationalized her decision to remain aboard ship by figuring that the magazine's readers would be just as interested in the use of whole blood, and motivated to donate, provided the wounded didn't look too wounded.

She had also, she believed, steeled herself against emotional involvement. She was going to shoot it the way Tony had taught her. The biggest hindrance to documenting war, he had explained, was the photographer's own emotional sloppiness. If she were going to call herself a war correspondent, she must learn to record whatever she saw as it was happening, without reflecting or weeping, because the minute her feelings got in the way she would stop being a professional.

"When I first began to work on the welldeck, I tried only to keep out of the way of stretcher bearers and to keep on focusing, framing, lighting, and shooting pictures," wrote Dickey. "The shapeless, dirty, bloody, green bundles being lifted and carried before me were not, repeat, not, human as I was human."

Every corridor was sardine-packed with stretchers, since there were not enough beds. The badly burned and gangrene cases had their wounds packed in ice to ward off infection. The bodies looked like hallucinations, flesh twisted and carved by mortars and grenades into surreal abstractions.

For most of that morning of the first day, Dickey hid behind the camera, rapping the shutter, taking light readings, and skirting the bloody puddles that marked the pitching of the seas; she walked around the bottles of blood feeding into the veins of the wounded, ignored the stench from body bags of the recent dead. She automatically hit the shutter, dutifully and swiftly identifying her subjects by the serial number on their dog tags. Every few hours, when her reserve threatened to yield, she would run outside and gulp the fresh air. Its sharp bite was a brief release from the ship and the horrible, hammering island.

"Hey, Dickey, what happened to those nice pink cheeks?" asked the ship's public relations officer that afternoon. It was all she could do to smile, wondering if she would encounter any new ways the human body could be horribly mangled. When she looked at those men, her mind refused to accept what her brain and her eyes knew to be true: "that there but for the grace of God go I." She later discovered that she had clenched and unclenched her teeth so often, she had ground the enamel off her back teeth. That night, huddled on her cot, she wrote, "I thought perhaps I should think myself a little more of a woman tonight. I am not able to do it, Tony. There is a doctor aboard who steadied my arm while I got the identification of the first bad one. He did not comment, then or since, on the fact that the ship was not rolling at the time.

"It is hard to imagine a kind of wound which has not bled on the after welldeck today. It is even harder to realize that the sheer bulk, the repetitiousness of human misery . . . represents a group of humans whose personal stories read like yours or mine; my mind, at any rate, is apparently shored against that idea. There must be something better that a woman could do with these men than to photograph them. I haven't cringed at their wounds, but at my lens." Then she loosened the rope belt on her khakis and signed the letter, "Once more and forever, I love you, your Dickey."

Before she went to sleep, she went over a routine she would follow for the rest of her life. She checked her camera gear, reloading it and padding it between pillows so it would not shatter if the ship were hit. She hung her helmet and life belt where she could reach them easily. The preparation no longer gave her the thrill it had only a week earlier. Then she rehearsed until she could find the camera controls with her eyes closed.

The ship had left Guam prepared for five hundred wounded and dying. By the morning of the second day over seven hundred were on board. The corridors smelled of stale cigarette smoke, sweat, and burned flesh, and another smell, "the smell of war, the smell not of death, but of people who have died."

The next afternoon, exhausted and shaken, Dickey had trouble holding her camera steady to focus on the face of a mangled young man on a stretcher. Transfused with blood from home, he was dying anyway. She tried again to focus on his face when she realized that he was trying to smile at her! All her pent-up reserve collapsed. "Uh . . . soldier—how are you?" she managed.

"Marine, I'm a fucking marine," he whispered. Dickey believed at that moment that if she could get him to smile, somehow he would hang on to life. "If *I* said *that word*." She wrote that she had never said it before. But this was no time to be coy. "Okay, you fucking marine, I asked you how you felt." And he did smile. He told her he felt lucky and grateful because his buddies had carried him out, willing to help him. They weren't thinking about themselves.

She watched carefully to see where they were taking him. One part of the ship was for the living, one for the dead. He was lucky. "After that, I looked squarely at each marine as I photographed him," she wrote, unafraid of that connection. She understood when they told her how lucky they felt. She knew Tony, her mentor, would disapprove of her lack of "professionalism," but she was no longer worried about the need to protect herself.

A chaplain was administering the last rites to a man with his abdomen sliced open like a watermelon. He opened his eyes. She wrote down his identification number, her hand trembling.

"Hey, who—you spyin' for?" he said. Dickey looked over the edge of the camera. Didn't he know? "The folks back home, marine." She felt his dimming eyes cursing her. "The folks back home, huh? Well, fuck the folks back home." Dickey didn't see him again, but she couldn't get his words out of her mind. Holding his dog tag number, she went to every ward, trying to find him. At last she came to a list of that day's dead. His name was at the top. "So I think I was the last person to whom he was able to talk. And I had heard him die cursing what I thought he had died to defend. It was my first and most terrible encounter with the barrier between men who fight and those for whom the poets and the powers say they fight."

Dickey knew she would never in a million years, on a million ships like this, ever understand what a man truly died for. Whatever the reason, it was not to be found on the deck. She reckoned it must be out there on the skinny-necked stretch of beach with its stunted trees, where smoke plumed up over the clay-and-humpbacked hills, over the blood-wet sand, until it puffed into nothingness over Mount Suribachi.

Two days later the *Samaritan* cast anchor for the nearly nine-hundred-mile voyage to Saipan, with seven hundred and fifty-three casualties. Eight would die before they reached shore.

About a week after the USS *Samaritan* docked in Saipan, which together with Guam and Tinian formed a trio of strategic island bases in the Marianas, 1,300 air miles southeast of Tokyo, Dickey was on her way back to Iwo Jima. In a letter written ten years later describing "the Pacific thing," she recalled that her Guam tentmate, Reuters correspondent Barbara Finch, had been making the trip to Iwo Jima on planes evacuating the wounded. She suggested that Dickey, who was understandably discouraged about ever being a combat photographer, accompany her to one of the three airfields on the island held by the marines. Dickey would be the third woman correspondent to be making this run, so she had no trouble getting orders, which specified she would be photographing the use of whole-blood procedures of the field hospital at Iwo's Motoyama Airfield 1, where marines who could not be taken onto hospital ships were being treated.

She flew out of Agana, Guam, where she was based, at three o'clock in the morning, scheduled to return by air-evac plane at three o'clock the next morning. Naval ingenuity dictated the ungodly departure time: it made certain she wouldn't be staying overnight with the troops.

When the C-47 "goony bird" arrived at Iwo, now D-Day plus thirteen, sniper fire laced up the field next to the Motoyama runway. The pilot kept circling, waiting for the firing to die down, and, after ten minutes of relative quiet, went in for a landing. As Dickey looked at the island's towering sand hills, all she could think was, What the hell am I doing in a fifty-thousand-pound airplane that's going to try a landing like this? As soon as the plane touched down, the pilot ordered her to hit the sand and keep running. That was no easy task: the ground was covered with ankle-deep volcanic ash.

The hospital consisted of three tents swimming on the ashy earth, with upended crates for operating tables. Even under constant attack, the medical staff had already saved hundreds of lives. Nighttime operations were performed with hand-held flashlights. One of the wounded men Dickey photographed had a leg so wrecked it would probably be amputated. He looked at Dickey as if she were nuts, not because she was taking his picture, but because she was unarmed.

"Here," he said, handing her his kabar, the eight-inch-long, marine-issue, double-edged trench knife. She was dumbfounded. He insisted she take it because he wasn't going to be needing it anymore. He showed her how to fasten the sheath to her web belt so that the leather-laminated handle of the knife almost touched the fingers of her right hand. Then he smiled. "Now I feel better about you." Overcome by the gesture, she had to get out of there before she started crying.

REALIZING SHE HAD TO GET A PICTURE of the hospital, the little island of hope surrounded by the bigger island of death, Dickey studied the undulating, endless sand ridges that surrounded it. All she had to do was climb atop one of the ridges, which she judged to be about fifteen feet high, with her eight-pound camera and her twelve-pound tripod. From that height she could get off a panoramic shot that might even include the front, if only she knew where the front was.

The bulky equipment made the sliding climb extremely difficult. For every three steps forward, she slipped back two. Gray dust went into her mouth, up her nose, into her eyes. The only way up was to bend with the burden, keeping the camera away from the sand. The thought of the marines climbing these same hills with seventy pounds on their backs kept her going.

From the ridge top came a startling sound: human voices. Heart pounding, knees jelly, she dived into the sand, still holding the camera up in the air. She looked up, trembling as she wiped the sand from her glasses, to see two marines on top of the ridge, a stocky captain and a leaner, younger lieutenant. They were looking down at her and laughing, rocking back and forth, hands on their hips.

Dickey smiled up at them. Surely if she could make two steps more, one of them would reach down and help her to the top; as the admiral had told her, men were so gallant. She was wrong. When she finally reached the ridge, the one with the quarterback's build grinned toothily.

"I'm looking for the front," she explained, spitting the sand out of her mouth.

"You want to see the front?" he asked. She nodded. "C'mon," he said, "we'll take you there."

She was too thrilled to speak. All she could think of, as she went sliding after them down the hill, was that very soon she, Dickey Chapelle, was going to be standing on the front of the most violent battle of the Pacific. Let "Peggy" tie that! She was far too excited to consider that she was now countermanding Admiral Miller's orders. For forty minutes she sat speechless and peacock proud beside the lieutenant as he drove the weapons carrier on the narrow lane toward Mount Suribachi. The constant traffic of heavy vehicles had cratered the road like a valley between the dark and sandy hummocks. There was no view of anything but the winding, miserable tube itself.

Dickey stuck her head out of the weapons carrier. "Boy," she said, cranking her neck to stare at the ocean of fifteen-foot waves of sand.

"Yeah, if it were any prettier," said the captain wryly, "I don't know if I could stand it."

The lieutenant swung the carrier to a lurching stop and looked over at her. "This," he said, waving at the vast, dark, soot-covered range, "is somewhere on the front."

All Dickey saw in every direction were sand ridges. She had spent forty minutes' driving time for this? No editor was going to buy it. Still, a shot from one of the ridges would at least give the scene some scope. She figured if it weren't safe, the lieutenant would stop her. But all he did was lean against the vehicle, smoke a cigarette, and watch her miserable, grunting climb. Once atop the slippery peak, she realized with embarrassment and horror that she had absolutely no idea which way to shoot. "The whole area was honeycombed with sand ridges, their overall pattern like a waffle," she wrote. She couldn't see what was happening from the bottom of one square to the next, and each ridge acted as a baffle, absorbing the sound. "I realized I'd forgotten to ask the lieutenant the most important question of all. In which direction lay the front lines? I thought about going back to find out, but that would mean I'd have to climb up again. No, I knew an easier solution. I'd take four sets of pictures, each in a different direction. One set and probably two was bound to show the front properly."

Nervously she set up her camera. All she spotted in that sea of sand were three marines who popped up and vanished like rabbits out of a magician's hat. That meant there were probably other people likewise camouflaged all around her. It was a scary thought. The wind whistled around her, carrying strange sounds like that of invisible winged insects. But the sound was not half as disconcerting as the view. Where *was* she? She saw three tanks so far in the distance that they looked like toys. One of them bounced. There was a blasting noise rolling over the ridge. But mostly it was desolate. Windy. Hot.

"It was hot now, and the wind carried a shout over to me. But it didn't sound as loud as my own breathing or the noises of bugs or the crunch of my boots in the gray gravel. I realized I was really frightened now." As soon as she finished her four shots, she stumbled down the hill.

The marine lieutenant, whom she knew only as Jameson, flicked his cigarette and faced her with a look of undiluted contempt. "That was the goddamnedest thing I ever saw anybody do in my life! Do you realize all the artillery and half the snipers on both sides of this fuckin' war had ten full minutes to make up their minds about you?"

He continued, "Didn't anyone, anywhere, ever pound it into your little head that you do not stand up on a skyline, good Christ in heaven?!

Let alone stand up for ten minutes? And do you realize that if you'd gotten yourself shot, I'd have had to spend the rest of the war and ten years after that filling out fucking papers?"

So, she'd been *standing* on the goddamn front. Lucky for Jameson she hadn't gotten herself killed and ruined his life.

"You know," she began shakily, "I don't think there is any sight sweeter to see than a fully committed marine coming at me with both arms flying." She wanted to burst into tears right there, but she was damned if she would give him the satisfaction.

BACK IN GUAM, Barbara Finch, the gray-haired veteran war correspondent, listened to her young colleague's story. When Dickey got to the part about the invisible insects whizzing past her and the sound of the flying bugs, Barbara shook her head and laughed. The dead volcano of Iwo had no winged insects. The sound whistling past her was sniper fire.

Dickey stumbled outside. She had been shot at—and not hit. A squad of prisoners was drilling nearby. Farther away there was the sound of target practice. Repeat: She had been shot at and missed. Suddenly her ears were ringing, her heart was pounding, the joints of her arms and legs felt weak. There *was* something to it, as Winston Churchill himself had said. *It was like no other feeling in the world.* She wrote a friend that as little as she understood about where she was, the atmosphere for literature was "odd and wonderful."

Down the hill from her tent was a Quonset hut called the zebra hut, so named for the four or five stripes running down the sleeves of its inhabitants, marine noncommissioned-officer combat reporters. The hut was strictly marine. The pressroom for civilian reporters was five miles away, inside Admiral Chester W. Nimitz's headquarters.

It was only out of the goodness of the hardened marines' hearts that Dickey and Barbara Finch were spared the five-mile trek. As long as the two women followed the tacit macho rule of zebra hut—which was to remain invisible, what Dickey called "speak-no-nothing"—she and Barbara could use its typewriters, telephones, jeep runners, and darkroom and drink the coffee. This was one male sanctum Dickey didn't even think about crashing.

When Dickey first entered the hut, she looked around at twenty combat-hardened marine correspondents, all of whom ignored her. As much as she wanted their attention, now that she had earned her first dateline under fire, nobody in the room was remotely interested. It quickly occurred to her that every inhospitable man in there had been under fire many times. Face it, she told herself, sitting on a creaky wooden crate and rolling a sheet of paper into one of the unused typewriters, these guys wouldn't accept you even if you had a couple of medals on your chest.

Nevertheless emotion welled up as she typed, "Dateline: March 5, 1945, Iwo Jima. Under Fire." When she finished writing and had labeled her photo captions, she leaned back and for the first time broke one of the sacrosanct rules. She listened to the marines. They were bitching about civilian correspondents who didn't go as far forward, or stay out as long, as marine correspondents. One of the marines, a big, broad-shouldered sergeant, shook his head and summed it up: "Civilians! Poor, frightened civilians! Damned if I know why we have to put up with civilian correspondents out here anyhow! What do they ever write about the marines?"

Dickey spun around to face the big man. She put her hands on her legs, looked around the room, and stood up, knocking over the crate. For the first time since she had walked into the zebra hut, every man stared at her. "If it was attention I wanted, and it probably was," she wrote, "I had it now."

"You marines make me sick. Sick!" she shouted. The room chilled, its inhabitants stunned. She had broken the rules by which she had been allowed into this hallowed circle. But they couldn't treat her any worse than they already had. Looking from one tough civilian-hating mug to another, she hoisted up her pants and paced.

"Don't you guys ever read anything beside *Leatherneck* magazine? 'Cause if you did, you gun-toting idiots, you would know that you got plenty of civilian friends." She spat out the names of the reporters and the photographers, the places they had covered, from Guadalcanal to Tarawa, Saipan to Iwo Jima. She reminded them of the civilian reporters and photographers who had landed on the beaches with them.

"I'm one of the people you've been sounding off about, and we women aren't writing about anything else, either," she added. "Even me. I've only been out here long enough to do six pieces. Five of them have been about marines and the sixth is about the corpsmen with marine units." When she finished, the room remained silent. She understood that from now on she'd have to make the five-mile journey to the civilian press-room. She put her hands on the hips of her shapeless fatigues and pushed her glasses back on her nose.

"Now you just tell me, is there anything else *this* civilian correspondent can do for the United States Marine Corps?"

"Yes, ma'am," chorused twenty voices inside the zebra hut. The marines doubled up with laughter.

It took a few seconds for her to realize what she had said to half a platoon of marines. She wrote that she envisioned the words in letters of fire, a scalding tidal wave washing up to the roots of her hair. The top noncommissioned officer, tall and in need of a shave, raised his hands. He walked the width of the room, looking at her. "Come on, I'll take you home now." She felt bad, even though finally being able to sound off had felt good. He escorted her up the hill to the turnoff path leading to her tent, saluted, then about-faced and set off the way he had come.

The next morning, as she walked down the path toward the mess for transient officers, she was waylaid by three of the combat correspondents. She figured they were going to block her way, punish her impudence. "Hey, Dickey," one of them offered, "you don't have to eat brass chow. Ours is better. We'll show you. Come on."

She was dumbstruck. They took her to breakfast in the big mess hall. She was astounded by the huge portions, but it all tasted so good that she ate as much as they did. After breakfast a dozen marines were standing around a big, good-looking, dark-haired sergeant getting into a jeep. He was Lew Lowery, the *Leatherneck* magazine photographer who had taken the first photograph of the marines raising the flag on Mt. Suribachi (although it showed a smaller flag than the one used by Joe Rosenthal, the Associated Press photographer whose famous photo would win him the Pulitzer Prize). Lew had covered nine assault landings and was en route to an attack transport ship for his tenth.

Somebody was holding his backpack so he could put his arms through the straps. Another marine held his belt, hung with two canteens, a first-aid kit, clips of ammunition, and a trench knife on either side.

"It always makes me nervous to watch a man go off to war," admitted the marine lifting the pack.

"Makes me nervous, too," said Lew. "More than usual when it's me." He looked up and noticed Dickey. She looked away, remembering that he had witnessed her outburst of the night before.

"Hey, come over here, girl," he said. He looked at the man holding his belt. "Let her do it," he ordered. "I'm going to be the only marine on the next operation who got his gear hung on him by a female."

Dickey nearly staggered under its weight as she struggled to close it; he offered no help. Finally she cinched the belt and moved back, pushing the hair from her forehead. Lowery patted her cheek, swung himself into the jeep, and waved.

"See you guys later," he called out, smiling at Dickey. "Take good care of our girl." He gunned the jeep down the road.

Dickey's hand froze in its wave. Had he said "our girl"?

A marine sergeant stood at her elbow with a scalding hot canteen cup. "I poured you some coffee," he said, passing it to her.

Still dazed, she lifted the cup. It burned her fingers, but she didn't drop it.

"Well," he said, "how you doing? You need any film or anything?"

6

The Limit of Human Endurance

L ATER that month, March 1945, Dickey was ordered by Admiral Miller to continue her stories on whole blood on Ulithi, the navy's immense base in the western Caroline Islands. It was 1,500 miles from Japan, 900 from Iwo, and 1,200 from Okinawa. The year before, it had been abandoned by the Japanese as useless. But for Admiral Chester W. Nimitz, the commanding officer of all Allied forces in that part of the Pacific, the unimpressive collection of coral-fringed islets and its deep, sheltered lagoon made a natural anchorage that could easily accommodate hundreds of ships at one time. Nimitz called the palm-dotted lagoon "the navy's secret weapon."

By this time Dickey and the other correspondents had been briefed on the next big operation in the Pacific, the invasion of Okinawa, the long, thin island closest to Japan. It was to be a huge, combined marine-army landing with heavy aerial and naval bombardment. It was scheduled for April 1, both April Fool's Day and Easter Sunday that year. She'd been to the front on Iwo—but she hadn't been there first. Her editor's instructions still burning in her ears, she once again appealed to Admiral Miller to allow her to go ashore—this time with the navy medical corpsmen on the first landing wave. Her audacious request was bolstered by the critical shortage of whole blood available for casualties.

"Admiral," began Dickey, "do you realize that the shortage of whole blood is so severe that members of the fleet, including doctors, corpsmen, and correspondents, are being bled regularly? Always on the eve of battle?" The admiral seemed sympathetic. "Well, I've been giving the problem a great deal of thought, sir," she continued, leaning forward on her chair to get a better view of him behind his wide desk. "If the folks back home could see the heroic way the navy corpsmen operate, coming ashore on the first landing wave to save lives, I believe we would get many more blood donors."

Many years later the admiral would recall that Dickey had a tenaciousness "beyond all belief" in her desire to get into the center of the action. He clapped his hands on the desk, fixed his steely eyes on her, and said, "Dickey, as soon as nurses go ashore, you can go, too." His face remained stony as he continued, "I am not going to have one hundred thousand marines pulling up their pants because you are ashore."

"Sir," she replied crisply, "it won't bother me one bit. My objective is to cover the war."

But Miller was adamant. He ordered Dickey to continue as she had. She would report to the USS *Relief,* another hospital ship, which would be arriving at Okinawa April 2, the day after the marines and the army landed.

Dickey looked down at her filthy boots, her salt-sprayed, muddy khakis. The admiral repeated his orders that she was not to precede the nurses, and he asked for her word. Instead Dickey persisted.

"I intend to keep on asking, Admiral," she announced.

The admiral, who would later be given a Gold Star in lieu of a second Legion of Merit for his many improvements in the navy's public relations, cheerily replied, "And I'll keep saying no."

When Dickey returned that evening from this disheartening chat, a patrol boat chugged alongside the USS *Relief.* On board, the nurses were running around in their silk dresses, getting ready to go to the war correspondents' farewell party on the islet of Mogmog at the former estate of the king of Ulithi, which consisted of a couple of thatch-covered shacks that had been liberated by the Americans to serve as their officers' club.

Noticing Dickey standing around glumly, one of them invited her. "Like this?" Dickey screeched. She was dressed in her usual stunning ensemble—her trousers with the thirty-six-inch waist and huge pockets at the hips gathered at her waist with a piece of rope, a GI enlisted-men's khaki shirt from Tanapag harbor, army trench coat from the post exchange in San Francisco, and socks from the USS *Samaritan.*

The war correspondents were leaving for Okinawa the next day, so the mood inside the former monarch's palace was intense and theatrical, part swaggering Hemingway, part unconquerable, terminal terror. There were 50 nurses, 150 officers of every rank, and all the correspondents still walking. Still in her fatigues, Dickey nursed a bottle of beer and watched the nurses grow drunker and louder as every man became fair game. The food was a sumptuous buffet, and the liquor flowed.

A fat tropical moon promised romance, and bodies around her locked into frantic eleventh-hour embraces. Next to her an officer grabbed a nurse, moaning, "Oh, honey, if you only had another two minutes." The party had all the urgent gropings, the gritty, unstoppable masked hysteria, that characterized war. The phonograph blared, and the dancing got dizzier. Guests who broadcasted their bravado were as transparent as glass. Dickey was dealing with her fear as she usually did. She nursed her beer and told jokes to a photographer from *Life* magazine.

She knew she had no right to pass moral judgment on anyone's behavior tonight but her own. Many of these crazed, drunken men and women would not be dancing another jitterbug again, and maybe she wouldn't, either. The Japanese attacked hospital ships, and she sure as hell didn't want to die on a hospital ship. But it was patently clear that she had no choice in the matter. Maybe she ought to get drunk and find herself a man, but staying unattached seemed the only way to safeguard one's sanity in war. She had seen too many soldiers on the hospital ships crack up over the death of a close buddy.

She stepped away from two nurses who were fighting over a falling-down-drunk correspondent, themselves so drunk they couldn't actually hit each other. They ended up with their arms around each other, crying.

THE INVASION OF OKINAWA on Easter Sunday, April 1, 1945, its landing called "Love Day" by the marines, was termed the "screwiest" of the entire Second World War. After three hours of heavy sea and air bombardment that destroyed most of the island's huts, sixty thousand troops landed on Okinawa's beaches without a shot being fired. "Never before had I seen an invasion beach like Okinawa," said famed war correspondent Ernie Pyle, landing shortly afterwards with the seventh wave of marines. "What a nice Easter Sunday after all," he said, beaming. He mentioned that the island was more American than anything the marines had seen in the past three years. To him it was fields of ripe wheat that recalled his native Indiana. On that warm, sunny day, fifteen hundred American ships soon lay anchored in silent symmetry at the Okinawa harbor. The lush island was sixty times the size of Iwo, its harbors excellent, its beaches wide, its climate temperate rather than tropical. It seemed to the Americans, 350 miles from Japan, that the enemy had vanished. On the beaches, with their mix of tropical and firlike trees, the troops were met by the island's ubiquitous goats and its natives, made homeless by the heavy aerial bombardment.

For the first two days the USS *Relief*, anchored one mile from the landing beach, waited. "We're ready for them," said one of the nurses, wrapping bandages and checking the bottles of plasma. Dickey fussed with her camera, cleaned the lenses, figured light readings. Not one casualty came aboard.

Dickey had received her first letter in weeks from Tony, whose orders to Chungking had been canceled; he'd be working stateside. Dickey had been gone two months, and he wanted her home, tempting her as always with visions of "all the cold milk you can drink." Much as she wanted to hurry back to him, and to stateside food, she couldn't leave yet—not until she made good her promise to editor Daigh, now, frustratingly, so close yet so far. As soon as she did, she would hurry home. With that decision made, she stuck her fork into a can of cold beans and chewed.

According to a letter from a friend stateside, her husband wasn't doing too well as a bachelor. "He seems lost and lonely without you. I must say you have that man wrapped around your little finger."

Dickey was lost as well, but not altogether from loneliness. "I wish I knew what was expected of me," she noted on April 3, 1945. "Am I to take the feminine psychology and do as I've been told—to be the first woman somewhere, which means I adopt the admired manly virtues— and grab the first shoreward vessel I can? I have a fine incipient case of split personality, the masculine lined up against the feminine. This is no place for the feminine. . . . Things are sure tough all over the forward areas."

Three days later, with waves that Dickey recorded in her notebook as "skyscraper in height" thrashing the sides of the *Relief*, she leapt from the ship's gangway onto a bouncing Higgins boat en route to the communications ship, the USS *Eldorado*, about one thousand yards away. She was carrying her camera, her kabar, and a life preserver. Ignoring the turbulent seas, she rode the handrails of the landing craft. Finally the silhouette of the ship loomed up, her superstructure interwoven with a weird muddle of antennae against a gray sky. Dickey tried two passes before she made the gangway, which momentarily depressed her. At the head of the gangway, she took a deep breath and spit out her ID and her request to see Commander Paul Smith, Admiral Miller's brusque deputy.

Although Dickey wrote in her notebook that the officer of the deck "gave me a smile as wide as the deck," Commander Smith was less sanguine. His first words to her were "Did you sneak aboard?"

"No, sir, I had the permission of the *Relief*'s commanding officer." She explained that with the absence of casualties coming aboard, the CO had given her permission to see Commander Smith about possibly going onto the beach in search of casualties. Then she dropped her pack onto the neat deck, making sure to find the spot where it would make the least mess. While officers and correspondents came to transact business, Dickey smoked a soggy cigarette. As always, the officers looked on in amazement while she sat smoking and entering notes in her reporter's book. She must write Tony and ask him to send money. She must write a letter to her folks. Then she must reread her notes.

Sensing that Smith was avoiding her, she went looking for him. He was standing near the officers' dining room, talking with an army medical officer, who suggested that she spend the afternoon at nearby Brown Beach, where army medics had their main blood cache.

Smith, probably glad to be rid of her, snapped out an okay. Then he ordered her to go eat lunch and be prepared to leave on the next boat for Brown Beach, a half hour's ride from the ship. There she would be able to photograph the delivery of blood donations to the army field hospital. While Dickey sat eating spaghetti and drinking lemonade at the chaplain's table, she could not get rid of a nagging thought.

"I hadn't expected conscience or jitters either to slap me down. . . . Commander Smith was Admiral Miller's deputy, so by custom whatever he said had the same force as if the admiral had said it," she wrote. "But I'd acted as though the subject of my going ashore had never come up before, and I knew better than that." After lunch she went belowdecks to see Commander Smith. She did not know what she was going to tell him. "He looked up across the deck at me and barked, 'Dickey, I distinctly told you the boat doesn't leave for the beach until 1300. That's half an hour from now. I can't do anything to get you there quicker!' "

Her conscience was now clear. She'd tried explaining her situation only to be ordered onto the beach. She'd be back aboard that afternoon with her photographs for Daigh and then—home to Tony, where she belonged.

As she boarded the Higgins boat, there came a shout from the *Eldorado.* Her stomach tightened. She looked up to see an officer running to the railing, holding a helmet. "You can't go forward without this," he shouted, tossing it down to her. There were two other correspondents on the Higgins boat. One of them, a marine correspondent, sat clutching the railing, every now and then leaning his head over the side to puke. The other, Jim MacLean, a tall, skinny, bushy-browed Australian war correspondent, managed in spite of the punishing waves to describe the lack of action on the beach.

The cox got them to an amtrac for the second half of the journey, shouting that he would not be able to pick them up that afternoon because an order had been issued to secure all small craft. The amtrac, an amphibious tractor, smashed its way over the coral reefs in grinding, monstrous motions. Two hours after leaving the USS *Eldorado,* Dickey and the two men were put ashore at Orange Beach.

Little did she know that in a few hours the placid island would be savaged by the most desperate kamikaze attacks of the war, which increased in intensity as America got closer to Japan. In the next two days seven hundred zekes would come screaming down the skies above Okinawa to meet the "divine wind."

Standing on the beach without maps, mess kit, arms, or the other gear usually issued to correspondents in combat areas, Dickey felt triumphant. Behind her, mysteriously, a tree burst into flame. Dickey and MacLean ran. The sand felt hospitable under her boots as she ran, sending a mental message to her editor in New York: "I am finally the first woman somewhere." She was also lost.

She turned to the laconic MacLean and asked if he knew where Brown Beach was. A seven-year veteran of the wars, MacLean traveled light; he didn't use maps, either. He carried only a cherished portable typewriter, given to him by the entertainer Bing Crosby. MacLean's method of combat coverage was pure expedience: he simply headed for the nearest outbreak of fighting and wrote. He'd never heard of Brown Beach.

MacLean and the other reporter hopped into a jeep heading for the captured Yontan airfield, leaving Dickey behind. To her right, a farmhouse burned. On the other side, some marines were hunkered around a campfire, barbecuing chickens. A goat walked over to her and nuzzled her wrist. Finally a jeep carrying two marine MPs picked Dickey up and headed for the marines' First Division command post, where somebody would know how to find Brown Beach. The ride was a rip-roaring one, the jeep screeching and tumbling over bad dirt roads, wallowing in mud on a road clogged with military traffic, six-by-six transports, amtracs, and other jeeps. They passed dead civilians, dead cows, stunted trees, sugar cane fields, cabbage patches, chalky cliffs, and terraced, unfenced green hills. The jeep stopped at a scruffy, exposed cliff, where the men of the First Division were digging foxholes for an expected counterattack. The commander of the division, General Del Valle, took one look at Dickey and barked to the driver: "Get that broad the hell out of here."

The apologetic jeep driver took her to Yontan, where she climbed a steep and narrow trail to a jerry-built tent that served as the Marine Corps press headquarters. From there she was escorted to a marine campfire for a field ration meal of hot eggs, biscuits, and ham.

By dark the kamikaze attacks had begun. That night the suicide pilots launched five attacks on the Yontan airport, strafing it in the pitch dark. "It's such a desperate act," remarked John Lardner, a tall, usually sardonic war correspondent. Lardner, a reporter for the North American News Alliance and *New Yorker* magazine, had landed with the marines at Iwo Jima and Okinawa. "I've never seen anything like this in my coverage of the Pacific," the journalist commented as the suicide planes ravaged the night. "The odds are three to one against any Jap plane returning to its base."

Dickey spent the first part of the evening drifting in and out of the tent as the kamikaze planes flew blindly through the night. At one point the correspondents raced across twenty yards of rocky ground to jump into a convenient shell hole. One side offered good cover if you kept your head down; however, being correspondents, they never did. After twenty minutes they climbed out and returned to their tents. Dickey asked John Lardner if there wasn't some other way for a broad to get her basic training besides the kamikaze attacks. She noted that the journalist, who, like most of the other correspondents, voiced his displeasure at her presence, responded to her offhand remark by yelling at her.

Being a condescending, gallant bunch, the correspondents gave Dickey the safest place in the tent to sleep, the middle. But haunted by the admiral's exhortations, she moved herself and her camera to a vacant cot at the edge of the tent, telling them she was protecting them from their selfless chivalry. She placed her boots so that she could slide into them the minute she sat up, then scrunched into a ball and slept.

At 0430 the strafing resumed. The men ran out of the tent as the kamikazes menaced above. The first man out knocked Dickey's right boot under her cot. While she was bent over reaching for it, the second man's knee grazed her head, knocking off her glasses. Fortunately they did not break.

Outside, the firing from a plane above the tent grew deafening. Dickey darted forward with one boot on, just in time to trip over the passing rifle butt of the last man charging from the tent, and fell flat on her face. It was too late to make it to the safety of the shell hole before the plane made a direct hit on the tent, so she rolled under the cot, banging into the cot leg. By this time ground fire had forced the plane upward so that it missed the tent completely. Dickey clambered up and onto the cot just as one of the reporters lumbered in. Bending down, he asked sweetly, "How did you get back into the tent so quick, kid?"

When dawn opened itself like a hibiscus, the mosquitoes had sucked every inch of humanity from the newsmen gathered inside the tent. One of them, James Lindsley, a correspondent from California, added to the already tense atmosphere with a long, racketing harangue on the evils of allowing women in a battle zone. Dickey wasn't upset by the irate newsman; she had far greater worries. She had not only disobeyed Admiral Miller's orders, she had committed a moral sin as well: she had spent the night with the troops in the field.

That same morning, at Guam, Admiral Miller was reading John Lardner's latest dispatch, filed from Yontan only a half hour earlier. Lardner wrote not only of the weird kamikaze attacks of the night before, but of the brand-new kind of war that was being waged: "We now have a woman in the front-line trenches, Dickey Chapelle." He described her as petite young woman with glasses and a helmet that covered nearly half her head, who yawned as the planes went strafing over them. But before Admiral Miller could savor the full extent of his outrage, he received a terse dispatch from Admiral Richard Kelly Turner, commander of the Joint Expeditionary Forces: "Get that woman out of there."

Unfortunately Turner's communiqué arrived after Dickey joined the correspondents en route by jeep to the Sixth Marine Division, headed by General Lemuel Shepherd. It was a two-hour drive up rugged piny hills that reminded her of Wisconsin. Suddenly she was homesick. Except for the sporadic fire from the big guns on shore, and the disquieting evidence of bombardment in the burning farmhouses, the countryside was as quiet as a picture postcard. Neatly cultivated fields of sugar cane, wheat, and sweet potatoes were everywhere. White goats trotted across the unfenced plots or stared blankly from the narrow dirt lanes. The chalklike cliffs leading to the sea were thick with tropical undergrowth and horizontal-limbed fir trees. Marines were moving along the roads shirtless, green utility pants tied over their boots. The tents of the Sixth Division were hidden under flat-topped trees, surrounded by muddy, boot-beaten paths.

Dickey wrote in her autobiography that the tanned and aristocratic-looking General Shepherd greeted her warmly as he strode from his tent, tucked into a grove of pine and pandanus bushes. "My dear," he said, "you are a very brave girl." In her notebook Dickey added that his greeting comforted and reassured her. In fact, the popular general was nonplussed by her appearance and wanted her out of his area. Although years later they would meet again and share a warm correspondence, his recollection was less than cordial. "We had a goddamn war to fight and she was in the way," he stated nearly fifty years afterward.

But as much as he wanted her out of there, reports of sniper fire along the road made travel too hazardous. She would have to spend the night with his division. It was cozy inside the tent. She and the general discussed the fine points of instruction at the Virginia Military Institute. They were seated on folding chairs at a jerry-built table—a plank of wood set over crates—sausages steaming on real, breakable plates, when a violent sound exploded over their heads.

"I looked up to see the world come to an end," she wrote. "But the trees and the sky were still there. The noise cut off and began rising again. My face must have showed exactly what I felt. Brave girl, indeed!" She then followed a ritual that would serve her whenever she was scared. She concentrated on her camera, checked the lens, squinted at her light meter. Though filled with terror, the mechanical nature of the acts calmed her down. She focused, ready to shoot. If this were the end of the world, the least she could do was record it. Her editor would be really impressed.

The general explained that the horrible sounds were coming from the division's artillery, its 155-mm howitzers.

"I was never a brave girl, then or later, about the sound they made overhead," she admitted.

That night Dickey slept fitfully inside Shepherd's blacked-out tent. The general slept on a cot surrounded by his staff so that no infiltrating enemy could reach him. Officers came and went, making preparations for the division's northward sweep to the Motobu Peninsula. She heard their muffled, staccato voices, the wind, the sound of the boots on the ground, cartridge clips going into rifles, a long barrage of firing. As if in a dream, she heard the general's voice on the field telephone, saying, "It's not the folks back home. We got to do something for the men over here."

The next day bad weather, kamikaze attacks, and reports of sniper fire and heavy traffic moving north along the road forced Dickey to cancel her return to the USS *Relief.* Over the next two days the "divine wind" scored thirty-three hits on seventeen American ships, miraculously missing the unarmed hospital ship the *Comfort,* though it would be hit a few weeks later. The death toll at Okinawa was 357 enemy and 367 American sailors. Four U.S. ships were sunk, seven damaged permanently.

The Americans retaliated. The streamlined Japanese battleship *Yamato,* capable of outshooting any ship of the United States Navy, went down in less than two hours of torpedo and aerial bombing. When it rolled over and exploded, it sent up a pillar of fire visible 120 miles away.

Dickey had been at the front for two days and had nothing to show for it except a dirty, sunburned face, dirty fingernails, and stringy hair. She dipped her helmet into a five-gallon drum of water, hallucinating about a cold glass of creamy milk as she spilled the water over her, then filled it again. Wrapping her wet hair in a military towel, she strode purposefully to the press office, a ruined house, its front yard on fire. A few combat photographers were wandering around the fire, checking out each other's photographic gear, bumming smokes, heads moving quickly, chickenlike, looking for a frame to shoot.

It was there that visiting *Life* magazine photographer Jay Eyerman gave her a rousing pep talk. He told her to keep on trying to get her pictures and to remember that a photographer was as important as a general. Then he told her to go to the division staff meeting for all the information she wanted about casualties. When she told Eyerman she'd never just walk in there uninvited, he shook his head in amazement. No photographer, he advised her, ever got any decent pictures waiting to get permission. Feeling dumb but encouraged, she went to the division staff meeting and learned about three critically wounded marines on the division front.

Despite the fact that marine officers all over Okinawa were alerted about Dickey's presence and united in trying to get her off the island, Colonel John C. McQueen, whom she described in her notes as short, flirtatious, and younger and more flamboyant than Shepherd, agreed to let her travel to the forward area hospitals to photograph casualties being treated with whole blood. "But are you sure you really want to?" he asked, adding, "There's no danger except for the snipers."

"Well, you take a chance crossing the street, too," said Dickey.

"It's your life, child," he answered. "I won't tell you what to do with it in my area."

A young-looking medical battalion commander, John S. Cowan, was planning to motor up to inspect the forward aid stations and to scout a location for a hospital. Dickey was the first person inside Cowan's jeep, determined to get pictures that would not only propel her stateside readers off their duffs and into Red Cross blood donor clinics, but would impress the hell out of her editor. Braced by these thoughts, she decided that the trouble she was facing was well worth it. She was squeezed in tightly as the jeep lurched along, encountering heavy troop movement. The weapons inside the jeep seemed extraneous to her: one Browning automatic rifle, five government-issue rifles, five .45-caliber handguns, two pistols, and six trench knifes. "Where on earth did they think they were going?" she wondered. "To no-man's-land?" They were only look-ing for a rear area hospital. The beauty of the terraced hills, the sloping cliffs, gave the trip the feeling of a Sunday afternoon outing.

"Heads down," shouted the commander as a bullet from a hidden Jap rifle whistled overhead. The jeep kept moving forward. Head down, heart thundering, Dickey clapped her hands together. Suddenly Richard Harding Davis's nineteenth-century dispatches of war's romance and sport came vividly to mind. She could see the ramparts standing, the flags unfurled. Beneath the sound of popping fire, she could also hear the sound of drums. As terrified as she was of the sound of fire, she never felt more alive. Or hungry.

The commander consulted his map. "We're four hundred yards ahead of the front," he reported.

So, she thought, we *are* in no-man's-land. She wondered if she would *ever* know a forward area. The road rose and she could see straight ahead. So could the enemy. One side of the road was verdant, the other rock. Steep clay cliffs rose behind rice paddies. They stopped at the village of Nago to look for a possible field hospital, but the American barrage had left only shell-splintered roofs behind. The gentle winding streets were black and smoking. Tile from roofs clattered into dusty stacks. Gaping holes replaced walls. And nowhere were there any people.

"Boy, we really did it, huh?" muttered one of the marines standing beside her. Dickey nodded, remembering Captain Orta's doomed plane and how what she was seeing now had also once been alive.

As mortar fire skittered around them, they ran for cover in one of the island's omnipresent cemetery caves carved into the cliffs. There was no better place to escape the artillery. Holding coffins and glazed clay burial urns, the cave smelled of wet earth and the dead. Everybody smoked to cover up the smell.

At dusk the jeep arrived at the forward hospital, once a schoolhouse. The two large frame buildings were set inside a huge courtyard, roofed with red tile and riddled by shells. The school was built on top of a mud-covered plateau overlooking rice paddies, set against the cliffs and looking down to the sea. Two generators rattled outside. There were rows of frame-and-thatch buildings around it. Foxholes lined one of the rugged cliffs.

When the doctor saw Dickey, he grimaced. Muttering "How the hell did you get here?" he grudgingly accepted the purpose of her mission. She felt as welcome as an outbreak of typhus. One of the corpsmen, a short, fine-boned pharmacist's mate, showed her around. In violation of the Geneva Convention, he had a .45 strapped to his chest.

About a dozen marines, none of them casualties, were in a long room with cots. Two were playing cards. The others were reading by flashlight. One was leafing through a three-year-old copy of *Reader's Digest.* They had toothaches, malaria, dermatitis. Two suffered from combat fatigue, and all were anxious to get back to their unit. The operating room offered wood boards for an operating table, under a single electric light. Windows broken by artillery fire and mortar attack had been mended with tape.

Shortly after midnight an arc of blazing headlights shattered the imperfect blackout of the schoolhouse. Dickey heard shouts outside, groans, the sharp crack of rifle shots. Vehicle doors slid open. She jumped off the cot and grabbed her camera. If this wasn't the enemy, they certainly would know where the Americans were by now with all this racket.

Corpsmen shuffled casualties into the room: four marines wounded from ambush—one with a shot-up leg, another with a broken arm, one bleeding badly from a head wound, one with a chest wound. The leg and arm wounds were patched quickly by the corpsmen, but the doctor shook his head when he examined the young lieutenant wounded in the face. His look said the marine was not going to make it.

Moving quickly in the little operating room, the doctor lit the white gas light and hung it near the bottles of plasma. He asked two corpsmen to hold the heavy navy flashlights, and they complied, grumbling.

When Dickey offered, the doctor shot her a look of annoyance. "It's too heavy for you to hold," he snapped. He also told her there would be a lot of blood and she would probably faint at the sight of it. By then as tired and annoyed as the doctor, Dickey replied that she had seen plenty of blood on the decks of the hospital ships. Reluctantly he agreed to let her help and turned to the man with the chest wound.

He was trying desperately to see well enough in the dim light to transfuse the patient moaning on the makeshift operating table. Dickey's hand trembled under the weight of the lamp. Two hours later the last suture was in place and the man's breathing was almost normal. When the doctor took the flashlight from her, Dickey nearly keeled over. She wondered out loud how anybody could stand this. Not looking at her, the doctor replied, "The limit of human endurance has never been reached."

Dickey stood there, her mouth open, hands still trembling. "Bullshit," she announced. The doctor looked at her, his grief-stricken eyes seeing her as if for the first time.

"Why don't you sack out," he suggested gently. "In the morning we'll help you get your pictures, however long it takes for you to show how a forward area field hospital works."

The next day, as promised, the doctor helped her. Dickey no longer jumped every time she heard the sniper attacks. The young, thin pharmacist's mate, to whom she became close—he confided that her kiss and his being shot at and missed occurred on the same day—also told her, "Sure they can kill you, but only you can scare you." Courage, she realized, was not the absence of fear—the fear never left her—it was the control of fear.

"A pool of blood, a clenched fist," she wrote in her notebook, "that wasn't war. None of those Hollywood trademarks of horror were valid here. Everybody out here had seen some guy trailing his innards. Every guy out here didn't anchor his faith to some machine of war, but to the odds." Passion out there wasn't a man's hand on a woman's breast, but "a man's hands around the enemy's neck."

Dickey, who so much loved being privy to what boys were thinking, luxuriated in her newfound camaraderie. The next day she moved with the corpsmen to another forward position to set up another hospital. By now her voice could easily be heard over machine-gun fire, speaking in the newly acquired vocabulary of a forward area marine. When not consumed by her new purposeful adventure, she would guiltily remember Tony and Admiral Miller . . . both of whom seemed a distant world away.

On the afternoon of her sixth day ashore, Dickey was eight hundred yards ahead of the front. While she was riding in a jeep with the chief pharmacist's mate, an MP waved them over to the side of the road. The MP looked embarrassed as he leaned into the jeep, peering past the driver and the chief pharmacist's mate. "You hadn't oughta ask us to do it any longer, Mrs. Chapelle," he said.

Dickey stuck her head forward in confusion. "Do what?"

He sighed, hitched his belt, cracked his neck, and smiled sweetly. "Say we don't see you," he answered. "Don't you know there's an order to arrest you on sight, ma'am? Every half hour I get asked have I seen you, and always I say, 'Seen a dame? Out here?' I say it so they think you ain't around."

Dickey nodded her head and lit a cigarette. "Right," she said.

"But today," he said, shaking his head, "you've been by me four times already. Ma'am, the admiral is so mad that at first the order was to shoot you on sight. But they said that was a mistake."

"Shoot on sight?" she exclaimed. "Marine, you've got to be confusing me with somebody else."

He only shook his head. "You're the only br—I mean, dame—we got out here. I think you better go over and talk to somebody at the public relations office. It's only a few miles down the coast road."

"Yeah, well, you shit if you eat regular, too," groused the driver. He turned to Dickey. "Look," he said with the authority of the righteously aggrieved, "there's no way they can bust a civilian for going too far forward or staying too long."

"You want to bet?" Dickey sighed. "It was just a matter of time before the admiral caught up with me. After all, I know I don't look too good, but I am the only woman out here." She turned to the pharmacist's mate. "As you boys say, my ass is grass."

At headquarters Dickey was placed under arrest by the division public relations director and charged with jumping ship. Admiral Miller later recalled, "She protested every foot of the way."

The next morning sniper fire laced the terrain, and rain rendered the road impassable. Nobody knew how to deliver Dickey until she suggested she be evacuated by sea with the marine casualties. She was held in quarters for two days aboard a hospital ship when the heaviest suicide dive bombing of the war began. Twenty ships were sunk or damaged beyond repair. Her ship miraculously escaped attack, although a destroyer escort ship five hundred yards away was struck. She watched it stream past "with the scorched naked bodies of her dead in rows on her deck."

A marine MP escorted her to a transport plane for Guam. He kept his .45 cocked and aimed on her until she was aboard the plane.

When she arrived in Guam, she was relieved of her credentials, though not by the admiral. He had been transferred to Washington and made a rear admiral. She cabled *Life Story* and asked if she could stay in Guam and write an article on how women could survive being on the front with the marines. The magazine wasn't interested.

She called Tony. Half-crazy with worry ever since word of her jumping ship had found its way to him, he'd begun a campaign of letter writing and long-distance telephone calls to navy public relations. It was Panama all over again. They all wanted her home, but how she was to be returned to Pearl Harbor became a battle of military egos. The navy wanted to send her back to the States by slow boat. The marines wanted her to go by plane, in style, at least as far as Pearl Harbor. While one of the ranking marines on Guam apologized for the behavior of the navy, a young private put her name on an air transport plane list to Honolulu.

"Erase it, marine," snapped Dickey, feeling dispirited by her unceremonious departure. "You don't want to get mixed up in this."

He shook his head. "You rate it," he said. "Besides, what can they do? Bust me?" He had one stripe on his sleeve.

She was flown to San Francisco courtesy of the army in order to annoy the navy, she was told. In San Francisco Dickey ate her first stateside meal: real eggs, milk. When she telephoned Tony, her first words were, "Tony! I just ate four eggs—out of the shell!"

Tony was waiting for her at Penn Station. His resolve to keep a scowl on his face crumbled the minute she stepped onto the platform. She looked skinny and tired; her wool coat, which once fit so smartly, hung loosely around her waist. Tony ran to her, tears streaming down his tough-guy face when he hugged her. Tears were running down Dickey's face, too.

"Oh, by the way," Tony said, reaching into his pocket and pulling out an official-looking letter. "I got this from the navy while I was going nuts trying to find you."

The letter, dated 30 April 1945, was from the United States Pacific Fleet and Pacific Ocean Areas. In answer to Tony's incessant inquiries about his AWOL wife, it regretted to inform him that "the credentials as a War Correspondent of your wife were revoked because she failed to comply with specific orders and regulations regarding her movements in this area. She was permitted to go to Okinawa on a hospital ship with the expressed understanding and direct orders that she not disembark while in that area. She did disembark—and caused a great deal of embarrassment to several responsible officers in the area."

Dickey dropped the letter into her coat pocket, already stuffed with her Cincpac officers' wine mess card, a book of unused mess tickets, bobby pins, a hair net, a crumpled-up copy of a cable she had sent to her editor, and a .45 bullet, a momento from the chief pharmacist's mate.

Tony hailed a porter, then grabbed Dickey by the hand and led her through the crowded station. "Well, pal," he scolded gently, "I hope you've learned something."

She stopped right there. "Oh, I did. I did, Tony. Wait until you see the pictures." She added that they were gritty and ugly, the way war was. She was proud of them, adding, "You think it was okay I stayed on Okinawa as long as I did, don't you?" A taxi pulled up. Tony opened the door for her, sliding in after her.

"I said, little goofy bird," he murmured, kissing her cheek and running his hand up her leg, "I said you shouldn't have gotten caught jumping ship in the first place."

"Jumping ship? Who jumped ship?" Dickey protested as the cabby moved into uptown traffic and over to Riverside Drive. She elaborated, her diatribe peppered with newly acquired marine vocabulary. This combat dialogue had become so ingrained that she would develop a long-lasting stutter trying to rid her everyday speech of it.

For the next several months Dickey wrote letters to Rear Admiral Miller pleading that he reinstate her credentials. Even though Tony was dead set against her returning to a combat situation, Dickey got him involved, no doubt by pointing out that his well-intentioned interference had fueled the naval fires. He sent Miller a letter defending his wife's actions, stating that she had gone ashore on "the verbal orders of the area public relations officer, Cmdr. Paul Smith." Even Ralph Daigh, Dickey's editor at *Life Story,* got into the act, noting in a June 29, 1945, letter to navy public relations that "it is our considered opinion that the decision to discipline Mrs. Chapelle was made largely because of her sex." Considering that she had proved her ability to work in a combat situation, the magazine requested that her record be cleared. All this was to no avail. Reports of her arrest and banishment from the fleet were reported by the wire services and picked up by a gossip columnist for the New York *Daily News.* The item, running in June 1945, quipped, "That gal photographer was sent home from Okinawa, Admiral Miller says, because he considered it wrong to have a gal there with 10,000 men running around naked trying to keep cool."

Dickey had been aware of the risk she was running trying to prove herself. If her hard-won photos found acceptance by magazine photo editors, the loss of her credentials would be somewhat mitigated.

But by July 1945 *Life Story* had fired Dickey. The break occurred when she showed them her pictures of wounded marines receiving blood transfusions. The young photo editor looked from the grim pictures to Dickey, shaking her head. "Dickey," she said, "of course our readers are interested in knowing that their injured men are cared for. But you should have known better than to have made *these* pictures. We can't use them. The wounded look too—*dirty.*"

Dickey was not that surprised. After all, although she believed that women should know exactly what was going on, the editors didn't.

Tony once again rallied behind her, dismissing her rejection with cncouragement to try another publication. And *Cosmopolitan* magazine published the photographs of the wounded marines in its December 1945 issue. *Seventeen* magazine did not buy any, but the fledgling publication offered her a job as its staff photographer. "Their *only* photographer," Dickey liked to add. The dirt of wounded men did not offend the Red Cross, either. One of the photographs Dickey had taken aboard the USS *Samaritan*—a before-and-after picture of a young marine whose life was saved by blood transfusion—was to be used by the organization for the next ten years to advertise its blood drives.

On August 7, 1945, the day after American fliers dropped two atom bombs on Hiroshima and ushered in the nuclear age, Dickey was still trying to get the navy to reaccredit her. "It's pretty obvious that half the newsworthy areas of the world will be under military jurisdiction for most of my professional life," she wrote the admiral that day. "And I don't think I care to leave this situation a matter of record indefinitely. No publication cares to consider . . . a byline which has been officially and ambiguously slurred in newsprint, and for that I do not blame them. . . ."

The loss of her military credentials, made public in a newspaper gossip column, had cast serious doubt on her credibility. She could not even return to writing aviation books, which she described as "my old line of endeavor, since there are plenty of aviation writers not in trouble with the navy. . . ."

Rear Admiral Miller, who was reported to have suffered great embarrassment because of Dickey's actions, was not conciliatory. Twenty years later he would write a glowing obituary about her in the *Overseas Press Club Bulletin* and remark that they had gone on to become good friends. But on August 11, 1945, three days before the Japanese surrender that would end the war, the admiral responded, "I sincerely regret that your professional standing has suffered. An excellent time for you to have given this thought would have been at Okinawa prior to the disembarkation following our many talks on the subject of women going ashore."

PART TWO

THE CERTAINTY OF
UNCERTAINTY

7

Leg on a Pair of Wings

T HE WAR changed many things. Years later Tony would comment that he lost Dickey at Okinawa. She returned from the island haunted by the experience, by the men. She described it as "a feeling of commitment"—a feeling bigger than herself, of being part of a group of one million people who in one time and one place shared a single aim, the land invasion of Japan, which was "more important than whether we lived or died." Other war correspondents shared the feeling; Marguerite Higgins described it "as close to being good as anything I know."

Postwar Eastern Europe was redrawn as the Soviet Union extended itself westward. Russia, America's fervent ally during the war, had become its enemy. "From Stettin in the Baltic to Trieste in the Adriatic, an iron curtain has descended across the Continent," reported Winston Churchill in his famous speech at a college in Missouri in 1946. "Behind that line lie all the capitals of the ancient states of Central and Eastern Europe. Warsaw, Berlin, Prague, Vienna, Budapest, Belgrade, Bucharest, and Sofia. All these famous cities and the populations around them lie in what I must call the Soviet sphere. This is certainly not the liberated Europe we fought to build up. Nor is it one which contains the essentials of a permanent peace."

At the same time, the first spasms of the cold war—the struggle between the United States and the Soviets for the stewardship of Europe—had begun. America's newly created Central Intelligence Agency operated a covert espionage inside Vienna and Berlin, the two cities legally open to East and West under the postwar four-power occupation agreements.

In addition, an estimated fifty million malnourished, displaced persons were moving across the war's burned-out landscape, searching for food and shelter. The wholesale starvation of these war-torn people had so impressed the United States that by 1947 Secretary of State George C. Marshall announced that "the United States should do whatever it is able to do to assist in the return of normal economic health in the world, without which there can be no political stability and no assured peace."

Marshall's words were acted upon with alacrity by the U.S. Congress. Billions of dollars of aid would go to feed Europe's people, most of whom were existing on little more than 1,500 calories a day. The Marshall Plan would also provide production start-up money to help the savaged economies of sixteen nations, including onetime enemies Germany and Italy. Once hunger had been banished, America believed, Central and Eastern Europe would have the strength to resist the spreading communist menace. American trade would also benefit.

Tucked among Dickey's papers are yellowed invoices from some of the more popular overseas relief programs of the day to which the Chapelles donated money—Save the Children Foundation and the Foster Parents Program, to name two. In exchange for their support they received letters of gratitude in stiffly written English from a young Polish war victim.

Since her ungracious return from the Pacific, Dickey had been employed as staff photographer and associate editor at *Seventeen*. Rarely home, she traveled to thirty states and Alaska, while Tony, having grown wealthy selling war surplus, film, and whatever else crossed his path that could be turned into quick profit, stayed in New York printing his wife's shots inside his darkroom and sending her telegrams of hungry love. "It's rainy and muggy and cold and all that's warm is that in my heart for you," he wrote to her when she was on assignment in Seattle. Followed by, "Alaska Kodachromes are swell. . . . Everything going smoothly except that I miss you too much. I love you, Tony."

Other than the outward display of confidence that came with her glamorous new life, Dickey was not personally fulfilled. Visiting his sister during that time, Dickey's brother recalled "those three-martini lunches." Dickey had become increasingly frustrated by the kinds of pictures she was taking for *Seventeen,* pictures she believed furthered the "gossamer illusion of global peace and plenty. . . ." She wrote, "Most people seemed to be pretending the war had never happened, or that its appalling consequences were the proper concern of somebody else."

Adding to her frustration was her relationship with Tony, which had made the inevitable turn. Tony had created Dickey, formed her, coached her, taught her how to make love—and now she was beginning to beat her wings against the cage. He grew emptier and more needy as her career flourished. The very qualities that had first attracted them to each other had evolved into fundamental differences.

Tony, the Orson Welles–size hustler, with his newfound wealth became a galloping consumer. He bought, reportedly for cash, their roach-infested apartment building on Riverside Drive, as well as the neighboring building. "My dad was either rolling in money or he was broke," explained Ron Chapelle. "He would pay for my schooling at a second-rate prep school for a year in advance. The next year he'd declare bankruptcy."

Tony gutted the apartment building, adding a pound of DDT for every ten pounds of plaster. With the roach problem solved, he entertained on a lavish scale. By all accounts he was a fine chef, insisting on only the purest, most expensive ingredients. Acquaintances recall him jumping into a taxi to hunt down exotic postwar delicacies. Years later even a chronic heart condition would not stop him from barreling into a taxi to find the perfect prawns for paella. When Ron came to stay with his dad for a few months, he recalled how Dickey would iron her dresses and drink beer while Tony performed culinary miracles in the kitchen. Ron's bride was so intimidated by her father-in-law's exotic dishes, she retreated into a steady diet of instant rice and peanut-butter sandwiches.

Tony decorated the apartment in what Dickey would later describe scornfully as "fake baronial splendor." Oriental rugs hung on the walls and covered the floors under expensive, unpaid-for leather chairs. There was air-conditioning and a weekly maid. A shiny two-tone green Buick Roadmaster was parked in the garage. Tony had guns, a rifle, and a couple of pistols. He used one of the two bedrooms in the apartment as his darkroom. The walls were painted Dickey's favorite color, hunter green.

They had enough money to indulge in Tony's favorite pastimes, shopping sprees and spur-of-the-moment vacations. In reaction to her husband's excesses, Dickey began encouraging her mother and aunt to send her their hand-me-down dresses, which would come to her at regular intervals. Now, instead of scorning Edna's homemaking projects, she eagerly hemmed and altered the used clothing, bragging to her family about how fashionable Aunt Lutie's dress looked on her. She did not like to buy new shoes, either, but preferred to repaint or resuede the ones she already had. Her only extravagance, acquired from her husband, was an addiction to taking cabs.

Tony's flirtations escalated with Dickey's job at *Seventeen,* fanned by his admitted jealousy over her high salary and the time she spent away from him. Despite the fact that he had made plenty of money, it hadn't been with photography, and his giant ego was irked that Dickey out-earned him in this arena. "Women did not find Tony unattractive," Dickey's brother pointed out. The sensual man with his soulful eyes kept busy with his photographic printing business and his photography classes, which were taught out of the Riverside Drive apartment and attended by what Tony called "photography-minded damsels." And these enthusiastic lady shutterbugs provided him with a steady source of bed partners. Tony excused his indiscretions to friends as due to nothing more than middle-aged angst, necessary in order "to make myself feel younger."

Dickey, so long aware of Tony's philandering, able to sniff it like an alien scent, developed her own form of defense: she slipped into what she later wrote Edna was "the indulgent mother to Tony's spoiled child routine," as well as "the role of indignant wife and cheated partner," a part she admittedly "went through often and most unbecomingly."

But she conceded partial responsibility for Tony's womanizing, admitting in a letter to her aunt Lutie to "a lifelong problem showing affection and love to those closest to me." Yet despite his infidelities, his professional jealousy, and his drinking, she needed her mentor and quite possibly still loved him. Certainly she treasured that first heady flash when they had met, the excitement of finding another being besides her mother who believed her to be wonderful. No matter how much she talked of adventure, she'd been on her own only during her brief stint at MIT and for a few months upon arriving in New York. Although she was feeling secure about her professional skills for the first time, she still depended on Tony for emotional support. She told her mother something far more "profound" than Tony's affairs would have to come between them.

One such factor was the discovery sometime in the spring of 1947 that Tony was still married to his second wife, Carmel. It came as a shock when Carmel charged Tony with desertion. He had left her and their son, Ron, when the boy was an infant, but it had taken her eight years to get around to serving the papers. Tony claimed that he had gotten a "quickie" divorce from Carmel in Mexico before meeting Dickey. It's uncertain how much he told Dickey about the other wife or wives as well as an alleged brood of children he'd fathered. No doubt Carmel's emergence was a rude surprise, albeit not the first. By this time Tony and Dickey had been "married" for seven years. Tony promised her they would legalize their union "at some future time," though they never did.

During the summer of 1947, a few months after this unpleasantness, *Seventeen*'s Quaker publisher, Alice Thompson, sent Dickey to photograph a Quaker work camp in Nashville, Kentucky. After completing the assignment, Dickey stayed on, writing that the camp "has stirred me as no other story since the war." The racially mixed campers, none of whom were Quakers, enfolded Dickey with their acceptance. "They never questioned why a person did something (any more than the lieutenant on Iwo Jima had questioned why I wanted to go to the front)—as long as you *did it.*" It was the feeling she had been searching for, "at once prouder and warmer than any I'd found behind a battle front," and she did not want to let it go.

The Friends was one of many American charities engaged in feeding Europe's postwar survivors, referring to itself as a "little Marshall Plan." In Dickey's mind, the feeding programs that the Quakers were starting up in war-torn Europe showed that there *were* people "willing to look squarely at the problems produced by warfare and then try, as individuals to do something about them." They were looking for a photographer to document their program in Europe and behind the Iron Curtain. Dickey immediately volunteered for the unpaid assignment. But the Quakers would not consider sending a woman alone. By this time Tony had joined her at the camp; and, knowing his wife was determined to get the assignment with or without him, he agreed to accompany her. Dickey was ecstatic. Finally, she'd be able to put her talents to work for a higher purpose than selling magazine fantasies. She and Tony would photograph this work and, she believed, "we could make others look and in that way, we could help, too."

By August of that year Dickey and Tony were courting John Kavanaugh, the public relations director of the Quakers' American Friends Service Committee. They were printing up dozens of publicity photos for the Friends and refusing any reimbursement. "Let's just say we're the friends of the Friends," Tony wrote Kavanaugh on August 26, 1947. The couple sent Kavanaugh their bios and a statement that although neither of them could support the group's position of opposing war— "I'd been no conscientious objector to warfare," Dickey wrote, since "I'd put on a uniform [as a correspondent] and so had Tony, twice"—they could certainly support the cause of peace. Dickey wrote Kavanaugh that she'd been "raised in the pacifist tradition, and I am in sympathy with those whose thinking is so much more certain then my own has been that they are able to hold this position, and I deeply wish to serve the cause they represent."

By early fall arrangements were under way for the couple to travel to Europe as the Friends' volunteer photo team. It would mark the first time Dickey and Tony would work together since their long-ago honeymoon. The Chapelles would be photographing feeding programs and the distribution of clothing and medicine where the scorched-earth policies of the Germans and the Russians had reduced entire cities to blackened heaps of rubble: Germany and the Iron Curtain countries of Czechoslovakia, Poland, and Hungary. The six-week assignment would begin behind the Iron Curtain, in Poland, where 80 percent of Warsaw lay in ruins and as many as thirty thousand of its fifty thousand corpses were believed to be buried under the detritus of the Warsaw ghetto.

Although the assignment involved a radical departure from their comfortable, sophisticated life, their combined incomes made it possible. It would also provide Dickey with a chance to get back to where the action was, without military accreditation. At this time few Americans were able to or wanted to get inside the Iron Curtain, the feared, malevolent domain of Joseph Stalin, the butcher of the Baltic. But Dickey thirsted for "the sheer adventure of seeing postwar Europe as few people would ever see it," as well as "a chance to interpret something bedrock real, the outcome of the war. . . ."

It was an impetuous and romantic decision for Dickey. Tony's motivation was less action-oriented. He was in the unfortunate position of a man chasing a shadow not his own, but of his design: the naive, obedient Dickey. He sensed that had he turned her down—she needed to be accompanied by a man to get the assignment—she would have quickly found someone else. So Tony had jumped into her scheme with the desperate hope that the rigors of the adventure would find Dickey disenchanted and eager for home. Had he been less desperate, he might have recalled how Dickey thrived with the marines on Okinawa—and saved his energy. He'd seen enough of war and its aftermath. Overweight and a heavy smoker, he was physically unprepared for the assignment. But he needed Dickey and she needed him. His presence would keep Edna's fretting to a minimum. He was still a damn good bulldog.

ON NOVEMBER 14, 1947, Dickey and Tony sailed past the Statue of Liberty as passengers aboard a Danish freighter. The ship's destination was Gdynia in Soviet-occupied Poland, a country that had lost one-sixth of its 32,000,000 people in the war—not from combat, but from Nazi slaughter and starvation. Setting out that sunny, breezy afternoon with a sense of real mission, they little realized they would spend the next six years traveling around the world, chasing Dickey's "feeling" and making pictures.

The trip on board the freighter *Falstria* was one last celebration of excess. While Tony indulged in the bounteous buffets, declaring, "I couldn't think of a worse way to prepare for our assignment," Dickey did tummy-firming exercises and studied Russian and German grammar. Somewhere securely lashed in the hold was a one-and-a-half-ton Dodge truck provided by the Friends. Dickey called it "the Angel." It was to be used as their mobile home and darkroom as they traveled the potholed and blasted-out back roads of Eastern and Central Europe.

After a few days' stop at Copenhagen, the *Falstria* docked at Gdynia, Poland, on December 6, 1947, a gray, foggy day. By three that afternoon Dickey and Tony had cleared customs, secured their truck, and driven to Sopot, where they checked into the Grand Hotel. Two days later, after a brief meeting with the local Quaker team, they drove on to Warsaw, which had been shelled and firestormed into what Dickey called a town of "horror and miracle." The horror was visible in the faces; the miracle was that the people were alive. Everywhere the odor of death issued from the burned-out buildings.

These were anxious times. America, the richest, most powerful country in the world, was waiting nervously for the Russians to come up with their own nuclear arsenal. Given these concerns, Tony and Dickey spent weeks in Shorewood outfitting the former ambulance truck. Edna helped Dickey sew the black velvet drapes to lightproof the truck, and Slug and Paul helped to install cabinets and shelving for their cameras and equipment.

Cooler heads than Edna's would have winced at the trip her daughter was setting off on. When Tony sat down with her and showed her a map, explaining in his calm, masterful voice that they had stored half a dozen jerricans of gasoline to have enough fuel to reach the Atlantic Ocean in the event of a Russian army invasion from Germany, Czechoslovakia, or Poland, Edna panicked. Later she would write to "atone" for her behavior. However, her hysteria was effective. During the Chapelles' time in Europe, they stayed in their truck, with Dickey's childhood hand puppet, Oscar, sent by Edna, swinging from the rearview mirror. Edna had wanted to include an old quilt made while Dickey was at MIT, but Dickey refused to schlepp a falling-apart, smelly old blanket through Europe. The Chapelles were traveling light. They turned down the comfort offered at the Quaker guest houses en route except as a last resort. Their desire, wrote Tony, was "complete mobility over food and warmth."

Six weeks after their assignment began, Dickey and Tony were not back in the States, as planned, but in Brno, Czechoslovakia, developing their film over a wood-burning stove. The Friends had asked them to stay longer. And, though Dickey noted in a letter to the gang back at *Seventeen* that "within one thousand yards of the continental hotels, all that you see is grim," she was charged up.

"Our job here is to get out and see what needs doing," she wrote to her colleagues at *Seventeen*, brimming with purpose. "I wouldn't be anywhere else on earth or doing anything else. Holy cow! There's so doggone much to get done!" In response to her fiery letter, the staff sent the Chapelles a donation.

They were faced with hardships at every blasted-out Eastern European road: scenery dominated by the lacework of burned-out buildings; wandering, vacant-eyed humans filled with disease and psychic despair. It shook Dickey's midwestern sensibilities. Aboard the *Samaritan*, the wounded and dying had been warriors, but the children and adults barely existing in the postwar rubble were bystanders, the victims of war. Tony wearily called it "all this damn misery." And then, absorbing his wife's concern, he banged out letters to friends in New York asking for donations of medicine and clothing.

Although Dickey was to write that she and Tony could never work well together or play well together, their work at this time proved otherwise. Years later, when Tony's situation was desperate and he needed Dickey to get a well-paying photo job—he told her it would be like old times—he'd do all the photography, she'd do all the writing. Their correspondence, however, verifies that they shared the photographic work, a total of ten thousand negatives—as they shared the credits. Dickey *did* do all the writing, though—captioning their double sets of thousands of negatives and their semimonthly letters to her anxious family.

Eventually their long reports to the Friends on the actual calories people were receiving—children and adults were being rationed food "too low to maintain body weight"—delivered important information to the administrators of these programs. Dickey and Tony provided the sole documentation of their practical benefit. Thousands of their negatives would appear as publicity photos in the States, raising funds for food, clothing, and medicine. Before insolvency and growing disillusionment ended their European relief work at the end of 1949, the Chapelles would shoot ten thousand negatives for a dozen other humanitarian agencies, including CARE, Save the Children, Christian Rural Overseas Program, the United Nations Children's Emergency Fund, and the Girl Scouts.

Their morale also suffered when six months passed without "a single reaction to any work we've done, simply acknowledgements that it had arrived." But for most of the sixteen months they spent working and living and photographing out of their temperamental truck, the couple believed they were making a difference. This belief was sparked by the slightest of responses—a letter sent to *Seventeen* in 1948 from a group of New York high school students moved to begin a school clothes drive after reading Dickey's article on teenage refugees. On one of their brief trips to New York in the summer of 1948, the couple was enthusiastically discovered by the media. They were profiled in the *New York Herald Tribune* along with pictures of their truck, as a husband-and-wife team photographing "Europe's misery from their 'White Angel' truck." That same week the *Christian Science Monitor* profiled the couple, and an exhibit of their photographs was on display at Girl Scout headquarters in New York, promoting the organization's "Clothes for Friendship" program. On June 29, the *New York World Telegram* described Dickey as a small, lively blonde who together with her husband brought back more than two thousand photographs and stories "of the people and poverty in war-torn countries."

After spending the day with a family living in a burrow and existing without heat or running water, coughing in tubercular unison, Dickey would hammer out long, solicitous letters of concern to her mother with unfailing regularity. Addressing them to "Marmee," she would coo over Edna's latest Eat Club wingding or tedious bit of neighborhood gossip—anything to keep her mother from going off on another hysterical toot. It was a difficult charade when all the time Dickey was herself shaken by "all the damn misery," so much so that by September 1949 she sent Edna a letter from Munich that exploded in a heartfelt rush for Shorewood. She was homesick for the scourge of her youth.

"The thing that keeps coming back to me is that the village of Shorewood and all it stands for (which I used to explain so regularly I wanted to get away from) seems to me now to be important to my whole world," she wrote Edna. "The community of ideas and standards which I learned there, and which I still feel is incomplete and stiff, is at the same time a thing of staunchness and fineness and reality, the kind of reality that you can believe in because somewhere it exists every moment. . . . The world of which my own family is a part, which their love and loyalty makes me a part of too, is a tremendously good world. If I didn't carry it around in my heart—which I couldn't do if it weren't for you, Marmee, and all you've given me—I wouldn't have very much to believe in and I'd start sounding like all the millions already over here who believe in nothing because they haven't had our kind of a family or a setting to put it in."

On April 1, 1948, Russian soldiers had begun turning back Allied vehicles en route to Berlin through Germany's Russian zone because they did not meet inspection standards or because a word was misspelled on a travel document. On the following day, American aircraft would begin airlifting supplies into Berlin. But on that first day of the Berlin blockade, Dickey and Tony were in a line of cars at the Russian checkpoint of Helmstedt, watching as others—who, like them, lacked correct papers—were turned back. While they waited, Dickey, ever the optimist, patted Tony on the shoulder and lifted her bulky sweater. His long-ago gift, the sterling-silver pin of a leg on a pair of wings, dangled from her bra strap, as always. "Don't worry, Tony," she told him, patting the charm and letting her sweater drop, "it's going to get us past the Russkies."

Tony was too sick to argue. In fact, since they had begun their assignment, few days had passed without some malady. He'd had the grippe in Paris, sinus problems in Munich, a liver ailment in Poland. Feverish and exhausted, he told Dickey he wished she would learn how to drive. A bottle of Polish schnapps sat open between his legs. He drank it like milk, cursing the afternoon drizzle, the truck, and the lack of something stronger to take for the pain.

Dickey, who would later claim that her insistence on remaining overseas had contributed to Tony's deteriorating health, found herself seeing a side of him that most people didn't. As much as he swaggered and was known as a guy you could lean on, he also complained endlessly and seemed to delight in having her nurse him, and whenever he faced a problem, she found herself unwittingly involved in trying to solve it. Feeling frantic, wanting to appease him, she searched the road for a store where she might buy a dessert with which to mollify him; but all the buildings she viewed on either side were shuttered and dark.

The Russian major standing at the Helmstedt checkpoint that rainy afternoon reminded Dickey of a character out of *The Three Musketeers*. He was mustached and erect of posture, and Dickey noted with envy his magnificent pair of black leather boots. He walked over to the truck and asked in Russian, then in German, to see their papers. Leafing through them and finding nothing that authorized them to drive through the checkpoint, he ordered them into his office.

"We're international," explained Tony, pointing to the Quaker sign he had painted on the side of the truck. His trouser pockets bulged with Hershey chocolate bars, and sensing the need for his powers of pursuasion, he rose to the occasion like a real trooper, casually unwrapping the candy and offering it to the Russian. The guard shook his head, saying, *"Bonbons auch schlect"* ("Bon-bons are bad"). He ushered them into a big room full of field desks, drafting tables, radios, and a dozen armed and unsmiling Russian soldiers. Dickey and Tony were quite a sight, dressed like twins in rumpled, mud-splattered herringbone tweed slacks and green wool hunter's shirts. Dickey, despite a recent "Toni" home permanent, looked unkempt in heavy walking boots made in Chippewa, Wisconsin, which Tony called her clodhoppers. The room grew claustrophobic as the soldiers rubbernecked and the little major studied the assortment of papers. Tony broke off pieces of Hershey chocolate with almonds, the American greeting in postwar Europe, and handed them around.

"*Nein, danke,*" said the dapper Russian, shaking his head, "*Bonbons auch schlecht.*"

The major picked up a huge silver microphone and held it in front of Dickey. "Why do you want to go to Berlin?" he asked.

Dickey answered, "To help relieve the suffering," which was how she viewed their work. If a single one of their pictures helped to provide food and clothes, then she had indeed helped relieve the suffering. But if the Russian officer saw their cameras, he'd think they were spies, so she did not mention they were relief worker/photographers.

"Your truck," he said. "I must inspect it."

Back outside, Dickey opened the door to the truck with the inviting gesture of a proud housewife. "It's our home," she trilled as Tony turned on the overhead dome light. The major stood in front of the hinged and padlocked crates containing their two Rolliflex camera outfits, the 16-millimeter spring-wind Bolex movie camera, the flashbulbs, and the Presto sound recorder and demanded that Tony open them. Stalling, Tony reached into his shirt pocket and fished out a crumpled-up pack of Chesterfield cigarettes. Flashing his most charming smile, he offered the soldier a cigarette.

"*Nein, danke,*" the major said. "*Amerikanski Zigaretten schlecht*" ("No, thank you. American cigarettes are bad."). Snapping open a silver cigarette case, the major smiled as the rich smell of Balkan tobacco drifted into the crowded truck. He offered the case around. Tony took one, inhaling it rhapsodically. "I bet these are Balkans," he said. "I've heard they're wonderful." Dickey took one, too.

She was hoping the Russian would pass over the containers holding their twelve hundred rolls of film and their twenty floodlights, praying he would miss the gasoline cans. Still smiling, Tony thrust his Dunhill lighter into the center of the group. "I don't believe in that three-on-a-match stuff, do you?" he asked. Now into the game, he crouched above the jerricans of gasoline, waving his cigarette. He took some keys from his pockets, jingling them. "Here we keep the gasoline and the machine parts," he said, cigarette puffing as he began calmly to fit one of the keys into the lock.

"*Ich rauche, du rauchst, und sie raucht, und jetzt öffnen sie die Benzinkanister?*" shouted the major in panic. ("You're smoking, I'm smoking, she's smoking, and you're opening gasoline cans?")

When Dickey wrote her family about this adventure, she presented it like a Marx Brothers comedy. She described the soldier as shaking his head violently, moving his hands wildly, backing out of the truck shouting, "*Las uns abhauen. Schnell!*" ("Go on, get out of here! Fast!") Tony and Dickey looked at each other above the pungent smoke.

As soon as they pulled onto the half-destroyed autobahn heading for Berlin, Dickey and Tony began to laugh. "Just like I said"—Dickey patted the silver pin under her sweater—"we beat the odds."

Tony squeezed her hand. His onetime child bride had a sublime smile on her face. He'd seen it once before, when she'd described going seven miles a minute.

But right now he had big worries: their truck. It had died on them twenty-seven times. They had no spare parts left. It was growing dark, and as usual they were the only fool vehicle driving on this unexplored, battered road.

As Tony's face tightened, Dickey could feel herself begin to tense, anticipating one of his explosive temper tantrums. After six months of life on the road, she saw nothing romantic about what she used to call "his Homeric wrath," especially since she'd become the unhappy recipient. To avoid more unpleasantness, she complimented him on his handling of the Russian soldier; Tony's face beamed with her flattery, and she relaxed.

After six months Tony had also grown disenchanted with their existence but was too frightened by what Dickey might do next to leave. He viewed his idealistic wife as too driven by her emotions, no doubt a trait inherited from her wacky mother. But at fifty years old, with his boozing and indulgences, he was having a problem keeping up with her.

His idea of camping out was a hotel without room service. Not Dickey. Every night she pluckily bedded down inside the truck in her sleeping bag, lauding its warmth and charm. Tony would have traded their entire picturesque adventure for one hour on his favorite green leather chair with its wide armrests. Whatever hopes he'd entertained about her growing tired of their life dimmed with the realization that Dickey had no need for the material comforts so essential to his existence. Except for a perm and haircut in Paris, his wife paid little attention to her personal grooming, content to wear the same unflattering clothes day after day. And though they spent an occasional romantic night out holding hands and drinking beer at village fairs, he'd stopped paying her the compliments he'd once lavished upon her. She didn't seem to fret, preferring to stay close to the Quaker relief teams they were document-ing. She eagerly volunteered to wash dishes, carry pails of water through the snow, and sew curtains, and she always piped right up to sing endless rounds of the nineteenth-century German *lieder.* He understood she was trying to recapture the burst of commitment she had felt that long-ago summer day in Kentucky or in Okinawa. But its sway over her worried him.

To new acquaintances like the journalists Charlotte and Denis Plim-mer, the Chapelles were enchanting, the kind of couple Charlotte rhap-sodized "that people write stories about, equally creative and exciting." The Plimmers saw what others meeting them in Europe did, a dynamic duo, a dedicated couple changing the world with their photographs.

DURING THE TWO YEARS Dickey and Tony spent abroad as relief agency photographers, they returned only briefly to the States—once for Christ-mas in Shorewood, Wisconsin, and a few quick trips to check on their apartment buildings in New York. In 1949 they drew up incorporation papers for their own nonprofit news agency, AVISO. The American Voluntary Information Services Overseas was their attempt to carry on with the work they were doing for the various overseas charities that could no longer afford to pay the expenses of a permanent volunteer photography team. AVISO's sole aim, as declared on an IRS form the Chapelles filed in 1950, was a desire "to spread perpetual peace." The logo was a handshake. Tony was the president and treasurer, Dickey the secretary. They worked strictly for their expenses.

AVISO would allow them to continue as a photo team, documenting postwar relief efforts for the charities still operating in Europe. But their altruistic business was ill timed. A year after they had begun AVISO, American assistance programs were ending and an ugly anti-American sentiment was sweeping Europe. For the first time, Dickey was becom-ing disillusioned. In September 1949, the same month the Soviets deto-nated their first hydrogen bomb, Dickey wrote Edna that "with U.S.

support of all the voluntary relief agencies plummeting down to its usual between-wars low level, it's hard for me to feel that what we have been doing *is* really useful. . . . Tony and I are supposed to be over here getting a job done, and when the job is growing tougher and the chances of getting it done less, it's hard to assess how and whether we are really helping or just floating around the map over here for our own amazement." Her weariness was expressed by guilt: "I feel that putting ourselves far enough away . . . to cause you anxiety is a dirty darn trick and hasn't any justification," she wrote, adding, "I think what you and Daddy had in mind . . . when you started your family . . . wasn't getting air mail letters from me with funny stamps. . . . Tony and I are at this point old-fashioned homesick." But as would always happen, Dickey's idealism overrode her physical and emotional considerations. So in the same letter, as though she had detoured but was now back on the main highway, she finished with, "But we are also even more deeply disturbed than we were a year ago over what we have seen here, and our conviction that the best thing a couple of journalists can do is to stick with interpreting peoples to one another is greater, not less."

A month earlier in Naples, while Tony attempted to shoot a 16-mm film for Save the Children Federation about the postwar homeless living in the Magellini caves, Dickey had been detained briefly by the police and charged with exploiting the poor. The beggars followed behind, chanting, "Down with the Americans" and "Rich tourists go home." Dickey found it difficult to take the charge too seriously, since most of the people she encountered in the caves had already been the subject of countless magazine articles; one family had even insisted she look at their clippings. By the end of the year, AVISO was eleven thousand dollars in the hole, unable even to cover stories assigned by relief agencies and magazines like *Junior Scholastic*. Dickey and Tony were stuck in Paris, trying to scrounge passage back to the States and hoping somehow to save AVISO.

Tony had already sold half their camera equipment to keep them and "the Angel" running. From New York, Aunt Lutie wrote that their apartment building was losing money. Tony did not want to spend one more Fourth of July picnicking in the wind and rain on some German riverbank eating hot dogs and potato salad while a batch of their negatives floated inside another borrowed bathtub. AVISO had been personally rewarding but disastrous financially. It was time to go home.

They were still trying to figure out a way to recoup their losses when they arrived at a Quaker house in Munich. Tony was encouraged by his mother-in-law, who believed that Tony and Dickey could make some of their money back by doing lecture slide tours accompanied by the Angel. Desperate to get her daughter home, Edna had already begun lining up some lecture dates for them in Milwaukee. While Tony sold off their remaining darkroom equipment to purchase tickets home, Edna wrote Dickey letters insisting she query American lecture bureaus. Certainly there was an audience for two relief photographers who had returned from the Iron Curtain intact.

But by then interest in humanitarian causes to Iron Curtain countries was considered unpopular, if not downright subversive. The United States that Dickey and Tony were returning to was astir with a need for security, protection from the "Red peril" now that the Soviets had their own arsenal of obliteration. While President Truman initiated loyalty checks on federal employees that would spill over to every sector of the American work force, the heavy-jowled Republican senator from Wisconsin, Joseph McCarthy, began rooting out commies under the auspices of the House Un-American Activities Committee. Dickey's letters to lecture bureaus were met with a lack of enthusiasm she pronounced "total." She was quite relieved. "The thought of lecturing terrifies me," she confided to Edna shortly before returning to the States. "Maybe I can talk my loving guy into it, but it would take ten years of coaching from you before I could imagine me doing it."

The Angel stayed in Europe. Dickey took the star-shaped piece of metal that had been attached to the truck's ignition key and used it as a key ring. She would keep it with her the rest of her life, "to remind me of the truck and how it was a bearer of mercy to the war-wounded. And that mercy still exists."

UPON THEIR RETURN to the Riverside Drive apartment, the Chapelles resurrected their cosmopolitan life, which for Dickey now rang hollow. After being lauded as a couple attempting to change the world with their photographic work, the high-speed, marketplace world of Manhattan struck Dickey, the onetime midwestern ogler, as unimportant, phony. Tony fared far better, welcoming the painless transition from truck to leather-upholstered armchairs. Although their long absence had created a serious dent in their finances, Tony made enough to keep the wolf from the door. Once again he busied himself with his photofinishing work; he shot publicity photographs, sold military surplus, and enthusiastically reacquainted himself with the noisy crowds of the Upper West Side bars and eateries. Dickey began making the rounds of magazines. So much about the States now confused her. For example, on television she saw women wrestlers engaged in phony violence, yet nobody wanted to print her photos of real violence. One of her first visits was to the photo editor at *Seventeen*. Dickey was no longer on staff, but she hoped they would be interested in what she had seen, although they had already rejected one of her photo stories on postwar Vienna teenagers with the comment, "Brr, just looking at these people gives me chills."

But in the summer of 1950 no magazine wanted Dickey's war-torn photos, even though American troops were fighting communist troops in South Korea. "We'll be one of the last to use pictures of the war," the *Seventeen* photo editor told Dickey. It was the same reaction that had greeted her photographs of combat casualties five years earlier.

"The hard-boiled illiteracy on the whole subject of suffering and violence is my real concern," she wrote indignantly on July 21, 1950, to Alice Thompson, the publisher of *Seventeen*, after her photos were rejected. Thompson thought Dickey "naive," which Dickey took as a compliment. "It's friendly and funny the way you say it," she wrote Thompson. "It always makes me feel as if we both understand what we're talking about perfectly (even if I probably don't).

"Perhaps there really is no very good reason why *Seventeen* shouldn't ignore the fact of war as long as it possibly can. But it's a service magazine, and while it can ignore the war, its readers can't." Dickey understood that her egalitarian point of view had been considered freakish by women's magazines during World War II, but she'd hoped things had changed by now.

In the same letter to Alice Thompson, Dickey wrote that she understood that *Seventeen* was dependent on its advertisers, and that advertisers were not idealists. "However, the increasing use of force among nations, and the fact that our readers can get killed that way . . . when something requires great effort and understanding to lick it, like VD or delinquency or bigotry or sexual maladjustment, all the stories you print, well, war isn't so very different from any of those things. It's more than that—war is all of these things with panic and personal death and suffering thrown in. My mother, who is a real pacifist, was so proud that

I grew up in a generation where illiteracy about violence would be fashionable, and was! I'm just not convinced that they really want to be illiterate any more."

She wrote Thompson that she understood what Mark Twain meant when he wrote, "There are some things a man must write or die," adding, "The more I study and learn about war, and write about it, the better I can come to terms with my own life. At least that's what I tried to do with all the other things that have threatened my serenity." In a fit of uncustomary candor, she wrote the same words to her mother. But Dickey did not have the military credentials to get to Korea, nor was any magazine willing to assign her there.

With a growing sense of frustration, and a gnawing need to return to work that she believed valuable, Dickey turned away from her former commercial outlets, for which she now felt herself "psychologically un-fitted." To alleviate their growing ennui, apparent in Tony's late nights out and Dickey's self-described "paralytic state," the couple decided to continue to work as a photo team, which provided them with a sense of purpose. They applied unsuccessfully to a Christian missionary organization, the Christophers, whose motto—"It is better to light one candle than to curse the darkness"—appealed to both of them. They sent their résumé to General Lucius Clay's National Committee for a Free Europe, whose intent, according to a July 28, 1950, New York Times article, was to "mobilize the American people for getting the truth behind the Iron Curtain."

Dickey and Tony had by now found a lecture bureau to sponsor them. They were able to give occasional talks on "conditions in Europe," though with the outbreak of what would become a three-year war in Korea, the refugee problem in Europe held little interest for American audiences. Dickey settled for a job as the Red Cross's public information director, resolving some of her frustration by making speeches to spur blood donors for the wounded GIs in Korea.

Finally, in 1952, a friend of the Chapelles working for the American government-owned radio network, Voice of America, arranged a job for them with the State Department's Technical Cooperation Administration, photographing examples of U.S. aid in the Middle East and India. The government job may have been pushed along by a photograph Tony sent to the Voice of America in January 1952—a shot of an anti-Voice of America float he had taken in Budapest four years earlier when he and

Dickey had been documenting the Quaker programs there. He had somehow managed to slip the film out of the country and away from its vigilant censors. The State Department appreciated his trouble and promised the photo would have a featured place in its office.

The original purpose of President Truman's Point Four, as the program was popularly referred to, was to administer aid without any strings attached. Eventually the program would become more politically motivated, trading technical aid for a mutual-defense policy, but in Dickey's eyes Point Four was "a bright light in a world grown dark with the cold war, Senator Joseph McCarthy's redbaiting witch hunts, and the Korean conflict." So while the Federal Bureau of Investigation began their interviews for the Chapelles' State Department clearances, the photographers set off for their new job.

"The Point Four effort was a national policy through which, in effect, all Americans had said to the world's underdeveloped countries that there was something *we* could show *them* which they would find it helpful to know," Dickey wrote, viewing their job as "the most exciting picture assignment since Matthew Brady packed a covered wagon and set off with his cameras to photograph the Civil War." When Dickey's uncle Hans asked her how Point Four could ever achieve its objectives, Dickey's reply arrived from Baghdad with all her old idealism intact.

"It never can," she wrote on May 18, 1952, "if you state the objective is care for millions of underprivileged—but if you speak of one such baby or one hungry family or one village that has suffered a drought, or a typhoon . . . then it works."

For seven months Dickey and Tony were ensconced like the minor foreign service diplomats they were in the great hotels of Iraq, Iran, and India. During the days they once again set out to change the world with their photos, chauffeured by jeep to mud-hut villages, where Point Four technicians were building wells, bridges, and schoolhouses or eradicating locust hordes. Tony wrote Ed Brown, his friend at the Voice of America, "It's a dream job," excitedly describing their location in Teheran as "right on the cold war front."

Only once did the going get rough, when the Chapelles were trapped in a canvas tent for three days in the Iraqi desert during a *shamal,* a sandstorm with winds up to one hundred miles an hour, while working on a locust wars story for *National Geographic* magazine. It was Easter Sunday. Tony missed most of the storm; he had a dangerously high fever.

As Dickey later recalled for the April 1954 issue of the *Reader's Digest*, while the storm raged she held her husband's hand, reciting what she could remember from the Sermon on the Mount. Miraculously Tony's fever broke, and he began to utter Jesus's words along with her.

Other than that singular display of married devotion, despite their important job, the two were growing farther apart. Yet Point Four proved the perfect job for the increasingly disparate photo team. Tony disliked roughing it. He relished the opulent hotels, palaces, cheap caviar, and booze, as well as his minor diplomatic status, hobnobbing easily with the Third World potentates. He relinquished much of the planning and organization of their work to Dickey, who assumed it with enthusiasm and admitted feeling "arrogant" with her newfound ability to make decisions. Often, sitting alone in her goat-hair tent typing up reports, she contemplated a solitary life off on some important mission, like her long-ago childhood fantasies; she didn't actually believe she'd ever leave Tony.

When Dickey wasn't encamped in the Iraqi desert or inquiring after "edible locusts," as requested by her aunt George, who seemed to know about such things, she could be found with the other Americans at Teheran's two-story Park Hotel. She would spend hours in the dining room, absentmindedly stabbing at a mound of caviar while she eavesdropped on the gossip streaming from *New York Times* reporter Albion Ross and his wire service sidekicks, speculating on the players involved in the country's recent CIA-engineered election of the pro-American Shah Zahedi. At these times Dickey experienced anew her youthful enthusiasm over the world of journalism, becoming the MIT coed listening in on the boys' "bull sessions." No matter how important she believed her diplomatic and humanitarian mission, it was not the work she longed for. It is evident from the detailed letters she wrote Edna about the supercilious Middle Eastern "expert" Albion Ross that it was acceptance by him and his cronies she craved.

But the competitive reporters, unlike the engineering students at MIT and the marines, didn't quite approve of her. They had no more room for her than had the newsmen on Okinawa. Her noisy curiosity made them nervous. "Each of the gentlemen . . . at various times assumes an avuncular discipline about your angel child," she wrote Edna from Teheran in August 1952. "I have a feeling I am quite a problem to these boys."

It was no wonder that Dickey became ecstatic when a woman reporter for the London *Daily Mail* arrived in Teheran. "She is a grand person," Dickey wrote Edna of her new friend, Annie Gallagher. "She has an unimpeachable wardrobe . . . for a female yakety I would be willing to cross quite a few streets and maybe an ocean. She's balanced the odds nearly equal."

Though the gap between Dickey and Tony was widening, Dickey still found pleasure in her husband, gushing with pride in another of her long letters home to Edna, "Oh, how handsome he is." Edna had been depressing her with a letter about "the passage of time," mentioning that she and Dickey's father had decided to retire. Dickey was alarmed by the decision. Her father was sixty-five years old, and as far as she knew had no plans for his spare time. "We know a lot of people who retire," she wrote to her parents, "not before they were ready, but before they were ready to do something else. . . . That seems pretty rough to me."

Dickey was enjoying the adventure of goat-hair tents, the mud huts, and the children, whom, she was certain, "can be befriended without the exchange of a word if you just take the time." She was never quite so happy as when she was sitting in her aba and sandals, cross-legged on a straw mat in a tent, after traveling three hours by camel trail into the Iraqi desert, drafting reports for the State Department on her eight-pound portable typewriter.

It was, wrote Tony, "a delightful existence, in spite of desert trips after locust stories." He was happy to report to his journalist colleagues and apartment sitters, Denis and Charlotte Plimmer, that he could get a drinkable sidecar, French onion soup, and chocolate ice cream in Baghdad. Tony's mellifluous voice boomed through the marbled hotels. He looked approvingly upon his turbaned servant boy, Hassan, waiting on his haunches to do his bidding. In the evenings, while Dickey played with children or hung on every smug word Albion Ross uttered, Tony would be at the American Club entertaining American tourists. Dickey described one of them to Edna as "a bleached blond divorcée with too much lipstick and a voice you can hear across the border."

Neither wanted this ideal life ever to end. While Tony indulged himself, his artistic fingers curled around a crystal brandy snifter, Dickey dreamed of the coming year. There had been talk that they would be returning to Iraq for Point Four for an indefinite period after going home for Christmas and receiving approval from the FBI. If not, their friend

Ed Brown, once on staff at the Voice of America and now attached to the legation in Libya as an information officer, might be able to swing something for them over there. By this time Dickey had chosen the mud hut she would live in as soon as their Point Four contract was renewed.

But the charmed life came to an abrupt end right around Christmas 1952. Amoebic intestinal infections would see each of them hospitalized during a three-month period. The Red scare had grown into full-fledged hysteria by the time of the Chapelles' return from the land of the Thousand and One Nights. With Eisenhower's election that year, his vice-president, Richard M. Nixon, announced, "We're kicking the communists and fellow travelers and security risks out of the government . . . by the thousands." Loyalty was now enforced among government employees with executive order number 10450, the "security risk." One could be a security risk by reading the wrong books—anything by Howard Fast, for example—or listening to the records of singer Paul Robeson.

In a letter, Tony referred to Joseph McCarthy as "the investigative blues." McCarthy's absolute panic power was so great, he even had President Eisenhower by the short hairs. Perhaps Tony and Dickey's bigamous state, and Tony's preference for exotic seasonings, compromised their status. Whatever the reasons, the patriotic Chapelles did not get FBI clearance.

In his July 24, 1953, letter to Roy E. Stryker, the pioneer documentary photographer and former director of the Farm Security Administration, Tony wrote, "No one has been cleared since the investigative blues settled over Washington. Basis of the whole thing, of course, is that everyone, either on contract or otherwise, is to have an FBI and loyalty clearance. For fear of errors, they seem to have decided to clear no one. From off-the-record sources, we hear again and again that several of the TCA missions in Near East countries have obligated funds for our return there, but TCA Washington can't seem to get around the rule that clearances must be issued, and no one is willing to issue the clearances."

Although both Dickey and Tony could not think of another job as "soul satisfying" as going back to Iran on behalf of the government, Tony was aware of other pressures. He wrote to Roy Stryker, "The demands of everyday living seem to dictate that we find one of those jobs that pay that filthy stuff the butcher, baker, and suchlike seem to think they must have in order that the Chapelles keep on eating and otherwise indulging in such sinful extravagances as cigarettes and clothing."

Two months later they were still hoping for clearance, but Tony seemed resigned to the inevitable. Point Four had been restructured, and Tony wrote to Stryker, "There is a grapevine report that a number of people are being processed for the vacant jobs. Their names are said to have come from a list supplied by Republican party headquarters. . . ." He was no doubt referring to Senator McCarthy's statement that the Democrats were the "party of treason."

By the end of the year Paul Meyer spoke up on behalf of his disappointed daughter. The lifelong Republican wrote his Senator, Alexander Wiley, as "a constituent who has voted for you faithfully and has supported your work on the Foreign Relations Committee." Paul wanted the senator to know that his daughter and son-in-law were lauded publicly by the TCA administrator during a series of their lectures under government sponsorship for "interpreting Point Four to the American people." He added he felt "parental pride" that his daughter had been singled out for her "remarkable work, under hardship conditions, as one of our 'shirtsleeve diplomats' and held up to the people of Wisconsin as somebody whose service to the cause of good foreign relations 'they could take pride in!' "

The situation was finally resolved on October 26, 1952, with a letter from Harold E. Stassen, director of the Foreign Operations Administration, to Senator Wiley, stating that "the current sharp reduction in number of personnel and reorganization of the Foreign Operations Administration makes it unlikely that the services of Mr. and Mrs. Chapelle will be needed by the program."

By the year's end the Chapelles saw their first article, "Report on the Locust Wars," appear in the April 1953 issue of *National Geographic.* Dickey had her own byline in the December 23, 1953, issue of the *Saturday Evening Post,* a story written while working with the Eastern European refugees entitled "There'll Be No Christmas for Them." They were heard on the radio and seen on the NBC-TV program "Mrs. U.S.A.," discussing their work for Point Four. They lectured to nearly one thousand people about the Middle East at the State Department as well as to the Department of Agriculture, the National Museum, and the League of Women Voters. But despite their lauded high-profile civic activity and their hectic entertainment of fifty-one visitors from eighteen countries, they could not find work.

8

"No Olympian Tragedy"

Losing the prestige of their foreign service job was a real sock in the chops for both Chapelles. The dreams that had brought them together—for Dickey, being part of something bigger; for Tony, helping her "to go, to be, to do"—were sustained by their exciting work as a team. Now everything that bonded them began to unravel. Dickey's fitful independence, fueled by Tony's excesses, flared anew in the ashes of what Tony called "the death of a dream." For six heady years they had managed to avoid their relationship's unpleasant realities. Now, at fifty-five, a fatigued Tony was being hounded by a cuckolded husband who'd hired a private detective to hunt down his wife's alleged seducer. Despite Tony's denial and allegations of being set up, Dickey didn't believe him. She'd been through too many such scenes, reacting as usual with screams and shouts that by now had a mechanical sameness. She could also feel herself retreating into traditional female martyrdom: silent suffering. A year later she would write to her mother, "Sure he was that kind of guy in the first place. But he might not have stayed that kind of a guy if I hadn't been so tolerant and so kind and so forth."

By now, as idealistic and loyal as she was, she had to face certain cold facts, writing to Edna the following year, "We weren't lovers or husband-and-wife any more; we were simply acting the roles of indulgent mother and spoiled child (in spite of our ages), that is the way it worked out." Added to this was an endless stream of professional rejections and Tony's resentment over what he called "growing to a complete dependence on Dickey," which he traced to their Point Four work together. Another major irritation was their finances. They were now heavily in debt from Tony's unchecked sprees. They sold their profitless apartment buildings, paid off the most glaring bills, and moved to a two-bedroom flat on West End Avenue.

Then, in January 1954, another pair of overseas visitors appeared at the Chapelles' front door: a young married couple from Berlin, Helga and Ernst. Helga was twenty-five and college-educated, a pretty, flirtatious blonde. Friends recall Helga as milky-skinned and speaking impeccable English. The Chapelles had met Ernst, who spoke no English, in Berlin, and had offered to sponsor him should he want to come to the States. Helga and Ernst moved into a rooming house until Tony arranged for them to house-sit for his friends, the Plimmers, for three months.

Helga recalled the Chapelles did not live "plush," but comfortably. "Even when Tony didn't have money, he lived like he did," Helga remarked, noting that his wallet often bulged with three or four thousand dollars.

But the comfort was illusory. Dickey's devotion consisted of always calming Tony down over some imminent crisis or nursing him through another illness. And though he could be counted on for income, the money often derived not from photography, but from one of his side scams, such as selling military-surplus handguns or setting up marathon poker games—for which she had little tolerance. And despite his often flamboyant show of wealth, his huge exotic dinners and fine brandies, they often had to rifle the piggy bank. So to provide some stability in their life and to boost her flagging spirits, Dickey went looking for a nine-to-five job, an unconventional step for an American woman in the conformist fifties. World War II had put them into the marketplace, but now articles in women's magazines were sending them back to the kitchen, cooking pot roast or shining the floor till it gleamed.

Dickey went to see John Kavanaugh, her old friend from the Quaker days, now working as publicity director for CARE. He offered her a job as his assistant at a moderate salary. She would later write Edna that ever since her job at *Seventeen,* over which Tony had kicked up such a fuss, she had made it a point, regardless of their finances, not to take any job that might trouble her husband's fragile ego, noting, "I was pretty happily martyred because I never looked for a job if I thought it was one Tony would have wanted, telling myself it wouldn't be considerate to get a bigger income than Tony."

In the afternoons, when he wasn't playing poker in the apartment or at the American Legion hall, Tony escorted Ernst and Helga to the Cloisters and other sights of Manhattan, teasing the young German girl about her use of American slang. Helga recalled she viewed Tony as her "hero," a man who explained to her all sorts of things, "like how the democratic system worked." He also, as he later told the Plimmers, "began to try to bolster up my own ego by trying to succeed on other and any other things that I did by my self alone . . . personal and business."

During this time, Selma Blick, a middle-aged medical receptionist, became friends with Dickey and Tony. The dark-haired Selma, a career girl who went by the name Stevie, lived at home with her family. She had met the couple through her married boyfriend, who was Tony's doctor. Stevie became one of Tony's adoring photography students. Like most people who met the well-traveled couple, the sheltered Stevie thought their bohemian ways incredibly glamorous. Indeed, Stevie was so taken by their exotic travels and their photographs, she once gasped that Dickey's work was similar to that of Margaret Bourke-White. She would never forget the look of intense anger that spread over Dickey's face. "She looked like she wanted to kill me. It almost ruined our friendship." Stevie, who managed to become a confidante of both Chapelles, was careful never to mention Margaret Bourke-White again.

Stevie had great admiration for Dickey's work, which struck her as highly authentic. "She really wanted to save the world." In contrast, Stevie wondered about Tony's motivation. "I always thought he was just going along for the ride or a good meal. But he could charm the birds out of the trees."

Stevie Blick lived on West Seventieth Street and passed the Chapelles' West Side apartment each morning on her way to work. "There were a lot of women around at that time," she remembers. "Dickey would go to work at eight-thirty in the morning and Tony would have somebody in bed with him by nine o'clock. I'm not exaggerating." One of the women Stevie often saw arm in arm with Tony was Helga, who had confided to Stevie that her marriage wasn't working out, claiming Ernst refused to learn English or look for a job. Tony, generous to a fault, was helping them out.

Despite Stevie's own affair with a married man, she had strong principles. In her circumspect opinion, Ernst was nothing more than a ticket to the States for the lovely, war-hardened fräulein, a money digger with the moral fiber of a gnat. Every man who came within breathing distance of her was fair game. Stevie glowered as Helga flirted with her boyfriend. "She would sit there and bat her eyelashes at men. She would look up at Tony and call him 'Daddy,' " recalled Stevie. Six months after Helga's arrival in New York, she had begun an affair with Tony. Helga, basking in being fussed over as the baby of the crowd, thought Tony possessed the same dash and vitality as Cary Grant. "Tony was so vital, so alive. . . . He was not the world's greatest lover, but he was one of the most active." Like Dickey, she sensed an element of danger about Tony that excited her.

By the middle of the year Stevie and Dickey had become good friends. Dickey confided that she wanted to leave Tony, but that she lacked the courage to walk out. Whatever confidence she'd once had was gone. She spoke about waiting for the "right opportunity." She also had to get up the courage to fight her conservative background and the tone of the times. In 1954 a divorce was a mark of a woman's failure to hold a man. Leaving Tony would also publicize their illicit state; they were widely known as a husband-and-wife photo team, and Dickey feared the professional consequences of airing her dirty laundry.

Stevie, unaware that Dickey lacked a marriage certificate, was not at all surprised that her friend wanted to leave Tony. What with the comings and goings at 575 West End, Stevie was amazed her talented friend had stuck with the porcine philanderer so long. Stevie thought of Dickey as a "marshmallow inside" and could never quite believe this was the same woman who would go on to parachute from planes as a famous combat photographer. Stevie was also convinced that Dickey feared Tony. "As charming as he could be was as nasty as he could be. He may not have wanted her, but he didn't want anybody else to have her. She treated him with kid gloves." Years later Helga would corroborate Stevie's suspicions. As his illnesses became more debilitating, he grew so jealous of the woman who became his next wife that he rarely allowed her to leave the apartment, except to walk their dog.

SINCE STEVIE'S BOYFRIEND was Tony's doctor, it was she who received the phone call when Tony suffered his first heart attack, on a sweltering day in May 1954. "I don't remember who the woman was he was in bed with at the time," Stevie said, "but she was hysterical, screaming into the phone, 'Help us, please, he's dying!' " Stevie telephoned Dickey at CARE. By the time Dickey arrived, the woman had gone and the ambulance was pulling away. "Of course once he got sick she couldn't leave him," recalled Stevie. "She waited on him. She cut up his food. She was very loyal."

But Dickey deeply resented her new role, which called a halt to whatever fragile steps for independence she may have been making. In a letter to her mother the following year, she described this period as draining to her energies, as she went through "all the motions of being a dependable nurse and the mistress of a household I hated and the holder of a job I didn't really want."

Along with his new condition, Tony's royal airs were on the increase. "He would sit there in his leather chair like a pasha and ask whoever was around to go get him another brandy or open a drape," said Stevie, a frequent visitor. "He never walked, except out the front door to hail a cab."

Stevie recalled with macabre humor how after Tony's first heart attack—there would be many more—he was outfitted with one of the first pacemakers, a clumsy electronic device he carried around attached to an implant that regulated his heartbeat. Often the pacemaker would beep off for a second or two, at which point Dickey and Stevie, and later Stevie and Helga, would jump onto Tony's chest and bang away on him until the machine kicked back on.

Tony's doctor friends supplied the increasingly incapacitated man with a variety of prescription drugs: phenobarbital, Valium, Seconal. Later he graduated to injectible narcotics such as Demerol and morphine. "I would go over there and he'd have boxes of the stuff all over the place," said Robert Meyer. "He didn't try to hide it."

Tony's descent into booze and drugs followed the script of any sodden television soap opera. There were drunken scenes at the Overseas Press Club, the foreign correspondents' organization to which Dickey and Tony belonged. Andrew St. George, a journalist and member, recalled one evening when a sullen, drunken Tony smashed a beer bottle at the bar and challenged another member to a fight. "It was sad," said St. George. But Helga didn't see it as anything more than a reflection of the times. "We all did a lot of drinking," she said. By this time the Chapelles' messy personal life was an item at the OPC.

While Tony and Helga were frolicking in bed, still unbeknownst to his wife, Dickey's pent-up rage over her role as nursemaid-cum-slave was intensifying. Dickey began lobbying CARE for a solo photo assignment in Haiti. Although she was understandably skeptical about the power of charities to change the world, she nevertheless believed that a technical assistance project sponsored by CARE and the United Nations in Haitian villages was a good thing. She wanted badly to document it so it could continue; and she desperately needed a worthy project to throw herself into to raise her shaky confidence. Not the least of its appeal was the prospect of escape from the apartment on West End. Tony was more than a little upset as he watched his wife getting ready for what she enthusiastically called her next "mud hut assignment." She began taking judo classes at a midtown gym and, despite her chain-smoking, was running two miles a day.

In October 1954, Dickey's father died. She noted it in passing, as one might comment upon the weather in Wisconsin, writing only that he was sixty-eight at the time of his death and blaming it, not surprisingly, on his early retirement. As quiet and unobtrusive as Paul Meyer appears in the memory of acquaintances, he was a staunch, unswerving supporter of his daughter, who referred to him as "Daddy" in letters and to whom she owed the safekeeping of her adventurous spirit. He would do anything he could to help her realize whatever cockeyed dream she cherished. Undoubtedly he spent much of his waking hours calming his wife's hysterical fears over her uncontrollable child. Dickey, who could write reams about a starving child with a belly bulging and flies in its eyes, could not muster a page about her loving father or any other people important to her. She was selfish with her personal grief, unwilling to share it with anyone. Yet the loss of her father, coming as it did when she was struggling to rediscover herself, had to be devastating. He was her biggest, most enduring fan. She also wrote that soon after she and Tony stopped working together as a photo team, "we came to what I guess is called the parting of the ways both personally and professionally."

Helga's recollection of her role in Tony and Dickey's split was that "their marriage was already over, it had grown sour." She added, "We did nothing to hide our affair." Indeed, Edna, a visitor during the Christmas holidays, had been struck by their curious behavior and mentioned it to her daughter. But Dickey, familiar with her husband's bearish affections, didn't take her mother's words seriously, and it wasn't until May 1955, after the affair had been going on a year, that Dickey found out—in the rudest possible way: she walked in on her husband and Helga in a compromising situation. It sent her reeling, despite her flip comment to Edna: "I must have been ready for it because it's no big tragedy." Actually Dickey fell apart when she and Tony broke up. Although Helga would later state that Dickey "wanted out" and greeted the breakup with "relief," Dickey's letter to Edna contradicts this. "I would have never believed it was Helga," wrote a stunned-sounding Dickey. The spark may have long gone out between them, Dickey may have been going stir-crazy as the wife of a semi-invalid, but the shock she felt, the sense of betrayal—not only by Tony, but by a woman she had befriended and sponsored to America—was profound. While Dickey's aunt Lutie dismissed Helga as "that tart," Dickey viewed her as "the first woman who—ironically—would let *him* play indulgent papa to *her* spoiled child role."

Another outcome of the affair was the breakup of Helga's strained marriage. Ernst moved to upstate New York and then to California, where he filed for divorce. But perhaps the real reason for Dickey's unsteadiness was that the affair provided the opportunity she wanted— and feared. If she walked through this open door, she would be facing the world alone. There would be no turning back. Fortunately she feared turning back more than the unknown.

Dickey moved in with Stevie for a few days—keeping her whereabouts secret from Tony, whose powers of persuasion she feared in her fragile state. Within a few days she rented a newly painted studio apartment on First Avenue, across the street from the mazelike, twelve-block-long Bellevue Hospital. Impressed by its spartan quality and its white walls, she ignored references to it as "dilapidated," though she later called it her "claustrophobic castle." She took only a few items from the old apartment: one of the Bukhara rugs on the wall, one of the prized green leather chairs, and her aunt Lutie's hassock. She also took the family heirlooms—crystal, a Gorham bowl, all of the sterling silver engraved with the initial *M*, linen, her father's office-model world globe, and her mother's bed with the green velvet spread—along with her two cameras, a small portable typewriter, five pieces of luggage, and all her clothes, jewelry, and books. She brought her framed photos, which she hung carefully, and one-half of the china.

On May 28, 1955, one hour after Dickey was packed and out of the apartment, Tony began a letter-writing campaign to woo her back. This would go on unchecked for the next ten months, even after he suffered another heart attack and moved Helga into his apartment. "How can I say, with all that has happened and with what I do to you that makes sense, that I love you?" the suddenly remorseful Tony began. "But believe me when I tell you that there is such a big part of my heart that is yours alone and always will be. . . ." In a follow-up letter written a few hours later, he added, "I know that I will be back some day on my knees. Don't please ever hate me for my weakness . . . and even if all of me doesn't completely love you, there is a big hunk of the heart that is left that will always be yours."

Fleeing the oppressive West End apartment had not, as she'd hoped, freed Dickey of her dependency on Tony. Although she wanted nothing more than to reclaim the straight path of her youthful dreams, opportunities did not magically spring up once she was freed from her tyrannical husband. Freedom and independence were not palpable, but frustratingly slippery abstractions. Intuitively she believed her best chance for salvation would be to concentrate on her professional life, which had also run into some problems. By late June the type of assignment she envisioned in Haiti, described in a proposal to Kavanaugh as costing $2,500 and taking "several months" to be covered "with camera and typewriter," was far more expensive than CARE could afford. Dickey wrote Kavanaugh that she felt "a deep personal concern" for the plight of the Haitian villagers and believed her coverage would be helpful to CARE for its Freedom Village campaign as well as to the UN for presentations to Congress and a major U.S. periodical. She was so committed, and so eager to get out of New York, that she volunteered to raise the funds herself. She requested a three-week leave without pay, beginning July 1, "for the purpose of trying to set up a cooperative sponsorship among these various agencies for such coverage by me as soon as possible." The first item, her airline ticket, was the biggest expense.

Lacking the courage to tell her mother she had left Tony, Dickey wrote about her upcoming trip, telling Edna she would be embarking alone on this job "for a ten-day shooting trip (by myself; there's no budget for two people to go) early or late in July." She then sent Tony a copy of the letter, asking him to add something so Edna wouldn't grow suspicious.

"I wish you were going together," Edna promptly wrote back, "and—precious, you must not resent my saying this—would you care to tell me who is to be *my* watchdog down there? Are you saying, 'Mother watches too many TV programs—they are all so full of intrigue and wrong thinking. . . .' "

Dickey responded to the worrisome Edna as if she were a child. Now that Tony was no longer running interference, it seemed the only practical way to handle her. "I am sure, for example," she wrote, "that there are no representatives of tyranny intriguing in tiny Haitian villages. And if there were, they would be kind of foolish, tactically, to interfere with a relief agency photographer. We relief and welfare people are much too small potatoes."

Although Stevie Blick was not surprised that Tony and Dickey had split up, the Plimmers were devastated. "It is no idle phrase to say that you have broken our hearts. You have," began a Plimmer letter on June 4, 1955. "Why was it necessary to do this murderous dreadful thing to the marriage that we had cherished, along with our own, as the finest in the world? How in God's name could you find any woman more eternally fascinating and kind and sweet than your own wife?" the Plimmers demanded. "Do you realize—have you forgotten—how rare such marriages are?"

"To woo and win sort of knocks off some of the years and gives me the feeling that I am not quite the helpless, dependent shell that I had begun to fancy myself," Tony wrote back on June 6, 1955, describing the breakup as similar to splitting up ham and eggs or salt and pepper. He spoke of having grown to a complete dependence on Dickey when his health failed, and it was the "reversal of our normal roles that has soured me. I'm just not the leaning kind of guy." He described himself to the Plimmers as "the big masculine rock that other people leaned on." He noted that now, "all of a sudden I stand on my own two feet and it's in a way a good thing. I needed it and had to have it," adding, "So I have it and now what? I can have a dozen women in my bed and it's an empty, hollow success. I just wanted the feeling of knowing that I could." Tony did not blame Dickey for his recklessness, he only raised an old grudge about her "interests": he'd been jealous of her job at *Seventeen*. "It took too much of her away from me that I felt was mine." He felt the same way about her job at CARE.

On June 10 Dickey wrote the Plimmers, reiterating the contents of Tony's letter. She wrote that in her fifteen years of marriage to Tony, she and he had somehow reversed too many parts "of our respective roles. Perhaps we always both thought we wanted it that way. I did, I know. I wanted Tony to train me to do the unwifely more and more, and he obliged I think largely because he always felt so very little confidence in his own health. Anyhow, as was inevitable, we did somehow forget about the fine joke that ends 'Vive la difference!' " Dickey sent this letter along to Tony for his approval, since the Plimmers were friends of theirs as a couple and she feared his wrath should he believe she'd gone behind his back. Then she added another page meant only for the Plimmers, explaining that she had not left Tony because of "an infidelity (chill word!) or a single series of infidelities." Rather, as she would also tell Edna, it was because they were both falling apart trying to be together, and that if she remained, she would not survive. "There were bits of each of us lying all around our respective lives, but neither of us was willing to pick them up and try to put them together." She believed that the result of their togetherness was illness—Tony had a heart attack and Dickey described herself as "a sort of paralytic." She saw leaving Tony as the best thing she could do for each of them, certain, she later told Edna, that once they were well and whole again, "I frankly can't imagine that either of us would pick the other for a mate. The way of life that Tony has come to like is too far from the one I want with all my heart." Not that Dickey knew exactly what kind of life would return her to a sense of certainty, except that it would have to be completely different from her life with Tony. She confided to the Plimmers that "with me around his . . . will seemed struck motionless. His integrity seemed buried under all the trappings of guilt. His initiative he seemed to pass willingly to anybody else, or to make it just an instrument of cruelty." She also informed the Plimmers that "while I am guilty of all of those same things"—she did not elaborate—there was no other man in her life then and she promised herself there would not be "for at least a year, if ever."

Dickey put off telling Edna for six weeks, waiting until July 4 and beginning with the banner headline "Independence Day." She prefaced her news with, "*How* I wish I could spare you this." She told Edna that the worse part of it was over. "I make a joke about it that you might smile at: I say there always was too damn much of every*thing* in that whole pattern of living; it was inevitable that the day would come when there were too many women, too. I must have wanted to do this for a very long time because it was much easier to do than I thought it would be." She saw the end of the marriage as "no Olympian tragedy. It's simply ended," adding, "I probably never should have married anybody."

Tony continued to see it otherwise, despite his deepening involvement with Helga, who would be living with him that summer after he suffered another heart attack. Helga claimed she'd done it "because I owed him." Tony had been paying her rent and had sponsored her to the United States, and now his doctor had personally requested she move in with him and nurse him back to health. Nevertheless Tony's letter-writing and telephone campaign to get Dickey back rolled on undeterred. Knowing full well that the passion between them was gone, he wrote her that he didn't want her back for "sex," which he lamented "seems to have gone out of me." He needed her for a far more frightening reason: she'd become his alter ego. To a man as egomaniacal and manipulative as Tony, retrieval of this loss became an obsession. It began with pleas for "a new shuffle and a new deal." He wrote, "Somewhere in my foolish ego I thought that I was remaking a young and foolish girl. I never did—I just subdued some of her less practical dreams and helped a little in some of the other. I am not equal to your dreams any longer. I want you to live the life that you dreamed about and let me help as I did a good many years ago."

Dickey emphasized in letters to her mother and the Plimmers that she was "shock cushioned." However, her actions told another story. Despite her claim to Edna that "I wouldn't go back there if it were the last place on earth, I can't stand the confounded place with its fake baronial air"—old habits died hard. She asked Tony for a year's "trial" separation and accepted his proposition that they get together once a week.

Helga, who would become Tony's next wife at a bedside ceremony in Tony's apartment in 1956, insisted that the split between Dickey and Tony was a "friendly" one and that Dickey came to visit on a regular basis. Unaware of Tony's fervent wooing of Dickey, Helga maintained that had she known, it wouldn't have bothered her. "I was not that deeply involved with Tony at that point, and I was never jealous of him."

The Haitian trip that would have removed Dickey from the suffocating reach of Tony and Edna (who was planning to visit her daughter in August) never materialized. Unable to raise the funding, and terribly upset about losing this opportunity to try her wings on a solo flight, Dickey left in mid-July on a month's leave with salary from CARE.

She shared her disappointment with her London friend, Charlotte Plimmer, who gave her a pep talk in a letter dated July 18, 1955. "What a damned shame that your CARE chores should go ploof at just this moment. . . . After our first distress over the news, it occurred to us both that it's probably a good thing—and that since you were putting yourself through a psychological shakeup anyhow, it might as well be a thorough one. Knowing you, we have complete and absolute faith that you'll turn up something both profitable and exciting in short order." Charlotte Plimmer was correct on one count.

A year earlier, when Tony and Dickey had been scrambling around for free-lance magazine assignments, Dickey had sent a letter to General Lemuel C. Shepherd, Jr., her acquaintance from Okinawa and then commandant of the Marine Corps. She wanted to know if there was "a Marine Corps story you would care to suggest . . . to serve the Corps." Although a letter was received from the marine director of information mentioning a possible story on the Corps Toys for Tots program, there is no correspondence to indicate the Chapelles followed through with this suggestion.

Feeling shaky, and desperately eager to lose herself in work, Dickey set off for Washington and some unsettled business. She visited with Commandant Shepherd and the pint-size gray-haired General John C. McQueen, the commanding officer of the marine recruit depot in San Diego, California. McQueen was the one marine on Okinawa who had seemed to understand her the best, and Dickey wrote that the two aging marines were "no less cordial in peace than under fire."

She informed them it was time to take care of a matter left over from World War II. A story on marine recruit training could gain her reaccreditation to the armed services and give the marines some publicity. What she wanted, she explained to the two gray-haired officers, was to show in words and pictures the marines' spirit, their ineffable esprit de corps. Although General McQueen, who had flirted with Dickey on Okinawa, was flattered by her interest, he cautioned her that esprit de corps "has never been truly captured even by many outstanding journalists." Dickey took the general's answer as a challenge, just what the doctor ordered, writing him later, "I wonder, what's the usual reaction of writers to being kindly reminded about a difficult story, 'It can't be told'? I trust most of us, too, feel, 'I know it can't—that's one of the reasons why I want to try to tell it.'"

9

Semper Fi

BY JULY 20, 1955, with the blessings of the Marine Corps, Dickey was making the rounds of magazine editors' offices, trying to get an assignment for pro-marine articles. The fact that her timing was off—after the folly of Korea, American readers were completely uninterested in the glory of the marines or any other of the armed services—didn't faze Dickey. The *Saturday Evening Post* had just run an article revealing that enlistment in the air force was at an all-time low. Managing Editor Bob Sherrod, a World War II correspondent in the Pacific, mentioned he might be interested in a piece on why marines were not reenlisting, which Dickey let slide.

Undaunted, and flying high on the Marine Corps endorsement, Dickey sent her agent, Marie Rodell (who was also Tony's agent), an outline for another marine article, which she was willing to do on "spec." It would be an exclusive, in-depth look at the marines' new Test Unit One at Camp Pendleton, California, the first marine aircraft carrier. This project would take her to the West Coast and cost close to one thousand dollars, including "first-class air transportation." Although Dickey snappily informed Marie that the marines were giving her an "exclusive" and that "I think it's my story," neither Marie nor Tony— now tracking Dickey's daily comings and goings in his campaign for repossession—was enthusiastic. Tony, who'd once urged Dickey to "keep trying" when faced with rejection, advised her to forget it. Dickey countered with a note to Marie that she was free "to roll on this" by August 15, after Edna's visit.

Tony, who'd trained Helga to work in his darkroom, was again flush from his photography and various side hustles. He offered Dickey financial help. He also offered to buy Dickey an air conditioner for Edna's visit, flinching at the thought of them sweating through a heat wave in her tiny seventh-floor studio apartment. He even invited the two to move into his apartment and take advantage of his air conditioner. Dickey turned him down.

Tony's losing battle for his Dickey entered a new, frenzied phase. After one of their weekly "dates" in August, when Tony was "convinced" there was no chance of being together again, he wrote Dickey he was "releasing" her "from whatever promises you made me." But he did not let up on his guilt-inducing behavior. His delicate ego was bruised by her refusal to drop at his feet. In the same letter he mentioned he had drafted a new will. "If anything happens to me," everything went to her, on condition that he was cremated and she kept in touch with his children. He said he hadn't meant to be morbid, but he felt he should get all this out of the way "once and for all." He once more stated his love for her and wished her a road of "love and kindness and bylines." He also promised that this would be "the last personal letter that I will write and the last time I will tell you I love you."

The next day, an anxious Dickey, hoping this new tone in Tony's correspondence heralded an end to his obsessiveness and ever mindful of his spiteful qualities, replied that she would gladly honor his requests. "What you asked of me of course I will do. It is such a small gesture— and I feel a need to make a greater and more real one to honor the wonders of having been so close to you for so long." And after wishing him a life filled with making "great photographs," she let her guard down. Whether it was a calculated move to keep this particular monster at bay, or a true expression of her confused heart, she added: "I feel today as I have felt for a long time, that the best way to do that is to be myself, the person you saw me as. *You* are paying *me* that compliment in so many ways! The irony is that, in so being true to ourselves and to our having-been-together we go—now—such separate ways. Perhaps, for me too, this is the last time that I can put that into words. Perhaps in fact tomorrow holds something quite different than either of us—such warm, such erring, such damn human people!—can think of amidst our urgent impatience of this day, this particular stormy moment! Do you mind awfully if I have faith that we will not be hurting like this always, either of us?" She wished him the same things he blessed her with "and one other thing—the consciousness of not-aloneness that you gave to me by reminding me that we will never, either of us, be without love for each other."

But these few quiet letters were only a lull in Tony's otherwise insanely prolific correspondence, punctuated by phone calls and surprise visits. Noticing during another of his unexpected visits that Dickey saved his letters, he asked her to destroy them. She kept every one. "As you no doubt know," he wrote her after Edna's visit in August, "I am unable to stand it around here any longer. There is too much of you and I in everything that I touch and see. . . . I know that you don't want me to call you up. . . . I am just a little crazy and mixed up—hoping you will come back and the other me says that you never will and I might as well let the torch go out . . . but so far the damn torch won't go. Your phone is too close to mine and you are too near to me. I keep hanging on to little things that I can do for you and feeling closer in doing them, but eventually I will have delivered everything to you that you will accept or that your apartment will hold and then I will run out of excuses and try as I will the damn apartment will always be full of you. . . . Is it that I am being pushed now in another way by you? I could keep this up all night or until I sort of collapse over the typewriter and I would still have to end it some time so I guess that it had been better never started or at least finished now. . . ."

He was again asking Dickey to marry him, this time promising to make it legal from the start. He offered to support her. She turned him down. "It was good enough to keep you in beautiful clothes and jewelry and enable you to do any damn thing that you wanted," he wrote when she scorned his offer. "But now all of a sudden it became tainted." He sent her jewels. These she kept.

By late August Dickey was desperate. Now without pay, she continued her leave from CARE, hoping to get an assignment for the marine story and squeaking by on her small savings. Despite the rejections, she stubbornly pursued the story, showing a tenacity she'd identified from her childhood as heroic, a tenacity so imbedded in her that it would eventually overpower her objectivity. For now, it fueled her determination to publish her story and revive her long-suspended journalism career.

The enthusiasm Dickey was generating among the generals in Washington had set the entire Marine Corps Public Information Office into motion. She had attended one or two marine functions, with the Corps picking up the tab for a trip to Parris Island, South Carolina, to do research. On August 24 she received a letter from Colonel E. N. Rydalch, the commanding officer of Test Unit One at Camp Pendleton, California, saying he would be pleased to have her do a story on his unit and would also do his darnedest to fulfill her request to shoot an aircraft carrier. He looked forward to seeing her at the end of September.

Although she was excited about Rydalch's response, Dickey's financial survival until the end of September was doubtful. Tony was pressuring her to take a well-paying job for the United Nations, which hinged on them working as a team; the man doing the hiring had no idea they had split up. Tony believed Dickey would go for it, as she had in Europe and India and the Middle East. "I do the leg work and the interviewing and the evaluation and you write up and index and recapitulate the reports," he wrote, relegating her to the helpmate status she assumed in his mind. But it was more than a job; it would be them together again, hour after hour, day after day. When she turned it down, he became indignant. "Without meaning to give offense, you are a very foolish girl," he wrote angrily. "Of course in your turning it down, you are also doing me out of my half."

Marie Rodell queried several general-interest magazines about a story on the Marine Corps, but not to her surprise, they were as discouraging as the *Saturday Evening Post*. Dickey argued that she did not see this as a strictly military piece anymore, but as a story about people responding to challenge. Her agent remained unconvinced. America was fighting the Reds in 1955, and women who wanted to go into the marine barracks to remind their country of its combat troops were seriously out of step. Yet Dickey refused to be discouraged.

Tony's pursuit of Dickey rolled along in its maniacal rhythm. Their once-a-week dates were, predictably, a disaster. Tony called them a "mistake," adding, "It's a lousy [sic] deal courting a gal that doesn't want to be courted and feels guilty about it."

Regardless of her besieged state, Dickey was determined to maintain her resolve and her mental health. She forced herself to sit down to three meals a day and practiced what she described to her mother as "a Quaker-like refusal to hate anybody." She bought herself a house-

hold expense book, describing it to her mother as exactly the same
kind as Edna's own. Whatever tranquillity this disciplined and apparently celibate existence brought Dickey was destroyed by Tony's spontaneous visits, phone calls, and steady harassment. Hoping to inspire a
social life, Edna sent black silk lounging pajamas, which Dickey
greeted with ambivalence. "You said it would be wonderful for breakfast. Breakfast *with whom?*" Besides, the slinky outfits were invariably
too small. "I have never had a twenty-four-inch waist, Marm; even if
I do all my exercises, I'll always measure twenty-eight inches." Dickey
returned them, which she would have done even if they had fit. How
could she ask another man to her apartment when at any moment her
estranged husband might show up?

In a letter dated September 12, 1955, General McQueen invited
Dickey to the Marine Corps recruit depot in San Diego and Camp
Pendleton for twenty days, "to get your story first-hand . . . and to
describe to the American public just what goes into the making of a U.S.
Marine . . . and the formula . . . for the esprit de corps. . . ." He
complimented her with magnanimous military assurance. She would be
under no restrictions in gathering her story "except for those imposed
by military security." On September 21 McQueen circulated a memo
to the officers at the recruit depot on Dickey's upcoming visit. He
described her as "a renowned free-lance magazine writer" and expected
the story that she would write on "the formula for the esprit de corps
which has made our organization famous . . . can be expected to appear
in *Reader's Digest* or some other top-ranking national magazine." He
instructed Sergeant R. B. Morrisey, the depot information officer who
would become one of Dickey's closest friends, to see that she "accom-
plishes her mission." The commanding general was counting on
Dickey's efforts to "prove advantageous in maintaining public support
of our mission."

The marines were turning somersaults for her arrival, yet Dickey was
broke. Even without Tony's continuous harping, she was aware that
proceeding on an expensive story without a publisher was foolhardy. But
she felt the way she had when eyeing Okinawa from the hospital ship.
The male and female parts of her (as she defined them), the assertive
versus the passive, were locked in combat. California was the landing
beach, an opportunity for her to prove herself once again. Eagerly,
against all odds, she accepted the challenge.

Although Dickey had written Edna that she would never go crawling to Tony for money, that's exactly what she did to get herself to California. Tony relished his return to even limited control over her. He would advance her one thousand dollars for the trip and her printing costs. She had put off his marriage proposals, obliquely hinting that September was to be a decisive month. Tony believed it would be in his best interest to let her get the marines out of her system. After a few weeks she'd be broke and, he believed, her idealism discouraged when reality didn't live up to her nostalgic memories of her heroic marines. Before her September 26 departure for Quantico (Virginia), San Diego, and Oceanside (California), Tony once again cautioned her about rushing headlong into a "spec" story without a firm assignment. "But I guess you have to learn the hard way," he wrote, hardly an inspiring send-off.

Whatever doubts Dickey may have had vanished upon her arrival at Quantico. When she asked permission to accompany one of the platoons on maneuvers, she was told, "We have no objection at all, Mrs. Chapelle. You can draw a sleeping bag and find a foxhole." It was music to her ears.

"Three young marines with four rows of battle decorations have told me," she excitedly wrote Marie Rodell, "that I am to be the first U.S. correspondent of either sex to be deliberately trained to cover warfare in three dimensions. I'm busier than a bird dog."

Months before, on a research trip to Parris Island, she had written Marie that "while I have been most literal in explaining that I do not have a magazine assignment yet, I think I ought to just stay here until I get one." Farther down she added, "I don't mean to imply that there'd be any embarrassment for me if my story didn't work out; I just mean that by this time I'm pretty deeply committed to me to do a Marine Corps piece and am going to be disappointed in me if we can't spin out an angle." At Camp Pendleton those same feelings were underscored by new confidence. She had gotten herself to California after all, writing her aunt George, "I'm taking the bull by the horns."

"I'm personally much more certain than I was a week ago," she wrote George, "that my trip here was a wise decision." She added that she found her time on the base "a fine vacation in many ways. I terribly enjoy my prestige, although I feel guilty about how little I've earned it."

Tony's assumptions about Dickey's speedy return were dashed by her friendship with Sergeant Robert Morrisey, General McQueen's aide. The young marine and his enthusiastic, pregnant wife, Mary Jane, adopted Dickey almost immediately. When Dickey told them she would have to cut her trip short because she was unable to afford an inexpensive motel room any longer, Sergeant Morrisey arranged for Dickey to be given a free room at the marine women's barracks. She was out of bed at five in the morning with the rest of the recruits for maneuvers, whipped by the Santa Ana winds and burned by California's merciless Indian summer sun. Within a few days she was "adopted" by the second platoon of Company C, who paid her the ultimate compliment of letting her march back from maneuvers *inside* their formation because she had spurned a jeep ride and hiked over a "small mountain" to the exercise.

The *San Diego Evening Tribune* did a feature story on Dickey, describing her assignment in her own words as "a sentimental journey." The October 17 article, subheaded "She's Taken Up the Challenge!" which she enjoyed immensely, mentioned she had come to find out "what happens in a man's mind when he becomes a Marine." The reporter noted Dickey had a voice like a drill instructor's bark, chainsmoked, and was in love with the marines.

She had finally left home to find home. After two weeks with the marines, she wrote Edna an exuberant letter, heady with her sense of self and a peculiar fellowship. She had come to answer a question gnawing at her for ten years. When she'd first seen the marines fight, she had wondered how human beings, with all their fears and frailties, could team up in a single concerted effort, so simple and so limitlessly hazardous, "until finally they are one moving, inexorable forward motion." That was, she confided to her horrified mother, "the story I wanted to do, an example of human endeavor that worked, because the older I get the fewer of that I see." And at the end of the two weeks she had discovered the answer. "On the sheer basis of my having shown a sympathy, all these people, six thousand of them, have so thoroughly identified me with them—i.e. with something bigger than any of us— that I am completely committed not to let them down. There is a richness and warmth in this position that I, as a person, find in no other."

Emboldened by esprit de corps, she expressed her desire that Edna would understand her and they could go beyond the "superficial" relationship necessitated by Edna's horror of all things military. The now-focused Dickey couldn't handle the strain of self-censoring or the constant need to explain herself to Tony and her mother. For instance, she knew that when she described "being jeeped" around Camp Pendleton, Edna would see it not as a means of getting photographs of people in the field, but as something "dangerous." When she wanted to tell Edna about a particularly nice general, she worried that her mother's bias would not allow her to see the general as a professional man who was helping her daughter get her story. She did not want to trigger her mother's concern, but how could she avoid it and still tell the truth? When Edna worried that one of the many "black sheep" in the Corps would try to seduce her Georgie Lou, now thirty-six, Dickey explained that the last thing the marines wanted was bad publicity. "We're all potentially black sheep," she wrote exasperatedly. "Even me."

On October 1 Tony left for Europe on a photo assignment for CARE. He wrote Dickey from Berlin that week, telling her he "loved her" and "was proud" she was doing the story. He would be returning to New York at the end of the month and couldn't wait to print up her photos. From there he stopped off in London to visit with the urbane Plimmers. When he told Charlotte that Dickey was doing a story on the marines and joining them in their field maneuvers, Charlotte dashed off a bemused note to Dickey.

"We are impressed and, as fairly unwarlike types, both intimidated and confused by your activities. It leaves us feeling inadequate and overcivilized. All our best to the Halls of Montezuma not to mention the gates of Tripoli."

Dickey had sent Tony her itinerary and telephoned him. She had confided, as she would have to any former photography teacher, that she was worried about her upcoming "big" shot—the setup of close air support covering the detonation of two hundred pounds of flaming gasoline jelly actually being dropped from a marine jet fighter, forty-six yards from advancing marine infantry in training. It would mark, she later noted, "the first time napalm has been air-dropped closer than 1/3 of a mile from human tissue in peacetime." She saw it as a magazine cover, an operatic composition of steel and flame. The frame's middle ground would show napalm being dropped; the background would be filled with helicopters and jets; and in the foreground would stand a marine with a raised bayonet, in silhouette. And she had calculated and rehearsed it down to the split second.

At the last minute the shot was moved up a day, and on November 1 the gods of napalm and photographers smiled: the shot went off without a hitch. Sure, standing one-third mile away, she had "gotten shook"—an expression she'd picked up from the marines and used often—but she had controlled it by concentrating on the picture. She felt true exhilaration when the other photographer, a man, "got shook," too.

On November 2, the day for which the shoot had originally been scheduled, she received a wire from Tony (then in London), in response to her anxious call of a few days earlier. Oddly, this telegram was not saved, but its message was clearly less than supportive. Dickey responded that same day: "I'm . . . sure that your so terribly dear wire would have made . . . a big difference in the way I'd have gone about what I'm here to do. And then I'd have felt trapped, not loved." Tony shrugged off his behavior as "unthinking." Dickey gave him the benefit of the doubt, writing that she believed he "had simply forgotten when you sent the wire that it could be so timed."

But having spent fifteen obliging years subject to Tony's various manipulations, Dickey had had more than enough of his games. He wanted her answer to the "Big Question." And with her budding belief in herself, no doubt buoyed by her militant surroundings, she gave him her answer: she had no desire at that moment to be anybody's wife.

"One of the reasons I think I got as far as I did [on the shoot] was because I'd had nothing on my mind except to do the best job I could on that picture," she wrote Tony. There was no point in asking him to wait around in case she changed her mind, either. She despised women who led men on. As crazy as it might seem, to Tony or anyone else, for that matter, she was happiest sitting by herself after a cafeteria dinner in a room littered with ugly field equipment. For the first time since their crazy correspondence had begun, emboldened by her environment, she had no desire to be coy. She finally knew what it was she wanted to do with her life, and the knowledge was giving her confidence. She'd begun calling the marines "my people."

"Like some of the crazy characters around me say, 'I want to be a Marine'—*I* say, I want to be a foreign correspondent," she wrote Tony. "I've even mentally added that that does mean a certain amount of war corresponding, and on this story, I'm glad, just plain glad—for the training I'm getting personally at what is probably the best and surely the safest place on earth to get it. I've always wanted to do it. I want to do it now; I'm trained for it, it needs doing. If I have to pay for this conviction with relative spinsterhood, then I'll have to just take the consequences."

Slipping back into the old insecurity, she quipped, "The truth of course is probably just that those nice people are flattering me into being so busy I just don't know my own mind. Their flattery is a very powerful psychological trick, of course, dangerous as hell, and the only reason I forgive 'em is because I fall for it—in other words, *I* think I can be a correspondent who can help them because *they* are so sure of it—there is no question. But it's good for me right now to feel a little confidence; that long stint of professional discouragement after the Point Four career just didn't turn into careering—that was bad for both of us."

So far, the consequences of going from insecure wife to trained combat correspondent were hardly distressful. In her nearly three months with the marines, she had learned more ways to safeguard her life in combat then she'd ever known existed. She had accompanied nineteen-year-olds on drills, marches, patrols, bivouacs, and airlifts. Much to her amazement, she could walk fast, run hard, climb, fall, roll, read a map, use a compass, and recognize weapons by sound. She could follow on a night patrol by silhouette and choose by reflex an earth hummock high enough to protect her from bullets. She realized that if she ever again went into combat as a reporter, she'd know exactly how to act. There were only two problems: She'd never managed to keep her film dry in a foxhole, and she had heard nothing from Marie Rodell.

"I don't get lonely here," she wrote Charlotte Plimmer, who by now was completely nonplussed by Dickey's enthusiasm for the marines. "I just sit and watch these miles and miles of beefcake parading in front of me, one of them always more handsome than the next."

"You can't spend the rest of your life as a gal reporter at one Marine Base after another," Tony notified Dickey three days after her November 2 letter of rejection. "What you forget is that you are among many new people and in a way you have become a center of attraction and respect. People are looking up to you and that's not a part of normal, everyday living," he warned. "It's fascinating, but don't you think it will wear off after a time?" Dickey had not only been gone far longer than originally planned, she had been shooting an incredible amount of film, a ratio of ten rolls shot and rejected for every one considered usable. Tony was overseeing its printing, and the cost was climbing dangerously. How long was she going to work on this story? He recalled her profitless habit of endless rewriting and how long it took her to turn out a story. "How many times can you do this, even if you are paid a normal magazine rate?" he demanded.

Tony was an albatross around Dickey's neck. The avalanche of letters, made fuzzy by his drug intake, continued. As his control weakened, his vitriol increased. He reproached her for the "childhood dreams that you got from that book by Richard Harding Davis of being a fascinating figure of a war correspondent instead of a woman." He also reminded her—despite the live-in status of Helga, his nurse-lover—that he was still her husband, "until you write and tell me that your heart is elsewhere and there is someone else that will play Bulldog to My Dickey. You can't wipe it out that easily." Ignoring her responses, he asked if there was already somebody else, and if that somebody wasn't Ernst, Helga's husband, who had gone to California at about the same time. Tony's delusional, drugged paranoia did not tickle Dickey's vanity. Instead it made her want to stay forever on her narrow bed in the barracks, dressed in dungarees and high-top boots, waiting for field maneuvers.

On November 10, 1955, the Marine Corps' birthday, Dickey put her domestic woes behind her to stand ecstatic on the turfy green of the marine parade ground at Camp Pendleton, photographing five thousand massed troops passing before the general. When the troops paraded, swords drawn and flashing, she felt an intense rush of camaraderie. "It was simply a spectacle of people paying a tribute to something they think of as bigger than they are," she wrote her family, downplaying its impact. But it was not that casual to her. She had been searching for it for years, for what she had felt riding in a jeep in Okinawa, when she heard the bugles and the drums and the marching feet pounding through her brain. She was there again.

Before Dickey left the nurturing climate of Camp Pendleton for Milwaukee, on November 20, Tony once again intruded on her curious love affair with "the Few, the Proud, the Brave." This time he wanted her to know that her black-and-white negatives were a mess. Although some of her shots could be saved, one batch had come up blank and the others were way underexposed. As to her color frames, he wondered if she had gotten careless and ignored reading the light meter. In a letter sent to her in Milwaukee on Thanksgiving Day, he continued his criticism, launching into a remedial lesson on how to take a light meter reading and how to use a wide-angle lens, hoping she would take it in the manner intended, as "a little refresher course to my best student."

These warnings, and concerns over Edna's health—the local doctor had discovered some "bubbles" around her liver—combined to shatter Dickey's resurgent optimism. Back in New York in her cell-like apartment, she felt the walls closing in on her. She had no job prospects and was surviving on unemployment insurance checks from her CARE job. A meeting with the Marine Corps public relations firm about how to market her work was a disaster. No magazine wanted her four photo spreads culled from her hundreds of shots or her half-dozen articles defending the Corps' discipline. As if this weren't painful enough, Tony's obsession was being unwittingly fed by Edna, who had been passing on Dickey's letters. Although that Christmas Tony wrote Edna he felt used by Dickey and was resigning as her watchdog, Dickey had a ton of letters proving otherwise.

She pleaded with Edna to stop letting Tony use her. "I don't want to be concerned that in expressing myself to you I might be indirectly communicating with him; please don't hand him any more ammunition for his profitless self-analysis." Dickey also urged Edna to see a doctor "you can talk to." Apparently Edna had cut herself off from doctors in Milwaukee, instead following the advice of the country's most famous positive thinker, radio personality and best-selling author Dr. Norman Vincent Peale. She had a hard time thinking positively about her daughter, though, now separated and without job prospects at thirty-six. Dickey tried to reassure her. "I have set a goal of Easter by which to have a clearer idea of where I stand on a lot of things."

Dickey enrolled in a night school class taught by a successful free-lancer. Perhaps she'd learn how to sell the marine pieces. Delighted, Edna seized upon it as a solution. Would she want to return to school full-time, with Edna bankrolling it? Dickey turned down the idea, writing Edna she was "seriously" looking for work and had dropped by the offices of *Seventeen*.

At the same time, Tony, like some demented Greek chorus, was demanding to collect on the "promises" Dickey had made in accepting his loan and gifts. "You want a man," he wrote her. "I had some illusions that I was and am. But I am not enough for you—can't compete with the youth and illusions of the Marine Corps or Admiral Byrd. You've developed into a pretty prim, proper do-gooder," he wrote after another rebuff. "All the things I have done that weren't quite honest or ethical really bothered you and caused you to think less of me. . . . But you are just as dishonest as I am . . . you won't even deliver what you accept payment for."

Writing her that she was now free to spend the night with any man she chose to, he demanded that Dickey, whom he referred to as a "cockteaser," pay back his loans and return his gifts. She returned the jewels and repaid half the loan, probably borrowing the money from her well-heeled aunts or her mother. According to Stevie Blick, Tony would still bound up Dickey's stairs waving his pistol and shouting for her to open her door. He had grown abusive on the telephone, maintaining that he had not called her a "whore," but rather had "said you were less honest than one of them." By mid-January Dickey could not take any more of Tony's dramatics.

Their relationship had finally descended to that ugly point at which shouting matches and allegations entirely replace passion. The hurt was too integrated and historical, yet that inexplicable urge to hold on to it like the tail of a kite remained. "Must you fight with me because there is something so satisfying in home-grown drama, urgent letters, unexpected visits, phone calls without limit?" Dickey demanded to know in a letter dated only "Saturday night, 12:45 A.M." "When will you stop delighting in proving you still have the power to upset me?"

Dickey contacted an attorney about getting a restraining order to stop Tony's continual harassment and also asking his fee for a divorce. Tony apparently paid for the visit, although he claimed he was through bankrolling her. Especially since they had never been legally married, he pointed out cruelly, "you are as free as you were the day I met you." Not in Dickey's opinion. She did not want to be responsible for any of Tony's mad bents. Even if it would do no more than ease her mind, she insisted on a legal end to their relationship. But she couldn't expect him to pay for that, and she could not afford an attorney.

As she had done as a teenager in Shorewood, with her first manuscript, she badgered Marie Rodell to send the marine pieces and photographs to magazines that had already rejected the material. She wanted Marie to cushion the marines' faith in her, to get a publishing contract for a book on the marines. She certainly had plenty of material.

Sympathetic, Marie understood Dickey's impatience. "But things cannot always move at the speed we'd like them to," she wrote. "I cannot say to *any* publisher, think up a book about the Marine Corps and give us a contract to write it." Marie also reminded Dickey that before her trip to California, "we explored the market pretty thoroughly and found no takers." Just because she had gone ahead anyway did not change things. "Sheer endurance, stubbornness, and determination won't do it," Marie lectured. "If *Collier's* doesn't want the material, sending it back there four times isn't going to change their minds."

Having gone through a breakup of a marriage, Marie knew how much of an upheaval it could be, how much resentment it engendered. She found Dickey "in a state of acute emotional hypertension" that was coloring everything she did and thought. "It takes time to get over tearing up years of one's life—why shouldn't it?" Marie asked her in an undated letter. "You're not any more of a superwoman than I was, or any other woman is. You can't just toss it over your shoulder. I hope you don't think you can."

Of course Dickey thought she could. Wasn't she as lean and tough as any marine boot? In the margin of Marie's letter she commented that "I can survive shock better than most people" but had also succeeded in putting herself into "a box."

Sometime close to her thirty-seventh birthday, a letter to Edna finally revealed the fragility of Dickey's mental state. She wrote that she wanted nothing more than to "pull a deep hole in over my head." Once again she felt "in a largely paralytic state . . . quite frightened of my own bad judgments and quite unwilling to go on making them." She had come to believe that there was only one "wise course," a job in some field "in which I do think I know something—the professional one—and let personal relationships alone for a while." She wanted to do nothing more than to avoid exposing herself to "everything and everybody that's a symbol of my past failure in human relations." This, along with financial security, would give her back the kind of confidence she'd believed she'd once enjoyed. When that happened, "or any success at all, I'll say, 'See—you're not so dumb, Dickey; maybe some of your other ideas will work out, too, even ideas about people and love. 'And . . . I won't be quite so scared at the idea of being close to another person . . . as I am now." She wanted the job to have something "special" about it—"I want a job that offers good professional adventure," she said, like a child wishing on a birthday candle. "It doesn't have to pay that much, but it does have to have something really good about it."

However, she could afford to wait no longer. Edna's condition, still undiagnosed, had worsened. Fearing the worst, George urged her to seek other medical opinions in New York, accompanied by Lutie. Although Tony called a halt to Dickey's repayment of his loan because of Edna's illness, he continued to berate her in daily letters over her failed marine assignment, addressing her as "big shot" and emphasizing that "it's probably the first time that you have ever been faced directly with the result of your own errors in judgment." Hovering over her like a black cloud was the fear that she might sink so low as to crawl back to Tony. Desperate, she returned to her job at CARE.

It was at this time that Marie Rodell introduced Dickey to another of her journalist clients, Julia Edwards. Also a member of the Overseas Press Club, Julia thought the photographs taken by Dickey and Tony overseas first rate. Julia felt that Dickey was an unwitting victim of the 1950s: the war was over, and "nobody was hiring women photographers." Julia had recently inherited a lot of money and quit her job as public relations director at the private business advisory organization Research Institute of America. She figured that Dickey—who always looked to be down to her last nickel—might be interested in replacing her.

10

Mission of Mercy

$\mathbf{D}$ICKEY was one of forty applicants for the high-profile, high-paying Research Institute of America's public information officer job. Having heard that the institute was intent on hiring a man, she had given up hope of receiving the position; a few weeks later she was on her way out the door to her CARE job when the phone rang.

On March 14, 1956, the week of her thirty-seventh birthday, she sent out her first official RIA press release, introducing herself as the author of seven books on aviation and "a writer and editor for U.S. periodicals for more than ten years" and, in a bit of true public relations hype, presented herself as having "reported on Asian economic developments in the *Reader's Digest, National Geographic* magazine, and *Saturday Evening Post.*" In private, she was less confident.

Dickey described the Park Avenue offices of the Research Institute of America to her mother and aunts as "the world's largest business research and advisory organization." Its great success hinged on its far-reaching intelligence-gathering capabilities, making it profoundly important—before there was an OSS or a CIA—for predicting the political climates of unstable countries.

Founded in 1935 by publishing entrepreneur Carl Hovgard to dispense advice to businessmen on how to profit from New Deal legislation, it hit the big time in 1939, when its whiz kid co-owner, Leo Cherne, dashed off a booklet entitled "Adjusting Your Business to War." By 1941, the RIA was reportedly grossing over a million dollars a year, with more than 25,000 subscribers.

A *Saturday Evening Post* article, "The Rover Boys," profiling Hovgard and Cherne said that one of the institute's "most profitable commodities is prophecy and its batting average has been high." In 1938, RIA operated a sophisticated intelligence network, able to predict that America's next big war would begin in the Far East, while its fall 1941 newsletter stated that America would become involved in the war in Europe "after a triggering event occurs in the Pacific," two months before the Japanese attack on Pearl Harbor.

According to the *Post* article, the institute was a great believer in psychotherapy, putting prospective employees through a battery of expensive psychological tests, administered by a psychiatrist: Rorshach, IQ tests, handwriting analysis, and exhaustive oral questionnaires that inquired into every aspect of one's life. The institute called it "getting to know a man."

Not surprisingly, the institute would appeal to the likes of William Casey, who'd go on to become the director of the Central Intelligence Agency. During World War II, Casey had worked as its chairman of the board of editors, crediting the institute with staying far ahead of the press when it came to mobilization of American resources for the war. Casey felt that the institute prepared him for his subsequent job with the wartime intelligence organization, the Office of Strategic Services (OSS), forerunner of the CIA. Casey would later serve as president and chairman of the institute's other arm, the International Rescue Committee, which was known in the 1950s for rescuing prominent persons from communist countries.

In a letter to Edna the week she was hired, Dickey shared her excitement at having found her dream job. The "opportunity to make a Big Thing out of it is really there," she gushed. "The catch in my joy, of course, is that I've never had such responsibility before (not the title, nor the private office, nor the salary, etc.), and I am really going to have to work hard to keep it. But I promise I shall—because, among other things, I think this job is my best chance to get out of the relief agency field—and at my age, for a working woman, it was time I did get out of it." Of her eagerness to test her recent marine training in the field as a war correspondent, she said nothing. For the time being, her need for adventure was subordinate to the intellectual excitement offered by her new job.

She was awestruck by the company of crack political analysts, believing all had "intelligence quotients probably averaging at the genius level." She wondered what she was doing in "such exalted company." She added that she believed she owed her fabulous change of luck "to my lucky hair-style, which I invented on the day I was hired." She pulled her long fine hair back from her face and wound it around a padded hair accessory known as a rat. Her lucky hairdo was to become her *only* hairstyle.

After two weeks on the job she was still on pins and needles, writing Edna, "I'm almost superstitious about my simply incredible good luck. It seems cobweb fragile." One of her fears was that the personnel department "will catch up with my inadequacies in about ten days. That's a joke, I hope!"

For the first time since being redesigned by Tony, she was again concerned with her image. She went to the gym on Saturdays to counteract all the business lunches. Unlike Edna, she did not give up smoking but assured her mother she was too busy to smoke much and was also cutting back on coffee. Her friend Stevie Blick was impressed by the Park Avenue office and found Dickey's boss, Leo Cherne, "a real lady's man."

Dickey had no desire to compete with the young, glamorous stenographers who paraded past her office. "I ain't that young," she confided to her mother, who was still ailing and undiagnosed in Milwaukee and contemplating a vacation out to New York for the purpose of convalescing. "The ground on which I think I'd make out much better is neither glamour nor sex—but rather a kind of sweeping queenliness, or at least precision." Although she was the first to admit she wouldn't know a piece of art if it stood up and bit her, she was impressed by the "wealth of taste" in the office. "I'm the only gal in the office right now who *always* has a clean lace handkerchief, polished shoes and handbag, ironed hair ribbons, and a smooth hair-do. This may seem an odd way to go man-hunting, but I don't feel in a hurry . . . such wonderful fun comes my way in my way!" she boasted to her mother, who was now concerned that her daughter was working herself to a frazzle with no social life, that her cubbyhole office was where "the top guys congregate," not "in the tight-sweatered gals' bailiwicks."

Other than the purchase of an expensive, dusty-rose-colored silk cocktail dress for RIA black-tie social events, Dickey hoarded her money. She stopped taking cabs, walking to work in stiletto heels. She needed every cent for an attorney.

A few days after the announcement of her appointment hit the papers, Tony returned the emerald cuff links, the gold Dunhill cigarette lighter, and the Cartier watch, which he'd been holding as collateral against the money she still owed him. It was, he wrote, only right, since "now you have a chance to wear them." But at the same time he warned that if she went through with the restraining order as threatened, he would do everything in a "legal" way to make her newly public life miserable. He dredged up her failure with the marines once more, telling her further that she could sleep with "whoever you want to if it will give you comfort or pleasure," warning patronizingly that her tendency to rush headlong into things would make her "sorry for it later." He himself was going to find another woman to marry. As for the annulment, she'd be wasting five hundred dollars since their marriage had never been legal to begin with, although "it will always be the closest tie that I ever had...."

Ignoring Tony's endless tormenting, Dickey plunged deeper into her job, still pinching herself to make certain it wasn't a dream. Dickey had her own secretary and a cubbyhole of an office, painted chartreuse and burnt orange and sporting a turquoise leather swivel chair and a private terrace. She felt self-conscious delegating typing, filing, and research to others. When she asked her predecessor, Julia Edwards, to whom she should report, she was horrified by the answer. "Nobody. You make your own decisions."

By the end of her first month on the job, the situation with Tony was improved by the fact that he and Helga planned to marry. Upon hearing the news, Dickey invited Helga to lunch. Helga believed Dickey viewed her replacement with relief, not jealousy. But as relieved as Dickey might be about being taken off the hook, she also felt protective toward Helga, whom she believed didn't have a clue about what she was getting herself into. Helga recalled that Dickey "tried to warn me about Tony, that he wasn't all that he appeared to be. She told me not to get burned. I didn't listen. To me, Dickey simply didn't understand him the way I did." But whenever Tony got sick, he yelled for Dickey. It usually happened, Dickey noted, "in the middle of the night, with all the usual drama." She would race out of bed and over to the hospital to hold his hand. "The doctor says it does him good," she explained in a letter to her aunts after a four-hour bedside vigil, emphasizing that this in no way meant she had become "close" to him again.

Leo Cherne, the executive director of the institute as well as the chairman of the International Rescue Committee, recalled Dickey as a rather stern, unapproachable woman. He remembered she had nice legs, but that her raw, throaty voice rendered her masculine no matter what she wore. He sensed, correctly, that she held him in awe, which he felt kept their relationship from being "easy going." He also believed that "personal intimacy with Dickey was not possible." He described the feeling in the office as collegiate and informal, which Dickey happily confirmed.

"One of the men, wanting to judge how much of the gambler there is in a new employee . . . likes to run penny-ante roulette games in the office," she wrote Edna. "He always finds out very quickly which of his associates is a plunger, who is slow and persistent, and who has an arithmetic mind that way. (I reveal myself as the steady, persistent, bet-doubling type who usually comes out of the game with just what I went into.)" But to Leo, Dickey was simply "a very private person with her own mind, whom you did not tell what to do."

Dickey seems to have had a schoolgirl crush on her dapper boss, who was not only a shrewd political analyst and adviser to leading statesmen, but also, at various times, an opera singer, songwriter, journalist, lawyer, economist, and sculptor. He was a flamboyant, brilliant man of action, a product of New York City's "dead end," a former poolshark, longshoreman, a pilot, a doer, hailed as a "Renaissance man" by the *Reader's Digest,* who viewed his chairmanship of the refugee-saving International Rescue Committee as championing "the cause of liberty by reaching out to the most helpless victims of oppression and deprivation." He worked with Franklin Delano Roosevelt to plan the country's industrial mobilization for war; he was assigned by President Truman to evaluate the needs of postwar Germany, traveling there "under cover" as a journalist; and for MacArthur, he developed a tax system for postwar Japan.

Dickey described her boss to Edna in the feverish tones of a lovestruck adolescent keeping a diary: she spent the entire morning "listening to Leo Cherne talk about women"; and she could tell that he was "shy." Her mooning over her dashing, silver-tongued boss, whom she described as a "star salesman," was just the medicine she needed to rid herself of the remnants of Tony. The RIA's clubby atmosphere, its discussion of politics—often going late into the night—awakened her childhood desire to be involved in great events. One of the highlights of Dickey's first month on the job was when Leo "liked" a five-thousand-word press release on Soviet stratagems, a subject she admitted to being "quite unfamiliar with." Leo would also be reading "exclusively from my copy" on a television show he was appearing on. "I can still get myself fired, all right," she wrote of the job that filled her nights and weekends, "but as long as this lasts, I don't feel the least deprived of the traditional female joy of being useful to a male she admires. . . . If the nights were cold, I might disagree with my theory. . . ."

That July, Dickey's expensive lawyer called her with good news. The Supreme Court of the State of New York had declared the Chapelles' nonmarriage void and had granted Dickey an annulment. Dickey hoped the news would not provoke another of Edna's emotional outbreaks, since Dickey herself did not consider it "worth an ounce." She assured her mother, who was still planning a trip to New York, it was "about the neatest, cleanest way to accomplish what I want—unquestioned, legally sanctioned freedom." For simplicity's sake, Dickey told her associates she had gotten a divorce. Tony told Dickey it would make him proud if she continued to use his last name. "It has served you well professionally and I would not complain one bit."

SOMETIME AFTER the annulment was final, Edna and Lutie arrived in New York to treat what had finally been diagnosed as advanced cancer. Dickey was so horrified, she could not bring herself to use the dreaded word. She wrote instead that her mother's fatal illness brought her to New York, where she lived with Lutie on posh Sutton Place, and that she did not live long enough to return to Milwaukee.

Edna's death in late September 1956 had a profound effect on Dickey, although she was characteristically silent about it. It left her wide open. Edna's endless worrying and annoying devotion had protected Dickey from herself. Now no one stood guard. It was different from the lonesome feeling she'd sometimes get as she cuddled up on her bed in the slinky black silk lounging pajamas. (Edna had sent them back, and Dickey had dutifully let out the waist.) To whom could she now recount the mundane details of her day in the office or how she had resueded her ten-year-old pair of shoes? Who else would think it important that

Dickey had learned to like buttermilk? Without the umbilical anchor, Dickey staggered.

Less than a month after Edna's death, on October 4, an event in Budapest had important repercussions in the Manhattan offices of the International Rescue Committee. It drew Dickey's gnawing emptiness like a magnet; it would change her life forever.

The ill-fated Hungarian uprising was by all accounts a spontaneous popular revolt against eleven years of brutal Soviet-backed repression. It began as a massive, peaceful demonstration. Thousands of students, including those from the Lenin-Marx Institute, where future communist leaders were educated, swarmed into Budapest's autumn-tinged streets for a march to Radio Budapest to present their demands: the withdrawal of Soviet occupation troops; freedom of speech, press, and elections; and the ouster and punishment of Stalinist leaders.

As the marchers sang and shouted for the reinstatement of their moderate premier, Imre Nagy, they were joined by workers and members of the Hungarian army. The crowd swelled to 200,000. The Hungarian AVO (secret security police) barred the way into the radio station. A student delegation admitted to the radio station was arrested. The crowd demanding their release was intercepted by AVO, which launched tear-gas grenades. Chaos ensued. The Hungarians—men, women, and children armed with rocks and the flaming grenades of Molotov cocktails—bravely battled Soviet tanks. The city's infrastructure disintegrated under the barrage of tank fire: buildings collapsed; rubble and glass and mangled tanks clogged the streets and bridges. So did the cries for liberty and human rights.

On October 29, as Israeli paratroopers began an operation coordinated by the French and British to regain control over the Suez Canal from Egypt's strong-arm ruler Gamal Abdel Nassar, Soviet tanks retreated from Budapest. Almost immediately the crowds began to attack the much hated and feared Hungarian secret police, which had also reportedly operated as a spy network, generating dread even among Hungarian's Communist party membership. Black-and-white photographs of AVO members routed and hung from the city's trees and lampposts electrified the pages of *Life* magazine.

In Budapest the dead were estimated at four thousand. A reported ten thousand were entering hospitals; supplies of antibiotics and food were in short supply. While Radio Free Europe and Radio Liberation, radio stations that served the CIA's propaganda efforts in Eastern Europe, encouraged the Hungarians with promises of imminent Western military assistance, the Hungarians, now heralded as "freedom fighters," appealed to the West and the United Nations. Meanwhile thousands of Hungarians fled to the mushrooming refugee camps in neighboring Austria.

The International Rescue Committee had been formed in 1933 after Albert Einstein, then in Germany, had sent a letter to two of his colleagues in America, academician John Dewey and theologian Reinhold Niebuhr, suggesting the formation of a temporary rescue committee to help his colleagues, and later others, flee Nazi Germany. During World War II the IRC rescued many illustrious refugees, including artists Joan Miró, Jacques Lipschitz, and Marc Chagall and writers Franz Werfel and Lion Feuchtwanger.

The IRC was reported to operate from time to time as a conduit for the CIA. According to a May 15, 1980, article in *The New York Times*, the IRC received fifteen thousand dollars in CIA money in the mid-1960s. In that same article Leo Cherne was quoted: "These bizarre efforts to identify me with the C.I.A. are damaging to an organization that is breaking its neck in seeking funds for refugees." In *Escape to Freedom*, the International Rescue Committee's official biography, the *Times'* account was amended in an apology by the article's reporter. However, the alleged connection between the refugee organization and the intelligence community continues to resurface. One of the last acts of duty for William Casey's mentor, General William "Wild Bill" Donovan—America's World War I hero and dashing "master spy" and founder of the OSS (Office of Strategic Services)—was to become IRC's honorary chairman after the 1956 Hungarian uprising. Despite failing health, Donovan personally appeared at the border area during the refugee exodus. As the national committee chairman of IRC's Hungarian rescue committee, Donovan collected $1.5 million for Hungarian relief.

The day following the departure of the Russian tanks from Budapest, Leo Cherne and IRC president and career diplomat Angier Biddle Duke flew to Vienna. They arrived in the Austrian capital carrying one hundred thousand units of Terramycin antibiotics, donated by the Charles Pfizer pharmaceutical company, to the Hungarian freedom fighters. The IRC chief in Vienna, Dr. Marcel Faust, then drove the two men in his

1946 Chevrolet with a Red Cross flag wrapped over its radiator—to indicate their neutral status—into Budapest. "It was a very exciting time," recalled Cherne, adding, "Dickey was in New York following these events . . . so moved by it and the urgency of it . . . in a sense it can be said that thanks to me, she risked her life."

Although Dickey ostensibly worked for the institute, she actually worked for Leo Cherne, who jockeyed between institute analysis and the IRC's activism. She wrote up the press release of her boss's journey, including his historic meeting with Cardinal Joseph Mindszenty, Hungary's moral conscience and a fugitive who lived as a permanent guest of the American legation in Budapest, and his journey to the secret hideout of the young, fearless Hungarian freedom fighters. Later Cherne would say, "Everywhere in Budapest, in everyone's eyes, I saw the gratitude for an American so quick to help."

The help that the beleagured Hungarians believed would result from the broadcasts of Radio Free Europe and Radio Liberty never arrived. It was an election year in the United States, and President Eisenhower, who was running for reelection, had no desire to risk war with the Soviets. The United Nations was embroiled in the Middle East and for them the far more important Suez crisis.

Within days of Leo's return to New York, despite Moscow's assurance that they would not interfere in the domestic affairs of another socialist nation, Soviet tanks rolled again. At dawn on November 4, some 200,000 Russian troops and 2,500 Russian tanks came steamrolling through the battered town. In an hour and a half fifteen thousand people in Budapest would lie dead, with twice that number tallied by the end of the invasion. "Russian gangsters have betrayed us; they are opening fire on all of Budapest. Please inform Europe and the Austrian government. They opened fire on everybody," came the lone, urgent Teletype to the Associated Press in Vienna.

The day after the Soviets installed János Kádár as premier, the first International Red Cross convoy bringing urgently needed medical and food supplies was turned back at the Hungarian border. Budapest radio announced it would not accept Western aid directly because "arms and munitions" and "agents" had been smuggled into Hungary on Red Cross planes earlier in the month. Although Red Cross officials denied the allegations, they did admit that it was conceivable planes using unauthorized Red Cross insignia may have landed nonrelief material in

Budapest at the height of the anticommunist insurrection.

Finally, after days of negotiating, the Red Cross convoys were allowed to drive the Soviet-controlled road to Budapest. A few weeks later the International Rescue Committee sent a million dollars' worth of penicillin donated by Pfizer to its headquarters in Vienna. The only way it could be transported into Budapest was via the Hungarian government–approved Red Cross convoy. None of the antibiotics would reach the freedom fighters once they were placed in the government warehouses. Western reporters were also finding their movements hampered. Journalists attempting to leave the country without Hungarian-issued exit visas and Soviet road permits for safe conduct were detained by the Soviet military.

The day after the second Russian invasion of Budapest, Dickey wrote up Leo's account of his visit to the freedom fighters. Appearing under his byline in the November 5 edition of the *New York Journal-American*, it likened the return of the Russian tanks to Hitler's march into Poland. How Dickey's heart must have pounded with envy and longing as she wrote of the heroic and beautiful nineteen-year-old Hungarian university coed, one of the leaders who would die "in their futile attempt to stop the barbaric might of Soviet armor." The crisis brought back all her recent marine training for covering just such an event, and its pull became irresistible, bringing with it a sense of mission she'd not felt since she'd sat in the radio room on Guam listening to reports from Iwo Jima. "Many of those . . . were soon destined to add their blood to the already crimsoned streets—before the Soviet Army withdrew and regrouped. . . ."

Destiny was bouncing toward her. She wrote in a notebook during the time of "the ache of an uncrossed bridge. . . . I know the Mongols ride. . . . Joan burns at every stake. . . ." Her childhood hero, Admiral Richard E. Byrd, served as the IRC's honorary chairman. From her fourteenth-floor office, she stood on the edge of the glittering pool where the men of action were making history and saving the world. Oh, but this was her time, *the* time. There was no Edna standing in her way. She picked up the ball.

"The IRC helps people anywhere on earth who are victims of terrorism," she wrote. "The committee's beneficiaries were always people in real trouble like those I'd known working for the Quakers." It was as if everything she'd ever done had brought her to this stage of readiness, not only the marine training, but her years in postwar Eastern Europe as well. All she needed was the right opportunity. But for the time being, she would have to wait. Like the other employees of the institute and the IRC, Dickey was working around the clock for Leo Cherne and Stop the Massacre, the IRC co-sponsored rally at Madison Square Garden to support the freedom fighters. She took very active charge of a substantial portion of the rally. An audience of ten thousand packed the auditorium, and it was hoped that one million dollars would be raised for Hungarian aid.

Addressing the rally were IRC President Angier Biddle Duke and IRC national committee chairman Major General William J. "Wild Bill" Donovan, whom Dickey would later refer to as "you know who." About fifty other patriotic, religious, and refugee groups co-sponsored the rally. Other speakers were Anna Kethly, the leading Hungarian socialist, in New York to ask for UN assistance; Henry R. Luce of Time-Life; and Alexandra Tolstoy, Count Leo's daughter, who made an appeal in Russian to Soviet troops in Hungary.

The speeches were interrupted by booing and shouts of "We want action!" The crowd grew menacing after Miss Kethly's interpreter used the word *coexist* to describe Hungarian self-determination with its neighbors, including Russia.

Jumping onto the stage, Leo Cherne asked the audience members to restrain themselves. "A near riot started . . . because of the universal feeling among the Hungarians that their cause had been betrayed, that despite President Eisenhower's campaign speech of using every political, economic, and psychological tactic to help the satellite nations, there had not been sufficient help from the United States," Leo said.

Cherne recalled that the outburst made a profound impression on Dickey, a woman he'd described as "aloof and professional and too complicated" for him ever to try to figure out. But "the Madison Square Garden rally was the precipitating event; it so moved her impulses that the journalist, the activist, could not be denied," he ventured. "Dickey was a romantic, an idealist, a person of unbelievable courage. . . ."

Dickey later wrote that "American business, on whose behalf I was so comfortably employed, wasn't in any trouble at all. In fact, the country's gross national product was exceeding all records. So of Leo Cherne's two interests, my heart clearly lay on one side and my paycheck on the other. The Hungarian revolution involved them both, and on the same side." She added that when the IRC and the editors of *Life*

magazine were looking for a photographer familiar with refugee problems to cover the border crossings into Austria, "they didn't have to look
far."

But the actual mechanics were not that cut and dried. Dickey's notebook contained a curious message for Leo: "Are your most severe critics
those who say you can only spend for political purposes? In ten days I
can get a picture story confirmed for a major magazine which will can
that canard forever. I need $5000 and two weeks' leave of absence and
no questions asked." Whether she ever delivered this message is unknown, yet the dispatch with which she was to leave for Vienna would
support it.

The details surrounding her departure were sketchy, made murky by
Leo Cherne's vagueness. "It was not at my request that she went," said
Cherne, a comment hotly denied by Stevie Blick, who claimed Dickey
went on his expressed instructions. However, Cherne acknowledged her
strong need, unsatisfied by a desk job, to become involved in idealistic
causes. "She came to me for whatever help I could give," Cherne said
in an interview years later, suddenly recalling a piece of puzzling information. "She was carrying a fairly substantial amount of money with her
into Hungary. My recollection says ten thousand. Did we of the IRC
provide it to her because she said she would try to get the money to the
Budapest resistance? I have no recollection that she ever frankly said to
me that she was going in to Hungary. She may have, but I have no
recollection. She probably felt, and I did nothing to discourage it, that
she was representing me not as the head of the IRC, but as an activist,
a role for which she had very great admiration; and this was her expression of that admiration.

"I would have loved to have a sense that this heroism was intelligently
motivated. I did not. But . . . it was absolutely *purely* motivated by her
personal agony at the destruction of this free Budapest after ten days of
freedom."

Leo Cherne's fuzziness about Dickey's trip to Vienna, which occurred within forty-eight hours of getting the assignment, as well as
her Mata Hari–type correspondence and unpublished material, sug-
gests that Dickey's mission was not, as she insisted publicly, to photograph the Hungarians fleeing into Austria or the transfer of IRC
antibiotics into the hands of Hungarian freedom fighters; it was something far more important—to the IRC. Since it was the IRC's position

to aid persons fleeing totalitarian governments, it is likely that Dickey's job—considering the large amount of money she brought with her and the continuing reticence of Leo Cherne and her predecessor, Julia Edwards—was to get somebody important to the IRC and American intelligence out of Hungary. Dickey would later refer to her trip as a "suicide mission," but it was said with pride, not bitterness. Regardless of the risks, in which she was well versed, she was eager for the challenge and confident she could carry it off without a hitch. Beyond the adventure it promised, the mission appealed to her idealism and her vanity. As she had once wanted to please Tony, she now wanted to please Leo Cherne. The message to him in her notebook is one of idealistic loyalty, of an urgent need to be of service to a man she admired and to whom she could be useful. Leo mentioned that Dickey struck him as being stubborn, that once her mind was made up "you couldn't argue with her," later writing, "You couldn't teach her prudence." Dickey's aim, she would write to Marie Rodell before disappearing inside Hungary, was to "help the IRC."

Although Cherne emphasized that Dickey "made all of her own travel plans," Dickey would write Tony that IRC influence helped her get a passport within twenty-four hours for an IRC-financed trip to Vienna to do publicity work for the organization. However, she denied that was the reason behind a hurried, unexplained trip to Washington. If it were Dickey's mission to spirit somebody out of Hungary, it would follow that while in Washington she was briefed by the CIA and given a Minox, a unique, expensive camera favored by spies because it was the size of a pack of chewing gum (an item not subsequently claimed on her breakdown of cameras and jewelry for a theft insurance policy).

She rushed back from Washington to visit Aunt George, who despite being hospitalized for unexplained surgery was pleased as punch about her niece's hasty, intrigue-filled trip to Vienna. It had become the pleasant duty of Edna's two elderly sisters to furnish Dickey with familial guidance, and the two far more adventurous women had always indulged Georgie Lou's desires. Of the two, Dickey was closest to George, her namesake and adventure mentor. Both sent her off to Vienna with enthusiasm.

"Do a good job, darling, and use your head—you know you've got a good one," wrote Aunt George. She had filled in Lutie, and sighed, "It's wonderful that you could have gone—and under such favorable conditions and auspices all the way 'round. It's wonderful to get to do what one wants awfully to do."

JULIA EDWARDS, Dickey's predecessor at the institute, likens Dickey's "purpose" to the Japanese movie *Rashomon*, in which four people give their varying accounts of a single crime. Dickey's trip to Vienna goes in and out of focus like a bad television cable hookup. "Everybody has their own idea of what the truth is. You must remember," recalled Julia, "Dickey was an extremely ambitious, dramatic woman. She wanted desperately to get back into journalism. Hungary was not her finest hour, but I'm not saying she wasn't motivated by high ideals." On the other hand, Richard Salzmann, an IRC officer at the time, claimed that Dickey struck him as "a trustworthy woman who did not exaggerate or brag, who was going on the trip to be the IRC's 'eyes and ears.' "

On November 15, while Budapest endured shortages of food, medical supplies, heat, and an absence of reliable telephone connections with the outside world, Dickey boarded Pan Am flight 27. She'd finally gotten an assignment from that biggie magazine *Life* for the next month's special issue on the Hungarian uprising, which included an expense check to her for four hundred dollars. "I've had my caviar and squab," Dickey wrote her aunts contentedly. "I have a berth for the night, so I'll arrive in Vienna fresh as paint. The weather far below us is just one thin serrated layer of clouds; up here it's glassy smooth, with moon and clouds yet." Although looking forward eagerly to her great adventure, she fell asleep as soon as she closed her eyes.

In Vienna Dickey checked into the luxurious Hotel Bristol, across the street from the Vienna Opera House. A letter from Tony was waiting. He had just returned from an assignment in Havana and told her she would not recognize the place, "it's so changed." It was an adult playground, a hedonistic delight, courtesy of the country's military dictator, Fulgencio Batista. Then he upbraided her for not saying good-bye. If she had, he would have loaned her his new Leica and good lens to take along on her assignment for *Life*. "I sincerely hope that you won't do anything as foolish as attempting to go into Hungary," he wrote. "I sure wish you luck on your assignment and hope that you have learned that there is always another picture if you stay longer; and if you stay long enough, you can make a life career out of a story! But how does it get published?

Please don't get sore at this—I really mean it as good advice knowing you as well as I do."

Dickey answered that she hadn't known she was going to Vienna until forty-eight hours before the plane left. She told Tony IRC was financing her trip to get publicity. (And what better publicity could there be than photographs documenting for *Life*'s millions of readers the delivery of antibiotics to the hidden Hungarian freedom fighters?) Not unlike the way in which she'd once soothed her mother, she assured her former husband that he could think of her "right where I oughta be, behaving myself with due regard for the calculated risks to which you so flatteringly allude. Thanks, pal. . . ."

Soon after Dickey checked into the Hotel Bristol, she went to see another Time-Life employee, *Time* magazine's Vienna bureau chief, Edward Clarke. Clarke, a hardworking, conscientious reporter, detested her on sight. She was a free-lancer, a loathsome species that he likened to "flies around garbage." Clarke had work to do, and he found Dickey "a dilettante and a pain in the ass."

Dickey's plan was to spend ten days at the Austrian frontier, photographing Hungarian refugees crossing into the Austrian village at Andau. The great exodus had gotten ample press coverage at the time of the revolution—nearly a month and a half earlier. But with Hungarian and Soviet soldiers manning the border posts, there was still some chance for action, so some reporters still hung around.

At about the same time, Dickey drafted a note to Marcel Faust, the IRC chief in Vienna, describing herself as prepared to undertake a "mission," one for which she was "trained and prepared." The mission, surmised from copies of her letters and cables, was to enter Hungary illegally, deliver IRC-donated medicine to freedom fighter doctors, and photograph the transaction for *Life* magazine and the IRC. She had acquired two thousand dollars from the International Rescue Committee for this purpose.

On the Austrian-Hungarian border, where thousands continued their frightened journey out of Hungary, Dickey worked with an interpreter named Ferenc Welsch, a thirtyish Hungarian student and officer at the Vienna offices of the IRC. From the beginning Dickey made her intentions to enter Hungary known to the other reporters, who warned her against it. Carl Hartmann of Associated Press asked how she intended to get a story out if she were in prison. Barrett McGurn, correspondent for the *New York Herald Tribune,* considered the people she was making arrangements with to be nothing more than smugglers.

In a letter from the Hotel Bristol dated "Saturday Evening," Dickey wrote her aunts that her accommodations at the hotel were a "brocade-walled room with my car-and-driver-and-interpreter at beck and call." She noted that "even the chow in this firetrap is good. And the company is superb—Rougier of *Life.* McGurn of the Hertrib and Gen. Donovan of you-know-what-but-you-mustn't-say." She added that the work was "progressing nicely . . . although—hectically."

Also guests at the Hotel Bristol were the lanky author James Michener, on assignment for *Reader's Digest,* and his Japanese-American wife, Mari, who liked Dickey immediately. Every afternoon at three the two women met under the crystal chandeliers in the Bristol restaurant for "coffee with schlag." From then until seven or eight in the evening, Mari recalled, Dickey and James Michener would interview the recently arrived Hungarians, either at the hotel or at the refugee camps. The tales of torture by the AVO at the infamous Fö Street prison were particularly disturbing. Michener would recall their sadism in *The Bridge at Andau.* Unlike the newsmen, the already famous author was impressed by Dickey's sensitivity during the interviews. "She provided enormous help and insights. She was a great investment," he recalled.

About ten-thirty every night, Michener and Dickey, sometimes accompanied by Hartmann and McGurn, would taxi the thirty miles from Vienna to the Hungarian frontier at Andau. Though Dickey had written her aunts of enjoying the life of a visiting dignitary, Michener recalled he would pay Dickey's fare because she was invariably broke.

"On the frontier, Dickey and I sometimes went far behind the Russian lines," Michener said. "I was cautious, she was totally fearless. I would draw back from spots of danger, she would always crowd forward. I was older than she, more experienced. It was her first time in the situation, yet she was quite extraordinary in her personal courage." Michener recollected that each time she would go farther and farther into Hungary, returning with Hungarians who had become fearful at the last moment. He thought she guided out "hundreds, maybe," and believed she saved their lives. "If she were a man, they would have called her a hero." Dickey wrote to her aunts that she and Michener had become "border jumping" buddies.

On December 1, three days before she disappeared inside Hungary,

Dickey wrote the enthusiastic George and Lutie that she planned to extend her stay another week, "not only because this is an exciting situation," but because she was having a real problem with the IRC's Dr. Faust. He was a "sweet man," she explained, "but he's making my job all the more difficult for the nice people who have paid most of my trip." She explained that a "new boss" for IRC's Hungarian program would be arriving the following week, and she expected he would prove more cooperative. Still, she was having a wonderful time. "You couldn't wish better fun for me if you'd planned every minute." She wanted the frail women to know that she did not only spend her time at the border in her old Quaker-days clothes, but also indulged in honest-to-goodness tourism. She window-shopped and yearned to purchase a few Viennese fashions—Paris haute couture left her cold. She also wanted them not to worry about her well-being because the marines posted at the embassy had already adopted her. As to her journeys behind the advancing Iron Curtain, there was absolutely no danger. "Every correspondent here has been into Hungary almost every day. We don't go far in enough to amount to anything—sometimes only one hundred yards—but we think we're heroic as hell and the refugees of course love us dearly and tell us everything amidst fantastic emotion."

Even though armed Hungarian border guards manned the wooden watchtowers, Dickey assured her aunts that "they turn their backs, and if they feel like firing, do so over our heads. So you see we know the game is safe as houses; the tragedy is that the men, women, and children, at this point, don't know it and have of course survived very real and hideous danger only a few kilometers back." Then, lest they think she was courting danger, Dickey added, "Actually as you might know your niece would exaggerate—I haven't been near the border in days, since the entire press corps, including Austrians, was kicked out of the most obvious border area near Vienna because the authorities wearied of our compromising their positions." She was delighted to report that everyone working the border was pleased with the continuing interest of Americans "in the saga of this hysterical migration over the frozen marshes. Suez may be a bigger story, but I'll remain loyal to this one."

Every night reporters, rescue workers, and CIA agents waited on the Austrian side with bottles of slivovitz, a Balkan plum brandy, to offer the frozen Hungarian refugees, who, under a bright harvest moon, children slung over their backs, arrived in shivering clumps of twos and fours.

Here General William "Wild Bill" Donovan, the IRC's national committee chairman, could (according to his biographer, Anthony Cave Brown) be found night after night, "helping refugees come through the great frozen bullrush swamps as Soviet tanks clanked in the darkness and flares arched across the night sky." Dickey, who'd written to her aunts about Donovan, met him in November on one of these cold, frenetic nights. She introduced herself as the IRC publicist and *Life* photographer. Perhaps this man's presence inspired the Mata Hari side of Dickey; the project ahead would call upon it.

11

Safe as Houses

At the border of Andau, across the Einser Canal a few hundred yards inside Hungary, stood a small wooden footbridge. Built by some unknown Hungarian farmer, it had become famous as far away as Budapest as the bridge to freedom. On the evening of November 21, Soviet soldiers began firing at the fleeing Hungarians, and a Soviet tank destroyed the bridge. In *The Bridge at Andau,* Michener tells how toward midnight three Austrian students lugged logs into Hungary and repaired the dynamited bridge. Michener also described Dickey as "a brave and daring photographer whose pictures helped tell the story of Hungary's mass flight to freedom." (To protect her identity in the original edition, Michener referred to her as a male photographer.)

When the book was first published, Dickey was in prison in Budapest. "[Dickey] would go anywhere. . . . Nights we patrolled the border together, bringing in hundreds of Hungarians. Sometimes we went well into Hungary, occasionally up to the bridge and always with an ear cocked for the sweetest of night sounds, the soft, tentative calls of men and women seeking freedom," Michener wrote.

"One very cold night we were on the watch when toward dawn we heard curious sounds coming from the temporary bridge. We crept up as close as we dared and saw a revolting sight. The communist guards, well liquored up, were chopping down the bridge and burning it to keep their feet warm. Then, as we crouched there observing them, we witnessed a tragedy that neither of us will ever forget.

"A band of some thirty refugees, led by a man in a fur cap, appeared mysteriously out of the Hungarian swamps and walked directly toward the drunken guards. These unlucky people had no way of knowing that the bridge was no longer a route to freedom, and we were powerless to stop them. Quickly, the guards grabbed their rifles and dogs, and the last refugees to reach the bridge at Andau were rounded up and carted off to prison. They had walked no one knew how far and had come to within fifty feet of freedom. Heartsick, the photographer and I crept back with the sound of communist axes in our ears, and by the time we reached the corner of Austria, the bridge at Andau had forever vanished."

Many refugees at Andau suffered, particularly the children. One evening Dickey watched a doctor inside one of the refugee shelters diagnose eleven cases of infantile pneumonia. Her mission, which would involve delivery of medicine, took on greater urgency. An injection of penicillin before the frozen crossing would prevent the illness. "I was not in Austria at all," wrote Dickey. "I was back on the deck of the hospital ship offshore at Iwo Jima."

BUT AS SHE MENTIONED to her aunts, she was having a difficult time getting IRC Vienna chief Marcel Faust to see her, let alone hand over any of the IRC-donated Pfizer antibiotics. This was not surprising, since the IRC and Faust personally had been, according to Dr. Faust's later recollection, "attacked on the Hungarian radio several times." In light of this Faust did not understand how Dickey, who desired to help the IRC, could still insist on carrying through her reckless scheme.

Dickey urgently requested official papers from the IRC "to cover her illegal trip to Budapest, which of course I couldn't do; the more so since it would have endangered her," Faust wrote in a letter years later.

Dickey wrote Faust, "I came at a cost in thousands of dollars on the personal urgent instructions of Mr. Cherne to do a special job. I am well trained, briefed, and ready to do it. It is urgent that it be completed as soon as possible. It cannot be done without the utmost frankness between you and me. It cannot be discussed in public restaurants nor in front of other people. My job, as I said, is to show U.S. materials given to IRC delivered into the hands of Freedom Fighters. Publication of this story to the largest audience in America had been set up and assured to

Mr. Cherne before I left." She asked Faust to burn the letter and to speak to her alone. He refused.

Frustrated, Dickey drafted several cables to the IRC in New York. One to Angier Biddle Duke read, "Would you advise Faust that I require his confidence and that Interescue is underwriting my mission with several thousand dollars. It still is not possible for me to see Faust privately and the original cable he received about me gives him no reason to believe me to be of any real potential usefulness. FYI, my mission here is, repeat, is possible at this moment, but without support from Faust, very difficult." At about the same time, she cabled Leo Cherne: "The full budget for this project was three thousand; have received only two. Can you cable additional thousand to me direct today as EYE [sic] unable to get support in any way from Faust. Unable to get anything from Faust. EYE [sic] expect to be accountable this sum but require it now."

By now Dickey's two-week leave from the IRC had run out. Another cable to Cherne requested additional time. She photographed Cherne's response, dated November 25, perhaps to test the Minox and infrared film. Her boss scolded her for taking an extra week in Vienna, adding, "We sure were glad to hear from you. It kind of made me feel you weren't taking too many chances. If I'm wrong, leave me to my delusions. I can just imagine the excitement of all the goings-on over there— and you in the midst of it. The reports here in the papers seem to show that you were right in thinking that things weren't going to calm down over there too quickly."

A week later, on December 2, a less sanguine Dickey sent her agent, Marie Rodell, copies of her cables to *Life* listing her shot breakdown on the refugee crossing story. "Presumably they have rejected all this material, including pix, except what has appeared in print—but I have no notion what that might be since I've not seen any new copies of *Life* since I got here." With her career expectations as a *Life* photographer doubtful and her important mission for the IRC stalled, a disheartened Dickey suggested Marie send the material on to the IRC, the actual owners of the photos, and to query *Life* to see "what kind of subsequent payoff exploitation we might concoct out of my having been here under these circumstances." Though there appeared to be little left for her to do, she told Marie she planned to stay on another week, returning to the States on December 9.

Although it is unclear who provided Dickey with the additional one thousand dollars, she received both the cash and papers identifying her as a volunteer worker for the IRC. On the evening of December 4, 1956, she set out with Ferenc Welsch and Zoltan Dienes, young Hungarian guides whom she described as freedom fighters and had promised to help emigrate to the States. She told acquaintances she was paying them one thousand dollars to take her across the Soviet-controlled frozen swamps to the Burgenland border, and she told Mari Michener she would be back in three days.

That same day, *The New York Times* reported that the Soviet Union was stepping up its charges that foreign plotters were behind the uprising in Hungary: "The United States in particular is being singled out by the Soviet Government through its controlled press as responsible for the revolt," the story read. *Pravda*, the official newspaper of the Soviet Communist party, was quoted: "American vehicles with Red Cross signs on them had distributed weapons on the streets of Budapest." *Pravda* also claimed that the "subversive centers" of Radio Free Europe and Voice of America were amazingly well informed about events inside Hungary before the uprising. It further alleged that "many foreign newsmen who went to Budapest during the trouble had no relation at all to the press and were just agents of the intelligence services, leaders of all sorts of reactionary organizations."

In this inhospitable climate, Dickey, wearing a girdle under heavy herringbone trousers and munching on chocolates and oranges, walked into Hungary. She had ten pounds of IRC-donated antibiotics stashed in her knapsack and a Minox camera loaded with infrared film taped under her arm. Her head was covered with a babushka, her feet encased in her old, sturdy clodhopper walking shoes; she wore a bulky sweater and a Hungarian-made overcoat. A contemporary notebook contains rough sketches of military outposts and fragments of information about Russian and Hungarian troops. This information was probably provided by the refugees met en route to assist her in the journey she was now taking. She was gambling everything on this hard-won trip, which if successful would prove that she could triumph—against all odds. Photographs would provide a much-needed professional benefit, but the thread that held all this together was personal. She believed that she was going to relieve the suffering of the Hungarians of whom she had written back in New York and had witnessed at the refugee camps. Believing she could, therefore, as she liked to say, "have her cake and eat it, too," she walked on, feeling warm despite the cold.

It was a silent, clear night with a fat white winter's moon. The calm night was broken every now and then by tracer flares whizzing overhead. After several hours of what she later described as "confused walking," one of the guides admitted he was lost. The hapless trio crawled over downed saplings straddling canals. The icy water soaked Dickey's shoes; her knapsack fell into the weed-clogged canals, and when she rescued it, she lost the chocolate and her glasses; after fifteen minutes of crawling around on her hands and knees, she located them. She was ten years older than her two guides, and she worried about keeping up with them.

They walked on. Suddenly four men, two in military uniform, fired submachine guns over the heads of the three travelers. In the confusion Dickey fell backward onto the snow. Zoltan Dienes escaped. Dickey's pleas of being on a mission of mercy fell on deaf ears. After a not-too-thorough search of Dickey's and Ferenc's knapsacks, the two were marched at gunpoint through the night. An hour later they arrived at a newly built military barracks less than fifteen kilometers from the Austrian border. Dickey counted this to be the sixteenth crossing into Hungary. The odds of fifteen to one cheered her. It was also her first trip without her lucky pin of a leg on a pair of wings. As she drifted off to sleep on the concrete floor of the barracks, warmed by a wood-burning stove, she was confident that by morning she would find somebody to "negotiate" with besides the soldier standing guard. She had her papers identifying her as a relief worker, and she was carrying the humanitarian gift of medicine.

The following morning one of the soldiers glanced at her passport and the letter identifying her as a volunteer for the International Rescue Committee. Ferenc Welsch sidled up to her. "They don't believe us," he whispered. "They don't think we came here to deliver medicine." Late that afternoon Dickey and Ferenc were separated. She was placed in the backseat of a black sedan, a Pobeda, which was the Russian word for victory. A soldier with a submachine gun sat next to the driver, who wore a Western-style suit. Under her arm the Minox chafed her; perhaps American currency weighed her down as well. After stopping at a farmhouse to pick up two more passengers, a wan-faced woman and child, the car lurched onto a dirt road. While the woman cried, Dickey held the baby. A Red Cross truck passed them, going in the other direction.

Dickey assumed she'd hitch a ride back to Vienna on one of these trucks. She was heartened as the car passed a road marker pointing to Budapest. No doubt they were taking her to the American consulate.

Finally the woman stopped crying, produced a tin of cigarettes from her coat pocket, and offered Dickey one. Dickey smiled gratefully. Fearing that smoke curling up in the frozen fields at night would reveal her position, she hadn't had a cigarette since leaving Vienna. In broken German the woman explained that she was a Czech whose passport was out of order. While the woman spoke, Dickey inhaled and wondered how to get rid of the camera, which would surely mark her as a spy.

"I rolled down the window in the locked car door at my side just far enough to flick out the ashes. The soldier in the front seat tired at last of watching this procedure, and turned back to gaze fixedly out through the windshield," she wrote. "Feverishly, I unbuttoned my overcoat, pushed up my sweater, wool shirt, and underclothing, and removed the camera from under my arm. I had used four adhesive bandages to hold the Minox to my skin and I counted them meticulously, not leaving one to tell its own story if I were searched." All she had to do was roll down the window—but what if the camera thumped against the rear fender? She wrapped one of her bulky knit gloves around the tiny camera. Rolling down the window, she flicked the cigarette ash with a shower of sparks and let go of the Minox. It dropped away silently.

The sedan drove onto Fö Street, the main street on the Buda side of the city. Budapest was actually two cities divided by the Danube into a residential west bank, Buda, and an industrialized eastern side, Pest. Her last visit had been in 1948, when she and Tony were working for the Quakers. When their Hungarian escorts had demanded approval of their exposed film, Tony had wanted to dump it in the Danube but had surrendered it in view of their goodwill mission, except for the roll secreted out and later printed for the Voice of America. Dickey remembered they had watched the May Day parade. There had been several anti-American floats, the most amusing one being a two-story-high figure of Donald Duck yawning on top of a pile of money bags, labeled "The Capitalist Press of the United States."

The sedan stopped in front of a fortresslike, U-shaped brick building. The five-story building was a block long and set back from the street by a courtyard and a high metal gate, topped by the letters *AVH.* Although Dickey could not read Hungarian, she recognized the abbreviation for the Hungarian state secret police. For the first time, she panicked. She was facing the notorious Fö Street prison, AVO headquarters. She recalled the refugees' hands, maimed by cigarette burns, the nails ripped off.

Like all secret police institutions behind the Iron Curtain, Fö Street was designed to resemble the infamous Lubyanka prison in Moscow. The main building facing the street housed courtrooms and hundreds of offices for interrogators, prosecutors, and judges, all on the AVO payroll. The officers of the MVD (Ministerstvo Vnutrykh Del, the Ministry of Internal Affairs), the paramilitary Soviet police assigned to keep a lid on civil unrest in Budapest, also had their offices there. An arrow of panic shot up from Dickey's ankles to her stomach.

Inside, a young female guard removed Dickey's earrings, her Cartier wristwatch, the Dunhill lighter, her lipstick, and other personal items and escorted her to a narrow elevator, which stopped on the fifth floor. It opened onto a Kafkaesque set piece: an endless, dim corridor buzzing with the indiscernible sounds of prisoners speaking languages she could not understand. On either side stretched thick, ancient wood doors centered by a small steel judas window, a peephole with small holes hammered into it for one-way spying on prisoners. At feeding time the "window" was opened for food. Dickey was deposited behind the rusted, creaky door of cell 504. The guard, after miming a hanging motion, removed Dickey's shoelaces. Dickey shook her head unbelievingly, her horror not at her surroundings as much as her ineptness. Once again she'd screwed up.

Though not immediately charged with any crime, Dickey was held at the state prison for the next five weeks. Her repeated requests to see the U.S. consul were ignored by the interrogator, who looked constantly from her to a Hungarian-English dictionary.

When Dickey did not return to the Hotel Bristol after three days, Mari Michener had her hotel room searched. Since all of her belongings were there, Mari began making inquiries. She was distressed by the callous indifference of the other reporters, finding Edward Clarke, the *Time* magazine bureau chief in Vienna, particularly unfeeling. "The attitude was that since she was not a full-time employee of *Life* magazine," James Michener recalled, "her well-being was not their concern. They completely disavowed her. It was reprehensible."

"She was looking for a story," said AP reporter Carl Hartmann. "She was on some kind of quasi assignment for *Life* and involved with a sort of spookish group, the IRC, who were getting important people out of Hungary. She believed she could get through and take her pictures and get out again. She knew it was a risk."

Hartmann confirms that neither the press corps nor the U.S. embassy in Vienna was particularly upset by Dickey's disappearance. When correspondent Sam Jaffe, a friend of the Plimmers also in Vienna at the time, inquired at their request, he turned up little. In a letter to the Plimmers on December 15, 1956, Jaffe echoed the sentiments of his colleagues. "We don't see why an intelligent (?) woman would take any risks in these days, as pictures are a nickel a dozen—every kind—and available all over. If she had business to take her there, her American credentials would enable her to get out of any ordinary misunderstanding. If she just went for the sake of thrills—I hope she got them. These aren't days to be playing *Front Page* or 'Stop the Press.' These are days when great, heroic action is being taken by people without even the encouragement one gets from support of like-minded persons. And one doesn't jeopardize anything in order to be personally exalted." Mari Michener visited the embassy and found them not very anxious to investigate Dickey's disappearance, despite her badgering. Then the Micheners left Vienna.

Zoltan Dienes, the twenty-nine-year-old Hungarian engineer who had escaped, spent the first night hidden in a frozen Hungarian canal. He returned to Austria the next day with a fever and stayed in bed for two days. Then he went to the border to search for a friend of Dickey's, a man with gray hair, who may have been James Michener or General Donovan. Unable to find him after several days, Dienes went to the American embassy and reported the incident.

On December 14 United Press wired a story about Dickey's disappearance. Picked up by the world press, the article mentioned Dickey's payment of one thousand dollars for a guide into Hungary and stated that she was employed by the International Rescue Committee.

Tony Chapelle, who had begun keeping a journal, wrote on December 15, "I managed to have the U.P. story killed by 9 A.M. because of the Rescue Committee angle. Cherne was frantic. . . ." With the help of Denis Plimmer, he got through to Vienna and was informed of Zoltan Dienes's report of arrest "by soldiers." Tony continued, "I had confirmation of this from the Hungarian Desk [State Department] in Washington, who later in the day reported that they now considered the witness to be unreliable. So again we were not sure."

All subsequent press reports identified Dickey as a free-lance photographer. *Life* magazine would use two of Dickey's photographs in their December 3 special issue on Hungary but denied that she worked for them in any capacity. Later, Julia Edwards would write, "Americans virtually disowned her in their rush to deny any knowledge of or involvement in her mad scheme. Before she crossed the Hungarian border, *Life* magazine had managed to get a staff correspondent accredited to Budapest. To protect his station, the magazine declined to defend her unauthorized trip."

As far as Julia and the other reporters were concerned, Dickey's actions were motivated not by journalism or humanitarianism, but by a desperate ambition to revive her stalled journalistic career, despite the risk to the IRC. Edward Clarke felt that "she got what she deserved."

The U.S. vice-consul in Budapest, Richard Selby, began making inquiries one week after Dickey's arrest (to which Dickey would always refer to as her "capture"). But another month would pass before the Hungarian authorities would acknowledge she was in custody.

Except for the first week, when two women informers shared the cell, in her nearly one and a half months at Fö Street, Dickey was alone. The only time she left the eight-by-ten-foot cell was for a morning trip down the corridor to fill a battered aluminum bowl with icy water, and for interrogations. All day, as ordered, she either sat on her sleeping platform, feet flat on the floor, watching her breath freeze, or she paced. Her tiny barred window was broken and could not be closed, but it hardly mattered, since there was no heat. At night she was required to sleep with her hands outside the coarse, foul-smelling blanket, a policy that prevented prisoners from slitting their wrists in the event they had found something to cut with. A yellow light bulb set inside a mesh-covered recessed box in the ceiling was always on. There was no way to reach the bulb. The metal sleeping bunk was bolted to the floor. Even if she were able to reach it, there was no way to break through the mesh protecting the bulb. Its psychological power over her was complete. She couldn't escape, either by suicide or by darkness.

Dickey divided up the day into its emotional components. There was the first horrible jolt of wakening, icy cold and stiff, to the reality of her surroundings—"the time of Panic." It would last a few hours, until the judas window opened and some warm gruel appeared in her bowl with a piece of black bread. As the food entered her body, the panic subsided and "the Long Wait" began, for the interrogation or cigarettes. She was allowed five. Then came the next meal and then, of course, sleep.

Cigarettes had to be lighted by one of the guards, and Dickey discovered a way of standing and arching her head so that the match would singe the jailer's eyebrows. It was a small victory, but such minuscule triumphs could make the spirit soar.

The three prison meals were no different from the fare being consumed by most of Budapest that winter, soup with cabbage or noodles, a piece of milky cheese, and a shriveled apple. On Sundays a piece of bacon, its fat glistening like jewels, arrived on her tray. She would use the rind to polish her boots to a marine spit-shine finish—until she realized her boots looked better than those of the guards. Such were the good times. She lost twenty pounds. She stopped menstruating. An old infection in her left ear began acting up. Refusing medical attention because the doctor did not speak English or German, she lost most of the hearing in that ear.

"The daily routine in Fö Street was grim and erratic," she wrote. "Erratic for a purpose. You never knew how long it would be before the next food or the night's rest. You did know, almost from the first moment, that you were being cut loose, systematically, from time as a pillar of sanity."

Defacing cell walls was forbidden. Guards searched each day to make sure she was not marking them. However, every twenty-four hours she made a vertical line with her fingernail in the plaster beside her sleeping shelf, where she sat most of her waking hours. The lines were visible only from one spot in the cell, where the unwinking light made a purple hairline shadow in the ridges. When she made her thirtieth line, she felt a sense of ironic triumph. The words she had first heard on Okinawa, "The limit of human endurance has never been reached," became for her the summit of all human wisdom. "If I could do one month here alone—I did not have to be afraid of doing another. And there on the wall was the proof that I had. . . .

"My being here had begun because there was something I wanted to see," she later wrote. "Well, how important was the job of being an eyewitness and a reporter? Would it really have mattered if I'd seen the delivery of the medicine into the hands of a doctor among the freedom fighters? Was one such image worth risking being killed or wounded or missing or imprisoned? The answer to the question was simply 'Yes.' I believed the picture I'd been trying to make would have moved someone who saw it to provide new aid to the freedom fighters." She may have also been asking herself if she had not been used. Certainly more than a photograph had been at stake in what she had set out to do and had written Dr. Faust she had been "trained" to do.

Whatever her exact mission, it involved the American intelligence community, which in those days was regarded with great esteem. She would have been one of dozens of patriotic and adventurous reporters recruited for purposes of spying at the height of the cold war. Whether she'd been sent to observe—at one point she claimed that her job was to *follow* the IRC medicine into Hungary at the behest of *Life* and the IRC—or to bring somebody important out of Hungary, given the activities and connections of the IRC, this would explain the shroud of silence around this episode, even decades later.

Sitting in that vermin-filled cell, she was not bitter. Her code of honor was as idealistic as a child's, filled with the same pure and irrational hope. In writing of her "capture," she mentioned how she immediately saw in her mind the faces of the people behind her assignment, and that she settled on one above all others. "It was a sound choice," she wrote, "symbol of greater cold and greater hazard . . . my ranking chief, the man who headed the International Rescue Committee, Rear Admiral Richard Evelyn Byrd." Her teenage hero was reassuring in the face of the bogeyman—her fear, hysteria, ignorance, distrust, prejudice—all the evil that shook in herself and others. *It* was the enemy. Her biggest worry inside Fö Street was that she would never get another chance to prove herself.

She was interrogated two to three times a week inside an office bare except for two scarred wood desks. She was not told what she was charged with, only informed that spies were shot and that nobody in America knew she was at the prison and that nobody need ever know. Twice she was threatened with hanging, and later she told friends that sadistic prison guards marched her into the courtyard at night, placed her up against a wall and aimed guns at her, doubling over in laughter as she stood terrorized and silent. She wrote that the people she loved were elderly and expected that by the time she was released from prison they would all be dead.

She refused to sign any papers, so the interrogator signed her name.

All her requests to see the United States consul were ignored. It was so bitterly cold in the room that the narrow-shouldered, hawk-nosed interrogator and the young female typist interpreter wrapped prison-issue blankets around their coats. When the man dipped his pen in the inkwell, Dickey expected to hear the sound of ice cracking.

When first arrested, Dickey had repeatedly been asked why she had escaped to Hungary. She explained that she had not escaped, "since the word means to flee in fear," but rather hers was a mission of mercy with the token ten pounds of antibiotics. She told them she was a representative of the IRC. Later she wrote that her interrogator knew that two men from the research committee, Leo Cherne and Angier Biddle Duke, had been in Budapest during the uprising. By this time the interrogator also knew Dickey had worked as a journalist, and pointing, he waved a copy of the December 3 issue of *Life* magazine.

"Why do you spread these lies against the glorious People's Republic of Hungary?" he demanded, threatening to hang her as an enemy of the state.

"I was not a journalist when you shot at me. You know I was only bringing medicine," she answered, suppressing the pleasure of seeing her photographs finally printed in *Life*.

"Did you not read the American newspapers before you came to Europe? Did you not know other Americans illegally here before you?"

"No."

"Last week you said it was yes."

She remembered distinctly that she had said "no" the week before.

"Do you realize that your employer already has betrayed you?" asked the AVO man, whom she called "Hawk Face."

"I have more than one employer," she answered.

"They have all betrayed you. They are doing nothing to help you."

As Dickey sat on her uncomfortable sleeping platform or paced to keep warm, socks worn through, her laceless shoes slapping against the stone floor, she realized that for the first time in her life she would not be spending Christmas with her family. The thought depressed her far more than any other so far. Not a young woman, she was living like an unkempt animal, her clothes ripped and dirty, her mind disoriented, and under the constant threat of being killed. *Nobody need ever know.* As she chewed on the Christmas rationed meal, a piece of bacon rind, she questioned anew the price she was paying.

In the sixth week Hawk Face told Dickey she was being charged with entering the country without a visa, a felony punishable by five years in prison.

Her cell measured seven paces from the reinforced door to the barred window. Compounding her isolation was the tapping on the wall next to her—another prisoner trying desperately to make contact. The tapping did little to satisfy Dickey's desperate need to talk to somebody, however, so she talked to herself.

A request, written in fading pencil on a piece of brown Hungarian wrapping paper, is illuminating:

Memorandum to my interrogator, January 4, 1957:

1. I would like to study your language. But I will need your help.

2. I need a book of phrases and/or a school-book about grammar, and/or a dictionary. (Hungarian-English as you used would be ideal. But Hungarian-German also would make my study possible.)

3. Also, I would need continued permission to have some paper on which to write.

4. I believe I would study with great diligence. Because my heart like everyone's needs urgently to be able to speak again to other human beings and to understand what they say, too.

Sure that one of the guards was always watching her through the centered, steel judas window, Dickey made a resolve. "Always, when I paced toward the peephole, it seemed urgently, desperately important that my chin be literally up even if it obviously was an empty gesture, with the truth plain in my expression. This led to one instant about which I still cannot think without shame. I turned at the end of my pacing, and was sure that I had successfully thrown back my head only to realize within a few steps that I was seeing the floor."

When Dickey ate sugar or fat, she could marshal thoughts of escape, though they always ended on a depressing note. What would she do in Budapest if by some miracle she did escape? How would she ask for a telephone book to contact the legation? If she hailed a cab, how would she pay?

She traced her fear to her stomach. If she could exercise, maybe the constant pain in her stomach would lessen. She removed her coat and took the blanket—bloodstained by a former prisoner—from her sleeping platform. As soon as she spread it on the floor, the jailer opened the judas window and began shouting.

"I stared hard at his young set face framed in the rusty iron. Slowly, out of sheer bravado, I answered bitingly, 'I don't need the blanket.' I swept it aside and quickly did a marine forward rolling somersault, starting over the shoulder and finishing standing up. I did the roll four times back and forth in the length of the cell, coming back to my feet every time. My shoulder ached, my head stung, I almost crashed into the wall, but it was worth it. . . .

"That's what happens when you give a woman a little bit of basic training," she later wrote her marine friend, Sergeant Robert Morrisey, "even if she's an old lady, she gets confident. Powerful stuff, that."

On January 7, 1957, Lincoln White, the U.S. State Department press spokesman, announced that Hungarian minister Dr. Peter Kos, who was being recalled to Hungary, had paid a visit to Robert Murphy, the undersecretary of state. Mr. Murphy told Dr. Kos there were reliable reports that Dickey Chapelle, an American photographer, was being held in a Hungarian prison and expressed the government's urgent concern that she be released. The minister said he would look into the matter and see what he could do. The following week the Hungarian government confirmed that Dickey Chapelle, a free-lance photographer who had entered Hungary on December 5 without a visa, was in prison. The State Department was relieved that she was not being charged as a spy.

In the meantime Tony and Leo Cherne were in daily contact. Tony's journal mentions extortion, a phone call he received offering Dickey's release on payment of one hundred thousand schillings delivered in Vienna. Tony wrote that Leo assured him that the money would get to Vienna, but there were no more phone calls. "Gosh, Dickey," Tony added wistfully inside his journal, "I thought that after Okinawa you were through with all that sort of foolish chances." Meanwhile Dickey's brother was writing to his Wisconsin representatives for assistance, and Lutie and George were fanning the home-front fires, having been told by Tony that Dickey was being well treated. By Christmas Tony was considering going into Yugoslavia and believed if he could get definite word of her location, he could "hire a few commandos and try to get you that way." He wondered again, "Dickey, oh, Dickey, why did you do this to us all?"

IN MID-JANUARY Dickey noticed that suddenly Hawk Face seemed to be in a hurry. She stopped answering any of his questions. On the evening of January 20 the judas window on Dickey's cell door slid open. A piece of bacon fat shimmered on a tray. Like an animal, she grabbed for it as the tray disappeared. A moment later the window opened again. On the tray was a glass of water.

A short time later a young guard entered her cell, holding a pair of foot-long plumber's pliers. He smiled sweetly and asked, *"Betteg?"*

She shook her head. "No," she answered, "I am not sick."

He asked her to open her mouth. She was puzzled. Still smiling, he set the pliers against his teeth, moving the handles up and down. Another guard entered the cell. After a furious exchange of words, they left.

The following evening the guard with the pliers returned and asked again if she were sick. She answered "No," shaking her head. He placed his cigarette between his teeth and tucked the pliers under his arm. He spread the fingers of his hand and nodded his head at her, suggesting she do the same. Dickey recalled the last photograph she had made, of a woman refugee's maimed hands, whose fingernails had all been ripped off.

The guard turned the steel teeth onto his own nail. Again he smiled. Dickey smiled back, reaching toward the pliers. At this point two other guards entered the cell. Gently she took the pliers. "Very carefully, as if it were important to do it right, I closed them over my own index fingernail," she said. "I rotated it until it stung, stopped, smiled, and looked up at the now staring faces of the guards. I said quickly in English, 'You do it like that, huh?' " One of the guards grabbed the pliers from her hand. After an awkward silence they left.

The next day Dickey was handcuffed, put into a windowless van, and driven to an industrialized section of Pest. She was booked at Marco Street Prison, which was within walking distance of the American legation. When placed in a cell with eight other women, she burst into tears. "They thought it was from sadness," Dickey wrote. "They put their arms around me with tenderness and said, '*Nem szabad sirni.* Crying is not permitted here.' " Years later Dickey would recall the experience as "crying because I didn't know there were really any other human beings left alive on the earth." She recalled that nothing ever happened again to match that moment of joy and relief.

On Dickey's seventh week of custody, Richard Selby, the young, blond U.S. consul in Budapest, and Hungarian attorney Karoly Havas visited the Marco Street Prison. Havas, who was on excellent terms with the prosecutor and would be representing Dickey at her trial, told Selby he felt "cautiously optimistic" about the case. A believer in timing, the wily Havas sensed it was an excellent time for Dickey. Since her capture the government had become interested in appearing reasonable, not repressive, perhaps for purposes of attracting much-needed American aid.

As the two men walked downstairs to see the American prisoner, the woman jailer accompanying them turned to Selby. She wanted to know what her chances were of getting into the United States if she were able to escape from Hungary. Selby was too startled to reply.

Inside a windowless room, Dickey, her thin, stringy hair lying greasy and limp on her shoulders, regarded the two men suspiciously. Selby understood her nervousness. But under her anxiety, he sensed, to his surprise, a very tough woman. He hadn't expected such resilience from someone with family on Sutton Place.

There were no other people in the room, but Selby believed it might be bugged. Dickey demanded to see his identification before she would talk to either of them. After studying Selby's diplomatic passport, she seemed to relax a little. Selby told her that even though she had broken Hungarian law by entering the country without a passport, Mr. Havas, the Hungarian attorney he had hired to represent her, believed she would be freed. Dickey was not so sure.

Selby thought Dickey seemed a bit confused, but he didn't think it unusual for someone who had been in a secret police prison, mostly in solitary confinement, for nearly two months. Disoriented or not, he also sensed she would make a bad witness for the Hungarian state, since she would not cooperate with them in any way. Besides, the government's whole judicial system was being examined, so there was no advantage to them in a big, splashy show trial. If she were guilty of anything, Selby decided, it was doing what women didn't do, wanting to get into the action. It was plain to him that she had taken the risk of entering Hungary without a visa to advance her career as a journalist.

A little over a week later, on January 26, Dickey and Ferenc Welsch, her Hungarian guide, were brought to a Budapest municipal court to stand trial. The trial, held on a Saturday, lasted six hours. Dickey wore a bright yellow sweater given to her by Selby's wife and spent the time counting the pieces of wood inlay carved into the panel in front of the bench. In her head she recited in its entirety Thomas Gray's poem,

"Elegy Written in a Country Churchyard." She made one mistake in the eighteenth verse and went back to the beginning.

Carl Hartmann of the Associated Press, the only Western reporter still allowed in Budapest, sat in the courtroom taking notes. He had worked on the story filing wire reports, ever since Dickey's disappearance, not because he was personally involved, but because "it was a helluva story."

Dickey identified herself as a representative of the International Rescue Committee. She told the judge she had no intention of breaking the law but understood from what she had been told that she had crossed the frontier illegally. She was sentenced to fifty days in jail. Since she had been in custody fifty-three days, the judge set her free and ordered her to leave the country within twenty-four hours and never return. When the judge asked what she would like done with the medicine she had brought, Dickey requested that it be given to the Hungarian Red Cross. She was still convinced she was not going to be released.

Ferenc Welsch, Dickey's co-defendant, was sentenced to eight months in prison. Dickey, whose guilt over Welsch's imprisonment was tremendous, called it a "tragedy." When she met with him briefly, the twenty-eight-year-old former university student told her his wife, Maria, was in Vienna with their child. Dickey assured him that if she got to Vienna, his wife would not be left alone. "I give you my word."

Accompanied by a female guard, Dickey reentered the cell. She was in no hurry to pack her belongings, since she was sure she was just being transferred to another cell. Not until the women gathered around, hugging her and crying, did Dickey comprehend that she was indeed being released.

A UP article appearing in the *New York Herald Tribune* on Thursday, January 31, 1957, datelined Vienna, reported Dickey's dramatic release as she reached "free soil" at the border checkpoint of Nickelsdorf, Austria: "American woman photographer Mrs. Georgette (Dickey) Meyer-Chapelle reached the free world Sunday after fifty days in Communist Hungarian prisons." The article described her as appearing slightly hysterical "with relief." As tears flowed down her cheeks, her first words were: "I thank God I am an American."

That same afternoon in Vienna, Marcel Faust visited with Dickey. One of the subjects they discussed was the welfare of Ferenc Welsch's wife, Maria, and her infant child, who'd been living as squatters in a vacant house. Faust, who had earlier warned Dickey against her trip into Budapest, assured her that Maria would be as well taken care of as the other destitute wives and children of Hungarian refugee students.

Dickey's return to New York was greeted by a phalanx of flashbulb-popping news cameras. She was a celebrity. Although she had cabled her aunts Lutie and George not to meet her plane, the two frantic women fought their way through the crowd to embrace their beloved niece and get her in a taxi to Lutie's elegant apartment on Sutton Place. Lutie recalled that her niece did not want to be alone.

"It came with great surprise to us that she ever got out," said Leo Cherne, adding, "I'm afraid I was not very helpful. But she didn't have a legal leg to stand on."

Tony sent Dickey the journal he'd been keeping, reprimanding her for giving the embassy all the credit for her release. "Many people and organizations helped get you out," he wrote, adding obliquely, "a few unnamed individuals over near the Suez Canal—who provided unnamed services with no compensation whatever." He believed she had gotten arrested in Hungary "because you wanted to." Although Dickey's brother believed Tony was entirely responsible for Dickey's release, Richard Selby and Helga both disregarded his claim as patently ridiculous. "Tony didn't do a damn thing to get her released," the former U.S. vice-consul stated firmly.

Dickey returned to the RIA and her old job as press liaison, but she was no longer the bright-eyed, enthusiastic employee. She was humiliated, and beyond her damaged pride, she blamed herself for Ferenc Welsch's imprisonment, worrying about his wife's well-being at Dr. Faust's hands. Then there was the frantic Zoltan Dienes, who languished in a displaced persons' camp. His letters threatened "another tragedy" if Dickey didn't help speed his immigration.

Meanwhile the gang at the Overseas Press Club was convinced she'd gone to Hungary for her own self-aggrandizement. Arguing her case would have meant exposing the IRC and *Life* magazine, the latter having forewarned her that they would disown her if she messed up her assignment—and they had. Later she would write, "I knew the conditions under which I'd been employed, I'm proud of taking my medicine and coming back for more. . . . *I* made the mistakes; *I* was punished. End of story." Despite friends recalling that she seemed no different and never discussed her imprisonment, Dickey was changed. She had disappointed Leo, who impressed her; and she'd been humiliated upon discovering that she was not any better at being "shock cushioned" in the face of calamity, regardless of all her tough marine training.

If the rambling, incoherent tapes that Dickey recorded at *Life* magazine upon her return from Vienna are any indication of her true emotional state, she had been broken emotionally by her time in the commie prison. The typed transcripts appear to be an attempt by some *Life* magazine employee to define the circumstances of her capture, but Dickey makes absolutely no sense. She sounds like somebody who has yet to awaken from a nightmare, who has suffered a mental breakdown. She called it "losing my girlish laughter."

Dickey's deliverance from communist barbarity at the height of the cold war made her famous enough for the American Legion Auxiliary to ask her to address a thousand women on the topic of national security. She refused, not because of stage fright, but to protect her employers as well as six other Westerners still in prison in Hungary. The only talking she did was the following May, at a Washington hearing of the Internal Security Subcommittee on the "Hungarian crisis," at the urging of Wisconsin senator Alexander Wiley.

In a letter written to Julia Edwards in March 1957, Dickey denied the popular charge that she had entered Hungary specifically to get arrested and then write about it. She assured Julia that fifty-three days with the secret police "to get a story is something I wouldn't do either, and not alone on account of the diet. I assure you my time among them, so to speak, was about as involuntary as you can get."

Dickey sent a letter thanking AP reporter Carl Hartmann for "triggering the whole incredible mechanism of getting me the hell out of there." She sent Edward Clarke an equally thankful letter. Neither responded.

Dickey left her job at the institute at the end of February. She told members of the IRC that part of the reason was the treatment Maria Welsch was receiving. According to her letters to Dickey, the IRC's promises were not being honored. Although Dickey had kept uncustomarily silent since her return from Vienna, by February 13 she could no longer contain her frustration. She sent a memo to Leo Cherne: "Ferenc Welsch had reason to believe that he was serving the interests of Americans at the time, and that I was associated with both *Life* magazine and the International Rescue Committee. . . . In part because of his association with me, he is serving a prison term. . . ." Dickey believed Dr. Faust was breaking his promise to Mrs. Welsch and cited his ongoing habit of breaking appointments with her. She felt that "both a matter of personal and organizational honor is deeply involved."

The day after Dickey wrote this memo, she sent money to Vienna for Maria Welsch and Zoltan Dienes and asked them not to feel "too bitter about the delay which we had . . . to take care of you. It was a bad accident. I have never been so angry at my colleagues about anything in my life as I am about this. . . . It will not happen again."

Dickey also quit because now doors were swinging open. By March 1957 she had appeared on a few local television shows and had given at least one interview to a magazine. But in a letter to Julia Edwards on March 10, she wrote that "the TV appearances, the magazine piece, and the other appurtenances thereto that you mention so flatteringly have not so far produced enough revenue to justify even my own far more modest predictions." Nevertheless she felt the time was right to try her hand at free-lancing again. She had written Julia Edwards that the story of her imprisonment was simply burning to be told. She viewed her split from the IRC, RIA, and *Life* unhappily. "I don't know whether my descriptive powers or my sense of humor are surviving *that* too well. . . . But again—we'll see," she wrote Julia Edwards.

A Washington friend working at the International Cooperation Administration wrote: "The ordeal has consumed some dross, and refined a lot of gold in you. You've mellowed—and not been hurt permanently. . . . Your story *must* be published. In years to come there will be others who will have to undergo fiery trials, and they will be sustained in them by the memory of *your* indomitable courage. Your story will keep us weaker souls from cracking. And so your action there in Hungary under pressure will fortify the whole line of fighters against oppression. [If it should happen to me], I would keep saying to myself: 'Dickey did it. You can't let her down.' And so I might stand up to it."

Six years later, in 1963, the IRC honored Dickey Chapelle with a medal acknowledging its "unpayable debt to one who tried to help from inside the inferno." The occasion, the IRC's thirty-year anniversary "in the struggle against tyranny," was to recognize "journalists who at great personal risk told the story of freedom." Also honored was Gene Farmer, Dickey's *Life* magazine photo editor on the Hungarian refugees assignment, who had subsequently disowned her. Dickey believed it was because his boss, "Mr. Luce, thinks he has to do it to cover *other Life* people who may get into hot water with Communist secret police."

A little over three thousand dollars, to be shared with her brother, remained in Edna's estate. Dickey withdrew some of it. "I am no longer associated with *Life,* the International Rescue Committee, or the Research Institute of America," she wrote to her brother in March 1957. "Please feel free to draw your own conclusions, as long as they are unflattering to all three outfits and, I guess, to me too, for not suspecting there was a Russian patrol in that damn Hungarian cornfield in the first place."

Upon Dickey's release from prison, the Micheners had cabled an invitation to recuperate with them, so Dickey went down to their farm in Tinicum, Pennsylvania. They enjoyed her visit, except for her incessant cigarette smoking. With Jim Michener's encouragement Dickey worked on the story of her imprisonment, managing to bang out a seven-thousand-word magazine article and an outline for a book.

The Hungarian episode, or what Richard Selby referred to as "the Chapelle Affair," had turned Dickey into America's first cold war heroine. Dickey hired a lecture agent, Elizabeth Byrd (no relation to the admiral), who would book a three-month lecture schedule for the American woman who had escaped from a communist prison. Edna would have been proud to see what a popular public speaker her daughter became in the isolationist Midwest. Cured of her fear of public speaking by the urgency of her message, she electrified audiences in the Rotary Clubs, American Legion Halls, Chambers of Commerce, Knife & Fork Clubs, and high school auditoriums from Tenstrike, Minnesota, to Mason City, Iowa. Pacing back and forth on the boards, she galvanized her listeners with her stunning tale of a horrible world dominated by human automatons who upheld the tyranny of totalitarian systems, who scared the shit out of her.

Dickey appeared on the ever-popular "What's My Line," where a witty panel had to guess her occupation. But as hard as she tried to look the picture of sophistication, there was always something askew; her overdone harlequin glasses glittered oddly, or her nylons sported a wide run. Tony, somewhat more charitable now that he and Helga were married, also embarked on a new pastime: critiquing his former wife's budding public persona. "I said I would give you a report and here it is," he said about one of her television appearances. "You were damn good, but you should smile more, with your real smile, the little one."

Yet her growing fame failed to project Dickey into the mainstream. In 1957 the women's magazines were aimed at readers whose duties and main occupations lay in providing comfortable homes for their husbands. A woman like Dickey Chapelle, now eager to write about "government by terror, the form of tyranny that held me and now rules more people than any other," was, regardless of her bravery and heroics, an aberration. And to *Look* and *Life* she was persona non grata.

That hot July, sitting in her tiny East Side apartment, Dickey worked on helping her Hungarian friends Zoltan Dienes and Ferenc and Maria Welsch. She urged the International Rescue Committee to sponsor Zoltan Dienes to the United States, which eventually they would.

In July Dickey received word from Richard Selby in Budapest that Ferenc Welsch had been released from Fö Street, and she wrote Maria that she would try and raise five hundred dollars for her. She wrote to the New York office of General William Donovan, apologizing for taking up his valuable time but stressing that her business arose out of her "capture by the AVO" and was "in the interest of the United States." Otto C. Doering, Donovan's law partner and the former executive director of the OSS, replied from Washington that Donovan was critically ill, but Doering would be happy to discuss the situation with her. By November Dickey was able to send the Welsches a check for five hundred dollars with a carbon copy of the transaction going to the Washington law offices of Donovan, Leisure, Newton & Irvine.

This correspondence, Dickey's association with the IRC and with the *Reader's Digest* (whose relationship with the CIA is well documented), and her future involvement with the intelligence branches of the military and the CIA's always curious Ed Lansdale evidences an ongoing relationship of sorts between Dickey Chapelle and the American intelligence community. It is doubtful that Dickey's encounters with the intelligence community were based on any consistent, well-reasoned political stance, but rather on enlightened self-interest, driven by Dickey's restless, private demons, an amorphous inner enemy whom she called "the bogey man." Whether embodied by the rigidity and prejudice of Shorewood, the rage of the dying marine off Iwo Jima, or the terror at Fö Street, to triumph over it consumed her, driving her to "write and study about the things that threaten my serenity." The bogeyman, she'd discovered, had many faces. She could not hide from it, nor it from her.

She'd failed in her mission for Leo Cherne, but she had survived the bogeyman. It gave her a feeling of real confidence. She'd come to understand the meaning of the words "there is no limit to human endurance," and she wished nothing more than to keep proving it.

As the summer of 1957 progressed, Dickey had no idea how she was going to make her next dollar. But "I find I have brought something very good back with me," she wrote her old friend from CARE, John Kavanaugh. "I have a real compulsion to both write about and study the kind of government that held me—government by terror." She told him she did not know how she was going to finance this activity, but she was going to pursue it for the next few months. She was no longer represented by Marie Rodell and had been sending the Hungary piece out herself. She wrote the Plimmers that her Hungary story "is still around kicking unprofitably," and that Jim Michener seemed to have given up on her. But, far from discouraged, she intended to stay with free-lancing "until I go broke!"

In this photo, taken about 1934, Dickey is the big, bespectacled kid, stopping with her friends so she could salute the flag at the Shorewood Village square as she did every morning.

The Life

This photo appeared in the summer of 1940 in the *Milwaukee Journal* under the header, "She's Ready to Defend America."

Tony Chapelle, whose charm was legendary, was Dickey's photography teacher, first serious lover, and later her husband.

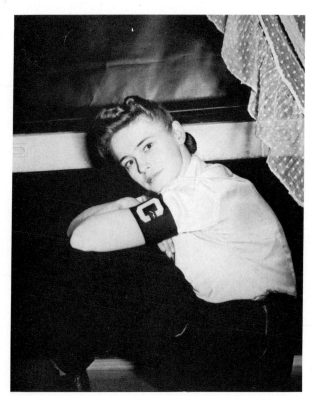

This photo was taken prior to leaving for assignment in Panama for *Look Magazine*. The C armband was the only badge of a correspondent's accreditation at that time. At the Chapelle's Riverside Drive apartment, 1942.

Taken in New York, at the 51st Street apartment of Grandma Engelhardt, 1943. Left to right, Dickey's favorite aunt, George (on the arm of the couch); Grandma Engelhardt; Dickey (seated); behind Dickey, her father Paul Meyer; next to him on couch, Lutie, Uncle Hans, and Edna.

This photo was featured in the July, 1945 issue of *Life Story*, a woman's magazine, for whom Dickey was employed as their war correspondent. She became the first woman photographer accredited to the war in the Pacific.

The Chapelle photo team: Dickey and Tony (1950–52), employed by the U.S. government's Point Four Program.

After breaking away from Tony, Dickey ran to the comfort and acceptance of the Marines. Here she is pictured at the U.S. Marine Corps Recruit Training Depot, San Diego, in 1955.

Dickey and Aunt Lutie embracing at Idlewild Airport, New York, days after her release from Budapest's notorious Fö Street Prison, about February 1, 1957.

In order to tell the story of the Algerian war from the rebel side, Dickey had to be smuggled through the French lines. Here she is inside the command post cave of the Scorpion Battalion of the Algerian rebels, in the Ksour mountains, the Algerian Front, in July, 1957.

"During the fighting for the town of LaMaya, I posed with Major Antonio Lusson, commander of one of the committed Castro battalions. While with the bearded ones, I kept my hair down since long hair was not a symbol of deprivation of femininity nor of femininity itself, since the men's hair was long." On assignment in Cuba, 1958 for *Reader's Digest*.

Milwaukee, 1959. "This is the photograph of me at work I like better than any other. It was taken covering the Marines on 'Operation Inland Seas' across the same beach where I learned to swim as a little girl."

Dickey and Leo Cherne, Hudson Institute, New York, 1962.

This photo appeared in *National Geographic*, November 1962 for Dickey's story, "Helicopter War in South Viet Nam." She was with the Sea Swallows in Ba Xuyen province, 1961. *(National Geographic Society.)*

Opposite page, below: On November 4, 1966, one year after Dickey was killed, Lieutenant General Lewis W. Walt and Lieutenant Colonel Nguyen Thanh Toai, Province Chief, Quan Tin Province, dedicated the Dickey Chapelle Memorial Dispensary. At the dedication ceremony, veteran correspondent Jim Lucas of Scripps-Howard News Syndicate remembered Dickey as "one hell of a girl," who refused to trade on her femininity to get her stories and didn't need to. "She beat us to death. We couldn't keep up with her. We ceased to try."

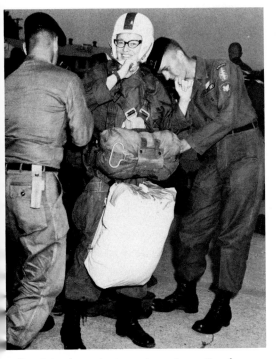

Receiving last minute pre-jump inspection from the 5th U.S. Special Forces Group, for U.S. Army Special Warfare School, Water Moccasin IV, June, 1963, Fort Stewart, Georgia. On assignment for *Reader's Digest.* About this photo, Dickey said, "This is the way I wished I always looked!"

Dickey Chapelle, the "bayonet border reporter," appeared on the Canadian Broadcasting Corporation's "Front Page Challenge," around 1963.

The Work

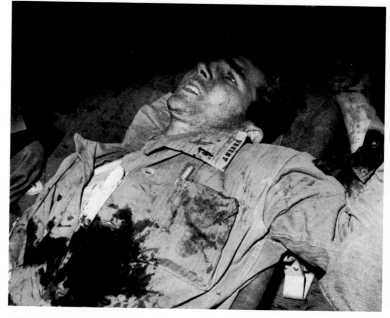

"Dying Marine," 1945, aboard the U.S.S. *Samaritan,* a hospital ship off Iwo Jima. U.S. Marine Pfc. William Fenton, Pittsburgh, Pa., lived and Dickey spent the following Christmas with him in a hospital in New York.

Dickey's love affair with the U.S. Marines probably started here, when she spent ten days in Okinawa "far forward" with this group of Marines, setting up a field hospital in 1945.

U.S. Marine training, 1955. Dickey had been invited by General John C. McQueen, the commanding officer of the Marine Recruit Depot in San Diego, California, "to describe to the American public just what goes into the making of a U.S. Marine . . . and the formula . . . for esprit de corps . . ."

Hungarian refugee flees into Austria, November 29, 1956, at the canal in the vicinity of the village of Tamsweg. Dickey shot this on assignment for *Life* magazine.

Nine thousand U.S. Marines landed in Beirut on July 15, 1958 to intervene in the country's so-called rebellion. Dickey covered the landing for *Reader's Digest* and *Argosy* magazine.

Cuba, 1958. Fidel Castro with Celia Sanchez, his constant companion (far left), and Vilma Espin (left of Fidel).

Cuba, 1958. Dickey wrote about how she watched in amazement as the rebels emptied their rifles and Browning automatics at Batista's American-made B26s.

Havana, Cuba, January, 1959. A jubilant group of Cubans celebrate Fidel Castro's triumphant approach into the capital. "I hope the revolution doesn't sit down and eat its children," Dickey told a colleague.

With U.S. Special Forces in Ban Hat Bay, on the Nam San river, Laos, 1961; covering "America's Secret War"; the chopper is the CIA-owned, Air America.

With the Vietnamese paratroopers in 1961–62, in a Mekong Delta village. "When paratrooper Pct. Cuu saw me check the dead man's eyelids, he wanted to make clear to me that such expressions of sympathy for the Viet Cong offended him. So he drew his .45 and just fired into the body of his foe when I made this picture."

This photo, shot in 1962 in Vietnam while on assignment for *National Geographic Magazine*, shows a combat-ready Marine. Despite U.S. government protests against showing what American advisors were actually doing in Vietnam, *National Geographic* decided to run this photo—the first ever—in their November, 1962 issue. The story went on to win the 1963 Press Photographer's Association "Photograph of the Year" award. (*National Geographic Society*)

"This is the sea of crab-laden mud in which the Sea Swallows set up the toughest ambush I've ever covered—almost twelve hours without moving. Reports on the ambush of the Sea Swallows were made by whispers and a man was permitted to move his arms and legs (if he did so slowly so he didn't make splashing noises) once every two hours. The men were in position for twelve hours."

Forward of Ban Hat Bay, Laos, 1961. "The trees and bushes make a cathedral vault over the road and a man cannot see a dozen yards to either side. A perfect ambush alley, miles of it . . . I still see with an urge to scream its story the terrible pathos of brave men moving inexorably into the lethal unknown—the tiny jungle patrol, the handful of parachutists plummeting at night into what they cannot guess but that it will be painful as well as deadly."

12

"Bayonet Border Reporter"

DICKEY described it as a rescue "right out of the *Perils of Pauline*," the silent-era movie serial in which the heroine was forever being snatched from the jaws of death in the last reel. Hobart Lewis, then assistant managing editor of the *Reader's Digest*, to whom Dickey had been introduced by James Michener, had that spring purchased one of her World War II articles, "The Quality of Mercy." The piece ran in the October 1957 issue. She happily wrote the Plimmers that the fee, around $1,000, "will keep me free-lancing for the summer."

Her efforts to write the article about Hungary fashioned at Michener's farm were still bouncing around collecting rejection slips "from some of the finest magazines," as she wryly wrote a business acquaintance. Nevertheless, all during the summer of 1957 she remained obsessed with the experience, wanting to write about "the human breaking point." She also doggedly dragged out her unsold marine story, telling one editor that "our assault force is being increasingly run by Momma," and that she believed this made the country vulnerable to better-prepared communist troops. But the editors at publications like the popular Sunday supplement *This Week* did not share her enthusiasm for tougher military training, nor her urge to alert the country. By now America was awakening to the threat of push-button nuclear annihilation at the hands of some commie maniac. The first inklings of protest could be heard among the poets and writers known as "Beats," but they were a tiny voice against the thunder of atomic tests being launched in the Nevada desert and defense drills in public schools.

Dickey was also trying to do some combat reporting. Most parts of the world were still settling differences on the ground. That's where she wanted to go—right into the warring belly of the "bogeyman." The *Digest* fee was sufficient to maintain her spartan life-style—her monthly rent was $85—while she tried to find an assignment to cover the one hot war on earth—the Algerian war on the rebel side.

The Algerian war for independence had begun in 1954, the same year their French rulers had been defeated by the Viet minh at Dien Bien Phu. For several years the French had imposed a successful censorship campaign, so that the only reports coming out painted the Algerian rebels as murderous barbarians, committing atrocities against the valiant, honorable French. In truth both sides were guilty of butchery, torture, and racism; but neither that nor the strong popular support for the rebels was being reported.

By the summer of 1957, the third year of the war, Dickey came to the story at the behest of Abdel Kadar Chanderli, the Algerian rebels' representative at the United Nations. By then the rebels were so desperate for Western coverage that they'd begun offering bribes to French correspondents. Dickey wrote that Chanderli wanted two things reported to the American people: that the fighting between the French and the rebels be explained for what it was—a war—and that the rebel side of the story be told. Dickey told him that she believed communiqués from any side of any war were untrustworthy, that there had to be another way to get the word from the rebels to the American press. Chanderli then told her that there was. He wanted to send an American journalist directly from New York to cover the fighting on the rebel side, but he couldn't find anybody willing to take him up on his offer.

A reporter would have to be smuggled in through Morocco (where French troops were massed in the nominally free country), and an Egyptian reporter attempting the trip had been caught and sentenced to death. Although the reporter was eventually rescued by the Algerian rebels, few correspondents felt a desire to follow in his footsteps. Then, in the winter of 1956, two enterprising American filmmakers managed to get through successfully and to document the rebels in a film later televised in the States. Dickey knew one of them, Peter Throckmorton (who would later introduce her to his photo agent, Nancy Palmer). After seeing the footage, Dickey no doubt recalled Tony Chapelle's commandment: "Be there first." She could taste a real scoop. If she could get herself over there, she would be the first American woman to cover the war from the rebel side, that of the FLN (Front de Libération Nationale).

Chanderli told her that he'd already cleared her through his people, who were impressed by her behavior in Hungary, telling her, "You have known terror yourself; you will understand how it is with us who are its victims, too." He outlined her method of discovery into rebel hands, which would begin with her kidnapping from Madrid. She was enthusiastic, telling him, "You're looking for a guinea pig with no dependents, no commitments, a little backing, and a positive taste for being a kidnapee." And for somebody with an assignment from a national publication.

But despite her notoriety and unquenchable enthusiasm, Dickey could not stir up any interest at women's magazines, which were busy running articles like "Why I'm Glad I'm Not a Man." Nor were newsmagazines and newspapers eager for coverage of the anti-American side. One editor cautioned, "You can't get that story! North Africa's not safe for any Westerner right now. The first Algerian soldier you see will cut your throat."

Dickey persisted, finally locating a small news syndicate who didn't slam the door in her face, but to whom she had to prove the newsworthiness of words and pictures from the rebel side. She spent hours in the New York Public Library reading back issues of newsmagazines to make certain her story would be an "exclusive," then typed a proposal, which convinced the syndicate's owner, Stirling Spadea, that her article would sell to some of his fifty-five newspaper clients. Spadea, who would place her long-languishing Marine Corps story "Momma Runs the Marines" in newspapers such as the *Kansas City Star* and the *St. Petersburg Independent* that August, advanced Dickey $630 for the plane ticket.

On a still, hot day, she took a short walk from her apartment at 487 First Avenue to a modern, sterile building near the United Nations, the U.S. headquarters for the Algerian Front of the National Liberation

Army. When she left her meeting with Abdel Kadar Chanderli, she had a new name, not "guinea pig," which Chanderli felt had "no poetry," but "squirrel," and became the first American to obtain accreditation to the Algerian rebels from the States.

Her "kidnapping" would follow the same intrigue-filled steps as those of Throckmorton's trip to the FLN the year before. She would fly to Madrid, meet her kidnappers at the unlisted Algerian embassy there, and be spirited to Rabat, Morocco, and thence to Algeria.

Dickey couldn't wait. It was a reward for her misery in Hungary, martial music to her ears, a page torn from the life of Richard Harding Davis, a true believer that "war is fun." The journey, which was begun in late July, went off without a hitch. Dickey described "being passed like a package through a working underground that, as Abdel Kadar had told me, spanned borders halfway around the world." She was moved by plane, car, truck, horse, and mule and on foot. She dressed as a German tourist and as a veiled Arabian woman. She was housed in Arab homes, stables, ammo dumps, and tribal tents of Berber herdsmen. Her escorts changed each day; they were European and Algerian refugees, couriers, and infantrymen in North Africa. In the Overseas Press Club's anthology, *How I Got That Story,* published posthumously, Dickey told of being flown from Madrid to Rabat, Morocco, with her young Algerian "kidnappers." Still blinking under the blazing North African sun, she was smuggled into the dark confines of a rebel harem. There, among Rubensesque veiled women with whom she was ordered to sleep, she waited with machine-gun-toting young Algerians for the next step in the journey, playing solitaire and listening to the sound of French army trucks and jeeps on the other side of the wall. The first questions from the rebels were "What do your people believe about our revolution?" and "When will America stop arming France?" In response Dickey asked them if they were terrorists. One replied, "Against terror one uses terror." She could understand that.

After signing a declaration releasing the FLN from any responsibility should she be maimed or killed, Dickey set off for the Algerian Sahara with her English-speaking guide. It was late July in the burning desert; only the four hundred troops and Dickey Chapelle would brave the white, blistering sands.

During a three-day walk from Morocco to Algeria, sleeping inside the rebel-held rock caves of the Ksour Mountains, Dickey prevailed in the face of extreme physical hardship. She proudly wrote that she learned to survive on a pint of water and two cups of tea a day in the North African Sahara, where the summer temperature easily climbed past 110 degrees. She limited urination to once a day. During the day she wrapped a thick blanket around herself to reduce and contain perspiration. She could walk five hours in the furnacelike heat without a break, on a daily ration of half a dozen dates and a chunk of sugar "the size of my hand"; she could sleep on a rock. The "pride" was important, if for no other reason than to help relieve the pain.

On night patrols the rebels hunted for undetonated NATO high-explosive aerial bombs, which Dickey returned to photograph during the day to show that the French aerial bombs were American made. "You know, your country really is my country's enemy, not France," the rebel commander told her. "We can bleed France white. But always America revives her with arms and money when she would faint without them."

Dickey's interpreter, Lamara, a lanky, easygoing junior battalion officer, started up a steep hill that she reckoned was as high as a ten-story apartment building, called Black Point. As the orange sunset washed the mountains around them into shadows, Dickey placed her feet in Lamara's footsteps, feeling as if she were on a ghastly treadmill. The commander's words rang in her ears.

"The hill had become a barrier," she wrote. "A high barrier that kept us from understanding what was happening here." She wondered if the barrier was only a lack of information about what was going on in Algeria, a story that few Americans knew or cared about. Perhaps it was what an editor friend had said: "Total distrust."

The only comfort was Lamara's huffing and puffing; between gasps he told her, "I've never seen anybody undergo such effort only to do their job. I offer you my admiration." Despite the compliment, she stopped, pulse pounding in her ears, and leaned against the rock, eyeing the top. It hadn't looked like much of a hill, just as distrust didn't seem like much of a barrier—until the chips were down. She made it, finally, when Lamara reached behind and extended his hand to her. Instantly she began to climb. Dickey wrote, "There—always—lies the challenge to meet, the hill to climb."

That evening, as they moved slowly down the hillside, they detected signs of a French patrol intersecting their path. Everyone threw themselves behind the nearest rocks. Lamara, who carried a Colt .45, shared her cover. It seemed forever until one of the scouts appeared, reporting that the trail across the valley was enemy free. Dickey asked Lamara about his little gun. He told her that his orders were to make sure none of the patrol was captured. "Especially not you."

"Why not me? My country is the ally of the French. They won't harm an American reporter."

"You don't understand, missy," Lamara answered. "That's just it. They'll cut your throat. But first they'll face you toward Mecca, and then they'll say *we* did it."

In the morning the rebels told her they were proud of her for climbing the hill.

On August 1 Dickey was taken forward of the battalion headquarters. Placed upon an unusually docile Arabian horse named La Coste, after the French governor-general of Algeria, and led by a boy holding the reins, she went higher into the rocky hillsides to photograph five tribes of shepherds, an estimated five hundred people who wanted to join up with the FLN.

It was here that she had her first experience with the rebel-held courts, where junior officers decided everything from wills and marriages to executions. Not too much later, inside one of the many rebel-held caves, she was asked to photograph the execution by firing squad of a seventeen-year-old "confessed spy." She had interviewed the slight young boy in a turban and torn blue jacket and made it last as long as possible, remembering "how welcome any diversion was to a person in custody." She listened to him admit his crimes, not believing the translation, that he had slit the throats of countless women and children. He was too young and beautiful, "with the face and grace of a Victorian poet."

She resented the request, queasy with the knowledge that the presence of a photographer and visible sympathy for the youth had precipitated his execution, yet aware that if she declined, she would break journalism's cardinal rule, to portray the truth of the moment despite personal revulsion. Immediately she began playing with her cameras, the reflexive habit she'd developed long ago to distract her in moments of fear. She informed the Algerian colonel in charge that she would photograph the execution only if she could photograph the trial, hoping for a time-consuming military trial that would drag on past her departure. But the boy confessed.

It was the hottest part of the day, moving toward dusk. Dickey smiled as she checked the light meter, trusting she would not have enough light. "I recalculated the light meter readings on the circular slide rule. There was no use arguing with the numbers," she later wrote. "Pictures were possible in this light. They might even be good," she added with a pro's cynicism.

The prisoner was led forward. The youth seemed more at ease than anyone. Now that he was facing his end, she noticed that his skin was clear and barely sweating. The planes of his face were curved like a child's, and there was no hair on them. His gestures were wide and graceful. Through a translator, he told Dickey that the French promised him food in exchange for identifying rebel villages. After the villages were burned, he was sent to slit the throats of the survivors. For each completed mission, he was paid ten dollars.

Dickey saw that the prisoner's brown face reflected the light from the pink walls of the mountains. Four guards led him down a rock-strewn hill. He did not stumble. Eight volunteers were selected for the firing squad. A low jutting stone was designated by the senior officer as the place where the prisoner was to stand. A sergeant fumbled to free the man's handcuffs and took the white turban off his head, making it a re-straint for his forearms, which were crossed at his waist behind him. The sergeant led him the final few yards, then pointed imperiously to the spot where he would die. The prisoner stepped forward and faced the east and the firing squad, erect and grave. In a photo essay for a 1961 issue of *Coronet* magazine, the popular digest-size weekly, Dickey com-mented that the barefoot spy marched before the firing squad "graceful and composed. . . . I sensed he felt obliged to make the job as easy as possible for his executioners. Professional courtesy, you might call it."

The officer began the commands at the instant his sergeant stepped free of the field of fire: "*Wahid . . . jeuj . . . tetta!*" The last word was lost in sound. There were no blanks among the rifles of the squad. The bullets tore into the assassin's smooth brown flesh, and he fell backward as if the wind had pushed him. Blood spread into a puddle. The only instructions to Dickey were "Please be sure your pictures show that the body was removed without being mutilated."

Upon her return to New York, Spadea placed her Algerian piece in fifty newspapers. It had not been unprofitable. Dickey later wrote of the rebels, who'd come to accept her, "They would now go back . . . to fight on. I would go back to a bed, shower . . . eat all the food my stomach would hold, and wonder why, in a world of order and plenty, it was so hard to tell of violence and want. Strangest of all in that moment was the fact that to try to do this was my profession." The pictures of the execution were subsequently purchased by *Life* and *Pageant* but were considered too violent to publish. However, *Pageant* did run her story, "Now I Know Why the Algerians Fight," in their April 1958 issue, while *Argosy,* the men's adventure magazine, ran her story and every grim frame in its October 1958 issue "The Executioners."

Dickey's reporting from Algeria finally established her as a combat reporter. This time her colleagues did not question her motivation. Even Julia Edwards revised her opinion of Dickey, whose tough-written pieces on Algeria for *Pageant* and *Argosy* were the envy of many less adventurous reporters. "She collected evidence that the French were dropping bombs supplied by the North Atlantic Treaty Organization for the defense of Europe, not for a colonialist war in Africa," Julia wrote approvingly, recalling that Dickey's success as the first American woman reporter to cover the Algerian fighters' side of that war "inspired several newsmen to follow in her footsteps. . . ." She returned to praise, not derision. *Pageant* called her "intrepid," *Argosy* hailed her as their "photographer-on-the-spot." *Coronet* heralded Dickey as a "blond-haired divorcée, a photographer-reporter . . . willing to go anywhere and risk anything for a story." The title over her *Coronet* photographs was "I Roam the Edge of Freedom."

In the meantime, Dickey's article "Nobody Owes Me a Christmas," the sanitized account of her mission into Hungary, finally found a home in the December 1957 issue of *Reader's Digest.* The piece won the magazine's First Person $2,500 award contest and would prove to be one of the publication's most popular articles. But when the *Digest,* famous for its scrupulous research, contacted *Life* magazine to inquire if she had indeed worked as a stringer for them in Vienna, the magazine denied it. To square herself with the *Digest,* Dickey, who never threw anything away, produced the magazine's check stub from November 14, 1956, marked "Advance for coverage of Hungarian refugees."

In a letter years later to her photo agent, Nancy Palmer, Dickey bitterly recalled the incident. "Why did *Life* do this? Because they said they would and at the time I agreed to it. I am convinced their practice is shameful, appeasing, and one of the most reprehensible and dangerous practices for journalists I can imagine. *But Mister Luce thinks it's neces-*

sary. Anyhow, the miasma of this difference in his and my approach to terrorist secret police still does shadow my name around *Life.*"

Her decision not to air those grievances proved prescient. It would only have jeopardized her golden opportunity by tarnishing her new relationship with the *Digest,* at the time read by sixteen million Americans. Better that she stick to her palatable slice of the truth: the tale of a steely American woman with ten pounds of humanitarian medicine in her knapsack captured by the commies. In any case, she had finally accomplished what she'd set out to do so many years before: to become a combat reporter—and a well-paid and well-known one to boot.

The *Reader's Digest,* America's ultraconservative monthly and self-appointed keeper of the flame, had warned its readers of the communist threat before the end of World War II. No doubt the editors found Dickey's patriotism a great asset, and her imprisonment in Hungary lent real cachet. But as they would come to realize, her patriotism was keenly personal, even idiosyncratic. Dickey believed, as did most Americans in the 1950s, that there was a slave world and a free world. Yet despite her extravagant enthusiasm for the military and avowed hatred of communism, her politics were naive and highly personal, not partisan. She viewed her position as "antigovernment by fear," adding that "if I knew what liberty and democracy meant in general terms, I'd be pro-them, but I only understand the terms as they apply to specific cases—so I can't make that claim. I side for prisoners against guards, enlisted men against officers, weakness against power. . . . I can't hope to change what our enemies do. But if I fail to point out where I believe we are contributing to their victories, I can't live with me. I'd call this the only patriotic point of view and any aberrance from it disloyal. I hope I can live up to it!"

The *Digest* provided that opportunity. It called her "one of the bravest women around, one of the best reporters and photographers in the business," whose "determination to be where things are happening has carried her into some of the most violent action in a violent world, and her sympathy for people in trouble has led her time and again to disregard personal safety." They saw a nobility of purpose about her, "humor, courage, pathos . . . the urge to report to people at home what the score is on the front lines of freedom." Just as long as her articles followed the *Digest's* policy—usually that of the government—they got published. The magazine apparently had no problem with her having written of the anti-American feeling in Algeria, articles that were published in *Pageant* and *Argosy*. Her position was not anti-American, but, as she wrote, that of a "neutral observer" who reported that the "tide of history was for independence in dozens of onetime colonies, and it was washing across many of them with little bloodshed." Yet in Algeria "it had meant war." The *Digest* accepted Dickey's quirky point of view, never doubting her patriotism; as it approvingly wrote, "What Dickey was doing . . . was getting at the story behind the story."

Although not under contract to the magazine, she was one of its steadiest contributors. Dickey couldn't have been more pleased. The *Reader's Digest* may not have been *The New York Times,* but it had millions more readers. Besides, Hobart Lewis, now the editor-in-chief, was a real fan of hers.

For the next four years the *Reader's Digest* was the main sponsor of trips and articles largely of her choosing. Her lecture agent, Elizabeth Byrd of Crawford Productions, was able to peg her midwestern lecture swings, which took up several months each year, to her latest *Digest* pieces.

Dickey, never secure with the *Digest* despite its praise, managed to overcome her nervousness with her growing recognition as a combat reporter, once mentioning she felt she was keeping score "from the far side of the cold war" as she fulfilled her own personal need to confront the bogeyman. "We have a war for the world on our hands," she wrote a friend in 1957. "[We] must be better than the enemy, whoever he is. . . . The idea is pure challenge, pure adventure." She believed that by her reporting on the ground battles of the cold war, she could keep watch and keep score and fulfill a promise "to make certain she would be the last woman held in a communist prison." The *Digest* enabled her to do so without—initially, at least—compromising her conscience.

It was no surprise when Dickey's brother turned on his car radio one Sunday night around Christmas 1957 to hear radio evangelist Billy Graham reading her latest *Reader's Digest* piece as part of his sermon.

Dickey was then in the Mediterranean, sent there in November by the *Digest* on a dual assignment, to cover the U.S. Sixth Fleet and its gunboat diplomat commander, the bible-quoting Vice Admiral Charles Randall "Cat" Brown, and to report on the status of the NATO-backed Turkish army.

In a letter to her aunts from Athens on November 24, Dickey first promised them she would not be indulging in "any games" and then went on to remind them that like her paternal grandmother, who wanted to perform as a tightrope artist in the circus, she, too, liked the "high-line." She had become a veteran, she wrote, of this "piece of rope from the upper deck of one warship across 100 feet of roiling water to the upper deck of another warship when both of them are moving about fifteen miles an hour in the same direction." She went on in more detail so that her aunts could really get a thrill. "From the piece of rope they hang a chair in which sits the person wanting to get from one ship to the other, and then the chair is moved, by sailors hand-hauling on one ship, over to the other across the water. I've now done eight such crossings between a carrier, two destroyers and a missile cruiser."

Right before her death, Dickey's octogenarian aunt Lutie recalled her niece as so filled with love of life and enthusiasm for her work that any attempt to enforce prudence would have been tantamount to cruelty.

Dickey's Mediterranean adventures also involved some imaginative helicopter landings when the weather was good and the decks large enough. "The pilots fly so low they have to *climb* before they make their landing," she wrote Lutie and George, "climb up the side of the ship so it looks like they were on an elevator. But not all ships have room. In that case, the 'copter hovers about thirty feet up over the deck. They put a piece of padded rope around me and I hold on to it while it is reeled down until my feet settle on the ship's deck. Then I let go of the rope, take off the sling and my life jacket. . . . If by all this you get the general idea that the Mediterranean Fleet is pleased to have its own female correspondent (as long as she represents 16,000,000 readers)—I expect you're right."

She could not have been happier walking the length of the ship with Admiral Brown in her new sable-colored trench coat. When the admiral asked if she enjoyed it, she first apologized to him for being a ham, then readily admitted "enjoying every minute of it." How different from last year's experience in Hungary; now she was representing the *Digest* in Turkey, whose geographic location "with the forces of communism on two sides" made it the most exposed country in the NATO alliance. "Yet," she wrote, "no military man—and few statesmen—prophesy military catastrophe for Turkey." Why? This was what she wanted to understand.

Like Algeria, Turkey was engaged in bloody combat, having fought its oppressor, Russia, at least thirteen times in eight generations. Unlike her position in Algeria, in Turkey she was a friend. Although she could not think of anything as monotonous as "staring across a trickling river at another soldier staring back at you"—which was what the Turks and the Russians had been doing along the border for the past thirty-seven years—she found the mood "that of combat troops who expect to jump off in assault at dawn." She patrolled where Russian soldiers "man the last tower of the Iron Curtain," finding herself close enough to the Red gunners "to count the buttons of their blouses." She wrote disapprovingly of Turkey's admitted press censorship and believed the reason its soldiers weren't pessimistic or apathetic was because "the Turkish soldier masters every military art but one, retreat." To her, this country with its twelve combat-ready divisions and NATO missiles was, except for the Sixth Fleet, the major force in the Middle East, "an object lesson in self-defense."

In a note to Stevie Blick, thanking her for taking out her garbage and turning off her electric coffeepot, she urged Stevie to stop dieting and come to Turkey, where Turkish officers were feeding Dickey six thousand calories a day and ignoring her protestations of getting fat with "We like you that way." She described a flight as co-pilot in an old Turkish air force C-47: "Fortunately it was a [short trip], so the outcome was happy after all." She asked Stevie to tell Tony and Helga "that I'm staying out of jail this year." To her ever-loving aunts, she wrote that she had spent her New Year's Eve marked with "real good fun." She went on patrol with the Turkish First Army along the Bulgarian border. "They've supplied me with a parade of accompanying officers, each more handsome than the ones before, and each assuring me that my comfort is his duty." With Stevie she was candid.

"Most of the officers are married and broke, I regret to say. But they are charming." When she told them she had spent her last New Year's Eve in the Fö Street prison, they presented her with her own tank brigade. She jumped off the tank, forgetting that "I wasn't twenty, and twisted my knee. I'd do it again any day for the sake of the utterly Turkish dialogue which went with it." The Turkish soldiers once held a concert for her by lantern light, singing of death and glory. Never so moved by music before, Dickey thought it was like a scene out of the Middle Ages. How could she ever be lonely when moments of such beauty bounced her way?

As the first (again!) American female accredited to cover them, Dickey was asked by the Turkish army to report that they were not abusing the planes, guns, and tanks received from the United States. Dickey's actual job, "to honestly see and say," came second on their list. She wrote her aunts that "they can't see, as long as I am swamped in tea, compliments, and [aerial] demonstrations, why I should need anything more." As a woman susceptible to flattery, she didn't. But as a reporter, it made her job difficult.

Dickey remained in the Mediterranean through February covering John Foster Dulles and the anticommunist Baghdad Pact meeting for the *Digest.* She wrote her aunts, "I swear Secretary of State John Foster Dulles winked at me avuncularly." Then she went to interview Turkish Prime Minister Adnan Menderes, whose approval of NATO nuclear missile sites along his border with Russia may have precipitated a bomb going off at the American embassy on January 26.

"I CAN'T SAY that I intended to be a 'bayonet border' specialist, but that's what seems to have happened," she wrote to an editor at Random House on March 15, 1958, before setting out on her midwestern lecture swing. "Now I wonder—if I go on doing this kind of story, as a woman— is there a book in it? At this point," she added, "I guess I sound a little confused. I am. I seem to be missing a boat I'd like very much to catch, and I simply don't know how to go about it." Random House offered no solution.

Despite this avowed confusion, Dickey Chapelle, the "bayonet border reporter," was a big draw on the heartland's rubber-chicken-and-mashed-potato lecture circuit, thrilling her growing audiences with her exotic adventures. "Nobody but me," she wrote from Clear Lake, Iowa, on April 26, 1958, "seemed to see any incongruity about getting up after a nice big lunch to talk about the attrition of diet in a Red prison, or the momentum of vengeance in Algeria."

The month before, she had elaborated on her trip in the Middle East and the Turkish army and air force for a group of marine intelligence officers specializing in the study of the Turkish language at New York's Columbia University. "Your informal and easygoing delivery was right up the gyrenes' alley," declared Lieutenant Colonel J. W. Eben. Eben, the organizer of the event, wrote Dickey from New York's Princeton Club to thank her for her "on-the-spot pix," which he believed brought the group "face to face with our fellow *asker*" (the Turkish word for soldier).

In the years to come, Dickey's "on-the-spot pix" from the front lines of Algeria, Lebanon, Cuba, and Southeast Asia, as well as her expertise on limited war capabilities and the motivational tactics of guerrilla forces, provided valuable intelligence at military briefings, the Pentagon, and the country's think tanks. Very quickly she came to believe that her privileged eyewitnessing gave her a better perspective on ground fighting than the defense experts she came to brief—which in many instances was true—and that if they knew what was good for the country, they'd listen to her.

"You asked me what would have worked in Hungary and Cuba, or might work in Algeria," she wrote an official at the Pentagon, directing him to one of her articles on "a weapons system I feel has a practical capability in limited war situations. . . . The *unarmed* opening gambit is what I'm suggesting . . . and not out of any idealism at all any more. . . . I'm not running down special weapons as a means of imposing will over will . . . but my country seems to be having a very dickens of a time reconciling our nonaggressive pretensions with any kind of effective military timing." She wryly commented that their usual response to her advice was "Oh, baby, why don't you go fry your hat."

Dickey Chapelle, the bristlingly confident, if totally bizarre, bayonet border reporter, began to appear frequently on local New York radio shows, including "Tex and Jinx," "Long John Nebel," Barry Farber's talk show, and WOR's newsman John Wingate's radio and television show, "Nightbeat." Wingate's television shows were formatted along the lines of Mike Wallace's hard-hitting "Interviews." Wingate's researchers were thorough, so much so that when Dickey left her lecture tour for a preinterview with Wingate for her appearance on his April 8, 1958, show, she was completely rattled by what she described to Stevie as "dragging in and bone-shaking every skeleton in my closet, from my casualness about Okinawan fronts to the end of my marriage. It wasn't libelous and it would have made a highly amusing show for everyone but me, my lecture tour, and the *Reader's Digest.*" On the air he didn't bring any of it up, except to tease Dickey about being on so many front lines, which she appreciated as the "best personal publicity. What on earth bought or scared him off?" she asked Stevie. "We'll probably never know."

Tony, bedded down with another heart attack, found it good therapy to keep track of his glamorous former wife. He had become nostalgic, almost paternal. "You were at your very, very best," he said of her appearance on the John Wingate show, noting as the erstwhile photography teacher that the lighting made her look as though she were in a police lineup. "I have never known you to be more completely at ease and to have a better command of your subject." Both he and Helga were "proud" of her. And should Dickey wonder where his heart lay, he wrote, "On the marriage question [that Wingate asked], it seemed you sort of hinted that marriage would be a more desirable existence than that of a foreign correspondent. It might be for some, but it most assuredly wouldn't be for you. I do not know of another man in the world with whom you could have had a measure of both as you did have with me and would have continued to have if it had not been that I burned out my bearings."

Dickey responded from St. Ansgar, Iowa, that he was "100% right. I don't know of anybody else, either."

Tony always wanted Dickey to know about his latest health problems, which Stevie, who worked as Dickey's part-time secretary, did her best to keep from her while she was on the road. But eventually Tony's insistence would pay off and Stevie would find herself writing Dickey about his latest "near disaster."

The formerly cavalier Tony must have felt that he'd burned out not only his bearings, but also his luck. He asked Dickey to return his long-ago juju, the pin of a leg on a pair of wings, "now that you are no longer superstitious about it. . . . Maybe it would bring me a charmed life. Although you stopped wearing it in Hungary . . . and still got by beautifully."

By now Dickey could afford nostalgia. Having survived Tony, she held on to the cornerstone of their relationship: he had been the first to believe in her. Dickey sent him the charm from Cedar Rapids, Iowa. "I have as of now telepathically transferred its benediction back to you, where it belongs," she wrote. "You must never think I don't or ever didn't believe in it."

13

"The Needs a Woman Has"

For DICKEY, life on the road was "ironic and curious." The lecture bureau of the University of Minnesota had set up a two-month hop in conjunction with Elizabeth Byrd, to whom Dickey paid a thirty percent commission. Dickey also paid her own travel expenses, but the lecture bureau supplied her with a 1957 two-tone "puke pink Chevrolet, with sick oyster white" to drive from one booking to the next. Dickey had no driver's license, but she was never one to let such details get in the way of her getting "from A to B," as Stevie Blick recalled.

The desolate midwestern interstate highways she drove in the spring of 1958 pulled at her memory. Her thoughts turned crazily to her parents as the gas guzzler sped from Worthington, Minnesota, into St. Ansgar, Iowa, "in the heart of the garden spot of Iowa." Her father had made his living driving a Chevy and staying in the same kinds of hotels. And Edna had lectured four nights a week to her adult decorating classes.

She wrote Stevie, "I keep wondering whether Dad and Mother would be pleased or horrified to see their child consulting road maps, reading mail, and writing lecture notes—all behind the wheel, which is how I remember both of them. There's one difference, though. If either of them had ever gotten a paycheck like I get . . . Lordy!" Out of character, she added wistfully, "Then I'd have had those dancing lessons Mother wanted for me, and that education in the local ladylike college, and . . . oh dear! things would have been different!" What an odd comment from this iconoclastic woman who wrote of her life as an adventurer, "The word means to dare in my dictionary—and I like the consequences . . . the sense of inner security that comes from having survived enough so that you can say to yourself that the next unknown or other threat won't panic you either." This is one of the only recorded times Georgie Lou Meyer bobbed to the surface, uncertain, belying the confident war correspondent, a "traveling salesman for Peace and Freedom." She was a good salesperson, igniting her audience as her harlequin glasses picked up the spotlights, pacing on her career-lady high heels, her croaky, smoky voice running rapid.

"It's not work, telling tales about machine-gun bullets clipping over my head and bayonets shaving my ear and Red interrogators shaking their fists in my face. I enjoy it," she wrote to Stevie Blick from Worthington, Minnesota, on March 22, 1958. "The trouble with my stories is that . . . by this time they even have a phony ring to me. But, God bless 'em, not apparently to my audience."

Along lonely, snowbound highways of Wisconsin, Minnesota, Iowa, and South Dakota, she stayed in motels and ate in restaurants called Chat and Chew. All the coffee looked like "blond dish water," she wrote her aunts, longing for the strong Turkish coffee she'd come to appreciate, "but it's hot," while the food was "grim but ample." She wasn't drinking and was getting to sleep by ten o'clock and complaining that there were "no vices out here." One night in South Dakota, she dreamed up a harmless amusement. In her third-floor room, a knotted rope on a hook was imbedded in the window frame. For fun Dickey hung on it, writing her aunts, "But I didn't succeed in pulling down the whole wall as I thought I might." But although her official line was that sex was something she had long ago dispensed with, it's unlikely that Dickey was celibate. She wrote a boyfriend she'd met in judo class at the New York YMCA, "There are no lost women, only mislaid ones. See you when I get back in New York." Not a serious lover, he had ingratiated himself sufficiently to have a key to her apartment. "He was younger than she," was all closemouthed Stevie Blick would later recall. His place in Dickey's life was no different from that of the other men Dickey hooked up with on her assignments and lecture tours. Most of them were either younger or married. After fifteen years of Sturm und Drang with Tony, she felt little desire for another permanent liaison. In her opinion relationships were a lot more dangerous than going on patrol in combat, where at least she could be aware of and prepared for the dangerous consequences.

Having discovered sexual liberation in a time when free sexual attitudes were not tolerated, Dickey was smart enough to keep that part of her life well hidden. She told television and newspaper interviewers that a woman could not be both a wife and a foreign correspondent, that correspondents were "created out of the simple compulsion to go see for themselves what is happening." Because of the competition for assignments, she explained, "The odds are heavily in favor of the man or woman who yields to the fewest distractions in obeying the compulsion. It's a twenty-four-hour-a-day task until a story's done, and you cannot know as you start covering an event where it may lead you. Till it's done, people you love always receive less evidence of love than the correspondent wants to give them." But despite this carefully crafted public response, which made her sound like a nun, and her insistence on wearing fatigues even away from the front (causing many acquaintances to wonder if she were a lesbian), Sergeant Robert Morrisey emphasized that Dickey was "all woman with all the needs a woman has." Letters to Stevie over the years to come reveal a lonely, if sexually active, woman who would write from Laos in 1961, "I know what I'd like to send you, one of these Special Forces types, but I won't because I haven't got my own yet."

The highlight of one of her lecture tours came when she was taken to lunch in Waterloo, Iowa, by two of the town's "handsomest" marines. In Mason City, Iowa, in her fanciest clothes, the local Kiwanis Club serenaded her with "Let Me Call You Sweetheart." She wrote Stevie that she didn't think "anything much better ever happened to an American career girl."

She was meeting machinery salesmen, managers of oil pipelines, and car salesmen and dating local school superintendents. In Cedar Rapids she ran into a former Point Four pilot to reminisce with over the inevitable watery coffee. But wherever it was she found herself, she'd draw a crowd—kids, mostly, listening in rapt amazement to her rapid talking. And after deducting her living expenses and income tax, what did she have to show? Glory and a dull pencil and a good feeling after she signed the autographs. "Because," she wrote to Stevie, "right away I want to get myself right back overseas and live up to the image of me I see in those sweet kids' eyes. Okay, okay, how silly can you be!"

But the risks she was determined to take, and her insistence on "eyeballing" events from the front line, did not guarantee Dickey her pick of magazine assignments. "She was a woman, and most photo editors were male," recalled Nancy Palmer, who became Dickey's photo agent in 1958. "Most of them simply didn't believe she shot half the pictures she did. And I must say that women editors were not much better. So she worked cheaper than the male photographers, because she wanted the assignments." Nancy characterized her arrangement with Dickey as "loose." She recalled that Dickey did a lot of her own agenting.

Back in New York in May 1958, Dickey wanted nothing more than to get an assignment to Cuba to cover the obscure revolutionary leader Fidel Castro. Having established contact with Castro supporters in New York, she found that her information conflicted with published reports that Castro's "motley" army was being slaughtered by better-armed government troops. She was distressed that neither the editors of the *Digest* or *Life*, with whom she conferred at length, nor the letters sent to *Look* and the *Saturday Evening Post* would assign her the opportunity to report from the rebel side. As she wrote her revolutionary contacts, "I have read every report from Cuba with my heart as well as my eyes, and I am sure the 'news' we are getting is not correct. I also believe that I might have, were I there, been able to learn and report more accurately the progress of the events."

She was also having a problem getting an assignment to the Mediterranean, her other area of choice, taking breaks in her flurry of phone calls and letter writing to go to the gym and the dentist and to learn how to use skin-diving equipment. She discovered a pool on Twenty-third Street and wrote Lutie, "With the market for underwater photography increasing all the time *plus* my needing the exercise, I'll give it a whirl. Just call me mermaid."

Citing the multitude of stories that she believed was about to erupt in Algeria, Greece, and Lebanon, she finally elicited some interest from the *Digest,* but not enough to cover an extensive trip, despite free transportation to the Mediterranean and the Sixth Fleet thanks to her relationship with Admiral Cat Brown. She beat the bushes offering her free-lance services to *Look,* the *Milwaukee Journal,* the *Chicago Tribune,* the *New York News Syndicate, Newsweek, Esquire,* and the *Saturday Evening Post.* All turned her down. Undaunted, she pitched her ideas to *Argosy,* to which she'd sold her Algerian piece, "The Executioners." The monthly publication advertised itself as the "largest selling fiction-fact magazine," but it was far better known for its blood-and-guts depiction of current events than its high literary standards.

"I think the greatest advantage of this project to *Argosy* is having your own writer-photographer in a 'hot' world corner this particular summer," she wrote to them in a letter proposing Mediterranean coverage. Although the jealously guarded men's magazine had historically shunned assigning women stories, its editors had been so impressed by Dickey's daring coverage of the Algerian rebels that it broke its long-standing rule. They sent her off and deposited a check for one thousand dollars to cover her expenses. For *Argosy,* her principal employer that summer, she would cover the Lebanese civil war, marine maneuvers on Crete, and the marines' final assault landing in Beirut on July 17.

Before leaving on the assignment, she was pleasantly surprised by a letter from the House of Representatives. It informed her that Zoltan Dienes was to undergo a final physical examination in Vienna before being issued his visa to the United States.

On June 26, 1958, the navy flew Dickey from Norfolk, Virginia, to Naples, Italy, where she registered at the Hotel Royal at the navy rate of six dollars a day. She had a terrace room facing the harbor and Mt. Vesuvius. She'd wrangled a *Digest* assignment to do a story on the Sixth Fleet's limited war capabilities, and she was anxious to begin—since before leaving she'd been briefed twice about the fleet's proposed future involvement in Lebanon, which she hoped to "do involved coverage on." On June 28, from Naples, she sent a letter to the Sixth Fleet's information officer requesting an update on their schedule of "upcoming events," so that it wouldn't conflict with her other assignments in the area. In response, a cable instructed her to be available "during 7–14 July . . . give or take a day." She was told to go ahead with her other plans: "Just keep us advised concerning your whereabouts. If the element of uncertainty is frustrating for you, it is doubly so for us."

By this time Dickey had become a confidante of the fleet's commander, Admiral Brown, who reminded her of a boy "winning the town's marble tournament," and whom she'd profiled in the *Digest's* March 1958 issue, entitled "Master of the Med." In it she described his fleet of sixty warships as "the most formidable striking power in the Middle East . . . NATO's right arm . . . carrying all the machinery of persuasion of our time, including nuclear ones." Brown would later send her letters signed "Cat" and share with her a denunciation appearing in the Russian navy's newspaper, *Soviet Fleet.* The Russians called the use of his ships to land the marines in Lebanon a "graphic crime" of American imperialism. Extremely sensitive to criticism, Brown wrote that he found the Russian article "an evil type of character assassination."

At the end of June Dickey was in Beirut, where Syrian-backed rebels, opposed to their country's pro-West president Camille Chamoun, controlled Beirut's Moslem slums, the cities of Tripoli in the north and Saïda in the south, and large areas of the Békaa valley contiguous with Syria. She had come to interview Saeb Salam, the leader of the Beirut rebels, who despite his formidable tank traps on the approach streets was anxious for press coverage. Dickey was escorted to his barbed-wire-enclosed mansion by some "tommy-gun-lugging teenagers." Salam, whom she described in a 1962 letter to a friend at the *Marine Corps Gazette* as a "greasy politician type billed as the president of Middle East Airlines," met her in the basement of his well-fortified command post.

"What are you going to do after you cover our war?" he asked.

"Going to cover some maneuvers of the U.S. Marines, Your Excellency."

"Oh?" he replied. "If you see any high-ranking marines, will you give them a message for me?"

"I'll probably see some," answered Dickey. "What's the message?"

"You tell those marines that if *one* marine sets foot on the soil of my country, I will regard it as an act of aggression and commit my entire forces against them." He then invited her to tour his bastion so that she could describe his resources accurately. She judged them to consist of about three thousand men, women, and children; a radio transmitter; assorted arms (about one-third automatics); and various tank trap positions.

About a week later she went to Crete for marine maneuvers and met with Brigadier General Sydney S. Wade, to whom she described her encounter with Salam. The general was only days away from deploying the marines into Beirut at the request of its beleaguered President Chamoun. Chamoun had attempted that May to amend his country's constitution so that he could run for a second term, which provoked rioting in the streets. A panicked Chamoun had pleaded for help from Washington and the United Nations, claiming that the demonstrations were part of a communist uprising, which would be supported by a Syrian invasion.

Almost immediately President Eisenhower ordered the Sixth Fleet into the eastern Mediterranean to stand by. But it wasn't until July 13, after the assassination of pro-Western King Faisal in Baghdad and the installation of anti-Western General Abdul Karim Kassem, that the situation became tense. By then Chamoun was convinced his would be the next pro-American regime to be eliminated, a feeling shared by America's other ally, Jordan's young King Hussein. Within days of these developments the warm blue Mediterranean began to churn with American warships and landing craft heading for Beirut.

When the nine thousand U.S. Marines landed in Beirut on July 15, 1958, to intervene in the so-called rebellion, Dickey was in Athens and, as she'd feared, unable to make the first landing. Her only consolation was that no other reporter had ridden in with the first two battalions. She arrived in time to cover the final assault by the First Battalion, Eighth Marines, as well as the defense of Beirut's port two days later by the Second Battalion, Second Marines. The day after the landing, after a brief encounter with local units of the Lebanese army, which had orders from their insubordinate younger officers to fire on the marines and were quickly dispersed by the Lebanese commander-in-chief, the marines made their peaceful entry into the Beirut port. They were soon dug in, guarding the Beirut harbor.

Five days later Dickey was in a foxhole surrounded by the Second Platoon, Third Battalion, Sixth Marines, defending a rocky hill they called Irene, which spilled down into terraced olive groves toward the beach road. The marines dug in beside her were concentrating north, on the main runway of the Beirut International Airport. She had her precious kabar with her, the World War II gift she had received from the marine on Iwo Jima, and slept with her hand around its leather handle.

The marines were ordered not to shoot unless fired upon and then to return fire only at a clear target. They were harassed by overhead shots and rock throwing, but there were no casualties and there was no shooting.

"We should be able to describe my material," she wrote her editor at *Argosy* the following month, "as the untold story of the Marines in Lebanon." Although there was neither a revolution nor a Syrian invasion and the two hundred news reporters gathered told of a beach crowded with carefree sunbathers eating ice-cream cones and waving at the troops, Dickey's eyewitness note to her editor claimed it was otherwise. "It was not the unopposed landing the censors have made most newsmen describe. . . . Probably no U.S. force in history has been subject to the harassment faced by our Marines here . . . the thrown rocks, the bullets overhead, the mysterious bombs close by. I did night patrol with them, learned how to throw rocks myself, dozed in a foxhole overnight with my knife in my own hand . . . kept my camera open, sighted down one of their machine-gun barrels night after night."

These anxious nineteen-year-old boys had again captured her heart and her respect. To *Argosy*—which called Dickey "our photographer on the spot"—she wrote, "The title of the scene is simply—Marines. Any night anywhere, almost any time in our generation . . . the eagerness, waiting, anxiety, the hours of cursing one's ears because they cannot hear farther and one's eyes because they cannot see without light all the way. . . ."

"They have pulled twenty days' peace out of eighty days' chaos," she told *Argosy*. "This is not a bad trick for a bunch of eighteen- and nineteen-year-olds. Their icy grip on nerves and trigger fingers may have given us a new tactic when we needed it most in the boiling Middle East: thunder without blood." She had to add, "Marine commander General Wade told me, 'Please feel free to tell your publisher that you have been farther forward with us and stayed there longer than any other reporter here—man or woman.'" The comment ran above her byline in the magazine's November 1958 issue, part one of a two-part "exclusive."

Several weeks later, as the situation in Lebanon stabilized and the phased withdrawal of the marines began, Dickey went to see Saeb Salam. After telling him she had delivered his message, she asked Salam why he had not fired on the marines.

"Because my judgment is better than that of your President Eisenhower. He was willing to start a great war. I was not."

She confided to her old adventuress, Aunt George, that she had been

shot at four times in Beirut: three times during firefights she was covering on the road to the Beirut airport and once inside Beirut. On August
15, 1958, unable to write in her lovely terraced room at Beirut's St.
George Hotel, she went up over Tripoli in a navy patrol plane, a propeller-driven Skyraider. As it was circling back to the attack carrier USS
Essex, it was hit six times by .30 and .50-caliber bullets. Dickey had gone
up to do a story on "how things were actually going in Lebanon."

The incident was quickly picked up by the wires. BULLETS FIRED AT
U.S. PLANE MISS AN EX-MILWAUKEEAN, reported the *Milwaukee Journal*
on August 16, 1958. *The New York Times* ran the story as well. Dickey
received a frantic letter from her aunts and a calmer one from Tony.
"We consoled ourselves with the thought that we would hear almost
immediately if you weren't alright," Tony wrote, apparently resigned to
Dickey's magnetic attraction for trouble. He did add, almost politely,
"Please take good care of yourself."

"Very similar things have happened before without stopping the
presses," Dickey wrote back. "The press reports . . . about my getting
shot at are grossly exaggerated." But to a friend at *Leatherneck,* the
marines' monthly magazine, she made it plain how very close she had
come to being another statistic. "We got six bullet holes in the plane
from ground fire, the nearest eighteen inches from the pilot's bottom
and another twenty-four inches from me." The next day she interviewed
Rashid Karami, the leader of the Syrian-backed insurrection in Tripoli
that past May. The smooth and dapper Karami, who would later become
the Lebanese president, complained to Dickey about the lack of American tourists.

"I can tell you one reason, Your Excellency," she answered. "I have
been shot at trying to visit you." Of course that wasn't strictly accurate,
but Dickey couldn't resist the opening. She rummaged in her handbag
and whipped out the official navy press release.

"I would like to meet the man who fired at me," she said after he
finished reading the press release.

Some time later a turbaned tribal elder, armed, bewhiskered, and
grinning, was brought in. He refused to pose with his weapon pointing
directly into her camera, but he gave her a great quote. Referring to our
plane's motion over him, he said in the tone of a father chiding an errant
daughter, "you do that again, and I won't miss by *any* inches."

"It is a strange Middle East," she wrote to her aunt Lutie from

Amman, Jordan, that August. *Reader's Digest* had dispatched her to do a profile of King Hussein, who, threatened by the assassination of King Faisal that July, had summoned protection by British air envelopment. Six years earlier with Tony on their Point Four trip, Dickey had been charmed by Jordan's romance, but now she longed to be "back living in a hole in the ground with the Marines."

"I try hard to remember Amman from 1952," she wrote her aunt, "before there was a big U.S. military force here, before the sky was full of howling jets and the streets packed with owl-eyed soldiers and marines. But it isn't easy. To me, the symbols of what's happened are two. One was a marine on a hilltop near Beirut bitterly telling his buddy, 'But it ain't right when I gotta take a BAR [Browning automatic rifle] to church.' The other was a British paratrooper today in Amman moving the barrel of his Sten gun out of the way so he could feel the sleazy satin of a pair of black lace-trimmed panties he was buying. . . ."

"I suppose the best real index of the tension is the king's conference," she wrote in another letter to Lutie. "There were thirty-three newsmen—and twenty-nine Royal Guards, carrying automatic rifles. Every time we opened our cameras to change film, one of them stood over us with the weapon barrel in line with our hands. I've been searched—not roughly, by women guards—eleven times in five days. And the king insists we quote him as saying 'The internal situation is perfect.' Phooey!"

WHEN DICKEY RETURNED to New York, she tried drumming up interest in another Algerian story, one of the rebels having written that despite her being an American, he'd found in her a "comforting communion of mind and heart, an actual sympathy for our dramatic struggle for independence." She had no better luck getting an assignment on that story than she was having convincing a magazine to send her to Cuba to cover Fidel Castro.

Like most Americans, Dickey had heard about Fidel Castro through the dispatches of Herbert Matthews, the veteran *New York Times* reporter. In February 1957, when Batista's censored press was claiming Castro's death and his revolutionaries' defeat at the hands of American-armed government troops and American-supplied B-26s, Fidel invited Matthews to interview him in his mountainous hideout in the rugged Sierra Maestra, at the southern end of the island. Matthews, a respected journalist who had reported on the Spanish civil war and a specialist in Latin American affairs, made the arduous climb in torrential rain. He came away with the quote "A bell tolled in the jungles of the Sierra Maestra." To Matthews, Fidel Castro and his large 26th of July army were "invincible" and would bring democracy to Cuba. Years later it was revealed that Castro had brilliantly stage-managed the interview to make it appear he was winning; in fact he had only twenty men and controlled little more than the ground upon which the interview was taking place. Castro had a great and loyal fan in Matthews, who long persisted in believing that the young fighter would come to his senses and prove to be the liberator of the Americas. The articles that followed this ground-breaking news journey, in *Life*, *Coronet*, and *Look* magazines, mirrored Matthews's enthusiasm.

As to Castro's fierce anti-American sentiments and the socialist beliefs of his student days (when he'd espoused nationalization of Cuba's U.S.-owned power and telephone companies), he told a reporter from *Time* magazine, "Some ideas I used to have would not be good for Cuba. I do not believe in nationalization." In the interviews he did with *Coronet* and *Look*, he vociferously denied that he was a communist. When Batista charged that Castro's revolt was pro-Soviet and procommunist, Castro pointed out that almost every man in his army was a practicing Roman Catholic. The Cuban middle class, the clergy, believed him. So did the CIA, which reportedly funneled fifty thousand dollars into the revolution in 1957 and 1958. So did Dickey.

Dickey had been vainly trying to get an assignment to cover Castro's rebel army ever since reading Matthews's stirring articles. The romantic story of this obscure bearded attorney and his young, mostly middle-class soldiers, holed up in the mountains of Cuba for the last two years fighting Batista, held little interest for editors and publishers. Those who'd known of Castro only through the heavily censored Cuban press were unaware of the rebel victories; thus *Time* magazine was able to dismiss Fidel Castro as the leader of a fanatic, ragtag force.

The real issue was the relationship between Cuba and the United States. Ever since winning its freedom from Spain in 1898, Cuba functioned as a corrupt protectorate of the United States. When Fulgencio Batista y Zaldívar seized control of the country in a military coup d'état in 1933, he merely fell into the role of his predecessors. He lined his pockets with bribes and created a secret military intelligence service known as SIM, which specialized in torture and castration. Batista ignored the needs of the poor, abolished civil liberties, and vigorously censored news reports out of his country. He grew fat off the American mobsters who controlled the lush island's gaming enterprises, the casinos, brothels, and racetracks. American investments in Cuba at the time of the revolution averaged one billion dollars. The Yankees owned ranches, forests, mines, and sugar plantations. America was the largest purchaser of Cuban sugar. At night, from a low-flying plane looking down on Cuba, one could see dots of flames—Fidel Castro had ordered his army to burn the sugarcane fields, beginning with those owned by his wealthy grower-father. By November, when Dickey managed to convince *Reader's Digest* to let her cover Castro, the magazine's editorial policy followed the lead of the American and Cuban middle class, which had grown tired of supporting Batista and now joined in the sweeping enthusiasm for revolution.

Dickey's excitement was shared by her New York contacts with the rebel army, two Cubans working at Bab's coffee shop on Forty-seventh Street and Third Avenue. They were only two of what Dickey estimated to be "thousands" of exiled Cubans working in the vast Castro underground. Castro's bearded fighters, known as the "26th of July," had taken on the stature of a formal army. Columns of rebels were advancing daily, fanning out of their mountain stronghold to win military outposts and small towns throughout the country. As they advanced, the troops of dictator Fulgencio Batista were deserting to join them. Dickey was to fly to Miami to meet with the Cuban underground and from there be taken by courier to Castro's mountain redoubt.

First she made a stop at Tony and Helga's apartment. Whenever she walked into her former West End apartment, there would be a flash of déjà vu, followed by immense relief. Though Dickey still felt as though the lovely German had betrayed her, far stronger was her gratitude that Helga was now on bedpan duty for Tony. Although most of Tony's days were now spent in bed, he continued with his photography business and had trained Helga to work in the darkroom when she was not nursing him. The woman had lost thirty pounds. Tony, on the other hand, had managed to transcend his invalid role, holding court from his bed with so much style that many visitors failed to realize he was bedridden. He had a chamber pot and a television set, and his voice remained commanding.

Ever since Vienna Dickey had made it a point to say good-bye to Tony before leaving on an assignment. His volatile temper, fed by booze and narcotic painkillers, had become increasingly unstable, and keeping in touch did wonders for his fragile ego. Besides, she still valued much of his advice; in many ways she remained his best student.

As always when Dickey came to call, Helga retired to the kitchen to brew some strong coffee. Tony, who'd recently declared bankruptcy, loaded Dickey down with requests. He wanted her to be sure to bring him and Stevie's brother, Morty, some cigars and as much Anejo rum as she could stuff into her luggage. He sent her off with a worried "Honestly, I don't know what you're trying to prove," followed by a reflexive "Take good care of yourself, please."

From Washington, on November 20, Dickey sent a letter to Lutie. She shared the good news about her "new" *Reader's Digest* assignment, "which leaves me with no mail address for a little while," and was also pleased to report that the magazine had purchased her Lebanon piece about the marines ("The Night War Didn't Come to Lebanon," February 1959), which made her doubly happy. "One because it's about the Marines, and I needed the $$$."

Dickey then returned to New York and left for Miami on November 28, sending a passionate note to her friends at Bab's coffee shop: "Your martyrs have not died in vain. Yours is an example of indomitable courage." She regretted leaving before she could meet with Zoltan Dienes, who had finally arrived in the States and slipped a note under her apartment door. He wanted desperately to see her and would come at a moment's notice "to spend hours talking, hours and hours, but you are somewhere else going."

At this point in her career Dickey noted that she had covered three revolutions—Hungary, Algeria, and Lebanon. Each had failed. "Hungary had fallen to the tanks. Brother still fought brother in Algeria. Rioting continued in Lebanon." Her weariness over the pointless butchery she'd been reporting, the longing for evidence that man had a nobler destiny, came after a meeting with Herbert Matthews. She believed Cuba would be different. Besides Dickey and a few other adventuresome reporters who were moved by Matthews's articles, myriad others flocked to the charismatic Castro: soldiers of fortune, a few AWOL U.S. Marines from Guantánamo Naval Station, and even Errol Flynn. One of Castro's supporters, a bookkeeper named Ramón Font working on a sugar plantation in Oriente province, recalled being disappointed. Nothing like the heroic "Captain Blood," Flynn was middle-aged and fat.

The headquarters for the clandestine Castro underground in Miami was in the Congress Building, the same building in which Dickey had worked decades earlier as city editor for the Miami Air Maneuvers. She spent five tedious days in a cheerless office interviewing victims of Batista's torture and waiting for the underground courier. She could not wait to see Castro's unpaid, underweaponed, barefoot *barbudos,* bearded ones, winning against three-to-one odds. She was excited by Castro's explanation that his army, unlike Batista's, was fighting for an idea—for freedom. For which they were willing to die.

Of the twenty reporters who attempted the journey to Sierra Maestra, half were turned back by government troops and escorted at gunpoint to Miami-bound airplanes. Dickey was concerned not with smuggling herself through enemy lines—after Algeria it seemed routine—but with the machismo rebel army's attitude about a woman observing them in combat. She hoped by now to have the discipline not to get sidetracked if one of them began to flirt or flatter. The minute some handsome soldier flashed a smile, all her resolve went out the window and she became as giddy as a schoolgirl.

When Dickey disembarked at Santiago de Cuba, the gracious old capital city of Oriente province at the east end of the island, she was dressed as a typical American tourist in spiked heels, tight-fitting skirt, low-cut blouse, and clunky earrings. She had purposely left her two Leica cameras and prized kabar knife with the underground in Miami. They had advised her she would have a much easier time getting through the Batista lines without them and promised to "smuggle" her gear to her by a "secret ammunition route" after she reached Oriente province.

When the airport security policeman questioned her destination, five hundred miles from Havana, where bullets had not yet dimmed the tourist industry, she flipped open her sequined wallet. A picture of a smiling young marine nestled between the plastic covers. Batting her lashes, Dickey explained that this was her sweetheart—the U.S. Navy base at Guantánamo was forty miles from the airport. The guard waved her through.

Dickey spent her first night beyond the farms and the burning sugar cane fields at the Motel Rancho, a tourist court on the edge of the city in Santiago de Cuba. It was near the foothills of the Sierra Maestra, seventy miles of jungled peaks rising to over six thousand feet and inhabited by a handful of pro-Castro farmers. Dickey cooled herself with daiquiris, listening to the cathedral chimes from the village square and waiting for her cameras. They never arrived. "Eventually my fury over the loss of my cameras simmered down," she wrote. "But to have let the trench knife given me on Iwo Jima pass into somebody else's hands—for this I can't forgive myself."

Also staying at the tourist court was her colleague Andrew St. George, the journalist who had followed Herbert Matthews to bring Castro's words down the Sierra Maestra for *Life* magazine. St. George, a burly Hungarian who, like Dickey, preferred action stories, admired her. She proved far tougher than he in sticking with a story, no matter what the risks. And although a lot of male reporters resented this attribute, St. George did not. "She was very good at what she did," he commented, "but she never did get the proper recognition or respect." She always struck him as insecure, worried less about getting shot than about where her next assignment might come from. That night he helped her locate another camera, a Japanese-made 35-mm loaned by a Castro sympathizer.

The following morning Dickey and her young female Castro courier, later captured and killed by Batista's secret police, drove across a golf course with contraband for the rebel soldiers—rifle grenades hidden under sacks of grain. After crossing the golf course at the edge of Santiago de Cuba, a bearded young soldier waited for her in a jeep that, like all rebel vehicles, had been liberated from Batista's troops. Like the other fighters she would meet, he wore religious medals on his cap. On his sleeves was a commemorative red-and-black *26 de julio* armband. (Castro's first, bloody, failed coup attempt in 1953, at the Moncada Barracks in Santiago de Cuba, resulted in the death and torture of many of his followers and his imprisonment for three years. The motto of the *26 de julio* armband was *Libertad o Muerte,* "Liberty or Death," the same words spoken by the American patriot Patrick Henry.)

Of the seven rebel infantry columns operating between Thanksgiving and Christmas 1958, Dickey covered two in combat: one commanded by Fidel, south of the Central Highway, and the other led by his brother, Raúl, to the north of the road. She witnessed five actions: the surrender at Alto Songo, the siege of La Maya, the burning of the San Luis *cuartel,* the mortar barrage at Maffo, and the assault at Jiguaní.

In Cuba Dickey truly began to understand combat; no longer was it "Gee whiz, I'm on a patrol." From this point on, her military perspective increasingly colored her notes and rough drafts for articles. Coverage of the actual battles she saved for the *Marine Corps Gazette*. She wrote up the Fidelistas' method of guerrilla warfare so extensively that her piece was later used as a primer in marine training. She would continue to write about limited war and counterinsurgency (topics of great interest toward the end of her life), accounts not intended for commercial sale, since they read more like military briefings—which they would in fact be used for. In Cuba, as she had suspected, the rebels were winning over better-equipped Batista troops. The deciding factor was their determination. It would become her canon: men, not weapons, won wars.

It is not hard to understand why her inclination to militarism blossomed six thousand feet up in the Sierra Maestra. It was the first time an army in no way restricted her movements, in fact doing everything they could to help her. It was also the first army with women fighters, doing what she had always *known* they could. One of the rebel sniper platoons—forty per platoon—was all female. One out of every twenty uniforms was worn by a woman. Although it was true that women mostly did housekeeping and ran supplies, hiding bullets under their skirts, they were still viewed as essential noncombatants. Dickey, who never consciously considered herself a feminist, nevertheless sounded like one when she later wrote that she had never been "more proud to be a woman than when I marched with Fidel Castro's Cuban guerrillas. I saw members of my sex perform breathless deeds of valor—squirming through enemy roadblocks with ten grenades hooked to their belts and fighting alongside the Fidelista troops, an eleven-pound rifle in their unmanicured hands."

If they were, like their male counterparts, loudly anti-American, Dickey dealt with these sentiments as she had with the hostility of the Algerian rebels, who despite their deep "inimical feelings to the U.S." came to respect her as an individual. "There is, happily, among you a race of pioneers, eager to help the small and feeble, and to unveil the truth wherever and whenever it is worth to be known," an Algerian rebel leader wrote her. "I really hope the stubborn work you perform all over the world will reconcile your country with many other countries which do not always find a generous support near Uncle Sam." The rebel soldier complimented her as a "gentle, lovely lady" who "shared the dangerous life" with him, so that she could return to her distant country "to enhearten them in [our] war of liberation by her human testimony."

Dickey believed that the Cuban's hatred for the Americans was, like that of the Algerians, rooted in distrust, exacerbated by the strafing by the American B-26s. She had exposed the illegal bombing of the Algerian rebels by French planes and intended to expose the illegal use of the B-26s in Cuba. She explained endlessly to the rebel soldiers that the weaponry had been furnished to Cuba by the U.S. government long before, under hemispheric defense pacts. It had never intended to be used to rain down flaming gasoline and bombs on the rebel-held towns, as part of Batista's last-ditch efforts. However, Dickey's repeated explanations did little good as she and the rebels came under attack from the B-26s. She soon found herself sharing their outrage, learning their epithets, screaming at the handsome pink flashes aimed straight for her. She believed that if the story of the rebels as she saw it were known in the United States—a folk revolution against a brutal tyrant—the distrust and hatred between the two countries would resolve itself. It was spurred by her own guilt as a member of the U.S. press, a group whose ignorance and indifference to Batista had only prolonged his tyranny.

The reactionary *Digest*'s policy actually reflected contemporary American public opinion in the winter of 1959, which could be described as warily pro-Castro, only because Batista had finally been unmasked, and because American interests wished to avoid the appearance of collusion with his regime. There was another reason for the *Digest*'s suspension of disbelief about Castro, rooted in sound business—the magazine's $1.8 million printing plant was located in Havana, which served as home base for its operations in Latin America. The publication was hedging its bets.

Shortly after her arrival in the muddy, rain-splattered hills, Dickey felt as if the first steps toward reconciliation had begun. The rebel women had come to treat her "like a sister."

Although a few years later, when her idealistic hopes about the revolution turned to cynicism, and she would dismiss Celia Sánchez, Fidel Castro's constant companion, as "febrile," that was not how Dickey first viewed the wiry Cuban. Dickey was impressed by the diminutive Celia, reportedly the first woman to fight with the rebels. Dickey observed Celia deploying soldiers and mortars like a man, all the while retaining her femininity. Celia, who reputedly could outwalk any man in Castro's command, designed her own field uniform: green twill tapered slacks and a V-necked overblouse worn with thirteen religious medals on gold chain necklaces. "She was a thoughtful hostess to me, although we had no language in common," Dickey wrote, "once borrowing a farm woman's clothing for me because my own dungarees had been soaked in a tropical rain." Raúl's wealthy girlfriend, Vilma Espin, who, like Dickey, had attended MIT, liked to neck with Raúl in the foxholes, on one occasion only a thousand yards from the active front. Dickey never saw Vilma without an automatic rifle in her hand and wryly observed that Vilma practically cooed when Raúl brought her a new, European-made para-trooper's gun with a special folding stock. "I think of them," she wrote, "first of all as I knew them, in the role of women at the side of their men. I've heard both tell their menfolk how to run a battle."

The six weeks she spent in the harsh jungle mountains toward the end of the fighting were "incredibly lucky." In twenty-three days Dickey was able to witness the five actions that would culminate in the linking of Cuba's main artery, the Central Highway, by Raúl and Fidel Castro's forces.

From Maffo, on the way to interview Raúl, the brakeless jeep Dickey was riding in crashed head-on into a bank, then turned over. She fell free, escaping with a badly sprained ankle; another passenger would die of his wounds. When she had suggested that they delay their trip until the brakes were repaired, the driver had told her he didn't know how they worked, and that unlike Americans, Cubans were not afraid of mechani-cal mishaps. This same driver had ordered her to take cover earlier when the road they'd been traveling came under mortar attack. As they'd waited in a mud ditch he'd said, chuckling, "I never thought to see an American in the mud like a pig, as we lie now." At the time Dickey hadn't replied since she'd been under his orders, but she'd felt indigna-tion; in his eyes she knew she'd compromised her country's face.

One of her companions located three horses, and she set off with him and the driver on a two-hour horseback ride to the single field hospital in operation—a former coffee-bean drying shed. It had a blood-covered floor and no lights, anesthetics, or beds for the wounded. After a bearded doctor examined the trio, he ordered them to crawl out of his way. Dickey's ankle was not broken, only sprained. As the casualties from the mortar attack arrived, Dickey was drawn to one man, a Dominican named Ramón Richirelo Mejia, who'd joined the battle to fight against

Batista so that later the rebels would join him to fight the Dominican dictator, Rafael Trujillo. His midsection was swathed in rags, and it was doubtful he would survive since the surgeon on duty, a young woman, explained there were no anesthetics or lights for the long operation. Three days later in a tropical downpour, Dickey arrived at Raúl's command post with fourteen other people in the battered, brakeless jeep.

Two years later Dickey wrote in a *Marine Corps Gazette* piece that Castro's riflemen time and again turned back Batista's tanks and planes by making every mistake in the book—but one. "They consistently delivered a high volume of fire. After they had started shooting, they rarely let anything—the enemy's reaction or their own commander's orders—stop them from continuing to fire until there was nothing left to fire on. They barely aimed and they did not conserve ammunition. But they unmistakably communicated their will to fight to an enemy whose superior equipment was unmatched by the will to use it."

They believed that if they went back to their homes while Batista was still in power, they would be killed. "The pattern was always the same," Dickey wrote. "The soldiers retreated behind their ultimate defenses and vainly waited for help from outside while the rebels fired round the clock from a ring of close-in positions until the garrison surrendered."

Outside the jungle-enclosed tiny town of La Maya (population eight thousand), Dickey watched one of the rebel soldiers try to fire homemade ammo through a 20-mm cannon. The cannon was being fired from a trench across a narrow strip of no-man's-land at a heavily fortified blockhouse—a complex of six buildings just over a low hill from the town where 325 Batista soldiers, with their wives and children, were hiding. Two hundred and fifty rebels formed a complete circle around the fortress. The blockhouse was on high-rising ground, which gave it an unexposed view right down through the town. It could therefore directly assault the rebel line.

Jerry Holthaus, a tall, blue-eyed, twenty-one-year-old, barely literate marine was directing the charge of the 20-mm cannon. Holthaus had first encountered the rebels that June, when he and twenty-four other marines were kidnapped by Raúl Castro's forces while returning from liberty on a bus en route to the American naval base at Guantánamo. Raúl Castro had orchestrated this kidnapping and a previous one to pressure the United States to stop supplying Batista with arms and planes. While Holthaus and the other Americans were held hostage, the

air attacks were halted. Three weeks later, with Raúl's guerrillas reinforced, Holthaus and the others had served their purposes and were
released. But by then Holthaus had reportedly fallen for a rebel girl and
had become sympathetic to the cause. In September 1958 Holthaus left
his post of sergeant of the guards at Guantánamo, taking a radio jeep,
two rifles, pistols, and ammunition and radioing his departure from the
jeep as he sped into the mountains.

The story of Holthaus's desertion was of interest to many American
reporters in Cuba, with intermittent coverage in *The New York Times.*
When Dickey walked up to the young marine, he greeted her with "You
must be the press. Drop dead." Then he went back to where a handful
of rebels was firing around the clock at the blockhouse. The battle was
in its twelfth day. Holthaus, who had wanted to fight since age seventeen
when he'd joined the Marine Corps, was acting as the rebels' big-gun
expert—because he was the only person there who had ever fired anything larger than a rifle. Overhead flew the B-26s. The rebels cursed the
planes and the Americans, but not Holthaus. They affectionately referred to him as *el loco americano*—"the crazy American." When
Dickey watched Holthaus, she agreed with the rebels that he was *loco*,
but wrote that "the word *americano* meant something else than
what I'd been hearing . . . the word meant a man, just one man, Sgt.
Gerald Holthaus . . . and not noted at all is the very considerable service
he performed for the image of his country in the eyes of thousands of
Latin Americans." Dickey had found a hero.

The rebel line described a complete circle around the fortress of La
Maya. In theory both sides could be supplied—the besieged by air, the
besiegers by road. The major tactic of both sides was to fire around the
circle and around the clock, and both had enough ammunition when
they started to go on for a long time.

Through the slits of the blockhouse, the government troops aimed
their rifles, always offering the threat of direct assault through the thin
rebel line.

"This was not a real circle," Dickey wrote. "It had a deep salient
which we called the Hole because part of a trench had been dug there.
In front of the trench, no-man's-land was at its narrowest, barely a
hundred yards across.

"The Hole was incessantly under blockhouse fire, of course. And it
always fired back." Dickey had heard about how Latin Americans

knocked off their wars for daily siestas, but she saw no sign of this among the rebels manning the Hole. "Jerry told me with deep respect in his voice that they were the little handful of men who were really fighting this battle; they fired around the clock, they were firing as we spoke.

"But the rifle bullets from the Hole, or from the entire rebel line for that matter, Jerry explained, would never reduce the concrete block-house. Grenades might, artillery should. For now he was searching for ammo for a .57 recoilless, wrapped against the dust in a plastic table-cloth, hand-painted with pink flowers and green leaves."

Dickey told Jerry that she had come up to the front in a captured jeep loaded with some garishly painted rifle grenades, but she didn't know what else it carried. Jerry headed off for the rebel motor pool, a former cattle pen with a board fence. Dickey reloaded her cameras, ducking from building to building out to the Hole.

The Hole lay between two gutted buildings; most of the position was not really dug in but consisted of a corridor ten yards wide with the mud underfoot beaten flat by bootprints. Rearward rose a half-burned barn with shingle walls. To the front was its main protection—two concrete walls, once part of a villager's home. Peering through the cracks, Dickey could see a football-field-sized area of littered sheet tin—all that was left of houses that once stood between the Hole and the blockhouse. This was no-man's-land.

The trench from which the Hole took its name was half a man deep, extending a dozen feet out from one of the concrete walls. The front of it was built up with a score of sandbags, and its rear was made from its own fill. At the far end, where the street paving led from one side of the war to the other, there was a full-length mirror braced upright on its long edge. Set at a forty-five-degree angle to the axis of fire, it reflected the squat blockhouse so a rifleman could see what he was hitting without literally sticking his neck out.

There was room for twenty men in the Hole, but it was usually crowded with more because the concrete walls offered the best security around. Lieutenant Cypriano, the heavy-bearded, massive-shouldered rebel commander, never had to scrape for manpower.

Dickey slid down the embankment into the Hole as Lieutenant Cypriano began delivering a speech of deep conviction to his knot of ragged riflemen. From the manner in which it was being delivered, Dickey understood it was an unflattering critique of their marksmanship.

"Beneath the dirt, the sweat and the beards, unease flickers under their skin. Their hands fidget." They carried captured rifles, two M-1's, the rest Springfields. Suddenly one of them fired accidentally. The muzzled blast passed the lieutenant close enough to ruffle his beard.

At this point Sergeant Holthaus reappeared. He crossed to the horrified firer and relieved him of his rifle. He tapped the safety lock with one grimy finger and, while the lieutenant watched gratefully, tossed the rifle back to the man.

Dickey began to photograph the riflemen, whose orders were to fire through the interstices among the sandbags at least once every five seconds. Up ahead came the deafening thunder of the B-26s. At the edge of the Hole, one rifleman retched unashamedly. "The sense of being small and helpless before pure malevolence, nightmare evil—this grips all of us," she wrote of this confrontation with the bogey man. "It flashes through my mind that we feel it in part because it is a fact; what we have to throw back is lead no bigger than half a pencil and what can hit among us are shells as thick as my wrist—and rained down automatically.

"I see the Marine, moving so fast he seems to have been born there, take a position beneath a heavy doorframe set into the concrete wall. Then he comes out into the open long enough to hi-block two rebels who seemed confused, back under it with him." The thunder of the B-26 became louder than the sound of Dickey's blood thundering in her ears. She sensed no other feeling "but the terrible embrace of sound."

Above them the strafing pilot swept inexorably from the unprotected rear of the Hole. A fifteen-year-old runner fastened a white rag to a rifle barrel and, running out from the Hole, waved it in clear sight of the blockhouse and the plane. The ruse worked. The plane shifted its aim to the far side of the street, its shells tearing the roof off an abandoned schoolhouse.

Then the firing from the blockhouse resumed, and Cypriano shouted for four men at a time to return the fire as fast as possible *over* the sandbags. While Dickey wondered if the men would obey the order, Cypriano grabbed a rifleman's M-1 and, striding into the trench, head and shoulders completely exposed, squeezed off a shot and moved back behind the wall. Nobody followed. Holthaus glanced up, and, in perfect imitation of the brave Cypriano, moved out, stood and fired, and returned. Suddenly all the men rushed to follow. A grateful Cypriano signaled Holthaus to give the firing order. Two teams fired in deafening, perfect rhythm while Holthaus handed out the ammo.

The volleys continued until a 20-mm gun was carried into the Hole by two weary runners. The baby cannon, which had been removed from one of Batista's downed B-26s, was a high-velocity, long-range weapon aimed by positioning the plane, and fired electrically. The rebels mounted the gun on a machine-gun tripod, fed it short-range homemade ammo, and fired it by hand. There were no sights, so the aiming was done blind; it was fired by two excited volunteers, who shouted the direction it would fall, then watched as it disappeared instead into some wild green jungle. The second time it exploded among the flinching faces of the rebels. After a dozen tries Holthaus's face, like the others in the Hole, was blackened and depressed. The cannon was disassembled and carried out.

Sacks of the homemade rifle grenades that had come up in the jeep with Dickey were brought into the Hole. They were firecracker-shaped sheet metal, painted bright enamel green with a bright red enamel tip. Once inserted into the rifle, the grenade stuck on the end of the rifle barrel with its fuse smoking and exploded within two seconds, going off cleanly between the Hole and the enemy. After half a dozen attempts, there was nobody within fifteen yards of the grenadier.

At this disheartened point, the legendary battalion commander Major Antonio Lussón, six feet tall with a rich beard and a long black mane of hair held by a tortoiseshell barrette, stepped into the Hole. Famous for his bravery, he'd led rifles and BAR (Browning automatic rifles) straight into the enemy's tanks and planes. "If you do not use the grenades," he told the men, "you will shame our dead." He fired two himself, each sticking on the end of his rifle and blowing up fifty yards out.

Lussón stepped back behind the wall, hooked his thumbs into his belt, and called for a BAR. The tension inside the Hole was palpable as he ordered a patrol. "Written plain on everyone's face," Dickey wrote, "was one question: How can you make a patrol in this bright sunshine on that tiny piece of disputed real estate in front of us?"

With Lussón leading and Cypriano at his heels, neither looking back, everyone moved out of the Hole.

"I will always wonder if there was anybody else of us on that patrol stupid enough to think as I do as I traipse along that Lussón means to move laterally. He doesn't. After we have run straight forward across half of no-man's-land, we see that there, dead in the middle, is a kind of cover, the building foundation of concrete stands a few feet over the litter of burned roofing."

Lussón ordered them to flop down while he emptied clip after clip through the BAR into the blockhouse. Dickey recalled that Lussón, head and weapon silhouetted against the sunset, made a splendid picture. After what seemed an eternity, Lussón led them back to the Hole. Two men had fresh bullet holes in their fatigues, but, incredibly, nobody had any in their flesh. And—morale was restored.

The .57 recoilless, with its two rounds of American-made ammo, was dragged forward and uncovered. Holthaus, who had waited so long for this moment, eyed the artillery piece and said, "Now it's just a question of marksmanship. My marksmanship."

After the heavy barrel was placed on the tripod, Holthaus swung back the breech, loaded and locked the weapon, then ordered everyone from the Hole. Meanwhile the soldiers in the blockhouse had had a full minute to gaze at the long muzzle of the .57 with its high projecting telescopic sight. Holthaus stood up, set his eye to the sight, and fired. The flame, the noise, the smoke, were tremendous—and the round fell short.

The Batista soldiers made lace of the burlap sandbag tops in front of the gun and gunner as Dickey and Cypriano gasped, watching Holthaus load another round and rotate the handle into the cocked position. Once again he stood up and began almost leisurely to readjust the sight. Beside him, the mirror splintered into a million shards. He fired, falling flat. Dickey was certain he'd been hit and was dead. A moment later, unharmed, he walked out of the trench. She did not think she had ever seen "a more furiously dejected human being." The second round had struck long. Covering his face with his hands, he shouted, cursing, "And I let the goddamn bullets shake me!"

Holthaus walked away, toward town. As Dickey watched she felt it seemed the best part of decency not to go after him.

The following afternoon the entire government force inside the blockhouse surrendered. Reasons cited were lack of air force supply drops, low morale, and fear of "the big gun." The sound alone had been terrifying. Holthaus perked up.

Dickey, who had once readily admitted to charges of being a sentimental dame, "and the day I'm not I'll be dead and it won't matter," found the kid's story pulling at her heart. Watching the big, awkward marine so intent on proving himself with the recoilless, only to have it fail, reminded her of her own humiliating baptism by fire on the hospital ship.

Holthaus had been in the marines for six years, he told her—six years of spotless service as a sergeant of the guard at the Guantánamo Naval Station, and all he had ever wanted to do was fight. After his kidnapping and his return, after telling the men back at the base not to cross the cyclone fencing and join the rebels, no matter how much they were behind the rebel cause—he had done it himself. Now he realized he was facing a dishonorable discharge. He didn't know what to do. There was only one thing Dickey could think of saying that might ease the kid's pain. "You'll always be a marine to me," she said softly. For the next ten days, in the fighting holes, on the ambushes, and in the artillery positions, she and Sergeant Holthaus were constant companions.

Dickey met others, "several score volunteer fighting men from America, waiving any oath of loyalty to Fidel . . . so that their U.S. citizenship would not be endangered." To her, the Castro forces paid the most sincere compliment to the United States by accepting the services of its volunteers. Although she could not condone Holthaus's desertion of his post at Guantánamo, she understood his frustration, which was not unlike her own when she had stood on the hospital ships looking out at Iwo Jima and Okinawa. She understood all too well how feelings of idealism and the need for adventure could overwhelm a person. Later, at Holthaus's court-martial, Dickey testified that at their very best, "those emotions served a greater purpose." Speaking as much for herself as for Holthaus, she said she believed those feelings "became inextricably bound up in their reasons for becoming freedom fighters."

The gangly Holthaus was definitely in a jam, and Dickey offered to write a story about his heroism under fire at La Maya, believing things might go easier for him. She also promised to discuss his "problem" with some colonels she knew from Okinawa. Holthaus didn't have much faith in her plan, but he wished her well. Malcolm Browne, reporting in Havana for AP at the time, recalled that Dickey became very involved with saving Holthaus; he likened her role to that of a "Marine Corps mother confessor."

Whenever Raúl Castro's troops won a garrison or a town, Raúl would stand on his gray Japanese-made jeep and make a speech. Like his brother, he would go on for hours, excoriating Batista and the Americans who were training his soldiers. "The great United States has sent our enemies planes and tanks," he began. "And we who were fighting tyranny as America's founders did—what have they sent us?" Dickey recalled that Holthaus sat among some sandbags cleaning a BAR. A villager caught in the light of a gasoline pressure lantern hanging from Raúl's jeep answered. "Here we have some help that comes from the United States," he said, pointing to Holthaus. "He is, I think, worth many planes and tanks." Dickey wrote of Holthaus's embarrassment at the comment. She found herself smiling. Though she personally liked the impish Raúl, his communist ideology disturbed her. She hoped he would come to his senses—he was only twenty-six—once the revolution succeeded. Being naturally optimistic, she hoped, but she also worried.

Fidel Castro's forces were not the band or mob portrayed in the press. There were 7,300 in uniform, and one in ten was a non-Cuban. The only way that a would-be Fidelista could become a *barbudo* was to disarm one of Batista's soldiers and hike into a Castro command post with his rifle, ammo, and canteen. There seemed to be no shortage of wanna-be Fidelistas, but there was definitely a shortage of weaponry, most of which was taken from raids on the enemy; only a small amount, she was able to ascertain, came in from gunrunners. Dickey watched a fifteen-year-old enlist by showing up with an automatic rifle that he insisted he'd gotten the hard way.

Beards served as a handy method of identification. The nucleus of Castro's forces had grown beards because there were no razors in their first hiding place on Pico Turquino. So a full-grown beard was cause for arrest by Batista's troops.

The Castro intelligence was incredible, so good that Dickey was convinced the Batista command could not go to the head without a perspiring runner showing up a few minutes later to inform Castro. Most were people of the countryside, unpaid volunteers—farmers, villagers. Ten- and twelve-year-old boys were battalion runners. Fidel placed the greatest faith in these messengers. The night that Dickey met Castro for the first time at his command post at Jiguaní, she found him and his command group standing next to a farmer's house, within six hundred yards of where a huge enemy patrol was searching for him. She assumed he would hit the patrol or cut it off.

"Oh, no," he explained, "it's too big. They are coming through the woods in a body, with men in pairs on either side. When the nearest pair is a few hundred meters away, people will tell me and we will leave." Ten minutes after he left, enemy scouts appeared and burned the farmer's house to the ground. "Before the ashes of his house had cooled," Dickey wrote, "the farmer came to the command post with a Springfield rifle in his hand."

Castro's command post was a deep, double-ended rock cave in a hillside overlooking a muddy side road sixty-five miles west of Santiago, a thousand yards from the front, along the Central Highway. It would never win the Good Housekeeping Seal of Approval. The cave was littered with radio equipment, food crates, cots, boxes of cigars, and belts of ammunition. Dickey quickly realized it was the last place to locate Fidel. His troops were busy seizing the town of Maffo and ambushing a relief column sent out from Bayamo, thirty miles to the west.

She watched the rebels blow up railroad bridges, mine the side roads, and finally mine the Central Highway, the main artery that crossed Cuba. They burned every bus, car, and truck. By early December the roads and most of the countryside had come under rebel control by night; by day only Batista's forces moved on them, never less than in a company and usually with tanks and air power.

Dickey would watch in amazement as the rebels emptied their rifles and their Browning automatics at the B-26s. She never saw a plane get hit, but she could see the psychological pleasure it gave the gunner. "The B-26s, no matter how poorly flown, utterly terrorized the province," she wrote, "and moral judgments aside, the fact is, we are heartily hated because they caused such fear."

Dickey thought Fidel Castro a huge bear of a man, as he sat on a hammock, swinging good-naturedly and smoking his cigar. When she inquired about her missing cameras and kabar, he quipped, "The revolution owes you two cameras." Later she discovered she was the third reporter "in a row" to have lost professional camera gear while "it was en route to its chief on his invitation."

But Dickey, like most reporters gathered around the fiery young Cuban, was entranced. "His command posts were always places of drama," she wrote, "with a shifting knot of intense bearded officers and messengers, hasty conferences, messages delivered, and orders sent out. He carries an air of tension in his every movement, even when lighting one of his Churchillian cigars.

"The normal state of ease for Fidel is a purposeful walk with a forty-inch stride out from the shelter followed by an equally purposeful walk back into it." The first time Dickey saw him leave his cave in this way, she assumed he was committing himself personally to battle and went running after him with her camera at the ready. But after she had followed him "perhaps half the length of a football field," he wheeled and strode back. "He was just pacing and planning," she wrote. "His movements are so fast that, to make his portrait, I set my camera shutter at the speed usually used for Olympic events."

But, despite his charisma and her own excitement, she sensed another trait that wasn't so attractive. Later she'd call it his "pathological personality." The young warrior who insisted she photograph the rebel dead "so their martyrdom will not be forgotten by the world" couldn't tolerate the absence of an enemy. "He had to stand or, better, rant and shout— against some challenge every waking moment." Dickey thought his tactical officers used his vast appetite for hostility to their own gain. She watched how a commander needing fresh ammunition could be certain he'd get it by charging up to Fidel and shouting up at the great bearded face, "Dr. Fidel, I tell you you have been a fool not to support me! You should have known I needed more shells." Dickey soon found herself behaving in a similar fashion. If she heard a rumor of a jeep heading for the front, but couldn't find it, she'd begin shouting at a bearded officer that she was tired of having Cubans lie to her.

"That this twist of farce would someday lead to political tragedy," she wrote, "that the Reds would make Castro's need for a powerful enemy a means of infiltrating his government, inspiring him to rattle their rockets against America long after Batista was gone—this I did not guess. Only its pathological overtones were plain.

"In the rare times when he spoke quietly, Castro revealed a fine incisive mind utterly ill-matching the psychopathic temperament which subdued it." His army returned prisoners without intimidating them. Dickey had first been told this by the underground and disbelieved it until she saw it occur at the surrender at La Maya. The Batista soldiers were sent back home through the Red Cross. Raúl Castro told them they would be sent back again and again, a sign of his utter contempt of their fighting potential. It was such an effective ploy that the captured troops often flinched as they listened. But other than Fidel's pathological need for an enemy, Dickey found his speech "distinct," his gestures "decisive," his humor "Jovian and soldierly." When pleased he would give bear hugs to his soldiers. When angered, his temper rumbled like an "earthquake." She never saw him "demand" any respect. She watched "iron-nerved" staff members stand up to his shouting simply by shouting back at him. He ignored maps, she realized, since he would need to sit down in order to read them. All this and his mastery of the media, she believed, explained his acceptance as a "folk hero at home, the larger-than-life Cuban. . . ."

Fidel and the reporters rode in a British-made weapons carrier. Almost daily he would set up his advance command post on the porch or the patio of a farmer's house, near enough to the front so he and the reporters could witness the bombing and strafing and listen to the sounds of the ground troops.

From the beginning of his struggle, Castro tried to offset Batista's attempt to black out news coverage of the rebels via Radio Rebelde. Grabbing his walkie-talkie, he would awaken the countryside with his hoarse voice booming down from the hills into the ears of the Cuban people: *"Urgente, urgente. . . ."* "He never spoke in code," she observed, "so that half of Cuba could follow the battle by simply tuning in on the Castro tactical transmissions. Before most of Cuba had seen his face, most of it knew his voice."

One afternoon she sat next to Castro on the wreckage of a sheet-metal outbuilding, while overhead the Cuban air force B-26s made strafing runs on the rebel forces barely a mile away. Castro told her that when he came to power he would make certain changes. She was convinced that his most sincere concerns were for "his country's rebirth without a secret police, without corruption, and without the empire of vice," that his way of going about it would be direct. "He will stand or fall on it," she wrote. He told her he would shut down all the gambling casinos. "We do not need it to attract tourists," he told her. "I do not want it. It is bad for my people." When she asked how he would employ all of the Cubans who were then working in the casinos, he shrugged.

Dickey fell in love in Cuba, not with any one individual, but, like her idealistic colleague Herbert Matthews, with the rebels' spirit. If they could win, then anything *was* possible. Castro's pathology may have disturbed her, but she did not recognize the jargon of communism in his followers' language. If anything, the rebels seemed indignant when such dogma was applied to the Castro movement, asking her dozens of times, "You won't call us communists, will you?" She heard her country excoriated for being aloof and indifferent to Batista's terrorism and for equipping the dictator's forces.

Dickey became famous all over America for broadcasting Castro's victory in advance, over a Cuban NBC radio affiliate. When she excitedly announced that the rebels would drive Batista from the island, Castro called her "the little American with all the tiger blood in her veins."

Dickey left the rebels at sundown on Christmas Eve, amid reports that the Central Highway, from the village of Jiguaní almost back to Santiago—sixty-five miles—lay in rebel hands. She was dressed in pressed tourist clothes, a white shirt, beige slacks, and shining oxford shoes. At the back of her head, she'd pinned a red ribbon. She was accompanied by a twelve-year-old *rebelde* carrying her plaid suitcase. She still limped from the jeep accident. It was a twelve-mile walk along a mud road back to Santiago, half of which was spent dodging the strafing of low-flying B-26s. "This made in the USA body has been dodging made in the USA planes and made in the USA bullets," she'd later comment, recalling how a bombing run sent her skidding into a gully, cans with her exposed film rolling around her, clothes from her suitcase scattered about. The clothes she wore and had taken such care to protect during her stay in the mountains were torn and dirtied. A rebel commander also hiding from the strafing in a nearby culvert whistled to her. She stayed with him, lying on top of her plaid canvas suitcase, until the B-26 finished its run. Then she brushed herself off, gathered up her belongings and limped toward Santiago. At a suburb she hailed a taxi, making it detour past the U.S. consulate in Santiago so she could see the flag.

When Dickey arrived in Havana, Ruby Hart Phillips, a *New York Times* correspondent, introduced her to Woolsey Teller, a Havana-based reporter. Teller, then in his thirties, was writing for a Canadian newspaper. He recalled that when he met Dickey she was smoking a big cigar in Phillips's office. At the time of their meeting, Batista was still in Cuba and Fidel was still in the hills. Two nights later, after Dickey interviewed Batista's secretary of state, who complained that the U.S. embargo on new arms shipments to Cuba had cut firepower critically, Teller had dinner with Dickey at the Ambos Mundo Hotel, where Ernest Hemingway had once lived.

Teller recalled that despite Fidel's charisma, Dickey had reservations about how the man would be as a leader. Teller said that unlike the male reporters under Fidel's spell, she was not blind to his galloping ego, nor to Raúl's communist leanings. She told Teller, "I hope the revolution will not sit down and eat its children."

Teller was married to a Cuban woman and though he denied ever having an affair with Dickey, his letters to her suggest more than a professional friendship. He hailed her as "my proud beauty," and "interesting witch." He thought she looked like a "tasty enough morsel to eat—in Macy's window at high noon."

On New Year's Day 1959 Dickey left her room at the Ambos Mundo Hotel to watch the raucous festivities unfold. She was now dressed in her reporter's garb, her Mark Cross leather handbag and a tailored suit. The dictator Batista, whom she'd arranged to interview prior to leaving New York, had fled the island along with the American military mission. The rebels' call for a general strike had shuttered every store, bar, and restaurant and halted every bus and taxi. Bursts of rifle fire assaulted buildings where gangster elements opposed to Castro were holed up. In front of half a dozen wrecked casinos, pinball machines and parking meters lay smashed in the gutters. Groups of shirtsleeved young men patrolled the streets, wielding firearms with what Dickey called a "great willingness to level them at anything which moved." Autos with horns blaring and rifle barrels protruding out of every window rocketed along the deserted pavement. These held not marauders, but Castro's militia, reimposing order upon Havana.

The next day the first bearded and uniformed men of the revolution marched into the capital. They turned the casino of the Havana Hilton into a mess hall. Gaily dressed but sober tourists were issued rations from the hotel's coffee shop and then detoured past a gun post bristling with .30-caliber machine guns set up on the marble floor beneath a potted royal palm. On the quiet streets, bare-kneed boy scouts directed traffic. Here and there fugitive Batista SIM officers disguised with false beards fired machine guns into knots of pedestrians. Rebel soldiers at the various checkpoints responded by stopping cars to pull the alleged rebels by their beards. By the fourth day the general strike order was lifted and the city began to function again.

Dickey left Havana a few days after Castro's grand arrival on January 8. He was televised walking, then riding, the length of the city on top of a captured Sherman tank. Dickey recalled seeing only two unhappy faces after Fidel's reception in the delirious city, those of the Castro-appointed provisional president, Manuel Urrutia, and the prime minister, José Miró Cardona, both glimpsed pulling out of the presidential palace grounds in a huge limousine with the license plate "1." The two men had expected that Fidel would travel the length of the city with them, and he had just told the cheering crowds that he intended to walk the entire parade route. On the night of January 8, Castro opened the gates of Camp Columbia, the huge army base that was the geographic seat of Batista's power. The people of Cuba could now walk through it unharmed. A crowd of thirty thousand stood on the parade grounds of the camp as army searchlights swept the night sky; they had been waiting for hours to hear Fidel Castro. To great cheers and thunderous applause, he spoke to them of the need for Cuban unity, promising firing squads for Batista's gunmen. As the sun rose, a pair of white doves reportedly came to rest on his shoulders. The revolution was over.

DESPITE HER CONCERNS about Castro's ability to govern, an excited, jubilant Dickey returned to New York and eagerly began the *Reader's Digest* piece. In an early draft dated January 19, 1959, she wrote that what she had seen in Havana was the overthrow of a murderous tyrant by a "genuine folk revolution surging toward a government with every kind of person . . . playing a proud part." Dickey dismissed the ever-growing concerns of the press that the revolution was communist-inspired. She wrote that she believed Fidel when he announced, "My country deeply desires the best of relations with the United States"; she also believed Cuba would not exchange diplomatic amenities with the Soviets. After all, the rebels were devoted Catholics. "The first words they taught me in Spanish were the Lord's Prayer. Few went into combat without religious medals safely pinned to their ragged fatigues." She was aware of Fidel's ego and his need to challenge, by pure reflex, even though it trapped him. She attempted to show him to her readers as he was viewed in his culture, believing that if seen that way, his impulses for expression, abrasive as they were to U.S. nerves, would not be taken as the full measure of the man as chief of state. Still hoping he would come to learn the diplomacy fitting his new position after the rough transition period, she found herself explaining his behavior. It was the action of a "larger-than-life Cuban," an explanation for his accept-ance as a folk hero in Cuba—with all his people's faults and virtues. But what really kept her defending Castro past the point of prudence was her insistence that her country own up to its culpability in Cuba. Its indifference, time and again, to Batista's terrorism, and its role in arming the dictator's forces, fueled her loyalty to Castro's cause.

14

Fire in the Wind

Toward the middle of January 1959, Fidel Castro began televising public executions of the enemies of the revolution. The first televised "show trial" of three Batista commanders filled Havana's sports stadium. Although the men were bestial thugs, responsible for the torture and murders of countless unarmed Cubans, the setting was grotesque. While 380 reporters from around the world watched, seventeen thousand Cubans inside the stadium jeered. Vendors selling ice cream and peanuts hustled the crowd, and one of the judges spent the recess devouring an ice-cream cone. The televised trials and executions of these summary court-martials continued throughout that year and into the next.

By February Dickey's original enthusiasm about Castro's future as a true liberator of Latin America had been shaken by the growing number of disturbing reports coming out of Cuba. Already the press was being censored by the country's "Maximum Leader." She felt an urgency to get back, not only to sift fact from fiction, but to save Holthaus, who had corresponded with her. The former marine guard was now stationed in Havana as a first lieutenant in the tourist police. He had decided to remain with the rebel government and make something of himself, he wrote in a letter that sounded desperate and dangerous to her. She queried *Argosy* magazine about doing Holthaus's story. Actually she wanted to get him back to Guantánamo before America's growing anti-Castro sentiment made it too late, and she wanted to peg his return in an article about his heroism, as originally envisioned in the pages of *Argosy*. By now she had discussed his case with the military, writing *Argosy*, "I've already made a little deal for him with Disciplinary Branch, Headquarters Marine Corps, in Washington. Now I need to go to Cuba, find him, rephotograph him. . . . He's one homesick guy. And without *Argosy* he can never come back." But the magazine turned down Dickey's proposal. One year later they would publish Dickey's cowritten piece on the marine, but at the time they were not at all eager to champion an AWOL marine who had chosen to follow a man most Americans were coming to view as bloodthirsty as his predecessor.

Later that month, during a speaking engagement in Richmond, Virginia, Dickey was described in the women's section of the *Richmond News Leader* as having gone to four revolutions in two years "because she wanted to bring to the free world the story of terror in its most alarming forms." Elizabeth Byrd had pitched Dickey by saying, "Here is your opportunity to have an eyewitness account of the Cuban rebel victory by a person well qualified to tell it."

"It's hard to believe that just ninety miles from the United States one could experience a terror so similar to that of the Red terrorists on the Austro-Hungarian border," Dickey told the reporter for the *Richmond News Leader*. In another interview that same week with the *Milwaukee Journal*, she blamed the press and the diplomats for Batista's terrorism. "That's been our real failure," she declared. "Our recognition of Batista's terror as a system of government is responsible for the antagonism of the rebels toward America." When the reporter asked her about Castro's public executions, Dickey's answer went over like a lead balloon. "No, I can't get very excited about the four hundred terrorists Castro has shot. Not when my own country refused to get excited about the ten thousand victims of Batista. . . . U.S. correspondents failed to keep the country informed about conditions in Cuba. Instead of taking a stand against Batista, we supported him. We have our own errors in judgment and interpretation to blame."

Later she wrote that while in Cuba with the rebel forces, "there were two groups of people to whom the rebels displayed no mercy, informers and the SIM." A rebel girl serving as Dickey's interpreter "with all the idealism of youth was not about to dispense with legal procedures even in the case of informers and murderers. She told me, 'We'll hold them, we'll try them, and then we'll shoot them.' Neither of us guessed at the time that she had touched on the issue that was to be the first cause of outrage by Americans against the Castro government."

While still trying to find a magazine to help Holthaus, Dickey went to Washington and met with General Lemuel C. Shepherd, Jr., whom she had recently acknowledged as having made her "think harder about Latin America than anyone else could have done. . . ." The former commandant had accepted the post of chairman of the Inter-American Defense Board, a twenty-member committee established for mutual military defense. She brought some of her pictures taken that past December, to help to "indicate some of Castro's tactics." The following month, still decidedly supportive of Castro's revolution, she addressed the deputy director of plans for special warfare at the Pentagon, as well as the Naval Reserve Association, on the Cuban revolution. Her audiences were given the chance to look over the shoulders of the revolutionaries in whom, less than six months earlier, nobody seemed too interested.

"People of our country owe a great debt of thanks to you and to other people like yourself who devote their time to strengthening the security of our nation," wrote Lester L. McDowell, the commander of the Naval Reserve, after Dickey's enlightening visit. Apparently her public support for Fidel had not dampened the military's enthusiasm for her intelligence-gathering value.

By now, as the executions in Cuba increased, a thoroughly horrified United States began gearing up to rid the hemisphere of Fidel Castro. The CIA's schemes would go on for years, ranging from the surreal to the absurd: exploding cigars, exotic powders that would cause Castro to go bald, anti-Christ religious apparitions rising out of the sea, and every variety of skullduggery with a cast of characters that would give new meaning to the expression *strange bedfellows*.

That April Dickey's long piece on Castro appeared in the *Reader's Digest*. Given the climate, it was surprisingly if warily pro-Castro, certainly one of the most in-depth ever written about the leader, giving a fairly balanced description of the events leading up to the revolution. Not surprisingly, the only mention of U.S. involvement with Batista matched Dickey's public utterances.

The article did not label Raúl a communist, only reported that he'd visited communist satellite countries as a student and was an outspoken critic of U.S. policy toward Cuba. It maintained that the Batista-led charges of Fidel's communism had never been proved by either Batista or the United States. In her wait-and-see position, she wrote that the "rough military justice, the executions," spotlighted "issues of both conscience and common sense." She went on to quote the governor of Puerto Rico, Luis Muñoz Marín, who, while not condoning them, understood "the deep feeling that . . . brought on the executions." Also mentioned were the sentiments of the American clergy in Cuba, enclosed in a wire to President Eisenhower: "The American silence on the crimes of the Batista regime has made the present criticism of the executions here offensive to Cuban-American relations."

Dickey recalled that Fidel Castro told her, "Our hardest work is not to overthrow Batista. It will come after we have won." As to Castro's intemperate attacks on the United States, she answered, "He does not seem to realize Cuba's best chance for a prosperous and stable future lies in the establishment of a friendly, working partnership with the United States. His attitude toward us may stem from his temperament, which essentially is that of a rebel." The article ended on a cautionary note. "Revolutions before this one have started out with brave ideals, only to end in a return to tyranny. Chief among Castro's problems will be the degree to which he permits the communists to influence his government."

Dickey believed the people of America would have demanded an end to Batista's corruption if reporters had informed them of the terrors. So, on her spring lecture tour through the Midwest, she continued to demand that America own up to its role in Batista's Cuba, and to understand how it contributed to Fidel's stance. Her appeal, issued in her usual outspoken manner, backfired. To her audiences and the media, her attempt at an explanation became a defense of Fidel's barbarous government. "Dr. Fidel is an idealist, he likes to be against something big," she'd say. "And the U.S. is big." On April 10 she addressed a group of staid women at the Knife and Fork Club in Davenport, Iowa, many of whom had seen her on "To Tell the Truth" the past February and were surprised that she was so tiny in person. The reporter for the *Morning Democrat* mentioned that Dickey still had a swollen ankle and a taped knee from her mishap with the Cuban jeep.

Like the rest of America, the reporter was horrified by Castro's public executions. She must have blanched when Dickey declared, "He is one of the few genuine folk heroes I have covered. To people in all of the Latin American republics, he is the arch-foe of dictators." But when the reporter asked Dickey about the summary executions, Dickey could no longer respond with an attack on Batista. Whatever she'd hoped to provide to the heartland with her view of Castro's Cuba curdled in the face of the unrelenting executions. "I do not condone those hasty executions," she answered. But she was not yet ready to denounce Castro as a tyrant and a demagogue.

When Dickey returned to New York that April, the country was abuzz with Castro's planned visit to the United States. Herbert Matthews had read her article in the *Digest,* and although he found a few errors in it, he wrote her that "only tyrants rewrite history. . . . What happened up to the present cannot be changed if it should turn out that Fidel does not make a success of his leadership. Personally, I think it is much too soon to judge. I have great hopes for his trip to the United States, both for Cuba and for us."

But for Dickey the mail from Havana held gloomy portents. Jerry Holthaus was still first lieutenant of Havana's tourist police. By now he realized the revolution had not created a new role. As at Guantánamo, he was still a guard. "Oh, what promises they made me when I left the base," he lamented to Dickey in a letter dated April 5, 1959. It had finally dawned on him that he was not going to be made a great hero, nor be favored in any way. Raúl Castro's anti-American speeches, which Dickey and Holthaus had listened to patiently during the struggle, had become deafening thunder.

When Holthaus appealed directly to Fidel for help in returning to Guantánamo, Fidel screamed at him, telling him he had no use for the American government and that when he was finished there'd be no Americans left in Cuba. Castro advised Holthaus to become a Cuban citizen, that he would be well taken care of. "All I have now is a beard and long hair," Holthaus moaned to Dickey. Besides clearing his name, he had only one desire, he confided: to have a chance to fight against Fidel Castro.

Upon his arrival in the United States, the bearded leader intended to visit New York and Washington. Dickey was now wrestling with Castro as with a technical problem. As a prisoner he had been one of the few survivors of Batista's terror, and she well knew and respected the resulting psychological scars. But she did not think Castro vengeful. "Our whole relationship with Latin America now depends on our relations with Fidel Castro," she told an interviewer in Davenport, Iowa. "And we in this country must remember this and act accordingly."

Dickey resented the widespread interpretation of her beliefs as blindly pro-Castro. "I believed recognition of what I reported from Cuba would prevent further Soviet takeover of the island-government," she wrote in an undated letter to an editor friend. "I resent being called anti-American, because I say the American government and people are making dangerous misjudgments in dealing with Castro." In the same letter she wrote, "If someday my alleged credibility is destroyed because I was demonstrated to be just plain wrong, I'll consider the fact of the demonstration my little private piece of immortality and I swear I'll shut up." She didn't shut up. But she was aware that the sentimentality of which she was so proud had tripped her up, once again overwhelming her objectivity.

But Dickey was not the only observer perplexed by the turn of events. Her consternation was mirrored by a letter from Herbert Matthews's wife, Nancie, written on April 12, 1959: "Well then, where do we go from here about Cuba and Fidel? It seems to me that I get a shock every day—and yet my faith in that man cannot yet be shaken." Nancie had accompanied Herbert to Cuba when he first interviewed Castro. "Herbert and I," she wrote, "are shivering about his coming visit, but we both feel that it can do a lot of good. . . ." Nancie went on to mention that she believed there was at present a need for patience about Castro and was certain that "all those groups who supported Fidel in his fight to throw out Batista and Co. will act against Fidel himself if at the end of some months they feel it necessary. One thing that few people here realized is that Fidel and his *barbudos* could not have won without the support of those many groups—and their support . . . their faith is being shaken . . . their sensibilities outraged. . . . They want Fidel to come to his senses. It is terrible how he resents any criticism—how little he seems to seek the advice of more experienced people, etc. . . . I never knew a case in history in which so many people want to help a revolutionary to succeed. Yet it seems to me, Fidel keeps slapping those people down. It shows the magnetism of the man." She ended the letter, "I don't believe Fidel is going to be able to end up another dictator. . . . It's going to be an interesting and disturbing thing to follow." Nancie looked forward to seeing Dickey at some of the "doings" for Castro that had been scheduled. She was certain, she wrote, that Dickey "would have an honored place."

When Castro arrived in Washington in April, he was resoundingly snubbed. President Dwight Eisenhower made a point of leaving Washington to play golf. Vice-President Richard Nixon, known to have Cuban friends with business interests unsympathetic to Castro, met with the Cuban leader. Although Castro had continued to deny he was a communist, Nixon, the fervid commie hunter, was convinced otherwise after their meeting and sent a memo to the State Department, recommending that the administration arm an exile force to overthrow the Cuban leader. This was not a new feature of U.S. policy. On the one hand, the administration had lent the revolution tacit support because it was unhappy with Batista. Yet while Castro was fighting Batista, the CIA had decided to go from its clandestine support of him—reportedly funding the revolution between October or November of 1957 and the middle of 1958 with $50,000 to key members of the 26th of July movement in Santiago—to a plan supporting other Cuban groups opposed to his takeover.

On April 18, with disenchantment growing over Castro, his executions, and the threat to the nationalization of American businesses, reporters who had covered the rebel army in Cuba were invited to Washington to a reception at the Cuban embassy. Fidel's charisma was undimmed by Eisenhower's crucial rebuff. He had addressed thirty thousand in New York's Central Park, appeared at the United Nations, and spoken widely at press clubs. If Dickey and the bearish Cuban exchanged any warm embraces at the reception, she never mentioned it. She and her colleagues were presented with inscribed solid-gold, football-shaped pendants, naming each as a friend of Cuba. Tony cut out the announcement of the awards ceremony that appeared in *The New York Times*, sending it to Dickey with a note: "Field maneuvers?"

"It looked like a little football. I think there was some kind of Cuban emblem on it," recalled Mary Jane Morrisey, whose husband, Sergeant Robert Morrisey, was then aide to Marine Commandant Wallace Greene. The couple, who had first met Dickey when she'd gone to San Diego on her Marine Corps story, were living in the capital and were Dickey's hosts the night of the embassy reception.

"Oh, it was real fancy," remembered Mary Jane. "She was all dolled up. A limousine came for her and everything. I remember she didn't know what the hell to do with that thing once she got it. It was just too damn big to wear like a necklace."

"I hawked mine," Andrew St. George admitted cheerfully. "It was pure gold. I don't remember how much I got for it."

ON APRIL 29, 1959, after a trip to watch marine exercises in Vieques, Puerto Rico, Dickey received a letter from General Lemuel C. Shepherd, Jr., who had missed her during Fidel Castro's visit. The general had met Castro and been impressed. "He . . . has a great deal of magnetism. I feel sure he will be a prominent figure in Latin American affairs for some time to come." But Shepherd had reservations. "Frankly, I am distressed at the turn of affairs in Panama," wrote the former marine commandant. He was referring to a crushed revolt "[which] I am certain his brother, Raúl, must have promoted or at least supported. If this sort of thing continues, it will cause much harm throughout Latin America and will undo all the good will Fidel has created in the U.S."

AS SHE OFTEN DID when real life became too intense, Dickey took a vacation in the military. On a sunny May morning in 1959, she stood in her high-laced field boots and fatigues, cameras around her neck, at a drop zone at Fort Campbell, Kentucky, where the noncoms of the 101st Airborne's recondo school were being trained in reconnaissance and commando tactics, under the command of General William Westmoreland. Dickey had arrived to do a story on the troopers' readiness, part of her research for the *Digest* for a piece on limited war. She'd glimpsed Westmoreland at the post exchange with his wife and thought the general, the most famous paratroop commander in Korea, movie-star handsome—looking exactly the way Hollywood envisioned its generals.

Above her, the paratroops were doing a mass training jump, the sunlight painting their billowing chutes cathedral pink. When the nearest man thudded down a few feet away, Dickey burst out, "Lordy, you looked good!"

For several minutes he ignored her, rolling up his chute with ultimate masculine superiority. Then he straightened up and put the chute under his arm. "Ma'am," he said firmly, "the hundred and first *always* looks good." And he strode off without looking back.

For the next two weeks Dickey rode in the jump planes making her pictures, "without thinking of jumping with them—consciously, that is. But they thought about it, though; each time I rode in those planes, I was required by regulations to don a parachute for use in case I fell out of the open door. Each time a veteran noncom would remind me that I had to wear the chute, 'but you do understand you will *not* jump.'"

The magic words had been uttered. Dickey answered, "Yes, Sergeant," mentally replying, Of course I'm not going to jump, but if you think I would even before I have, hooray for me.

One morning, among the troopers misshapen by their parachutes, there appeared one erect figure walking over to planeside as Dickey waited to board. People moved out of his way, and Dickey, able to see the two stars on his fatigue blouse, realized why. It was the general himself. He stopped, faced her, gazed purposefully at her boots, and said, "You do understand that you will not jump."

She mumbled, "Yes, sir."

For a split second the general looked almost hesitant. "You do understand also that I'm always a little suspicious of anybody who gets on one of my airplanes wearing a parachute and those field boots."

Clear as a bell, Dickey heard herself answer, "Well, I sure hope you're right to be suspicious," adding quickly, "sir."

The order to move aboard the aircraft interrupted any further conversation. Airborne, Dickey sat unmoving, repeating to herself with scorn and horror, "Do you realize the only implication of what you just told that general? You—you—volunteer."

Within a week of leaving Fort Campbell, a terrified but determined Dickey plunked down $150 to cover a week's lodging and parachute training at a jump school in Orange, Massachusetts, recently opened by a former marine captain. She was its 111th student. She later told a reporter for the *Milwaukee Journal* that the thirty-six hours before her first jump were among the worst of her life. Terror, not fear, accompanied her. Undoubtedly Dickey's famous phrase—"Courage is not the absence of fear, but the control of fear"—was chanted repeatedly as she braced herself on the lip of the open door of the airplane. Did she also recall her father's instructions never to look down?

Beyond the real, ongoing need to conquer her fears, the way an athlete must forever exceed previous records, plus the challenge set during her brief exchange with General Westmoreland, Dickey was driven by another, colder logic. The guerrilla conflicts she wanted to cover, the so-called brushfire wars, were waged mostly in inhospitable terrain. As a forty-year-old woman hoping to be taken seriously in a young man's game, she could get there first only by jumping. She also had to honor her own credo: if she were going to communicate to readers what was really going on, she had to share the danger. And with this humming in her brain, she braced herself, closed her eyes tight, and jumped from the plane.

In July 1959 Dickey returned to Fort Campbell, clutching in her hands the first approval in years from the Pentagon for a reporter, and the first for a woman, to jump with the troops. Her instructor prior to a scheduled military night parachute jump, who would determine if she was adequately trained, was the fabled Major Lewis Millett, a Congressional Medal of Honor winner in Korea, who'd once told a reporter that he'd won the medal for the same reason he'd gotten divorced: "cruel and inhuman behavior." The mustached Millett, commandant of the school, inspired fear and awe in Dickey, who first had to prove herself capable of jumping from a 150-foot practice tower.

"Up in the air on stilts thirty-four feet long is a little wooden shack overlooking a sandy field in Kentucky," she wrote. "To enter its back door, you climb five flights of worn, winding, wooden stairs. To go out the front, you jump off into thin air." Dickey added that one out of every sixteen volunteers for airborne duty would fail to leap—despite the knowledge that a harness link to an inclined trolley limited free fall to about twenty-five feet.

On this hot July afternoon, Dickey was poised on the tower, waiting for Major Millett's command. She noticed his boots were gleaming as he looked up and shouted against the hushed air, "How far down does it look?"

"I fixed my eyes on him, smothered a flinch (it looks about a mile; it always does), and made the ritual answer. 'Thirty-four feet, sir.' To this, Millett shouted, 'Go.'

"I seem to have jumped late and slipped into a state of panic, besides," she wrote. "But when the harness jerks me upright, my ankles touch, my hands clutch the reserve chute strapped to my waist, my chin cuts into my chest." All this time she recalled her breathy voice was shouting, "One-thou-sand-two-thou-sand . . ." Millett ordered her to repeat the jump. Standing once again high above him, she realized that what displeased him was not her hesitation, but the fact that her eyes were closed. How could she, despite her panic, have forgotten this cardinal principle for reporters as well? "His shout is . . . surely the litany of my work as one. There is absolutely no reason to close your eyes. . . . If you call yourself a correspondent, your reason for being is first to see. And then, of course, to tell." Eyes wide open, she jumped.

On her trip to Fort Campbell and subsequently to Fort Bragg, North Carolina, where she would jump with the First Special Forces of the Eighty-second Airborne as part of her continuing research for the *Digest* on the limited war capabilities of American soldiers, Dickey would acquire a certificate accrediting her as a military parachutist. At the time few correspondents and surely no other women reporters were so qualified. Dickey publicly downplayed the risks, mentioning that the ripcord was yanked automatically and that she had an extra chute just in case. . . . However, she seemed ready to drop everything at a moment's notice for a chance to go diving out of an airplane. At one point she merrily suggested a team of her parachutist pals accompany her on a mass jump onto the wide green lawn of the *Reader's Digest* offices in Pleasantville, New York. It didn't happen, but what a perfect drop zone that big green patch would have made.

Like others who parachuted, Dickey had come to desire nothing so much as the great quiet out there beyond the lip of the exit hatch. She called parachuting one of the "greatest experiences a person could have." The only drawback was that it was over too fast. One of her proudest moments, besides the day she finally landed with the marines (in July 1959 in the choppy waters of Lake Michigan for part of the St. Lawrence Seaway celebration), was when she received her wings from the 101st. She hung her paratroop certificate on the wall above her typewriter. It was signed by Major General William C. Westmoreland, who would command the first U.S. combat forces in Vietnam.

By the summer of 1959, Dickey's growing identification with the elite forces of the military and familiarity with its bigwig generals had become a source of annoyance to her loyal friend Stevie Blick. Stevie worked at Bellevue Hospital, right across the street from Dickey's apartment, and would often spend her lunch hour visiting her well-traveled friend. Often, as she climbed the stairs, Stevie felt as though she were visiting the mess hall at Camp Pendleton. Stridently issuing out Dickey's doorway were the rousing strains of John Philip Sousa's "Semper Fi," the Marine Corps hymn. The bewildered Stevie asked Dickey, prancing about in combat fatigues, why she couldn't dress in a more feminine manner when not on assignment. Stevie didn't buy Dickey's answer that it was to benefit her career. "What career?" she asked, looking around the tiny apartment. It needed paint, a maid, a new spread on the bed. She would lecture that Dickey was getting too old to go jumping out of planes, that Dickey should stay put and start earning some money. "But she never worried about money," recalled Stevie. "Only with keeping up with the troops."

Stevie recalled that her tailor father made many of Dickey's suits, dark, severely tailored, made of expensive cashmere or gabardine. The whole image—pulled-back hair, husky talk, now peppered with crude if colorful jargon—seemed phony to Stevie. "She wanted the attention it brought, I think. She was overplaying her role." But when Dickey had to attend any kind of fancy "do," Stevie would often find herself running around looking for exaggerated, gut-busting, wasp-waisted, low-cut satins and silk, as overplayed as Dickey's military garb.

FINALLY, IN AUGUST 1959, the *Reader's Digest* sent Dickey to Cuba for an update, one year after the revolution. Anti-American feeling in Cuba had come to equal the anti-Castro sentiment in the United States. Many early Castro supporters about whom Nancie Matthews had written Dickey had fled to Miami. Wealthy Cuban landowners and U.S. business interests who had supported the revolution were impatient to collect their spoils. That same month the United States made an unsuccessful attempt to mobilize the governments of Latin American against Castro. Meanwhile, Castro seized American-owned properties. The reaction in Washington was swift. Cuban assets were frozen and American markets for Cuba's sugar were also closed. All that remained was for diplomatic relations between the two countries to be severed, which happened the following year. Idyllic, libertine Cuba, America's playland and dominion, ten minutes by jet from Miami, was turning to the Soviets.

When Dickey arrived in Havana on August 13, 1959, she expected warm greetings as a friend of the revolution. A letter from Tony, who despite his infirmities managed to keep up with Dickey as if by radar, was waiting in her hotel room. After reminding her to bring back the usual cigars and rum, he asked if she had yet flashed her gold medal from Castro around the town, if it gave her special treatment, and if the tourist business was picking up. She could answer that quickly enough. There were no tourists.

She had arrived on the island of white sand beaches and turquoise water amid American news reports that there was increasing turmoil on the island and opposition to Castro's revolutionary government. Attempts had been made on the life of Raúl Castro, and there had been actions by anti-Castro forces at a sugar mill in Las Villas province. The prisons were crowded with counterrevolutionaries. Only the day before, Fidel had foiled a bizarre coup attempt backed by his old foe, Dominican Republic dictator General Rafael Trujillo. The coup was to be led by two commandants of the rebel army, formerly fighters among the Guerrilla Second Front of the Escambray, one of the factions opposed to Fidel Castro in the fight against Batista—the American mercenary William Morgan and the former commander of the Escambray, a Spaniard, Eloy Guttierez Menoyo. The two would-be conspirators, now supposedly loyal to Castro, had told him about the plan when it was hatched. (Morgan, always the opportunist, had reportedly collected a down payment of $500,000 from Trujillo.)

Amid this flurry of paranoid intrigue, Dickey was anxious to begin her interviewing. From her room at the Hotel Nacional, she sent a letter to Carlos Franqui, editor of the formerly clandestine rebel newspaper *Revolución,* now personally edited by Fidel Castro. Franqui, a communist and early Fidelista who would eventually flee Cuba, had directed Castro's Radio Rebelde from the Sierra Maestra. He had been Dickey's previous contact to the rebel forces and was still working as liaison to the press. Apparently Franqui, described by Dickey as a "small, fiery man," had earlier offered to accredit her to the Cuban military, promising she'd enjoy the same access to military news sources and trips with the military forces as the *Revolución*'s reporters.

"There is much false reporting—or rather reporting of speculation instead of fact, about the current crises," she wrote Franqui five days after Castro's security forces had rounded up a thousand soldiers loyal to Batista and with connections to the Dominican Republic, to which Batista had fled. Dickey wanted to interview the captured soldiers and asked Franqui also to grant her access to Fidel and Raúl Castro. "I can only be useful in contradicting the reports in the U.S. press . . . if I have access to the military sources before—not after—the crisis is ended, so I can again tell my readers in both North and South America that I *saw* the truth just as you enabled me to see it when it was Batista's censorship we were fighting against."

Franqui refused. "My government doesn't have anybody doing that kind of thing," he told her. "We don't need to do it. It's just a propaganda device."

The rebel army may have looked warmly upon Dickey's efforts to publicize its struggle, but postrevolutionary Cuba had no need for the *Digest*'s fierce conservatism and its well-advertised CIA connections. To boot, the magazine's $1.8 million Cuban printing plant had been lost to Castro's nationalization. Of course Dickey was fully aware of the *Digest*'s politics, but she had yet to feel compromised. She had returned to Cuba "as a friend," as the author of "a wholly approving and very long story about the rebels for sixteen million people!"

It struck her as curious and ironic that the Castro cabinet, the same men whom she and other reporters had risked their lives to cover during the revolution, had now cut themselves off from the American press corps. "After all, these men were fighters, not administrators, so some delay in organizing press facilities was to be expected," she later wrote. "But time passed, and like almost every other segment of the American community in Cuba, the press found its needs pointedly ignored."

Still, Dickey proved resourceful. Her notebook is filled with details about the failed coup d'état plot. She interviewed its participants and "leaders," now praised as Cuban heroes, William Morgan and Eloy Guttierez Menoyo. Morgan was then being protected against an attack by Trujillo with twenty Castro-supplied guards. The adventurer, a certified parachutist like Dickey, stroked his .45 while assuring her he was not afraid of Trujillo. Dickey hoped to profile the colorful Morgan for *Argosy*, which turned her down. Two years later he would be executed for involvement in a "counterrevolutionary" conspiracy. Menoyo—who sent her a warm greeting in a flowery handwritten note upon her arrival, translated as "We salute you in the name of the people of Cuba and from the government of the Revolution"—would also desert the revolution. He was captured in 1961, during the Bay of Pigs operation.

The country evidenced little violent opposition to the new government. Dickey noted the existence of an anti-Castro underground as well as a rumored Soviet presence in Cuba, but she was unable to verify it. A few months later an item in the Hearst-owned *New York Herald American* reported the presence of Soviet engineers in Camagüey.

Dickey sent a note to Raúl that she now had become a "jumper." It failed to get her into the inner circle. So she left for Las Villas province and then the onetime revolutionary stronghold, Santiago de Cuba in Oriente province, to find out about the growing counterrevolutionary activities.

Back in Milwaukee, Aunt George, sixty-eight years old, and Lutie, ten years older, did not let failing health diminish their support of Dickey. But in George's August 18 letter, she told Dickey she was counting the days until her return. George's tone of concerned perplexity was new. George asked if her intrepid niece had uncovered anything about the failed revolt that would make sense of the conflicting news in the States.

Dickey replied from Santiago on August 31. The Motel Rancho, where she had stayed a year earlier, was to her surprise now completely overrun by other Americans, mainly, she wrote George, "professionals"—oil people, scientists, students, and probably more than a few spooks. The trip was disappointing. She had turned up nothing and was worried, as always when two weeks were becoming three and she didn't have a bead on what was going on. Nevertheless she squeezed out five thousand words about the unverifiable hearsay and sent it to the *Digest*.

"What you're reading from Cuba is mostly balderdash," Dickey wrote George. "I don't yet see how I can assemble a *Digest* piece from reasonably factual stuff which will make sense against the background of what other publications are writing. I'm not saying everyone's out of step but me (though I'm sure I have to fight to keep from feeling that way)." It was, she added, impossible to get "any solid information out of this blessed government, and hence what you are reading is compounded of equal parts of fantasy and frustration by every reporter around. Too many of whom never set foot out of Havana. And of course, the story is not in Havana at all." She was putting in her share of running around and being run around, but as far as she could see, even in Santiago "nobody was shooting at anybody."

She eventually did spend time in the presence of Fidel Castro, busy as both Cuba's president and prime minister; it was an encounter she later described as "bordering on farce." She managed to see "the biggie" only surrounded by bodyguards. And Raúl—who had sworn never to be civil to an "Americana" when the revolution was over—actually "kissed me on my widow's peak in public—my one reaction being that it had been quite awhile since I was kissed on the forehead by a terrorist." But other than Raúl's perfunctory greeting, she was snubbed and "blind furious" about it, "since I had treated them very well in print."

The meeting occurred at a televised trial of captured Trujillo conspirators, which Dickey attended with her Havana-based colleague, Woolsey Teller. Teller recalled that Dickey told him the "invasion" incident was a "trumped-up" job to keep Cuban emotions stirring while Castro consolidated his power. In the studio, she sat next to a young security guard who slept, sitting up, with the barrel of a sweat-rusted German Schmeisser submachine gun across his hips. She noted that the television studio had become the real seat of the new government, where blazing lights and cables provided Castro with a new "command post." His televised appearance took on the "same web of hypnosis, the same almost liquid spell," that had been present during the revolution, but this high-tech atmosphere lent it an air of stifling megalomania. "The enemies are overstated where he used to understate," she observed reluctantly. "Now his microphone weighs a ton and takes a crew, now his audience is millions. . . . Nothing, but nothing, that takes away the magic will be tolerated." The revolution had sat down to eat its children.

Though she hoped there would be an end to the violence, her observations told her otherwise. "Fidel Castro is not a deity as the influential Cuban magazine *Bohemia* pictured him (with a halo), nor is he mad or just-another-small-dictator. He is a national leader entrapped in an outworn role. But he will not fade away like his TV counterparts at the turn of a switch. As a reporter, I see as one of the crying needs of our world men who—like Castro—are unable to take a backward step on a course they believe in." Two years later she still thought it was the man's ego that was the real enemy. She wrote a friend that "Russia is not behind him, but simply is using his overweening vanity for the Soviet's own purpose of burying us of the free world."

The defendants in Castro's odd courtroom drama struck her as "disbelieving that they would soon not exist. It's written in their eyes." It seemed obscene to her that the last act of a man's life should be spent inside a television studio with a live audience, while Fidel Castro joked, needled, and rearranged papers on his desk with the audience laughing, jeering, and hissing. She watched Morgan, "sitting like a schoolboy while his recent companions in adventure act their last scene."

Before leaving Havana, Dickey found the woeful Jerry Holthaus at a milk bar. She had spoken to her marine friends at headquarters in Washington, and though the charges against him were serious, they were not insurmountable. But he had to get back and face the music if they were to have any success in fighting his dishonorable discharge and cutting his jail time. "You made me damn proud to be an American," she told him. "And even prouder to be accredited to the marines." The next month Jerry Holthaus surrendered at Guantánamo.

Inside the lobby of the Hotel Nacional, Dickey ran into the rebel army commander, the heroic Camilo Cienfuegos, who showed her something curious. It was a metal insignia he had pinned to his shirt pocket, an enameled white rose belonging to an anti-Castro secret society. Membership brought execution by firing squad. He told Dickey it was a joke, an expression of his ultimate contempt for his enemies. She didn't think the joke would be any good if the threat to the revolution wasn't real.

Dickey's piece appeared in the January 1960 issue of *Reader's Digest.* She described Castro's response to her question about his views on communism: "Just because Karl Marx had a beard and Castro also has a beard, Americans should not jump to conclusions." She wrote that the government of Fidel Castro was "a regime . . . threatening . . . the unity of the entire Western Hemisphere. . . . He is . . . providing impetus and leadership to anti-Yanqui movements throughout Latin America." As far as she was concerned, Cuba was doing the Kremlin's top-priority work in the Western Hemisphere, "which is to wreck hemispheric unity. . . ." Gaining the perspective of her cold war colleagues, Dickey saw only that the United States was being used as a "scapegoat" to aggrandize Castro's liberator role. How could the Cubans shake America's investment in their country? She admitted Cuba had its "rational grievances" with the United States—its arming of Batista and indifference to his excesses, for example—but she did not support the "grotesque caricature of Uncle Sam as a fat exploiter of weak neighbors and blood-partner of Latin dictators. . . ." In summation she described the Castro regime as "wide open to infiltration," writing hotly that "while the sky is the limit in attacking the United States, no Castro leader ever attacks Soviet Russia or Red China."

Fidel Castro, known to be sensitive about his image, also read her article. "Somehow Castro got word to Dickey," recalled Sergeant Robert Morrisey, "that if she ever wanted to come back to Cuba, she had better bring the marines." Dickey, who took a great deal of pride in being kicked out of Hungary, experienced a similar thrill about Cuba. She sent a message to Castro—who had demanded that the United States remove its naval base at Guantánamo despite its lease in perpetuity—that she intended to return, with the marines.

15

With Her Eyes Wide Open

Dickey, whose business card read "Overseas News," was spending less and less time in the States. When at home, she could be found at midnight hammering together orange crates for bookcases and doing her filing—she now had half a dozen metal cabinets and there was room for no more in her tiny apartment—picture framing, clothes mending, shoe sorting, and copper polishing. She was a guest on the television quiz show "To Tell the Truth" and joked with her aunts about one day being famous enough to appear on the "Jack Paar Show," with its fat fee of $350. She'd also been approached by a radio producer about the possibility of having her own show. Although this did not materialize, it underlined her growing celebrity as an "interpreter of violence," her self-described role. She turned to her stacks of mail, some of which, she noted ruefully, was three years old. She got letters from girls eager to emulate her, one so intent on entering journalism so that she might sacrifice her life "for a cause" that an alarmed Dickey began writing her on a fairly regular basis, gladly looking over the girl's term paper and gently guiding her into another field. Others she also tried to discourage, disparaging her career as demanding, not glamorous. If her sober tone did not frighten them away, then she'd offer some firsthand advice. "Learn to type and take very, very good care of yourself physically. Like a soldier. And roughly for the same reasons." She had by now carved a very special niche for herself as a combat reporter and viewed her assignments as what they were, military operations. Dickey missed her two aunts in Milwaukee and their indulgences. "Heck," she wrote, "I've even put my spice shelf up properly, all of which makes me homesick for both of you. . . . It's terrible to do all this work and not to have you to dinner to show it off to." But in truth, she couldn't wait for her next faraway assignment.

On October 11, 1959, only four days before leaving on a *Digest* assignment to the U.S. Seventh Fleet to patrol near the islands of Formosa and Quemoy, which were threatened by constant bombardment from the Chinese mainland, Dickey dropped a note to *Argosy*, hoping to arrange the same setup she'd made with them in Beirut. She wanted to hop from the Pacific fleet to Ventiane, Laos, because "a Special Forces paratrooper just back from Laos told me it is much hotter than the public news reports indicated." She told *Argosy* she wanted to do a "big story" in Laos "about the effort of Laotians to counter Red infiltration with 'village development teams' trained in part by us." Since there were no navigable roads in Laos, six- and eight-man teams parachute-jumped into their assigned areas and walked out. Dickey had connections with one of the U.S. Special Forces trainers, who had told her he could set things up so that she'd be able to jump right in with the Laotian army teams. But she needed somebody to pay the freight, which she estimated "would cost about as much as I've known *Argosy* to pay me for a two-part cover feature." She believed it would have "the same real advantages as the deal we made in Lebanon—that is, you'd have a reporter *belonging* to you on a global hot spot." If not, she would settle for a five-hundred-dollar advance from them for an exclusive personal story with the U.S. Seventh Fleet—since her work for the *Digest* had to do with "destroyers." Her letter was ill timed, and the cost involved was not attractive to *Argosy*. Dickey left for the Pacific without an assignment for Laos, spending a month with the fleet and the Chinese navy on its patrol operations in Kinmen and Matsu.

While in Quemoy, only four miles from the Chinese mainland and suffering heavy bombardment, Dickey interviewed a French missionary as to why he insisted on staying. He replied, "How did *you* feel about the communists when they released you?" The man, whom she'd never met, seemed to know all about her experiences in Hungary.

"I intend to spend my life making them sorry they let me go," she answered.

The priest smiled. "Then surely you understand why I stay."

A note from Aunt George dated November 12, ringing with her old enthusiasm, caught up with Dickey in Taiwan. "Gosh, I'd like to have snuck along with you for your Hong Kong visit," chirped George. "Shall I send you a new box of hairpins for the destroyer fixings?" George further informed her niece that thanks to the *Digest* she had one thousand dollars in her savings account. "Think of it, a whole thousand between you and the poor house!" Also, Dickey's brother had confided to George that he'd really come to "like and appreciate" his big sister and that he felt her writing had also improved tremendously. The only unpleasantness was the prospect of an avalanche of letters from Tony, who had split with Helga for the moment and was, according to George, "feeling *very* sorry for himself without any present lady friend to hold his hand." Knowing her niece's weaknesses, George warned, "Don't stick out your little sympathetic finger—there are plenty of others to console him."

As often happened to the increasingly rootless woman, Dickey did not return from the Pacific fleet as she'd planned but went on to Okinawa for the *Digest* to finish her article on limited warfare ("Our Secret Weapon in the Far East," June 1960), which she'd begun earlier in the year at Fort Campbell. Now concentrating on unconventional warfare training with the First Special Forces, Airborne, she was the only reporter allowed to accompany this elite group of professional soldiers. These were the men, she wrote, who were "preparing to train guerrilla forces deep behind enemy lines if war, limited or nuclear, comes back to Asia. . . ."

"Preparing" was the word she used in her article, although she knew there were covert Special Forces teams already in Laos, whose secret mission was to set up a Laotian army. She had every intention of going over to see for herself. She was on the verge of being indoctrinated into this special group of men—men who like herself were no longer young, "who swaggered even when they were sitting down from looking hard for a long time at hazard"—she would be covering when she got herself to Laos. She felt tremendous excitement. This was the very apogee of her training as a combat reporter, and the *Digest* was paying for it.

By now Dickey was plugged into a humming clandestine forces network; the men she had jumped with kept her informed about brushfire wars. One of these covert fighters had been so impressed by her that he wrote to the *Digest,* proposing Dickey as one of their "unforgettable characters." At times she herself stood back, amazed by what she could do. She feared looking too long, lest she get scared and quit.

After a briefing inside the clandestine Okinawa classroom, she and the men were driven by truck with their chutes and battle gear to a Special Forces section of the Naha Air Base, far from prying eyes. Hidden by a row of hangars, a C-130 Hercules waited for them. In less than two hours they would be over their practice target in South Korea. Dickey had been cleared to jump with a Special Forces inspection team on one of their night exercises from an altitude of twelve hundred feet, to land on a sand island in the middle of the Han River. She would have nine seconds to live if her chute didn't open. The quiver moved from her stomach to her knees, and she could feel her heart going thump, thump, thump. . . .

Unlike the other eight-man teams inside the big C-130, Dickey's team consisted of herself, Special Forces Colonel Francis P. Mills, a onetime legend in the World War II Office of Strategic Services, and Staff Sergeant Virgil Postelthwaite, the operations officer and a former OSS officer, who would follow Dickey out of the plane.

Leicas cross-strapped over her chest, Dickey had not felt so special in years. It wasn't just jumping over Korea, the war she had missed reporting on years before, but a delicious smugness in the face of Tony's former warning—that she couldn't be a gal reporter forever going from one marine base to another for the rest of her life—that she had proven him wrong. Her two crusty jump partners weren't marines, but she sure as hell had found a way to be a gal reporter, with one military outfit after another, albeit an admitted "plumpish, forty-one-year-old one."

It wasn't that she didn't like women, it was simply that she had not met any who could share this kind of delicious, forbidden fun. Anyway, she would have hated to have to share any of this. Inside the darkened plane she watched the men strap rifles and submachine guns into elongated canvas covers tied to shoulders and legs. They wore RANGER and AIRBORNE shoulder patches, badges of their secret society.

Earlier she had torn a page from her notebook, releasing yet another government, this time her own, from any liability. The group's intelligence officer back at Naha Air Base had instructed "Posty," "If we lose her in the water hazard, recover the body. I'm signed for that jacket she's wearing."

Her box lunch of chicken tasted like the cardboard container it was packed in. Outside, the sky was darkening. A faint light from the cockpit shone down the plane's corridor, glinting on the polished leather pistol holster of a man whose helmet showed a captain's bars and on the handle of a trench knife on the thigh of a mustached sergeant. The harnessing-up resembled a ballet, and Dickey felt the nervous excitement waiting for the curtain to go up. She was the female lead of this ballet. The plane went dead dark twenty minutes from the jump zone, to accustom them to the blackness outside the plane. Posty had removed the cameras from her neck, explaining they were not allowed. Although Dickey didn't like being separated from her cameras, even by Special Forces, she felt sure she could replay the evening a dozen times, frame by frame. She sat on the rivet-marked floor, chuted up, her harness so tight she had gasped when it was cinched.

She studied the two rows of anonymous, suddenly misshapen human beings, like her so vulnerable. It was a twentieth-century military ritual "by which there is a place in time for everything that still needs doing," she wrote. All she needed to do was concentrate on the colonel, his legs braced, his hands grasping the door frame. Luxuriating in the total trust she had granted him, she fastened her ripcord to the taut, braided-steel wire passing over her shoulder that would open the chutes.

The heavyset airman slid open the door with a grunt. The wind outside howled like a hurricane. Suddenly Dickey's static line, the second safety bar to her ripcord clip, seemed to be missing. But it had only slipped. Her hands were shaking, and she was grateful not to have fumbled the connection in front of the men. From behind her, Posty signaled the colonel, who disappeared into the darkness. Suddenly Dickey was confused. She wanted to do the jump correctly. "Step. Pivot—" Now was it the left or the right foot last? She put her head down to check that her feet were together and was still wondering if she was doing it right when Posty shoved her out.

She was alone, her eyes open, the plane gone, the earth somewhere below. She was the center of the universe of rushing darkness. "The engulfing blackness is not unkind," she wrote. "You sense with an ultimate clarity that nothing can happen that hurts." She was being engulfed by night, quiet, and exploding emotions: joy! panic! She began counting, "One thousand . . ." Above her the umbilical cord from the plane, fifteen feet of nylon ribbon, the static line, pulled back the cover from her main chute. "Two thousand . . . I am a rag doll." Almost a thousand square feet of nylon, thin as a pencil, stronger than steel, unfurled. "Three thousand . . ." The nylon canopy trembled, reaching, stretching out. "Four thousand . . ." She was tugged upright, the harness straps spreading the shock across her body. The chute opened and spread; it was a flower, an umbrella, a cool helpful sun-shaped blanket, a perfect circle. Dickey thought it the work of a master draftsman against the starry night. She hung like a Christmas tree ornament, rock steady, but her heart was pounding "with an exultant shout edged all around with sun bright silver!" Looking down and seeing lights, she said to herself: "So this is Korea."

She later wrote the London-based Plimmers that after her jump in Korea she received her ceremonial Special Forces wings, the dagger and flame, "without regard for the legality of a broad and a civilian getting them." She didn't think any "teenage paratrooper had any more fun than this old lady. The problem with such unseemly conduct is that once you've got your story out, what do you do with the left-over enthusiasm?" She wasn't kidding.

Dickey rarely allowed herself the indulgence of introspection. When she did, she'd inevitably find herself worrying about some black day when she'd have to give up her joyous existence—the day when she wouldn't be able to keep up. The thought would send her into a state of real panic.

When Dickey returned to Okinawa after her thrilling jump and practice drill in Korea, a sergeant rushed over to her with two urgent messages. She was summoned to Guantánamo to appear as the only character witness in the court-martial of Jerry Holthaus; and Tony was in jail.

Dickey was flown on a military plane to the big U.S. naval base at the island's southern tip, which in answer to Castro's demand for its removal was now cut off from the rest of Cuba by twenty-seven miles of barbed-wire-topped cyclone fencing patrolled by thin-lipped marines. There were seven thousand Americans on the base, which employed three thousand Cubans. Sailors and marines by the thousands had once poured through its gates into the Cuban towns and villages whenever the fleet was in. No more.

At the court-martial, Dickey reminded the presiding military of the prevailing sentiments two years earlier, when "most freedom-loving countries assumed Castro would also have a free country." If that had happened, she believed that the accused, Jerry Holthaus, would have been in Officers' Candidate School at Quantico, Virginia, rather than facing a court-martial. The prosecutor questioned Holthaus's motives for going AWOL in the first place; as far as he was concerned, this oversize, under-IQ'd kid was a patsy. "The only thing about America that the people saw was the strafing planes," explained Dickey in response. "The consequence of [Holthaus's] actions . . . believing he was fighting imperialism, particularly at great risk to himself, changed the meaning of the word *American* at that time. If Americans stop acting that way, I as an American and certainly as a reporter, I am not going to like living in the world that much. . . ."

Dickey did not know if her emotional speech had influenced the court to halve Holthaus's original twenty-four-month sentence, but she knew it hadn't hurt. After thanking her for all her trouble, the bungling kid had one more favor to ask. He wanted her to drop him a card from time to time, with a few words on it, "like, 'Hi, Jerry, still alive, Dickey.' "

By the time Dickey got back to New York, Tony had already sprung himself from Chicago's Cook County Jail. As he told it, the trouble had started when Helga had left him for a younger man, adding insult to injury by taking all Tony's Revereware pots and pans. Tony, tanked up on booze, Demerol, and phenobarbital, had threatened the two on the telephone. Waving a gun as he'd disembarked the plane in Chicago, he'd been quickly arrested, and now he was thinking about getting Helga deported. He said he had some compromising pictures that he could bring to the INS. Dickey advised him to "burn it all" and take care of himself instead. "No one could hold my hand but you and make it come out all right," Tony wrote her after his release from jail. Luckily a temporary reconciliation between Tony and Helga spared Dickey a return to nursing duties. But as difficult as Tony would become, retreating woozily into his past and tracking her like a psychopath, Dickey would never discard him. Stevie Blick was certain that one of the reasons Dickey kept traveling was to stay out of Tony's clutches, but he continued to do her photographic work until 1963, when he sold all of his equipment after filing for another bankruptcy.

During her 1960 lecture tours, although discussing the man she now called "a Nasser" was low on her priority list, Castro was a popular topic on the midwestern campuses and in its auditoriums. On March 5, 1960, Dickey wrote George and Lutie that the Soviet Union's public overtures to Castro's revolution were giving her "great twinges."

Her body was, too. Jumping had badly damaged a ligament in her knee, and the spill she'd taken from one of the *rebelde*'s jeeps hadn't helped. It was swelling and it hurt. A well-known neurosurgeon had advised her to remain in bed for ten days and to gradually strengthen her muscles by lifting ten-pound weights. She made the best of this unusual period of quiet by catching up on correspondence from young girls who wanted to know if being a woman made it harder to be a combat reporter. "I haven't found my professional way made harder because I'm a woman," Dickey answered. "I do think women as observers work a little differently, perhaps more intuitively than men. But this is not a disadvantage to a trained professional." She encouraged them all to learn to type, "not because your writing is hard to read, but because it's still the most essential act."

Ten days of inactivity were ruining Dickey's "joy-in-life." She scuttled the doctor's advice, turning to the more practical ideas of her marine drill instructor friends, who suggested she work her muscles past the comfortable stage. The no-pain, no-gain exercises did wonders for her morale, but probably overstressed her banged-up knees.

In April 1960, while she battled the effects of gravity on her body, she made a deal with publisher William Morrow and Company to write two books—one, as she described to a paratrooper buddy, "a howling tome on military training in the United States"; the other, encouraged by military affairs analyst Brigadier General S. L. A. "Slam" Marshall and to be delivered within the year, an anecdotal autobiography. Upon signing the contract, Dickey was paid a fifteen-hundred-dollar advance.

The following month Dickey hobbled over to Parris Island to begin her research. The military training book would never be completed, but nevertheless she enjoyed telling the story of how she'd gotten the contract "by a parlor trick that should amuse you," she wrote her friend. To emphasize the army's "present depressed physical fitness standards, I . . . performed the push-ups, squat jumps, situps, and squat thrusts actually in the editor's office. Thank God he didn't have a pull-up bar or the whole trick wouldn't have worked, what with I still can't do 'em."

Sometime in July 1960 Dickey got a note from another Special Forces pal. For the life of him, he couldn't understand why she wasn't covering

Cuba or Léopoldville—or Vietnam, where Major Millett, her former, shiny-booted jump instructor, had been ordered to set up a Vietnamese ranger school. The paratrooper asked Dickey if she could imagine Millett's "delight . . . in actually patrolling in the communist-ridden environs of the area. If your travels take you there," he continued, "and the story potential might warrant it, he'll be tickled to take you on patrol, I know."

Her reply, after being stateside for more than a few months, was predictable. "The *Reader's Digest* and the country have both made a tragic mistake, as our mutual addresses at the moment indicate; that is, neither of us is in Laos, Vietnam, the Congo or in Cuba." She went on to say that she was leading a sad and solitary life "writing the inevitable books" and "you sure shook me up to the cursing-out-loud point by telling me where Major Millett was. Oh, how I'd rather be there." Her book contracts could never compete with a chance to see action.

By 1961 Dickey had every reason to believe she would finally be able to use her paratroop wings in reporting combat. John Fitzgerald Kennedy, the World War II navy hero and Pulitzer Prize-winner, was a man of her generation, who viewed the world as she did. At his inaugural address, hatless despite the solemn occasion and the inclement January weather, he said that the word should go forth, that "the torch has been passed to a new generation of Americans." His words sounded like music to Dickey's ears: "In the long history of the world, only a few generations have been granted the role of defending freedom in its hour of maximum danger. I do not shrink from this responsibility—I welcome it."

Kennedy's black-and-white view of America as the defender of the free world and the Soviets as drum-banging tyrants greatly appealed to Dickey's sentimental, idealistic gung ho nature, offering her direction in the stormy seas of an ever-changing world.

The free world would win, that was known. Yet to be revealed was its plan for victory, a secret web of plots and hidden wars, strange shenanigans, secret agendas created by a vastly powerful intelligence community run amok. In those spangly Camelot days, the Kennedy years, the Central Intelligence Agency was not an adjunct to the government. It was a nation unto itself, an invisible presence that was everywhere that Dickey went.

On April 17, 1961, thirteen hundred CIA-trained anti-Castro Cubans known as Brigade 2506 stormed the Cuban beaches of the Bahía de Cochinos, the Bay of Pigs. The plan was to have these troops set up a beachhead while supported by overhead B-26s. At the same time, as divined by the CIA, a spontaneous revolt to overthrow Fidel Castro would occur among the Cuban citizens. Then the Cuban Revolutionary Council, the CIA-supported Cuban government-in-exile, would return to take control of Cuba.

For a number of reasons, including bad communication between Washington and the landing forces and President Kennedy's reported indecisiveness, the Bay of Pigs invasion was a bloody disaster. The promised air cover arrived too late. Instead of restless Cuban citizens waiting to revolt, a well-prepared Cuban army under the leadership of Fidel Castro met the invaders on the beach with a hail of gunfire. Three days later nearly twelve hundred survivors of the brigade were placed in Cuban prisons.

Dickey and a few other reporters had learned of the U.S. govern-ment's plan for the invasion weeks earlier, from contacts among Florida's talkative and zealously patriotic Cuban exile community. But it had been decided that press coverage would jeopardize national security. Newspa-per and magazine publishers fell into line and quashed any stories that might tip off the public.

Two days before the scheduled invasion, at the Hotel Lexington in New York, Dickey's credentials had been acknowledged by José Miró Cardona, the exiled first prime minister of Cuba under Fidel Castro and now chief of the Cuban Revolutionary Council and Castro's U.S.-based successor.

The next day Dickey walked into the New York office of publicist Lem Jones, who unbeknownst to her was the CIA-salaried press liaison for the command of the Bay of Pigs forces. He began dictating the following information, claiming it was "hot off the Teletype from Miami: The Cuban Revolutionary Council announces a successful landing of military supplies and equipment in the Cochinos Bay area of Matanzas province. Overcoming some armed resistance by Castro supporters, substantial amounts of food and ammunition reached elements of internal resist-ance forces engaged in active combat."

Suspicious of Jones's information, the next day Dickey flew to Miami. Upon landing, she was already beginning to feel the awful certainty of a wild goose chase. She visited the public relations offices of Osborne

Associates, the Miami press liaison for the combat unit. She thought it odd that the offices for an allegedly desperate and destitute fighting force of exiled Cubans were located in an expensive building, with newly decorated wall-to-wall carpeting, indirect lighting, a modern architecture desk, and a pretty blond receptionist.

She watched a well-groomed, athletic-looking man cranking the brand-new mimeograph machine. A guy with a crew cut and flat gut, who looked nothing like an office clerk, was manning a mimeograph machine and squinting at her. She stared back. She'd never seen him before.

"Dickey Chapelle!" he shouted. "I can't tell you how much I enjoyed that last article of yours! About Cuba, wasn't it? My, you surely called the turn!"

When admitted to Mr. Osborne's private office, she spoke right out. "If there's one agency on earth whose minor employees are required to memorize the face and recent reports of every correspondent from a major U.S. publication," she told him coldly, "it isn't some ragtag revolutionary force, it's the CIA." Livid now at being taken for a perfect fool, she stabbed the air with the cigarette. "Tell that mimeograph operator to cut that stuff out," she advised Osborne. "He's breaking your cover."

Osborne told her he didn't know what she was talking about. He advised her to go to the "recruiting office of the Cuban Revolutionary Council, to stay away from Cardona's house," to which she had been invited personally, and "to stay away from the naval station at Key West." Upon leaving Osborne's office, Dickey scribbled, "Why is it I keep running into the Company?"

Dickey visited the Cardona residence and was told that he was "in the hands of the American government." Right before the invasion was scheduled to begin, the CIA, who were known to distrust their Cuban associates, had spirited Cardona away. Whatever assurances he had given Dickey prior to his disappearance were no longer valid.

It was the first time in her years of combat reporting that she had knowingly been thwarted by what she called "agencies of the United States government." The fact that none of the other fifty reporters in Miami were getting any closer to eyeballing the action was of little comfort. She understood only that she was being prevented from covering a news event by a device she called "management of the news," a dangerous precedent. Moreover, it was hitting her right in the pocket-book. If she sometimes cooperated with the intelligence community as a patriotic American, she did it without ulterior motive. When they began getting in the way of her getting her story, all bets were off. She was first of all a reporter and one whose reputation hinged on her reputation for eyeballing. "If Ernie Pyle were alive today," she scornfully told a friend, "he wouldn't be able to make a living."

In a letter to Hobart Lewis, her editor at the *Reader's Digest,* written two years later and detailing how from this assignment onward she'd found herself increasingly battling government interference, she told of hiring a light plane to fly her over the naval station at Key West, taking aerial shots of five navy destroyers in operational formation. On landing, as she had learned to do during wartime, she submitted her film for censorship at the naval base, but the master-at-arms told her the navy could not officially acknowledge the photos. Also, her presence was beginning to embarrass the base security guard. She left.

In a last desperate act to get the story, Dickey and a photographer for the French magazine *Paris-Match,* who happened to be an ex-para-trooper, considered jumping into Oriente province, but without any drop zone information they gave up on the idea. At this dispirited point, Dickey telephoned Hobart Lewis and ran down the sorry state of her research, asking if he would let her go to Laos instead to cover the reported cease-fire between the Royal Lao Army and the communist Pathet Lao. "I don't imagine the United States is intervening there any less," she told him, "but perhaps the government isn't trying to conceal the intervention as much as they are in Cuba." Lewis gave her the green light, and within hours Dickey left Miami for the Pacific.

PART THREE

AGAINST
ALL ODDS

16

Face to Face

O N MAY 3, 1961, when Dickey stepped off the plane from Saigon into the blistering heat of Vientiane's Wattay Airport, she was stepping into a twilight zone. The ancient kingdom of Laos, the "Land of a Million Elephants," sits on the southern border of China, sandwiched between Vietnam and Thailand. It is a fierce land of impenetrable jungle and towering mountains dotted with reed-and-bamboo huts and rice paddy fields; it also cultivates the world's third-largest opium crop. The people of this remote, mysterious land represent many opposing tribes that have clashed repeatedly throughout their history as foreign armies invaded and conquered, hungry for control of Laos's strategic location. The landlocked country borders not only China, Thailand, and Vietnam, but Burma to its west and Cambodia to its south. Another prize is a rutted dirt road crisscrossing the Annam mountains into South Vietnam and Cambodia. This route, called the Ho Chi Minh Trail, was North Vietnam's impregnable supply artery during the Vietnam War.

In 1959 Laos was seen by President Eisenhower as the cold war key to Southeast Asia—the first domino that, if allowed to fall to communism, would topple all the rest of Southeast Asia onto the Philippines and right up the beaches of California. When the corrupt, right-wing Lao government alleged that it was in mortal danger from North Vietnamese– and Soviet-backed troops called Pathet Lao, U.S. Special Forces disguised as civilian "technicians" were dispatched to the country to whip the pro-West, anticommunist government troops into shape. So began America's secret war.

As the years passed, America poured more and more money into Laos, bankrolling its entire Royal Lao Army, while the Soviets covertly armed the Pathet Lao. A third faction, the neutralists, was also swirling inside this steamy cauldron and inclined toward communism, despite the stream of American aid. President Kennedy, warned by Ike about the domino theory, had publicly pledged to protect Laos.

With President Kennedy's sponsorship, a secret Special Forces–led army of Hmong tribesmen, reportedly numbering nine thousand troops, was being formed, led by CIA-trained Thai and U.S. Special Forces called Green Berets. In exchange for tribal support, Air America (a CIA front whose pilots for the most part had no idea for whom they were working) air-dropped supplies and matériel to secret bases and transported opium.

Dickey checked into the three-story ferroconcrete Constellation Hotel, the backwater's highest building. Situated on Avenue Samsen Thai and partially covered by bursting bougainvillea, papayas, and coconut palms, the hotel maintained an open-air restaurant bar that sheltered the round-eyes of the Western press corps, the crew members of Air America, diplomats, and a few snakelike opium smugglers for good measure. Outside, at Vientiane's single traffic light, black Mercedes-Benzes driven by Laotian officials grown rich with American aid battled bullock carts and pedicabs. Like everything on this northern bank of the Mekong River, the traffic moved to the swell of Laotian pan pipes in slow, shattered movements.

Dickey had arrived on the eve of cease-fire talks among the country's three warring tribes. But the declared cease-fire, like many things in this exotic, mysterious kingdom, was an illusion, a trick of mirrors. Even as an international conference for the peaceful settlement of Laos opened in Geneva, the fighting continued in inaccessible mountain regions—a situation undisclosed to the Western world because most of the handful of Western reporters inside the country did their reporting from the bar of Vientiane's Constellation Hotel, where rumors, like beer, floated amid the greasy chumminess of its guests.

Dickey was eager to get up north to see if the reported cease-fire was working. Desire was not enough. The only way into the mountains was by plane—on Air America—and that required connections. On May 14, after cooling her heels for two weeks in Vientiane and trying unsuccessfully to make the right contacts, the three fighting factions signed a cease-fire agreement. On the following day an NBC newsman, an Air America pilot and mechanic, and at least one Special Forces officer were taken hostage by the Pathet Lao.

By now Dickey was acutely aware that duplicity veiled all transactions in Laos, and western journalists often reacted by going to pieces, as witnessed by the amount of staggering around that took place in the Constellation's bar. Dickey knew her editor, Hobart Lewis, had expected better from her, because on May 19, he sent her an urgent cable: "Want you to cover all aspects of guerrilla war, theirs and ours." She wired him back that his cable had been received with "great joy."

Ostensibly Dickey was in Southeast Asia as a journalist, but the cable explains the reason the magazine kept her there for ten months. Knowing the *Digest*'s relationship to the government and Dickey's intimacy with the military, her job was to gather military intelligence, and do her articles. For the moment, the cable did not make her feel compromised. If anything, her ego, made insecure by her other failed assignments, swelled with the request. It meant they trusted her and her alone to get vital information. But her joy at their endorsement was nearly extinguished by her being stuck in Vientiane. She was also distraught at news from a friend. Her aunt George, who had been battling cancer for years, was dying and asking for her favorite niece. If ever Dickey needed a friend, it was now.

Edward "Clancy" Stone (not his real name) sat at the Constellation's open-air, fly-riddled bar, where acrid smoke from a Gauloise Bleue cigarette hung over his head. As was often the case, the twenty-seven-year-old photographer had a whopper of a hangover that he was treating with an old family recipe, Scotch on the rocks, the tried-and-true "hair of the dog." After seven years in Indochina shooting for wire services, Clancy thought of himself as the grand old man of Southeast Asia. He liked showing newly arrived press the ropes, introducing them to the various lines of information that hummed under the bar's insect-splattered fan, on the dice-playing patio, and in the subterranean caves of the town's whorehouses and opium dens. If one of the press happened to be a good-looking woman, all the better. It struck the Canadian-born Clancy, whose wife lived in Tokyo, as sinful not to take advantage of the loose mores of the anything-goes capital of the world.

A British reporter had been trying to seduce him for weeks, but he hadn't found her in the least attractive. Now Clancy shoved his hands under his Australian bush hat, mowing back his curly blond hair, and turned to the tanned woman next to him. Dickey was wearing rubber flip-flops, a flowered shirt, and khakis with many pockets. Big cat-shaped glasses covered half her face. He wondered what she would look like with her hair down.

Dickey soon brought up her desperate need to get up north. Clancy bought her a beer and told her to relax—"I'll get you out there." He instructed her to meet him the next morning at Wattay Airport. "If they would tell me I couldn't go up where the troops were or I couldn't get on the helicopter, I would say, 'The hell I can't,' " a more subdued Clancy Stone commented years later. "I'd say, 'By God, you get out of my way.' And if they didn't, I'd punch them out." Clancy knew that Dickey liked that about him. "I'd get us where we wanted to go."

The next morning a bleary-eyed Clancy met Dickey where Air America housed its abused and unfit H-34 helicopters. Hitching a ride with the choppers was the only safe way to get to a battle. It was too dangerous to brave the constant shooting and land mines on the rutted paths that passed for roads in Laos.

Clancy and Dickey choppered north over the palm trees of Vientiane and the wide brown band of the Mekong River. An hour later they landed in jungly Ban Pat Lak, where Dickey wrote that for a steaming day and a rainy night, loud, racketing gunfire between two barefoot, tattered-uniformed "Lao groups" testified to a violation of the cease-fire agreement. The American military adviser and his team of blond, blue-eyed sergeants were squatting beside the young officer of the Royal Lao Army when the enemy shelling hit. Dickey grabbed Clancy.

"I think gunfire turned her on. She'd come closer and closer as the guns came in there," recalled Clancy. "I understood. I'd been with a few women in combat. I think you need reassurance when gunfire's going down. I had been with Maggie Higgins in Korea. Maggie didn't stay up front the way Dickey did."

Air transportation in the field was iffy at best, and Clancy remembered that they "got shafted out of their transportation back." The commander of the Royal Lao Army gave them a hut for the night. It was late June, the monsoon season, damp and only slightly cooler than the blood-warm dry season. The night fog was as white as a sheet and would stay that way until nine the next morning.

"We threw our bags on the floor, and we were going to stay in there—the foxholes are right outside the door—all you got to do is to make a running leap and hit it. From then on, we had this thing. But I wasn't the only guy she was involved with. There were a couple of others, military types."

Over the next few months Clancy recalled he and Dickey would go out to the field together in Laos and Vietnam. "You could get the best loving in the world if you could keep her under gunfire for a little bit." Sometimes she would stay behind while he went back to file. If she were somewhere where something was about to go down, she would send him a message through military communications. They worked out a code: "C'mon up and have a drink."

Clancy prided himself with gleaning entire life histories off throwaway lines. Dickey's anxious "I'm only forty-one" made it clear that she wanted desperately to make up for her late start as a combat reporter. He liked her, the way he would an older, sexy tomboy, though realizing that aspect was the part of her that seemed to offend the other reporters. But it didn't threaten him; he got a big kick out of it. Later she showed him her photographs. From the way she talked about her ex, who had taught her to "make pictures," Clancy got the feeling that the divorce had been nasty.

He advised her to forget everything Tony had taught her. "What you're shooting looks stiff," he said, not to insult, but to be helpful. "It looks like birds on a fence." At that point in her photo career, Dickey's photos did have an artificial, posed feeling, which she lost about this time. Whether or not this was due to Clancy's coaching or simply a matter of confidence is unknown. But by all accounts Dickey never did develop the conceit that she was a great photographer; her pictures were tools to prove what she'd seen with her own eyes. If sometimes the outcome was artistic, it was largely incidental. In the case of a haunting double-truck shot for the *National Geographic* article "Water War in Vietnam" (published posthumously in February 1966), her photo editor, Bill Garrett, flipped the negative. "You got a good eye," Clancy told her. "You just got to trust yourself more."

On one of their forays he'd given Dickey an Australian bush hat, the kind the U.S. Special Forces wore, to protect her face from the sun. He had no idea that from then on she always wore the hat on combat assignments. Later Dickey sent her aunts a picture of herself in her new hat, "so you can see what a weird specimen your niece is," noting that the Pathet Lao had placed a bounty of $25,000 on said hats.

Dickey soon realized that nothing in Laos was as it appeared. The letter to her friend Stevie Blick set the tone: "This trip is the wackiest, least predictable one of them all. I started out for Cuba and ended up a week ago counting high explosives coming my way with hostile intent in a hole in the ground in Laos. This is, in case the newspapers didn't make it clear, the noisiest cease-fire I ever covered."

Dickey resolved to try harder. It had worked in the past. She had no idea that endurance was no match for this CIA production.

In late May, Dickey spent a week with the U.S. Special Forces at Ban Pa Dong, fifty miles behind enemy lines, where she'd been airlifted above the dense, rainswept forests to witness a truce violation. Amid heavy artillery fire, a threatened cholera epidemic, and massive refugee movement, two Green Berets were killed in a helicopter crash. Dickey was numb when she returned to her room at the Constellation on June 4. It was just as well. Waiting for her was a cable. George, her favorite aunt, had succumbed to cancer. Although George had been ill for a long time, the loss was gigantic. The next day Dickey wrote her aunt Lutie, expressing her grief. "I hope [this note] says how much I love you and how badly I feel to have been so terribly far away and useless during so much of the bad time. . . . I hope the report I am writing will make up for being away from you . . . wishing I could write a letter which would say what is in my heart, or at least let you know the yearning to hug you and hold on tight. . . ."

Shortly afterward Dickey took off again for the mountains. Once she'd grasped from Clancy the workings of air transport, she could get herself out to the men in green utilities, where her reputation preceded her. She wrote of one occasion when an officer had asked her if she would be willing to eat bats. Without hesitation she snapped out, "Yessir." So, unlike the other reporters covering Special Forces, whom she saw ordered out by helicopter whenever action appeared imminent, she spent three weeks covering them by pole boat, on foot, by supply drop planes, and in helicopters.

She returned to Vientiane on June 26, her ears ringing with mock admonishment from the military that "you've been too far forward too long." But with her privileged access came a real confusion of loyalties. The closer she got, the farther away from the pack, the less what she saw corresponded to what was being passed off as news.

The official story was that the American military in Laos, in mufti since 1959, were civilian instructors. In the spring of 1961, when the royal Lao government asked for direct U.S. military aid, the Special Forces/Green Berets got into uniform. Officially they were there only for a short time—weeks rather than years—training, not leading, the Laotian troops. It was, as one admitted to Dickey, "a thin story," but the only way their presence would "jibe" with official policy.

A year earlier Dickey had written to an editor friend that "not once has a general ever offered to trade me a secret operations order for my fair white virtue, and if it sounds as if I'm complaining, I guess I sure am. You get bitter in your old age when you hear all about your irresisti-bility in this situation and it turns out in a few decades you can't find the damn thing." Personal needs aside, in Laos she had stumbled onto a real secret, all because of her insatiable need to be in the heart of it. Dickey confided to her aunt Lutie, all that now remained of her familial fan club, that she was deeply conflicted. "I feel privileged . . . and terrifyingly challenged since what I have seen isn't exactly the way it's been told in the newspapers by less privileged reporters, and I am puzzled on how to reconcile what they've made their readers believe with what my own eyes have taught me."

As long as the spooks didn't obstruct her as they had in Florida, Dickey's interest did not lie with uncovering the serpentine workings of the CIA's clandestine war. Her rationale at the time was that they each had the best interests of their country at heart. As far as she was concerned, the best example of American foreign policy was being *practiced* in the Laotian mountains, where unnamed, anonymous Americans were fighting communism and dying alongside native armies. That was the *only* story she wanted to tell, from Laos and later from Vietnam. Naively she believed it possible. Nonetheless, she was to find herself caught up in a censorship shuffle that would make the Bay of Pigs look like amateur night.

Despite President Kennedy's pledge, it had become clear that Laos was being lost. "We somehow undertook in Laos a test of will against communism which we were afraid to win," she wrote to Hobart Lewis.

The planes and weaponry being used by the Royal Lao Army were dangerously antique—and despite reports in the global press of an "inhuman wave" tactic of communist invasion, it "had not and could not occur considering terrain with which I was personally familiar." She had also seen U.S. "transport-type aircraft and helicopters take off and land daily and hourly at Wattay Airport, while claiming we were not intervening," and that "both sides have intervened in Laos covertly. . . ."

Bearing all this in mind, as well as Hobart Lewis's earlier cabled request, Dickey gave him a report on all aspects of the guerrilla war, "theirs and ours," as well as putting together a magazine piece on the Green Berets, entitled "The Men Who Didn't Give Up Laos." She was passionately inspired by the men she had seen killed, by their committed "will," and by the memory of Aunt George as well.

"I want to try and tell the way it is out here," she wrote Lewis in a six-page, single-spaced letter from Vientiane's Hotel Constellation on June 29, 1961. "The little handful of flesh-and-blood Americans—a few hundred alive and at least nineteen dead, wounded, missing, captured—who I've seen daily risk their lives to carry out U.S. policy in Laos. They're the tough, inexorable answer to those who think Americans today seek adventure only by flipping TV channels. There are three groups, all volunteer: the veteran transport pilots, the young helicopter pilots, the U.S. paratroopers of Special Forces who lead and teach and risk and die beside Lao soldiers."

Was it vanity that led her to believe that her account of America's phantom soldiers engaged in a secret war in Laos would be printed by a magazine that operated as a veritable organ of government policy? It was the vanity that all good reporters require, the ultimately destructive, chronic condition that what they see they must tell, despite the knowledge going in that the odds are against it ever being told. And it was on that deadly mission Dickey was now engaged. She'd seen too much and she'd never been good at looking the other way to please her editors. If anything, she'd always looked too hard. She was filled to the bursting with the great, desperate, driving need to tell America about the boys it had twelve thousand miles from home, and a belief that their heroism deserved to be told. She responded to the magazine's rejection emotionally. It would mark the turning point in her relationship with the *Digest.* She now felt compromised, frustrated, as more of what she saw went unpublished. She had yet to realize that more and more this was the price she'd be paying for her privileged viewing. She *was* being censored, but it was illogical to liken it as she did to her experience with the gritty World War II photos: nobody had ever denied the existence of the Second World War.

Despite Clancy's allusion to her many affairs, Dickey was lonely. When Lutie wrote asking why some nice man didn't grab up her warm, loving niece, Dickey wrote: "Here in Vientiane I have met dozens of the nicest men on earth; that's the trouble, they come in dozens." She had been in the country for two months and claimed that she knew so many people that "when I take a walk around town, they hail me like an original Laotian settler . . . but I don't have one for my own." She had big ugly sores all over her legs from the country's vicious mosquitoes. She was eating too much and gaining weight, sitting day after day at her typewriter. When she finished her piece on the Green Berets and had captioned the one thousand photographs taken in the field, she sent them on to Washington for the censors at the Department of Defense. She would never dare publish a word or a picture that would in any way compromise the security of her country.

After six weeks in Laos Dickey arrived in Saigon, South Vietnam, in the last week of June 1961, where American presence was seen in the form of military advisers. Once known as the "Pearl of the Orient," Saigon endured a tropical heat that demanded a languid life-style; businesses were closed from an early lunch hour until the sun set above the West-facing treetops. At those times the city of broad, tree-lined boulevards and imposing villas created by its onetime French overlords was empty and ghostly quiet except for the whir of unseen electric fans. But with the sunset it cooled and the town came alive with traffic, pinging bicycle bells, autobuses, pedicabs, and motorcycles. Men in white linen suits sat with beautiful young Vietnamese girls at sidewalk cafes; vendors and beggars crowded the streets.

The war Dickey had come to report on was elsewhere, not yet close enough to shatter the opiated pace of the city. She registered at the Hotel Majestic, fronting the Saigon River, close by the U.S. embassy and down from the Hotel Caravelle. It was air-conditioned inside the hotel, and she sipped a Pernod, cabling Hobart Lewis that she intended to cover "Americans' adventurous role guerrilla fighting" among others. After attending a few diplomatic bashes in Saigon, she grew restless, and on June 28 she left for Laos, where she knew the lay of the land and where, according to Clancy, "she had a few things going." Two weeks later, on July 12, she returned to the Majestic.

As much as she wanted to hurry out to cover how the Vietnamese troops were fighting the war, which her government downplayed as a "brushfire war" or "skirmish," Dickey gritted her teeth and locked herself inside her hotel room with her typewriter, croissants, and strong black coffee, pounding out a series of long reports on guerrilla warfare and captioning the photos for her autobiography. Every now and then she would take a well-deserved break and hit the hotel's rooftop bar, with its view of the muddy Saigon River, where peasants fleeing the fighting in the countryside had come to live in sampans and shacks on stilts and cholera thrived in the malodorous waters.

She had finished the last chapter of her autobiography that March, though another chapter about her experiences with the Vietnamese airborne, written from Saigon, would be included in the *Digest*'s condensation of the book that would run the following year. Julia Edwards, Dickey's colleague, recollected that upon signing the book contract Dickey went around the Overseas Press Club, looking vainly for a ghost-writer. Though she ended up writing the book herself, her search didn't strike Julia as odd. "She was busy with her reporting jobs, and she had never written a book."

Nancy Palmer, Dickey's photo agent, found that scenario improbable. "Dickey was far too possessive of her work and too proud of it to do anything like that." But her so-called possessiveness had not brought her to New York during the last critical stages of the book's prepublication. She was being kept up to date by long letters, often weeks old, from Larry Hughes, vice-president of Morrow. Each letter filled her with mounting dread.

She was disturbed by the crew of women Hughes had assigned to work on the book, two editors and a publicist. In addition, the title they had cooked up—*What's a Woman Doing Here?*—set her teeth on edge. Hobart Lewis had suggested *The Trouble I've Asked For.* She'd wanted to call it *With My Eyes Wide Open.* But Morrow believed its title made the book more attractive to their targeted audience, women. Dickey wrote Hughes that the usual cry of greeting to her was "What the hell *are* you doing here?"

On July 25, after writing Lutie that "my time of desk-sitting in this plush-lined foxhole is over . . . what I'm doing in Vietnam is not very different from what I did in Laos—trying to cover the struggle against the Reds," Dickey left her hotel to be flown "sixty miles from Saigon" above the shimmering rice fields to the Vietnamese marines, with whom she would spend ten days on patrol, on the border of Cambodia, walking twenty-five miles a day and coming under fire three times. "Brush fire war, my foot!" she scoffed upon arriving back in Saigon. Over the next few weeks she made an effort to be social, inviting the marine officers with whom she had just sloshed through the mud and their wives to a Chinese dinner, in the fancy Chinese suburb of Cholon—courtesy of the *Reader's Digest.* She had dinner with an infantry colonel who was teaching her the finer points of guerrilla tactics. He also took her dancing, which she wrote Lutie "was good for my morale, though I can't say the result should be called dancing."

Her morale was pretty low, not only from her frustrating career with the *Reader's Digest,* but also after the shattering experience on patrol with the Vietnamese marines. The senseless death of the young, utterly brave Lieutenant Lien became in its sickening meaninglessness her metaphor for all that was wrong with the way that the war in Vietnam was being fought.

For the first time in her writing about men in battle, she struggled for satisfactory answers to what she'd witnessed, only to be frustrated by the unacceptable turn of her reasoning. His death had nothing to do with bravery but with an impersonal long-range hit that might have been fired from a passing spaceship; by the inefficiency at command level and a scandalous lack of backup support. She didn't question why it was that the death of this young soldier in a hellish jungle clearing disturbed her so; it underscored all that was wrong with the way the war in Vietnam was being fought.

She wrote up the experience, entitled "Death of a Marine," and declared in a letter to Hobart Lewis on August 11 that it had "implications sadly more significant than I like to say. This one mission which I accompanied illustrates more sad truths about what is happening over here than you usually find in a single anecdote." She'd found no lack of toughness, training, or bravery among the marines, "but they just aren't able to kill the enemy under the present setup." She brought up the poor quality of their commanding officers and their woeful use of conventional tactics in a guerrilla war, where the only man the guerrillas killed was "the man in front." She wrote that nobody ever *saw* the guerrillas, so they couldn't be pursued; moreover, the medical care was bad. Lien had died because there was no blood transfusion, no helicopter evacuation. "In short, the Vietnamese Marines, trained by ours, are first, just as impressive and second, just as ineffective, as ours would be. I'm sure this isn't all of the story in Vietnam, but the newspaper stories that the war here has reached a turning point find no echo in my experience."

She was seeing what was wrong, but she couldn't grasp *why*. Her midwestern solidness and her experience in the straightforward Second World War made it all the more difficult. The patrols she accompanied might as well have been fighting a war on Mars. The government in Saigon that the United States was backing was as corrupt as any of the tyrannical dictatorships she'd denounced, but Dickey was not in possession of that fact. She only sensed it, agonizingly.

In Vietnam in 1961 there were less than a dozen accredited Western reporters. A nervous South Vietnamese government would pull accreditation and allegedly rough up and arrest reporters writing hostile stories. These tactics were fully endorsed by an equally nervous American government, whose official policy in 1960 and 1961 stated that transportation and other coverage facilities commonly extended to the press were to be denied any correspondent doing unfavorable stories. Most stories about Vietnam were being written by a New York public relations firm representing the Vietnamese government, hired to conceal the full extent of American involvement and to stem criticism of Diem's government.

President Diem had no more interest in standing behind his fighting units or in bringing democracy to his country than had Batista. He had his palace revolts, his underground dealings. America would bring in its thousands of advisers and scratch its head over the inability of the South Vietnamese troops to fight, but it couldn't correct the fact that Diem and his miserable successors didn't inspire loyalty. Two years later it was estimated that 80 percent of the rural population was under the direct influence of the North Vietnamese guerrillas. If Laos was an illusion, a Third World rendition of "The Emperor's New Clothes," then Vietnam was its oozing-mud sequel. Most Westerners referred to the country as a peculiarly seductive lunatic asylum. Under the earth that Dickey so bravely patrolled, the enemy went unseen and unpursued in hidden tunnels. Bewildered by the fact that the soldiers seemed so badly provisioned, their uniforms in tatters, their weaponry antique, she eventually realized that most of the U.S.-donated matérial was being stolen, only to show up later during an enemy ambush.

The following week Dickey returned to the Cambodian border, attaching herself to the Vietnamese airborne, a group Clancy referred to as "too crazy" and one Dickey had been wanting to cover for two years. She earned her second set of wings parachuting with the Vietnamese airborne troops and their two American military advisers from the U.S. 101st Airborne. "Here, we are going out to hunt down live human beings," she wrote. "Human beings who otherwise, tonight or a decade from now, will hunt us down here or perhaps somewhere closer to home." She would later remark she did not enjoy jumping with the Vietnamese. "With Americans, there's a lot of banter, joshing. It helps when you're scared." But she found the Vietnamese silent, broodingly quiet. "They sit passively, giving you nothing. They're awfully good. But you do it all by yourself."

She made six jumps with them, one with two cameras and full field gear, into drop zones reclaimed by other Vietnamese riflemen. With them, she walked nearly two hundred miles through head-high jungle and knee-deep swamp. She was fired on from ambush, watched the airborne return fire seven times, and slept seventeen nights in the field. The jump pack she carried was a gift from the airborne, the first ever designed by a military force "just for a parachuting combat correspondent." When she returned to New York, she put the wings and those of the 101st together with her family jewels in the vault of New York's Chase Manhattan Bank.

DICKEY HAD READ ABOUT the South Vietnamese village of Binh Hung in an article entitled "The Report the President Wanted Published" in the May 21, 1961, issue of the *Saturday Evening Post* magazine. Bylined "An American Officer," it was actually written by air force general Ed Lansdale, who under CIA auspices had come to Vietnam in 1954 to mastermind the promotion of staunch anticommunist and Catholic Ngo Dinh Diem to president of South Vietnam. Since 1961 Lansdale had been working at the Pentagon as an assistant for special operations to Secretary of Defense Robert McNamara.

According to an editorial sidebar, the article was published "at the suggestion of President Kennedy, who saw a story of human valor and dedication to freedom, a reminder that Communism is *not* the wave of the future."

Lansdale's story, which had arrived on President Kennedy's desk in the form of a classified memo, described the leader of the Binh Hung village, a stocky, bespectacled Chinese-born Catholic priest named Yuan

Lo-Wha. A former lieutenant colonel in the Chinese Nationalist Army, the dynamic, middle-aged priest called himself Father Hoa. He had found his way to the mud sea of South Vietnam's Ca Mau peninsula under the auspices of Colonel Bernard Yoh, another former member of the Chinese Nationalist Army, who was married to an American and worked in Saigon as an adviser to President Diem.

The fighting priest wore a steel helmet and a pistol belt over his robes. In 1958 he had led a band of his followers out of South China, through Cambodia, to Ca Mau. This area of mud flats and mangrove swamps, two miles from the tip of South Vietnam, was given to him by President Diem. Father Hoa's army, using Boy Scout staves and knives, repulsed the Viet Cong guerrillas who dominated it. From then on Binh Hung—which translates roughly as a "flat area of land rising from out of nowhere"—became famous for its fighting irregulars, called "Sea Swallows." The army was so well disciplined that it soon became a thorn in the side of the Viet Cong.

As its reputation spread, so did its support. Malcolm Browne, working for the Associated Press in Southeast Asia at the time, was an early visitor to Binh Hung: "The American Central Intelligence Agency took a keen interest in Binh Hung, and through its Combined Studies Group in Saigon and the U.S. Army Special Forces, regular air drops of supplies began to pour into Binh Hung." At times Binh Hung received supplies even before the U.S. forces, wrote Browne. The Sea Swallows were given high-velocity AR-15 Armalite automatic rifles and unsinkable fiberglass assault boats with outboard motors. The U.S. government supplied air support to assist the Sea Swallows whenever the Viet Cong mounted a full-scale attack.

Shortly after Lansdale's article appeared in the *Saturday Evening Post,* journalists flocked to the village, most for no longer than two days. Dickey Chapelle, who'd met the priest at a U.S. embassy tea a few weeks earlier, wrote Hobart Lewis, "He [Father Hoa] has built a defense perimeter 45 miles across guarded by three battalions (1,400 volunteers) in which some 8,000 Vietnamese also live. This is a reclamation of free world territory previously a Red stronghold." She added that "I seem to be the first journalist invited to actually live for a few weeks in the village. Two others have visited for a few hours, but there's been no first-person tale. . . ." If she didn't hear from Lewis or stumble upon anything better, she was planning to accept the invitation, since she believed their story would be acceptable to the *Digest*, as "simply a story of brave anti-Reds successfully making a place for themselves in Asia."

For Dickey it became more than that; Binh Hung became her salvation. She would have gladly stayed on because it reassured her that the war was about fighting the Reds, that there were no hidden agendas. And in the face of the disheartening lack of commitment she had witnessed elsewhere, the village's mud walls and mud streets represented to her "a place of real decision—irreversible, nonnegotiable, unequivocal, final. . . ." She felt, inexplicably, that she'd come home. She regretted arriving in a plane, "sissy" fashion, not by parachute. She wrote of the poignancy and inestimable value of a spoonful of tea, a new belt buckle, a handful of cigarettes, and "of course a letter, when it has come to you strapped to the body of someone hurtling through the air. Maybe the way to cure people of equating happiness with *things* would be to deny us any object we weren't willing to jump ourself or have jumped for us by someone we loved." She jumped whenever she could.

She believed, as did the other American supporters of Binh Hung—one-fourth of their arms were supplied from the American arsenal—that the village was "one of the few places on earth where there is *only* right and wrong, *only* good and bad."

After Laos's and Vietnam's confusing "shades of gray," the surreal battles and long-distance death by remote triggers, the certainty that in Binh Hung "nothing is relative" gave her tremendous psychological comfort. She was not beset by confusion in Binh Hung, only by mud and mosquitoes. It was a village that worked, miraculously, on a schedule. A huge drum outside the village chapel of "Our Lady of Victory" sounded the people to worship, and an all-is-well signal rang every hour, "just like criers in a medieval village used to do." Every morning she was awakened by the sound of a military bugle serenading the raising of the gold-and-red South Vietnamese flag. To her, the 160 Chinese-born Catholic families living in bamboo-and-reed huts were as much Red terror victims as had been the Hungarians and the exiled Cubans. She did not want to see America abandon them, too.

"THE FIRST TIME I saw Dickey she was parachuting out of a helicopter into Binh Hung," recalled Stan Atkinson, then a Sacramento, California, television reporter, another of the village's early visitors. "It was a tough place. Just mud and every adversarial creature known to man. She went out on patrols with those guys. I don't know how she could do it. I guess if any woman could ever call herself a marine, it was Dickey."

Father Hoa, whom Stan Atkinson recalled being "the most incredible character I've ever met," greeted Dickey when she first arrived with the admonishment, "You go too gently, my daughter." She accompanied the Sea Swallows on nine patrols through waist-high water and mud that sucked her boots to her thighs. She wrote in a journal she kept during her stay that she was finding it "hell on wheels to *make myself* keep up speed." But it was the only way she could see how these fighters managed to triumph over the always elusive enemy, and it soothed away the peculiar anxiety she'd come to feel over the world outside the village.

In her journal, which she called "Binh Hung Diary," she wrote about setting off one morning from the village on a patrol inside a twelve-foot-long pole boat loaded with vintage guns and soldiers. The children and women waved them off. On the bank there was a Chinese woman, not too young but still pretty. She was wearing green print pajamas, and she held a dishpan in one hand. When she saw the boat Dickey was on chugging by, she saluted the captain and smiled at Dickey, blowing a kiss to the man standing behind the French submachine gun on the boat's bow.

"I nearly cried," Dickey wrote. "The man was obviously her husband. Her man. It was the classic 'Go-do-what-must-be-done-but-come-home-safely-to-me' gesture of any woman to any man she loves committed to danger. Here human beings depend so tangibly on each other . . . and live or die because of their skill and character. In my civilized way of life, the dignity of these affairs has been reduced to a shadow." She thought it odd to be having this kind of reflection about marriage in a battalion of battle-bound troops, in a culture that had as one of its proverbs "Women are the slaves of men."

When the patrol reached its destination in an open grove of trees where the buttercup-choked canal joined a a river, Dickey grabbed at the blossoms. She wanted to put a bouquet of the delicate petals onto her field hat. Too fragile, they fell apart in her hands. A mortar was set up, and seven ancient shells were fired to the east and west. Two misfired. One of the 81-mm mortar shells was American made, and she cheered as it went off.

She wanted to go on night patrols, but it was difficult for her to keep up in full daylight, let alone in the pitch dark. Besides, orders from Binh

Hung's press liaison, Bernie Yoh, were to protect her. She wrote of fighting back tears when he denied her request to be moved from behind with the command group to the front of the patrol. But after she had been there awhile and proved herself, Bernie Yoh issued her a carbine and allowed her to follow the squad leader of a four-man patrol. "Falling ass over teakettle," she wrote of a patrol with twenty-one water fordings, "and of course we never slowed or stopped. I ruined the lens hanging around my neck. But I wouldn't have been there at all if I hadn't known it was the only right place for the photographer to be. And it still is." She also concluded that the photographs she would get would be well worth the exertion. "If not," she wrote, "I'll be greatly surprised."

Patrols always made her nervous. There was always the threat of booby traps, trip-wire mines, and *punji* stakes. There was always the possibility that the point man up front would set off a booby trap, springing a chain reaction to the back of the patrol. She had to be alert, hunched and waiting, her body a tight spring wire. When they came onto ambushes, she would guide herself through her camera. The bullets flew around her, but as long as she saw them through the viewfinder, she felt invulnerable.

The immediate challenge was staying on her feet, achieved by keeping her nearsighted eyes on the fixed shoulders of the man in front of her. The surrounding swamp produced clouds of mosquitoes. A slap would echo like a shot for miles in the stillness. She had twisted her camera straps so that she could put the camera inside her shirtfront, buttoning the top two buttons. She was careful with the upper buttonhole; that was where the shoestring tied to her glasses went, so that she wouldn't lose them when she fell. The black, squirming mass of mosquitoes across the mosquito-net head covering was so dense that she couldn't see, even in daylight, to adjust her camera, so she didn't want to wear it. But despite the misery, she had never seen such "ineffable beauty." The jungle of brush-topped reeds, higher than the heads of the patrol, gleamed, rain-wet in the silver wash of the moonlight. "So we were at once enfolded, wrapped, engulfed in rustling, luminous sweeps of holiday tinsel. There was nothing to be seen but the black silhouettes of men and guns against the gently nodding fronds of the reeds, each looking like polished precious metal—and touching our hands and faces as we passed no more firmly than a breeze."

It wasn't always so. One day she waded four hours with a company of Sea Swallow troops through a lily-padded canal. Though the sun was well up from the horizon, the wild reeds had grown so high that they met overhead and the only path through them was forward motion under the bent reeds and mud puddles to a neighboring village encircled by enemy flags. Scattering the enemy, the Swallows presented Dickey with one of the captured Viet Cong banners. Upon leaving the village, they were ambushed. "Three deliberate shots from behind us," she wrote, "then a veritable storm of fire." She began to run, not once looking down. I can get killed like this, she thought, skipping into the slippery mud, the high grass humming beside her.

From the opposite side of a canal, the enemy hurled grenades. Dickey heard the sound of an American-made M-1 among the enemy fire. The counterattack from troops in the trees and bushes opened up, "burst after burst of their automatic rifles. Then came the detonation of what I took to be a grenade and finally—deep, shocking silence." After the enemy scattered, Dickey discovered that what she had taken for a grenade was an enemy-placed mine. Two members of her company lay dead on the other side of the canal, while sheets of rain pelted them. It gave her even more respect for the deadly enemy-placed weaponry, made her realize she had always to pay attention.

When she and the men entered a friendly village hours later, under torrential rain, Father Hoa was there to greet her, arms outstretched as when she had first met him. Word had reached him that the ambush on the canal was part of an attack by more than three hundred heavily armed Viet Cong against two companies of Sea Swallows. At a wedding banquet that evening, Father Hoa invited her to sit beside him. Her fatigues dripping, her boots sodden, her camera wet, and feeling a need to sneeze, she demurred. Then he commanded her to sit down, and she obliged. The villagers wanted to give her a gift to celebrate her survival. She sneezed and asked for a handkerchief. "Wouldn't you know it," she wrote. "My one chance to play Joan of Arc—and I get the sniffles." Later she wrote, "Even if war is the only game around, it's a grubby game."

Looking at the line of Asian profiles, she felt very close to these people, with the highest admiration for the bridal party. One of the women stepped out of her high black rubber boots and stood up barefoot on a stool to pick up the drinking duties where the happy couple had left them upon slipping away. Amid cheers, she kept at it—there was a bottle of white lightning sloshing in a disposable 500-cc human blood container. The woman had one delicate spasm of vomiting before falling off her perch, recovered herself gracefully, and stepped back into her boots without tripping. She was the most elegant drunk Dickey had ever seen: "A great woman, that one."

The Sea Swallows gave her their shoulder-patch insignia of a sea swallow against a bamboo in a blue sky. Father Hoa told her she was the first non-Oriental to receive it.

That October, while Dickey was in Binh Hung, Hobart Lewis sent her a letter with another "urgent" request for another article on the subject of guerrilla warfare, which was becoming a subject of keen interest for General Maxwell Taylor, who would be arriving that month in Vietnam to appraise the situation for President Kennedy. Since Dickey knew far more about the subject than he would ever hope to, Lewis declined to suggest how she write it for the general.

At the time, President Diem wanted to increase his army and expand the American advisory group. American advisers to Vietnam began as the U.S. Military Assistance Advisory Group (popularly called MAAG) in 1954. By the time Taylor arrived, there were at least three thousand American advisers in the country without any actual authority over their Vietnamese counterparts; they could call in air and artillery support but could not relieve incompetent South Vietnamese officers. They were also supposed to be strictly noncombatant, an order that they, like their counterparts in Laos, ignored. They were fighting and dying, too.

Before Taylor left Vietnam (no doubt having read Dickey's report) with recommendations to increase U.S. military advisers and thus create a "limited partnership" between the United States and South Vietnam, he planned to visit Binh Hung. Dickey was so excited that she herself raised the American flag. Although she had met Taylor casually at the Overseas Press Club, she felt close to him "as one old paratrooper to another." When the general's plans changed, she acknowledged the trip—more than five hundred miles south of Saigon over enemy territory—was dangerous, but "we could have protected him for the two to three hours he was here," she insisted to a friend when she returned to New York. "It would have meant so much [to the Sea Swallows] to know the Americans were supporting them."

Back in Saigon after the blessed simplicity of Binh Hung, there seemed to be nothing but bad news. Dickey read the galleys of her forthcoming book, and what she had feared was now shouting at her in black and white: her story had been "feminized the hell out of." She'd spent her entire career convincing the military that gender had nothing to do with understanding their operations. Finally, after years of hard work, she'd found acceptance with the least objective group of males she'd ever met. Reading the edited version, she discovered that all her hard-earned reporting on war from the grubby perspective of the soldier in a foxhole had been scrupulously disinfected by her editor in New York. She felt burning indignation at being portrayed as a dizzy, if gutsy, broad who just happened to show up whenever she heard the sound of guns. To her, her sex had nothing whatsoever to do with her role as a military observer, and now she felt as though the publisher were making *that* the only point of the book.

From the Majestic she wrote Larry Hughes, "[Both] editors edited tales of infantry warfare with a sense of taste which you and I surely understand has no place in any accurate reporting of the real thing. . . . Now if you, my own beloved editors, cannot resist so loudly emphasizing the woman bit, why in God's green heaven should any bookseller, reviewer, TV interviewer, or reader take me seriously as a combat reporter? . . . My alleged future as an alleged observer . . . on military subjects which I know the most about . . . cannot depend on my being a broad, but rather on my being a story-teller of integrity, in mood at least. . . . A woman won't buy my book because a woman says it's good, nor will men, of course. But they might if they felt I had impressed a male with my reflections on a male subject. . . . Can you try to reduce this emphasis on femininity, preferably to near zero?"

The publisher declined to run on the book jacket the photo of her seated in a breeches buoy on her ship-to-ship transfer in the Mediterranean, hoping to soothe her by explaining, "It was just too cute." In fact it was probably one of the most unattractive pictures ever taken of her, and Hughes probably knew no other way to excuse it than to try backhanded flattery. He also declined to run her photo of the Algerian execution, since the consensus was it was "too gruesome." "You may be right," Dickey wrote Larry Hughes, "but just for the record let me say I think you are right for the wrong reason. I am entirely willing to be criticized for photographing the obscenity of homicide if that is what happens in front of my camera (think how I would be criticized if I failed to photograph it). That I've subsequently failed to convince my publishers they should print said pix—and I have failed—is interesting."

That same day she wrote to Stevie Blick, her surrogate Jewish mother, who was nagging her to return to New York because she had been gone six months and "don't you think it's time a woman of your age should be earning some money?" But Dickey was not yet ready to come home. The *Digest* wanted her to remain and so did she—to return to the refuge of Binh Hung.

"I am terribly unwilling to end my research on a downbeat, and all I could conscientiously report right now—after covering three operations against live enemy and walking one hundred sixty-five miles cross-country in seventeen days with infantry—is that the issue of military victory is genuinely in doubt," Dickey wrote. "There simply is no doctrine for licking guerrillas, and either the Viets—not we Americans, but these little brown men of South Vietnam—evolve one or we lose the confounded war." Besides, her financial situation was better than it had ever been. She had close to $12,000 in the bank, some of which had been left to her by her aunt George, who of all people would have understood her tenacity.

She was still there in late October, sitting in Tan Son Nhut, Saigon's big airport, waiting to go parachuting with the Vietnamese airborne. She wrote Hobart Lewis that despite reports to the contrary, "there is a war in Vietnam. It is a war against live shooting enemy, and from the testimony of my camera and my eyes, people on both sides are daily, almost hourly, getting killed. . . . What is happening here is not a series of local disorders about which to temporize, or that demand . . . political chess moves to be countered. The only adjective this war lacks that others out here have had is 'declared.' " Acknowledging her desperate tone, she nevertheless emphasized her belief that it was important Americans realized "Southeast Asia right now is a time and place of decision." She'd been galvanized by her month at Binh Hung and was afraid, she wrote Lewis, that unless America committed itself wholeheartedly to the country, it would become "another Hungary" or "another Cuba." The thought was too terrible.

Dickey spent a busy, stress-filled seven months in Laos and Vietnam. Besides supplying the *Digest* with that additional chapter on the Vietnamese airborne brigade, she wrote six other articles. From Laos she completed a long article on the U.S. Special Forces, a primer on guerrilla warfare for unnamed Special Forces types wherein she discussed the need for a counterinsurgency doctrine (at the time a pet idea of President Kennedy and the Pentagon's Ed Lansdale) for the South Viet-namese and declared that the enemy had a much better one.

Clancy Stone, whose wife had recently given birth, was leaving Viet-nam. For the first time in his vagabond life, the photographer accepted the fact that he wouldn't be much of a father if he were dead and that he would be killed if he stayed. Sitting on his bed at the Caravelle Hotel in Saigon, the lanky, quick-fisted young man decided to request a transfer back to the States.

A few days later he ran into Dickey in her fatigues at a diplomatic bash in Saigon. "I think you wear your fatigues more than you have to," he told her. "I guess you feel you've got to prove you're a field person."

She told him she was leaving early because she was getting up early in the morning to parachute with the Vietnamese airborne. Clancy asked if he could come along. At four in the morning he and Dickey went jumping with the airborne in the marshy highlands. Clancy sank up to his thighs. Dickey was perched in the chopper ready to follow when he frantically waved her off.

"Don't jump, don't jump!" he cried. "You're too short. You'll go right down to your ass," he yelled.

So she waited for the chopper to find more solid ground, then leapt. Clancy waded through the mud over to her, pulling off leeches. "I guess I owe you one for that," she told him, grinning.

Mud-splattered and giddy, they returned to the Colonial decadence of the palm-filled Hotel Continental bar. The usual crowd of male reporters stopped their drinking to stare at the disheveled couple, won-dering where the two had been. But as soon as Dickey began talking in her speedy, excited fashion, they turned away.

"She'd be trying to give her opinion and some of the guys would ignore her, like they didn't think she knew what the hell she was talking about or something," Clancy recalled. "They'd ask me about the same operation she'd been on, too. They were rude enough to tell her that they were talking to me, not to her," he said. "She'd take it very personally. We'd walk out and she'd say, really hurt, 'That bastard.' "

Clancy reflected with a chuckle, "Well, most of these guys were not going to the front. Dickey was. That's always a little tough on male egos. There would be this little gal coming back from an operation with firsthand information and all they know is what they're told in some government briefing. The guys would just sort of want to walk away because they were embarrassed. And Dickey never concealed her feelings toward the bar-line reporters, which didn't help. I didn't like a lot of them, but I didn't let it show."

Clancy saw Dickey one more time. He was with a Vietnamese girl at one of the hotel bars when Dickey walked in. Dickey was feeling pretty good—not drunk, but a little high. She looked at Clancy and said, "Tell that floozy to get out of here. I've got something better for you."

Clancy and Dickey went back to her place at the Hotel Majestic. "I was a pretty selfish lover back then," he recalled. "The next thing I knew, she came out of the bathroom. She had a towel around her and she dropped it. She looked at me and said, 'Okay, now it's my turn. So the next time we get together we'll be even.' "

Clancy gave her a little ivory Buddha, saying it would bring her luck. "I always had this feeling that she was trying to catch up on things. That she was trying to prove she was as good as anyone else. But she was taking too many chances."

Dickey returned to Binh Hung the first chance she had, at the end of October. On one of the patrols, as they waited between gunshots, one of the officers asked her if she ever got homesick. He added shyly, "I think you are willing to die for your duty."

Dickey added, "quite gaily and with a little banter, 'We might both live through our whole careers,' which I realized immediately was not the right thing to say."

She went racing back to Washington on November 7, 1961. Two months later she taped a meeting in New York with an old friend, Chester Williams, whom she had known when she and Tony were a photo team. She told Williams, then assistant to the director of the military think tank, the Hudson Institute, that she had hurried back because "I saw a spectacular change in our tactics that I thought somebody in Washington should know about. I didn't know whether it was classified, so I committed it to memory."

She told Williams that she had rushed over to the Pentagon to make a tactical report and to show photographs "to prove this was the kind of fighting we were doing." There she met with Ed Lansdale, author of the *Saturday Evening Post* piece on Binh Hung and staunch supporter of its militia.

The former advertising executive, who had helped crush communist-led rebels in the Philippines after World War II, tended to treat Third

World turmoils like an advertising campaign. Using slogans and other public relations ploys he termed "psychological warfare," he spent seven years in Vietnam silencing opposition to Diem's government through his CIA-backed Saigon Military Mission, a covert group of American intelligence agents and soldiers who were reputed to be experts in "dirty tricks." He was "the only person President Diem trusted," according to his associate, Bernie Yoh. Lansdale—an enigmatic cold war character whose exploits as a counterinsurgency and covert action specialist served as the main subject of two novels (Lederer and Burdick's *The Ugly American* and Graham Greene's *The Quiet American*), saluted Dickey as one of his own, another action-romantic. He acknowledged her warmly in their correspondence as "a good girl guerrilla and fighter of the good fight."

Dickey greeted General Lansdale with breathless instructions that she would appreciate his letting her know if she was making "an ass of myself," but she thought what she had seen was "so important I should take up your time." Neither Lansdale nor Walt Rostow, an aggressive hawk who helped forge White House policy under President Kennedy and whom she was sent to see in a White House car, laughed at her. "Neither one of them said, 'Baby, why don't you go home and fry your hat,' " Dickey gushed excitedly to her friend Chet Williams. "They were not unsympathetic." In fact, she added pointedly, "General Lansdale asked for twenty-one of my pictures to show to President Kennedy." Actually Lansdale had not seen Dickey immediately; he'd sent her a penned note of apology on November 19: "Sorry you went home mad. Honest Injun, I wasn't trying to duck you—but had a fast action on the move. When I looked around again, you had left. Will you please accept apologies from a guy who gets absentminded about other things when following an operation?" Then he put her onto a group in Newburyport, Massachusetts, that had adopted the village of Binh Hung as its sister city.

In a letter to Ed Lansdale dated December 14, 1961, Dickey good-naturedly accepted his apology. "Any time a general even so graciously explains his preoccupation with his own military operations to a correspondent, one of them is in the wrong business. You aren't. Honest, I didn't go away mad (why should I? I got what I came for). The copy, 'The Men Who Didn't Give Up Laos,' your men kindly checked for me will go into the *Digest* in February" (it would never run). The ever-optimistic Dickey was returning to Washington the following week to complete research on a *Digest* report about antiguerrilla doctrine in Southeast Asia and hoped to see him at that time. She "bragged" that her pictures of Vietnam firefights were being used for Special Forces briefings in Saigon. She also wanted him to know that she "was playing ball with the Newburyport, Mass., people [and would ride in their parade] even to the point of hamming it up in my Binh Hung arm patch and hat tomorrow."

Dickey told Williams that she'd also gone to see the marine chief of staff, who told her, "Baby, this is too important for my ears only." He authorized a briefing in which Dickey again described what she had seen and showed her photographs. "From one end of the military to the other, everybody said, 'Let me see, oh . . . my God, there is a shooting war in Vietnam.'" In the tape-recorded interview with Chet Williams Dickey added, "that is not the kind of reception I usually get."

After her visit to Washington, Lansdale wrote her on December 26, 1961, thanking her for the "fine Christmas surprise of your wonderful pictures." He wrote Dickey that he had thus far shown them, not to President Kennedy, but to Deputy Secretary of Defense Roswell Gilpatrick. Secretary of Defense Robert McNamara was out of town. "They speak volumes," he wrote, and he was passing them along for "the big boss to see." He thanked her for riding in the Newburyport parade and for "firing up the local citizenry about their adopted town in Ca Mau." By this time Lansdale had also read a draft of Dickey's *Reader's Digest* piece on the U.S. Special Forces in Laos. "I'm passing it along to my staff," he wrote, "with the injunction that they can't go running out to volunteer again when they've finished reading it. (I almost lose them every day anyhow.) It is a grand bit of writing you did. . . ."

She returned to New York, typed up a report she entitled "Course of Action, Laos and Vietnam," and sent it to Marine Commandant General Wallace M. Greene, Jr. The report suggested that the conflicting philosophies of the departments of State and Defense come to agreement over Laos and Vietnam, and that more American advisers be sent to lead the Vietnamese troops, whom she told Greene under separate cover "I challenged for being underaggressive in one way or another." Greene thanked her and told her, "I think that you are a good marine." If she at any time entertained the thought that these men were treating her with condescension, no matter how benevolent, it didn't stop her.

She had come to them for their attention, and she was getting it, wasn't she? There was no reason not to believe they wouldn't heed her eyewitness reports.

But six weeks of running from New York to Washington left her six weeks behind in her work and embroiled her in eighteen months of "acrimonious correspondence" with the Department of Defense, as she tried to retrieve the one thousand photographs taken in Laos that she believed showed "we could win there." Eight hundred of them, she was told, were "missing in censorship." It took ten weeks for the departments of State and Defense to review her article on Laos. In 1962, while leafing through a copy of *Army Digest*, she spotted one of her "lost" photos credited to the army. Whether or not the "big boss" ever saw her photos she never found out; she only knew that Lansdale's people, whom he described to her as "a limited and select group whom I felt needed to catch a bit of your spirit," finished reading her manuscript by January 31, 1962. Lansdale returned it to her only after she'd requested it back. He told her it had gathered some "interesting fingerprints," and that "between the two of us, it's a beautiful piece of writing."

Years later Bill Garrett, her photo editor at *National Geographic*, called her willingness to submit to censorship a "carry-over from World War II, where it was ingrained in everybody." He and Dickey would frequently argue about the war in Vietnam. "She was sort of a commie hater . . . and I'd say that's not why we're there at all."

Garrett viewed Dickey's ideas about Vietnam as simplistic, a refusal to seek the real truth. Garrett was speaking in journalistic terms of "the big picture," the ability to put what the reporter sees into historical context. That criticism was justified. Dickey was the first person to admit she had no interest in the big picture. However, she didn't avoid truth. Indeed, her life was one tireless pursuit of truth, her personal truth, and by this time she believed there was only one place to find it—with men in close combat, where even if the battle made no sense, at least death did. When she spoke of the urge to shout out the story of men on a jungle patrol, it was with the urgency of need. Dickey, a loner moving through the miasma of Southeast Asia with clandestine forces, was continually stumbling over secret governments and their agendas. Aware there were shenanigans going on, she came up against wall after wall as she tried to move farther into stories, finding only the pieces of a puzzle that would take decades to decipher. Her confusion growing dizzying as each corner she turned brought illusory confrontations, she found comfort only in the clarity of the small story of men on a jungle patrol.

Garrett faulted her for this. Yet few journalists knew any more than she about what was really going on, and those who got a whiff of it were shorn of their accreditations or, like her, censored. There was also a generational difference between Garrett and Dickey, which would become a real point of controversy as the war continued. It pitted the younger, far more cynical reporters against those whose view of Vietnam, like Dickey's, was tempered by the recollection of World War II. "She was superpatriotic; I was extremely critical," Garrett commented. "She wasn't totally adamant about it but . . . if the president says go to war, we go to war. And follow orders. That was the mentality."

17

Cold Warrior Woman

C HESTER WILLIAMS listened with a shudder to Dickey's description of her trip to Vietnam, her seventeen patrols and thirteen ambushes, of having seen an eleven-year-old boy hung by the enemy. He was fond of her but declined to subscribe to her view that Vietnam was similar to Korea's Pusan perimeter: the last domino before the Philippines fell to communism. Williams believed that communism was in bad shape and would collapse of its own accord. "All we have to do is sit on our hands and grit our teeth," he told her. So why did she insist on taking all these risks?

She dared not tell him the truth. He'd never understand. He'd think her mad if she opened up her soul; that she believed the bogeyman was Vietnam, that the only chance of winning lay with the fighters of Binh Hung; that the world outside the little village had grown unfathomable. Or, more to the point, that danger was as addictive as any other drug. So, she answered him with something he'd understand. Dickey responded that her personal motivation was purely self-serving, "to make the world safe for Dickey Chapelle. I have no other. I would like the world to go on being the kind of place where an overemotional woman reporter who overidentifies with people who are fighting for her life can

326

run around the country and say all kinds of outrageous things because she believes them. And for no other reason. I have no motivation more glorious than saving Dickey Chapelle's ass."

When her aunt Lutie, far more cautious than the enthusiastic, adventurous George, suggested her niece turn her talents to the safer madness of writing fiction, Dickey said she'd like to, but she didn't have "the imagination." She explained that "the intellectual feat of imagining a person and what happens to them is incomparably harder than following real people to see what happens to them, even if you have to do the latter on the end of a parachute." Stevie Blick had a more cynical suggestion: "Why don't you do an article on 'War Zones I Have Revisited'?"

Dickey's body itself had begun to rebel. At the end of January, while cruising the windy, ice-swept highways of the Midwest on a lecture tour following the release of 8,500 copies of her autobiography, she was suffering from incontinence caused by a relaxed bladder and bleeding from fibrous tumors that had grossly enlarged her uterus. She told Chester Williams that every time she thought about the title "I get physically sick to my stomach." It wasn't only the title that bothered her, it was the military men who had been asked to review advance copies of her book. "They were patronizing as hell," she complained. "I've never been patronized by those people before." She even resented the dust cover's moody shot of a paratroop drop zone, since she wouldn't be identified. "It's set my career back ten years," she groaned.

The book received favorable reviews in the *Saturday Review of Books* and *The New York Times,* which said her "photos are splendid . . . so is her capacity to supplement them with words" and advised its readers to "put it on your reading list." It was condensed in the *Reader's Digest* that same month. Yet it received dubious support from the publisher.

While fascinating, Dickey's unorthodox life-style had concerned her publishers from the start. Although the women's movement had finally gathered enough momentum to persuade President Kennedy to create a Commission on Women, Dickey Chapelle was one of those patently unsettling women best ignored. The following year she would take exception to feminist writer Betty Friedan's article in *McCall's* magazine entitled "The Fraud of Femininity" and would request permission to write a rebuttal since in her opinion, "femininity is not a fraud!" It would have given insight into Dickey's ideas about her gender, but the editor at *McCall's* expressed no interest. Her book was conceived, like most women's books of the time, to be without controversy, a cute-gal-adventurer book.

"What's the matter with being a frankly controversial character? Will it sell less well?" Dickey asked one of her editors in an undated letter. "Let me look at this business of writing an autobiography which won't attract criticism. Such a goal can't be one which I ought to take seriously. . . . I must have somewhere along the line . . . done a slew of things for which I damn well ought to be criticized. If all were eliminated from the book, it seems to me the accuracy of the document would be highly suspect." Her concerns were justified. And between her careful omissions and her publisher's cold feet, the reader is left with a two-dimensional adventuress, a comic strip character, Wonder Warrior Woman. The book's superficiality, its overemphasis on her sanitized travails in Hungary, and its lack of marketing doomed it before it got out of the gate. Irate about Morrow, Dickey was also aware that "the real fault after all is mine," as she wrote to Stevie while on her lecture swing. "I knew their apathy and I still did leave New York, walking into the situation of being in their flaccid hands with my eyes open! I'm simply not there when from the book standpoint I know I should be."

Years later Larry Hughes recalled that Dickey's book sold 7,100 copies, was published in Norwegian and Dutch editions, and that it never did get into a mass-market paperback, nor was it taken by a book club.

"It's difficult for me to recall exactly the expectations we and Dickey had for her book," wrote Hughes. "I do know that she did quite a lot of personal publicity, because I remember accompanying her to Washington for a radio interview." The tape of that unnamed radio show and its anonymous female interviewer bubbles over with a lot of "Gee whiz, you're quite a gal" incredulity, just the attitude to work against sales in those early self-conscious days of women's consciousness-raising.

"It's possible she was also on television," wrote Hughes. "Why didn't the book sell better? My answer has to be that 'it just didn't catch on' with the public. Why was Dickey upset? Frankly, I had quite forgotten that she was upset. My guess is that friends tried to buy the book in certain stores and it wasn't available, or she wanted more advertising— when from the publisher's point of view there weren't enough copies to justify a large advertising budget. Her complaints of lack of distribution and promotion are not at all uncommon in the book business, particularly when an author has expectations that are unrealistic." Hughes recalls taking the book on less because he thought it would be a best-seller than because of its immense interest. He believed Dickey's book was "given a good launch," and that after the booksellers had sold whatever copies they had, they didn't reorder. "Dickey was a feisty, aggressive personality, and I believe that anything less than big best-seller sales would not have satisfied her."

While in the greater Milwaukee area, where less than two hundred copies had been ordered, Dickey hunted vainly for her book. She also consulted a hometown doctor for a second opinion about what she called "that little vaginal tumor." The opinion was that she needed a hysterectomy—but she didn't know when she could fit it into her schedule.

After committing Dickey to six months of lectures for the University of Minnesota Lecture Bureau, her lecture agent, Elizabeth Byrd, had died suddenly. Some weeks Dickey was scheduled for as many as fifteen appearances, other weeks only one. At a fee of $200 a lecture plus expenses, less 30 percent to the lecture bureau, Dickey was losing money unless she had fifteen lectures booked every week. She fired Crawford Productions, Byrd's employers, but honored the commitments.

It was not surprising that the articles Dickey wrote from Laos and Vietnam, all of which were confrontational about American policy, were suppressed by the *Reader's Digest* and waylaid by the Pentagon, nor that her photographs were "lost" by the Defense Department. When Dickey returned to Vietnam in 1962, she wasn't surprised to discover that the Vietnamese government was no longer paying a publicist. According to the publicist's man in Vietnam, the job had been taken over by the U.S. government.

Although her growing audiences weren't able to read her articles or see her pictures from Laos, nor for the most part her material from Vietnam, they could *listen,* and she used her lecture tours, the one uncensored avenue left to her, like a politician in the hustings. Surely if the people knew there was a war going on to which the United States was already committed, they in turn would commit themselves to winning, as they had done with World War II. She did not let the glaring differences between the two wars shake her faith. If by accident the truth slipped past the censors, she believed it would show up before any others in *The New York Times,* because of its foreign desks. "Buy it," she urged her audiences, "even if you end up lining your cat boxes with it."

Fueled by her sense of mission, she would whip her captured Viet

Cong flag from her black leather Mark Cross bag and wave it above her metal helmet like a drum majorette. "Don't kid yourself," she'd tell her audience of mothers with draft-age sons, "we're already at war in Vietnam." She'd compound this shocking information with "The trouble is Americans don't know whether we want to lead the free world or what we want in Asia." The audiences in North Dakota, Illinois, Minnesota, Iowa, and Wisconsin, startled and upset, nevertheless listened. She advised that America must either get in there and win or get out, not drag its feet. "The communists know what they want; they want the real estate. We've got to make up our mind about South Vietnam. It's our last piece of real estate on the Asian continent," she told reporters. "What happens there can very well decide whether or not I live out my life in a free society that can afford an outspoken free press."

When she repeated this speech on the "Jack Paar Show" on January 24, 1962, the popular late night national television host shot back, "But isn't the problem that it isn't *our* real estate? Aren't these sovereign people?"

She expressed the same views on Mike Wallace's television interview show on February 15, 1962.

"South Vietnam today is . . . in my mind, almost as much 'my' real estate as Minnesota," she wrote to Chester Williams, to whom she had earlier recounted, "When I was in Binh Hung, they kept wondering each morning if this was the day the Americans would leave. We cannot abandon them." Having set up Dickey's guest appearance on the "Jack Paar Show," Williams was deeply disturbed by her comments. So was the popular liberal periodical *The New Republic*. Its March 5, 1962, issue commented that "If this comment had appeared on a news show, the networks in their effort to appear objective would have let it pass without comment . . . but the opinionated Mr. Paar didn't." The article went on to praise Paar as a "voice of sanity" to late night viewers.

Dickey agreed that she was "mongering, selling—a war, even one on foreign shores," in an undated letter to Williams from Minnesota. "I believe there is a shooting war in Vietnam which the U.S. should fight and win. Not with U.S. ground troops, but with advisers . . . leading the very good Vietnamese troops. Ten years ago I had been taught not to say 'our real estate,' too," she informed Williams, who would eventually break with Dickey over her increasingly strident posture over Vietnam. "But this is now. The tired outworn sin of Western imperialism for which the use of the pronoun is a symbol in your mind is *not*—the fancied sin for which your country is distrusted. . . . It is the shiny new sin of saying in the voice of our President that we, America, will help countries defend themselves against communism and then not meaning it as we did not mean it in the cases of the Hungarian revolution, the Laotian betrayal, the Vietnamese foot-dragging. And the very symbol of those failures is our refusal to think 'our.'

"Vietnam *is* the last piece of the free world's real estate on continental Asia (as my unprinted rebuttal to Jack Paar made clear). As long as I am a citizen of that free world and some members of it are doing my fighting for me, it would be ungallant of me not to at least recognize our common cause in speech."

Upon Dickey's return to the States from her first Vietnam trip, Nancy Palmer had tried hawking her photos of her patrols with the Vietnamese airborne, the marines, and the Sea Swallows. Despite her penchant for being where artillery rained down, to document that there was a war going on, her photos showed the little brown Vietnamese, not the big strong American fighting men. There was little interest in the war to begin with, and Dickey's unglamorous portrayal of the Vietnamese troops was not commercial.

Nancy Palmer, with whom Dickey had a loose arrangement, always believed that her client's strong suit was her writing, that her photographs were simply a means to help her with her writing ambitions. Dickey liked to say that she took pictures because she was too lazy to write, which was not true. Friends recall her writing and rewriting every story she ever worked on. Nancy managed to sell one of the Sea Swallow patrol photos to *The New York Times Magazine* for its February 25, 1962, cover. Two other photos taken when Dickey jumped with the Vietnamese airborne brigade ran on the inside pages to illustrate the cover story. A few more sales were made to small magazines. The *Reader's Digest*, which had requested Dickey's presence in Laos and Vietnam for seven months, ran her story on the Vietnamese airborne, along with the condensation of her book, in February 1962. Two years later they would run her photo story on Father Hoa, "The Fighting Priest of Vietnam."

At the time, Nancy Palmer handled two other women photographers, Jill Krementz and Marilyn Silverstone. "Selling their photos was as tough as selling Dickey's photos," Nancy recalled. "Mostly, you had to

convince male photo editors that women could shoot as well as men."
Nancy was very fond of Dickey, but she described her client as ambitious
to the point of "not letting anybody get in her way. If you did, she'd
steamroll right over you." Nevertheless, she sympathized. "I would show
Dickey's portfolio to the photo editor at *Life* magazine—before he knew
who had taken the pictures," Nancy said. "Then he would ask who the
photographer was. When I said, 'Dickey Chapelle,' he would do a
double take."

"I have been thinking," wrote Nancy Palmer to her client in January
1962, "that there must be a magazine somewhere which would use your
actual 'operation' pictures to show up these would-be reporters, three of
whom we know turned in their stories half done, if that, as *the* feature
story of Father Hoa and his irregulars in the *Saturday Evening Post,
Look,* and *Life.*" Nancy had submitted Dickey's material to *Look* and
Life and was stymied by their rejection, "since your story was the more
accurate because it was *complete.* Now why???"

Dickey replied from Milwaukee in February 1962, "I'm delighted by
your indignation. Now about why my pix, although taken at greater risk
and effort than other people's, don't sell as readily. Neither *Life* nor
Look in the more than ten years I've tried to do business with them has
ever said or done anything indicating that they trust me (with the single
exception of the time *Life* sent me to cover what they considered a
second-rate news event at the time, the Hungarian refugees crossing into
Austria, and then it was frankly a suicide mission—on which they didn't
want to expend a good photographer).

"*Look* has always treated me cavalierly . . . that is, with a kind of
discourtesy and doubt . . . a barely hidden challenge that my pix were
acquired by some boudoir legerdemain from a man who *really* took
them. . . . As to *Life,* you must not forget that the biggies are still trying
to deny I ever worked for them. . . . If someday I do win some recognition
from my colleagues, say an Overseas Press Club award, we may get the
stupid problem solved." She suggested that all of this might be an
excellent reason for Nancy not to want to represent her. "I hope you will
go on, though. Anyhow, I'm not quitting."

Still fired up by Nancy's letter, tired of the road, and nervous about
her health, Dickey sent Stevie a cranky letter from Ely, Minnesota.
She'd decided to submit her book and work from Vietnam for the
Overseas Press Club's annual awards. She was ticked because she had no

idea how to submit them complaining, "Goddamn it. I would have liked to know how material was supposed to be submitted and then done something that important *with precision.*"

Although in most ways, Dickey continued to be the "good marine" and "girl guerrilla" that Commandant Greene and General Lansdale dubbed her, her adoration of the military could not compete with her role as journalist and the stronger urge to see and tell for a publication that would be willing to publish her. Having been duly "screwed around" by government censors, she'd leave it to her colleagues to decide the worth of what she'd witnessed. The decision to submit the censored material was sparked not only by her vanity, but by the condolence letters she'd been writing to the growing legion of widows of anonymous American advisers. She'd been chosen for the job, as one government official wrote her, "because you know better than most the sacrifices [he] gave for [his] country." Her frustration over her knowing and not being able to get it out there had cleared up her priorities. "We must constantly defend against those who would control the press to promote their own interests," she'd write the following year as a member of the Overseas Press Club's growing Freedom of The Press Committee, "whether they be crooks or saints, right or wrong."

About this time Dickey arranged for a Green Beret to accompany her on the lecture circuit. It was no longer enough merely to champion advisers; now she was recruiting. The young, broad-shouldered sergeant would stand beside her, later making a recruitment pitch, while Dickey hyped the marines and, for the less warlike, the Peace Corps. She had also taken to challenging the teenage boys in the audience, insinuating they'd never beat the Vietnamese communist troops, who walked twenty-five miles a day through steamy jungles.

"Of course American boys wouldn't dare be made to walk that far," she'd say. The warrior standing beside her would smirk. "Because their mothers won't let them. Tapioca training is what we're giving our American boys." At a Minneapolis high school, when Dickey ridiculed her audience for being soft, two boys challenged her to a twenty-five-mile hike. "If the commies can do it, we can do it better," one of them boasted.

In late February Dickey, looking unusually glamorous in dark glasses and a kerchief, hands tucked into her cashmere coat and no doubt in pain from her uncertain health, set out with the sergeant and the two boys. They completed the march in twelve hours. "I don't know what a woman guerilla is doing giving lectures," wrote retired Admiral Arleigh "31 Knots" Burke upon hearing of Dickey's latest challenge to the nation's youth.

Burke, described by writer Warren Hinckle as a "stone-age cold warrior," also spent a fair amount of time doing public speaking and, like Dickey's other colleagues, tilting at windmills. He addressed her as "a good-looking guerrilla," letting his fierce guard drop to confide in a letter of March 15, 1962, "I get a feeling of futility and sometimes even the desire for personal combat . . . when I look down on the upturned, cynical, unbelieving faces of some of the undergraduates. I think I should ask you for a course of instruction on how to convince unbelievers."

Dickey replied, "You see, you are *not,* I gather, permitting yourself to accept those physical challenges from among those upturned, cynical, unbelieving faces. And I *am.*" She added proudly that one of her young hikers was going to join the marines as soon as he graduated.

That April the Overseas Press Club presented Dickey Chapelle with the 1962 George Polk Award, the organization's highest award, "for the best reporting in any medium requiring exceptional courage and enterprise abroad," for her coverage of hostilities in Vietnam and for her book *What's a Woman Doing Here?* She was the second woman to be so honored. She was lecturing in Carlton, Minnesota, when the announcement was made. Stevie wrote gleefully, "I can't wait to see the look on Tony's face when he finds out."

Despite the jocular comment to Dickey by Bill Laurence of the OPC's awards committee that "one of your old parachutes will do nicely," this was one event she did not treat in her usual cavalier style. She intended to look every inch the vision of "sweeping queenliness." She purchased a formal gold-and-white gown "with a prow-type long skirt" and a gray-green velvet fitted bodice, "strapless type but with straps," confiding to Stevie she didn't have the "guts" to wear a strapless gown. She sent Stevie shopping for her. The list was specific. She needed an evening bag of gray-green velvet, "plain envelope type" on which to attach her two pairs of military parachutist wings, "which have much to do with getting the award." She sent Stevie her charge plate from Saks for purchase of purse and gloves, "long dead-white doeskin," and authorized Stevie to take five hundred dollars from her bank account (covered by the OPC's cash award of five hundred dollars) to purchase the earrings she had already chosen at Tiffany's. Dickey remarked, "This is roughly the same amount of work as getting married, isn't it? All that's missing is—the honeymoon." Dickey's dates for the April 13 "do" were Lutie and Stevie.

"There's no other award in my business I've ever coveted," she wrote to the editor of *Leatherneck* on April 29, 1962. "And to receive this one, alive and unwounded, still hardly seems real. All I can do now is to try like hell to live up to it. And to thank the people who trained me, which brings us right back full circle to the United States Marines."

Tony was still keeping tabs on his Dickey, noting dates of her departures from and arrivals into New York—though he was married once again, this time to Kay, whom he wrote Dickey "takes good care of me." He sent Dickey a warm, fan-mail-type letter on May 15, 1962, finally abandoning advice on career management. It was, after all, rather difficult to argue with her success.

"I sure bask in the reflected glory of having once been the husband of a celebrity," he wrote at about the time she was having a hysterectomy at New York Hospital. Her pathology report was "satisfactory," but additional surgery was called for to stop further unusual bleeding as well as to support her bladder and urethra. The doctor was concerned because she was planning to leave the country for an unusually long period.

Two weeks later, the additional surgery completed, Dickey left New York for Vietnam. The award had done what she had hoped: the "biggies" were beginning to take an interest. *National Geographic* magazine assigned her a piece on the role of U.S. Army helicopter pilots. Like most photographers, Dickey was thrilled to be doing a story for the magazine and getting red carpet treatment, even if the magazine retained ownership of all the photos and wasn't paying top rate. She received a guarantee of $3,000 plus expenses and a minimum of $150 per color page and $75 for black-and-white, though Nancy Palmer had suggested she ask at least $6,000. Nancy was nevertheless happy, writing, "Maybe this means that if they jumped on the bandwagon, others will."

Dickey was anxious to get back to Binh Hung, whose irregular army's many victories had created problems for Father Hoa with jealous South Vietnamese army officers. The past February she had snagged a Chicago millionaire's support, or so she implied in correspondence with Colonel Shaul Ramati, the Israeli consul in Chicago, with whom she hoped to meet "about . . . how we can best put some Israeli products manufactured in Burma into the hands of the Vietnamese freedom fighters."

By this time the military situation in Vietnam mirrored the state of Diem's government—desperate. But as Dickey rode inside a U.S. Marine helicopter over the sunlit rice fields of Ba Xuyen province, south of Saigon, she felt hopeful, if tense. Thousands more U.S. military advisers had been dispatched to shore up the faltering government troops, and she was riding in one of sixteen choppers surrounded by professionals—a combat-ready American marine helicopter team and a squad of veteran South Vietnamese infantrymen. Above the deceptively quiet mirrored standing water of the fields, she thought that "this was the place . . . where the fate of millions of people was being decided—in blood, the blood of the men around me. If their battles were won, Southeast Asia might remain free." Looking around at the quiet men, she thought, "Each of us, made dumb and separate by the thundering engine and rotor, shared a certainty. Somebody was going to be hurt. And each man was resolving: It isn't going to be me . . . or this photographer," she noted wryly, sitting cross-legged on the corrugated metal floor, changing her film and waiting for its smooth tedium to deliver her, if only for a moment, from her fear.

They were choppering to the village of Ap My Thanh, once a river-pirate stronghold, more recently a shelter for communist guerrillas who'd taxed and terrorized the inhabitants. According to the marine intelligence officer, earlier sweep missions had reported moderate ground fire. The final words of the senior officer were "You will not—I say again not—fire until you are being fired on."

The major chewed his gum at double cadence, the sergeant looked calmly through the open hatch of the chopper, the soldiers shifted their weight, crouched to spring. As they hedge-hopped at one hundred miles an hour, Dickey concentrated on the rush of the grass tufts on the ground. The noise from the engines and rotors and the heat had become insufferable. Then the Vietnamese corporal shifted his position, using Dickey's hand as a brace as he pushed himself toward the hatch edge. His hand was ice cold and wet.

"The helicopter's wounded-banshee howling rose to a scream as the laboring rotor held us at a hover, probably the loudest noise the human ear could bear," she wrote. "Then we touched down." Jumping from the chopper as it rose behind her, she struggled for balance, fell, picked herself up, and raced after the men. She was supposed to be accompany-

ing the American advisers but could only make out the squad of Vietnamese. She ran through the tall grass to catch up with them as the first
firing rolled over, an automatic burst that she discovered later was one
of the squad, firing into what he believed to be the enemy's rear guard.

She stumbled into the squad's skirmish line, heeded the corporal's
command to stay in formation and keep moving. She dogtrotted over the
uneven ground of a plowed rice field and was heartened by what she saw:
"From the far right and left, letter perfect by U.S. infantry standards,"
the men were running forward, evenly spaced.

By the time they reached the thatch-roofed houses at the edge of the
village, there was a flurry of activity. Not surprisingly, the men had
cleared out, leaving dogs, chickens, and hogs running in all directions.
Women and children were frozen, appearing more patient than frightened. "They'd been through such visitations before and seemed to trust
the government soldiers not to loot or kill, and this trust was honored,"
Dickey wrote.

Her squad came upon fifty-odd camouflaged foxholes at the edge of
a field and other squads' captured prisoners. Flying back to Khanh Hung,
a town one hundred miles from the southern tip of Vietnam where the
American base consisted of map-walled tents, Dickey thought the action
she'd seen "bespoke a shift in the winds of a war." She believed that with
the infusion of U.S. advisers, the isolated villagers sensed "their government's efforts to defend them."

Dickey's optimism evaporated upon her brief return to Binh Hung.
The CIA-supported village, a favorite of Diem's, eloquently bespoke the
political reality in Saigon. She'd come to attend a funeral. Thirty Sea
Swallows had been killed after guerrillas attacked one of their outposts
with captured American arms. U.S. Marine helicopters close by were not
informed of the battle until it was hours old. With the village's position
now precarious, Dickey recalled Father Hoa's spirited words to his
fighters as they prepared for a battle. "Do not fear death, my sons. You
came here to fight for all humanity." Father Hoa had been successful
because his fighters were loyal not to something as vague as the government in Saigon, but to the priest himself.

She remembered choppering out the year before and arriving in Cholon, Saigon's Chinese district, part fancy suburb, part shantytown, to
find a message from a clandestine transmitter linked to Binh Hung. It
said: "Please forward these words to the fighter of Binh Hung named

Dickey Chapelle. We extend our best wishes for your success." The message went on to add that a heavy battle was being waged with assault groups and companies of the Sea Swallows against a possible enemy main force. They had named the assault the Chapelle battle, but the outcome was still unknown.

The funeral was held among nineteen candlelit coffins in a tin shed as the rain outside drummed against the metal. The men had been killed by enemy-captured U.S. weapons. There were other Americans in attendance whom Dickey knew. Like her, they always seemed to turn up in the same beleagured places, the warriors, the aging, elite fraternity of windmill fighters, the only people outside of Binh Hung she could still relate to: a U.S. Special Forces lieutenant she'd met in Laos; a helicopter pilot who had flown her during the Lebanon landing; and, ironically, two marine officers who had come to visit Binh Hung as a militarily successful village. Many noted that this funeral marked the beginning of the end of Father Hoa's experiment. Dickey also noted that twenty years earlier she had been told by the U.S. Army that there were no facilities for women in the field—and that, that afternoon, at Khanh Hung, she'd be provided with her own private toilet, an enclosed trench. That same afternoon she met three young marines, telling her eagerly that this was their first overseas duty. Then, incredibly, each told her that his *father* had met Dickey when she was covering the battles of Iwo Jima and Okinawa. Shockingly, it dawned on her that "I was now covering my second generation of combat marines, again, on embattled ground half a world away from home." If anything, the information only reinforced her commitment to the country.

She spent seventeen more days on the military helicopters. Four times they were fired upon. She made her own base of operations first among the marine choppers deep in the southern plain, then later with the army helicopter company in the northern mountains. She covered air-evac of the wounded and delivery of food and ammunition and spent four days deep in a guerrilla-dominated province with U.S. Army Special Forces, urging them to eat the native food since they were already sharing the danger (but not all of them thought Dickey's instructions relevant, preferring to eat Spam out of tins).

Dickey was inside a chopper with a squad of Vietnamese riflemen and a U.S. Marine captain as they approached the river junction village of Vinh Quoi, thirty miles west of Khanh Hung. They'd come, with a second chopper, on a reconnaissance, after the transmitter in the village had ceased functioning. The reason was obvious as they got closer: the sky above the village had turned red with banners of flame and popping ground fire from the guerrillas inside the village. Even with the marine and Vietnamese gunner firing back with Browning automatic rifles, the guerrillas had the advantage.

In a moment of cease-fire, Dickey grabbed the headset from a hook on the compartment wall. She heard the captain shouting, "See them go! I bet I can count two hundred!" As he took the chopper out of gun range over the burning village, she made out scores of the enemy, noting they wore helmets and carried packs and were using a pattern of dispersal that marked them as trained soldiers. So finally she'd seen it—the ghost force of North Vietnamese conventional forces, miles from the north, where by treaty they were required to remain. The men in the helicopter were raging with helplessness. Dickey wanted to get closer.

By the time they returned to Vinh Quoi with more than a hundred airlifted Vietnamese riflemen, the enemy was gone, although the village still burned. Inside the smoking ruins, the villagers had been hacked to death. The silent survivors were gathering the bodies into reed mats. Dickey counted the bodies of six women and children. Two widows of Vietnamese soldiers were taken aboard the helicopter, and Dickey held one of their babies. Four days later she covered a helicopter mission led by an American adviser that ended in success, in an area near Vinh Loi village, where a guerrilla leader was captured. Upon leaving, Dickey wrote of feeling she'd "walked out of a theater before the curtain came up. I hoped to come back for the show."

DICKEY RETURNED to the States by way of Allentown, Pennsylvania, so she could attend the annual reunion of the U.S. Marine Corps Combat Correspondents and Photographers Association. The organization presented her with its award for "her brave endeavors, and professional excellence in reporting the cause of combat marines everywhere." The previous year the award had gone to astronaut John Glenn.

Dickey's *National Geographic* article entitled "Helicopter War in South Viet Nam" was selected to be the magazine's cover story for November 1962 and would mark the first time a combat-ready American marine in Vietnam was shown. In a Leica camera newsletter recalling the assignment she mentioned flying in a chopper twelve hundred feet above the Mekong River, when the engine "in the chopper I was flying in conked out. We began plummeting down out of formation, and this gave the picture an angle you would never have normally seen. Scared? Of course. This was one picture I did not make for any journalistic reason. I just felt that if I kept on shooting, I would be less frightened. Finally the engine caught and we limped into a friendly air strip."

Prior to its publication, the U.S. Pentagon requested copies of the photographs to be used with the article. They would be using one of the photos, which would appear in the magazine as a triple-truck spread, showing marine helicopters "swarming out on a guerilla-trapping mission, with a squad of Vietnamese regulars inside, waiting to attack," as part of a presentation for President Kennedy. But government security review officers objected to the photograph of the combat-ready marine crew chief cradling his automatic. They requested that *National Geographic* omit it from the published article.

Dickey was outraged. Every frustration she'd felt over government interference, from her first run-in with the CIA during the Bay of Pigs affair to her eight hundred "missing" Laotian photos, resounded in this latest attempt to stifle what she'd seen. She had once told an acquaintance that "indifference to proof, the refusal to look for it, the unwillingness to commit to any but claims—these are the real sins, the real wrongs against which the profession of journalism ought to be fighting, and against which I hope I have truly—to paraphrase a fine old American document—pledged my life, my fortune, and my sacred honor." She was not even remotely bothered by an attack of her usual blind loyalty. The photo she'd taken was exactly the kind of documentation she'd been fighting for since her first eye-opening trip to Vietnam. And finally a national magazine was going to show Americans what was actually going on.

On August 8, 1962, Dickey wrote to Lincoln White, the press officer for the State Department, and to Arthur Sylvester, press officer for the Department of Defense: "The implications of the approved version are not what I reported. I'm given to understand that the reason for this deletion is to avoid embarrassing U.S. 'cold war' negotiators by showing such a degree of combat readiness. I respectfully point out that such negotiation about Viet Nam now is governed not by illusion, but largely by hard-fact military performance of troops actively engaged in hot warring. My protest is exemplified by the case of a photograph judged objectionable because it shows an American marine helicopter crewman aloft over Viet Nam holding his weapon as he has been ordered: in the normal military-ready position. I am alive to make this protest only because of such readiness, and I have witnessed it on not less than 23 recent flights (four times we did come under hostile fire, and returned it) in Viet Nam. I cannot accept any effort to bury these facts." The photograph ran. "Helicopter War in Viet Nam" won the 1963 Press Photographers Association "Photograph of the Year" award.

Another photograph taken on the *National Geographic* assignment showed an officer of the Vietnamese airborne brigade about to execute a supine prisoner with his .45 automatic. Dickey referred to the photo in a September 26, 1962, letter to Nancy Palmer as the "atrocity Kodachrome from Vinh Quoi—on operations." The photo was discussed in an article in the winter 1984 issue of *Aperture* magazine entitled "The Photography of Conflict" (Fred Ritchin), as predating by six years the classic Eddie Adams, Pulitzer Prize–winning execution photo of a Vietcong prisoner, "Guerrilla Dies." But in 1962 *National Geographic* had no interest in presenting such a graphic definition of the obscenity of war. Nor did any other general-interest magazine. According to *Aperture*, the photograph was finally published in an obscure magazine.

Nancy Palmer could not recall its name. Dickey became involved with many such magazines as her gritty photos and articles extolling the Vietnamese fighters met with increasing rejection, while her photos of U.S. Special Forces engaged in guerrilla warfare were censored. Her frustration, and her narrowing vision about the war, began to dictate her decisions. Nancy recalled one occasion when she urged Dickey to avoid a lurid one-shot magazine called *The Face of War, Vietnam,* "Exclusive Inside Story," the patriotic inspiration of a North Hollywood, California, porno publisher. Dickey contributed her Vietnam photos and articles to the magazine.

In the fall of 1962 *National Geographic* magazine offered to send Dickey to Cambodia for a general piece on the country, from December until March 1963. Obviously flattered by the high-paying, prestigious assignment, she nevertheless refused it. She had been invited to Vietnam by her Special Forces friends during those months, when she believed heavier fighting "involving Americans" would occur in South Vietnam. She explained to *National Geographic* that she looked forward to South Vietnam as "the place of decisive testing of the single U.S. war tactic actually in use—our military adviser system—against shooting communists. I'm afraid the emotional pull on me toward that story would prejudice the results of any comprehensive general assignment in Cambodia."

As it happened, the biggest battle to date was fought in January 1963, at Ap Bac in the northern Mekong Delta. Unable to get an assignment, Dickey did not witness the engagement. Three American advisers were killed as they attempted to lead an armored column of South Vietnamese troops. Five American helicopters were shot down. The Vietnamese troops that Dickey had pointed out to Commandant Greene as being underaggressive lost one hundred troops. It was a terrible defeat.

18

The Angel of Hialeah

ALTHOUGH by now Dickey had collected enough awards for her journalism to open a museum, the last months of 1962 and the first of the new year were marked by increasing frustration.

Despite the anguish of her time in Laos and Vietnam for the *Reader's Digest*, editor Hobart Lewis continued to assign her bayonet border stories, for which she was grateful. Yet each fresh story she pursued eluded her. Always insecure about her relationship with the magazine, one of the few wealthy enough to support her kind of journalism, it was now magnified by her inability to produce and the growing gap between their editorial policy and her journalistic sensibilities. The publication had been responsible for bringing her to the public's attention and making her practically a household word, ensuring her success on the lecture circuit and the notoriety her vanity and her pocketbook required. But it seemed the harder she chased a story, the faster it disappeared. It was as if she were jinxed.

She spent most of October racing back and forth between New York and Washington as the Cuban missile crisis loomed. With confirmation by President Kennedy that a ballistic missile launch site was being built at San Cristóbal—rumors fueled by Cuban exiles who told the CIA that the Russians were planning to attack the United States from Cuba—it looked to Dickey as though D-Day were only hours away. She had her assignment from the *Reader's Digest* to cover the first army paratrooper or marine to land on the Cuban beaches. She hoped to cover the first marine landing in Cuba by boat or helicopter, if one occurred, or any eyewitness story from Guantánamo during the crisis.

By this time U.S. amphibious and ground forces were put on military alert and preparing for exercises in the Caribbean. On that same day the leaders of the CIA-backed Cuban Revolutionary Council were meeting with representatives from the Pentagon and the State Department. According to a witness, the United States wanted a massive enlistment of all exiled Cubans of military age.

On October 22, the day President Kennedy was announcing a blockade of Cuba to prevent further shipments of Soviet military equipment and demanding the removal of Soviet missiles, Dickey was again in Washington pestering Mac Kilduff, the assistant White House press secretary. She had received her accreditation from the marines and the army to cover any invasion story. Now she wanted confirmation of a planned invasion. Not wanting anything to do with her, Mac Kilduff passed her along. Not surprisingly, she was unable to get confirmation from any of the designated press secretaries.

At the same time, newspaper reporters standing by in Puerto Rico were being flown back to Washington by the government. Dickey found it a real bore explaining to the public affairs assistant for the secretary of defense how she was prepared to put herself into the hands of the marines or the army and to cut herself off from all outside communication, as she had done when covering the Sixth Fleet and Seventh Fleet in Lebanon and Laos. In a letter she would write to Hobart Lewis about increasing government interference, she described how the public affairs assistant and another man, a navy admiral, appeared amazed that she knew how to parachute. Uneasy around Dickey, the men told her they'd keep her posted. She never heard from them. On the other hand, one of her marine friends had offered to get her a brief trip to Guantánamo. As much as she wanted it, she declined. How could she possibly tell the story without exposing someone on active duty?

A year later Assistant White House Press Secretary Mac Kilduff spoke at the Overseas Press Club. When he was introduced to Dickey, she recalled that he smiled faintly and asked not to be seated "next to that crazy parachutist." She sat opposite him. Later he explained the White House policy: one shouldn't expect to have an eyewitness observer "when you drop an atom bomb, for heaven's sake."

In reply Dickey, a member of the OPC's board of governors and its Freedom of the Press Committee, pointed out that fellow OPC member Bill Laurence had won a Pulitzer Prize for doing exactly that, flying in the bomber over Nagasaki.

Then, on November 6, 1962, Dickey and nineteen other reporters were flown from McGuire Air Force Base in New Jersey to Dum Dum Airport in Calcutta at the invitation of the Department of Defense. The reason, ostensibly, for this exhausting press flight was to cover a U.S. arms airlift to India. Although there had been no eyewitness reports, India was charging China with attacks along its border. The *Reader's Digest* assigned Dickey to make an eyewitness report of the fighting in the border areas between Indian troops and the Chinese. Right before leaving Washington on this press junket, she wrote Hobart Lewis, "I want to *see this invasion* by waves of Chinese, the concept which since Korea has been the second-ranking nightmare, I think, of us Americans (Russian nuclear attack being the first). . . ."

Two weeks later, from the Ashoka Hotel in New Delhi, India, Dickey reported to Hobart Lewis that she never saw "any evidence of a single U.S. weapon reaching any troops on the Sino-Indian border." Nor were any newspeople allowed to witness "any Indian outposts" where fighting was reported. One month later she wrote her aunt Lutie, "I've been running around like mad all right—Tezpur, Assam, and Jammu have enjoyed the doubtful pleasure of my company. As a matter of fact, half a dozen reporters and I were about the only defense force left in Tezpur a few weeks ago, when the communists decided on a cease-fire just in time to avoid capturing all of us. I not only haven't actually seen any U.S. arms in the hands of Indian soldiers—I actually have to this day never seen an Indian soldier on duty!"

Bill Garrett, Dickey's photo editor at the *National Geographic,* was also a member of the press party. Garrett recalled the trip to India as "rotten, really." There was a lot of flying and being turned back and sitting around and waiting. Garrett finessed a flight to the border area of Ladakh, posing as a member of a cartographic party since no journalists were allowed. A little later he heard Dickey pounding on his door.

When he opened it she yelled, "You goddamn son of a bitch!" Non-plussed, Garrett asked how she'd found out. "Never mind," she answered, "I've got to go along." Garrett refused.

"But then she said she would actually help me," he said. "She'd shoot pictures and make them available to me because she didn't need pictures for the *Digest*."

Dickey prevailed. When they arrived in Ladakh, they were obliged to spend the night together. "We weren't just sharing the room. We were sharing the bed," remembered Garrett. "It was the most sexless night of my life in those terms, because I don't think Dickey even took her boots off. Everybody kind of giggled and whispered about it the next day." Needless to say, they never got off shots of any fighting or of weapons being delivered.

Back in Calcutta, Garrett invited Dickey to dinner. "We deserve it," he told her. They went to a night club. "I remember she wore a blue jersey knit dress. I couldn't believe it when she let her hair down. When she got out of her fatigues, she was well stacked. But you never saw her that way. There was nothing coquettish about her." Garrett, a charming, worldly man, thought of Dickey as without the vanity of most women. In preparing her eulogy for the magazine's February 1966 issue, he was surprised to learn that she'd been married. Though she'd been a frequent houseguest, always eager to help chop wood, Garrett had no idea how she lived when she wasn't on assignment, wondering if she didn't spend so much time with the military, living in barracks, "because she was always broke." He liked her especially because she laughed a lot, although she reeked from cigarettes and had a hacking cough.

After five pointless weeks in India, Dickey returned to New York, uncharacteristically down about the recent nonstories she'd been chasing. Friends like S. L. A. "Slam" Marshall, the brigidier general and military reporter, suggested she try another kind of career. Barry Farber, radio WOR's talk show host, who'd become one of her fans and with whom she'd become a fairly regular guest, told her that maybe it was about time she stopped collecting war stories, chidingly adding that she certainly had enough to tell to her grandchildren. She told friends she wasn't ready to give up just because her luck had been bad, but the thought crossed her mind when she was sitting at her desk. As horrifying as it was, maybe she'd become too old to run after stories. It seemed the harder she tried, the more walls sprang up. Her legendary toughness and humor, her tenacity, no longer seemed resilient. She departed from her public image for the first time when she shared her nagging self-doubts with Hobart Lewis, who, despite their differing points of view, she trusted as a friend. She asked if there was any place for her at the *Digest.* "It isn't good business for you to send me far places to see something historic happen and have me turned back." She listed the trips to Miami in 1961, the trip to Washington during the missile crises, and the latest junket to India. "Is the press powerful enough—or the objective of maintaining eyewitness integrity to printed fact important enough—so the trend can be stopped?" she asked.

DICKEY FOUND A RESPITE from her professional problems among young people, particularly the budding photographers to whom she looked to "carry the torch higher than we of my generation ever did." She wrote those words for a speech she delivered to a photography class in 1963. "It is so good to be with you," she wrote, "to know that there is still somewhere that it is okay to feel and to believe that being a photographer is the most important statement a person can make."

On March 18, 1963, the *Reader's Digest* asked Dickey's new lecture bureau, Colston-Leigh, to book her as the keynote speaker at the Eighteenth Annual Conference of the Girls Club of America, which they were co-sponsoring in the grand ballroom at New York's Hotel Roosevelt. The theme was not the war in Vietnam, nor the burgeoning civil rights movement, nor what some considered the biggest boon to women's liberation, the "Pill." It was "The Challenge to Excellence— Building Today for Tomorrow's Citizens."

Dickey was wearing one of the severely cut suits tailored for her by Stevie Blick's dad. She had on her theatrically thick pancake makeup, her false eyelashes, her gold Cartier tank watch, and gold-and-emerald cuff links. With her hair tied in a topknot, she could have been selling war bonds. She had been chosen to speak because she epitomized a woman who upheld her own sex under the most trying circumstances.

Dickey told the women and girls and the handful of men assembled before her that excellence didn't always win. Looking above the hopeful, listening faces, she told them that when the famous Notre Dame University football coach Knute Rockne wanted his team to perform excellently, he would gather them around at half-time and fire them up by saying, "Well, girls . . ." Dickey said she was relating that story because she didn't like it, that it was a story she had heard fairly often among the armies of the world. "And it always enrages me."

She had come up with another version of inspiration for herself, one that hadn't let her down. "Sometimes, if there's something I have to do that I'm not real enthusiastic about, like stepping off, especially at night, into absolute nothingness from an airplane because the troops I'm covering are doing this, I say to myself, 'All right, all right, let's not do this like a bunch of boys. They have to have a jump master, a brass band, three slogans, and a sergeant. You do it like a girl. Just go do it.' " The room applauded her speech. She noticed that some of the men present were also clapping and she admonished them, "You weren't supposed to do that.

"I grew up in the heartland of the United States," she continued. The room had turned silent, as it usually did when she spoke. "I believed that I could do anything I really wanted to do, and I still believe it. Nowhere else in the world can a woman of seventeen or an old lady in her forties, as I am, say 'I can do anything I want to do.' But I am going to condition it. You can do anything you want to do if you want to do it so badly you'll give up everything else to do it. Because it's only true if you accept the whole proposition. That's how great the freedom is for being an American woman at this time."

She spoke about the women in Hungary and in the mud huts of Binh Hung. She remarked that in the forty-four countries she had now visited, she was constantly revitalized and amazed by the "sisterhood of women" that made a common language unnecessary. It was the job of a war correspondent to spot the heroic acts and the heroic people in any situation and "to pass them back because those are the ones who can inspire the rest of us. The ones we'll remember." As far as she knew, it was a peculiarly woman's job. She ended her speech by bringing up the women in the Marco Street prison: nothing as exciting had ever happened to her. "I didn't know there were any other human beings left on earth." The motto of those women had become her motto as well: "Tears are not permitted here."

THE FIASCO of the Bay of Pigs and the end of the Cuban missile crisis did not alter the Kennedy administration's obsession with Fidel Castro. Indeed, it had become a cause far more important than Laos or Vietnam. Spearheaded by the CIA and Dickey's friend General Edward

Lansdale, and given the name Operation Mongoose, the clandestine program to rid the world of Fidel Castro brought an estimated six hundred CIA case officers and as many as three thousand contract agents into the Miami, Florida, area. In 1962 Lansdale envisioned a great triumphant march into Cuba and had proportionately wilder schemes to ensure this march. His imagination running wild, he planned to unleash rumors that Christ was about to make his second appearance—as soon as the Cubans got rid of Castro. The signal for the Second Coming would be rockets bursting from a U.S. submarine off the coast of Cuba. The plan was scuttled, but others as harebrained and arrogant persisted. Fodder for Lansdale's plans and those of other CIA movers and shakers was the raw talent of Miami's rapidly growing, factious Cuban exile community.

On December 23, 1962, Fidel Castro released the eleven hundred "freedom fighters" of Brigade 2506, captured one and a half years earlier at the Bay of Pigs, in exchange for $53,000,000 worth of food and medicine. They were met in Miami by José Miró Cardona, the CIA-endorsed leader of the Cuban Revolutionary Council, who stood under a burning sun shaking each man's hand. One week later President Kennedy and his wife, Jackie, greeted the returnees and forty thousand of their supporters at Miami's Orange Bowl. The tanned, beaming president and his beautiful young wife were handed the blue-and-white flag of Brigade 2506. As the crowd went wild, Kennedy held the flag firmly and told the hapless fighters, "This flag will be returned to the brigade in a free Havana." (It was in fact returned years later after a lawsuit on behalf of the brigade unearthed the flag from storage at the Kennedy Library in Waltham, Massachusetts.)

Boosted by Kennedy's apparent promise to support the exile cause, the steamy streets of Miami's Little Havana vibrated with intrigue. While tough, athletic Cuban exiles like Tony Cuesta and the bull-necked Ramón Font sipped their tiny cups of sweet Cuban coffee, CIA agents encouraged them to pursue one or another well-financed raid. Despite the cash flow, most of the raids failed. But some, like the March 27 sinking of the Russian freighter *Baku*, timed for publication in *Life* magazine, succeeded.

Life magazine's April 12, 1963, cover story featured the "eyewitness story of the attack on the *Baku*." Tony Cuesta and Ramón Font, the hot-for-action leaders of the action group Commandos L (L for *libre*), were old friends and former supporters of Castro. Well financed by the CIA, they boldly attacked the seven-thousand-ton *Baku* at the northern Cuban harbor of Caibarién. For the magazine's cover, Andrew St. George shot the grainy color photo of Tony Cuesta aboard his twenty-two-foot-long speedboat, *Phoenix,* fondling his automatic rifle.

The *Baku* had loaded its cargo of sugar and was ready to sail when the *Phoenix* opened fire at two hundred yards, angling closer until it pulled alongside the *Baku.* At close range, while Cuesta and the others threw grenades onto the deck of the ship, the bald-headed Ramón Font placed a magnetic mine onto the freighter's hull, below the water line. The mine exploded, ripping a hole in the hull.

Pravda, the official Soviet communist newspaper, branded the sabotage the work of "CIA bandits and Cuban malcontents." *Life* heralded it as a great act of "derring-do." Tony Cuesta later wrote that he did not appreciate being reduced to a buccaneer when in fact his had been an act of war. But he didn't complain too loudly; he understood publicity.

President Kennedy and his brother Robert, then attorney general, were not anxious to have another confrontation with Russia. So instead of lauding the Commandos L, the United States reaffirmed the Neutrality Act. The State Department issued a release on March 30, 1963, denying that any of the raids against Cuba had been launched from U.S. territory. Moreover, the release confirmed that the FBI, the Immigration and Naturalization Service, the Coast Guard, and the U.S. Customs Service would "take every step necessary to ensure that such raids are not launched, manned, or equipped from U.S. territory."

It further stated that although the government was sympathetic with those Cubans "who hope to see their country freed from Communist control," the United States could not tolerate any activities that "might provoke armed reprisals, the brunt of which would be borne by the armed forces of the United States." The twenty-odd members of Commandos L were stripped of their privileges and completely cut off from what Tony Cuesta called "those fat CIA checks." Since the *Baku* incident, the CIA had selected its own exile units from within the teeming population of émigré Cubans and opportunistic Yankee paramilitary adventurers. The word was out on the Calle Ocho, inside the cafes and coffee bars of Little Havana, that the unmanageable Commandos L were not to be allowed any more outings.

Every morning when the thirty-six-year-old Cuesta left his house, two

FBI agents were waiting in their parked car. One morning he walked over to their car, leaned in, and asked if they would take him where he wanted to go, "instead of using two cars." They replied politely that personally they wouldn't mind, but they had orders to follow him.

At this dismal point in his career, Tony Cuesta received an odd message through the Cuban underground. Some woman photographer wanted to take his picture. His instructions were to come to the appointment armed. Interviewed in 1989 in the tiny government-subsidized apartment in Miami's Little Havana that he rarely leaves without a bodyguard since a reported attempt on his life, Cuesta—who lost his left hand and eyesight during his thirty-third raid into Cuba (in 1966), where he was imprisoned for twelve and a half years—recalled his first meeting with Dickey.

It was a June day in 1963, in an abandoned lot that the Commandos L used for firing practice. There, amid a shimmering swamp of abandoned appliances, Dickey waited. She wanted a photograph of Cuesta firing his .45 carbine above her head. Cuesta, a six-foot-five-inch former Olympic swimmer, and onetime intelligence officer for Fidel Castro, did not want to shoot at her.

"But she shouted at me to fire," he said. "There were jets thundering over our heads and she kept yelling, 'Go on and shoot.' Cuesta still couldn't do it, although he thought she was one of the strongest-looking women he had ever met. He recalled that even standing still, a fierce energy emanated from her. Hair pulled back from her plain face, he found her not beautiful, but feminine. Her blue eyes flashed at him from behind her glasses. Raising her camera, she yelled again.

"So I thought, All right, since she's asking for it." Cuesta pointed the gun at her head and pulled the trigger. "The flash of the camera moved over the flash of the gun," he recalled. "As it whizzed past her head, no more than an inch from hitting her, she smiled at me for the first time. It seemed as if my firing at her were of no consequence, that it was a routine."

She told him she wanted to cover the Commandos L in their next raid on Cuba. "She didn't just want to ride the pony horse of danger," Cuesta said, his voice etched with machismo awe. "She wanted to put on the saddle."

Dickey wrote that "because American pressure was so heavy on them [Commandos L], to cover them I lived eight months under a false name, not even letting my editor know where I was." She introduced herself to Cuesta using her long-abandoned given name, Georgette Meyer. On this assignment there would be no long letters to Aunt Lutie or Stevie. Tony Cuesta shook his head at the tough woman before him and her flowery name. Later, after he explained the sorry state of the Commandos L, Dickey offered to give Cuesta a thousand dollars for rent on a new headquarters for his demoralized cadre. The money had been advanced to her by the *Reader's Digest* for expenses.

When Dickey met Tony Cuesta it was a toss-up as to who was the most desperate for action. Except for a picture story the *Reader's Digest* planned to run later in the year on Father Hoa's Binh Hung village, none of the projects the magazine had assigned her during the past three years had seen print. Her pieces, always written from the heart, were becoming less and less objective with her tendency to overromanticize her subjects. While insisting on accuracy, she was nevertheless losing credibility with her penchant for overidentification. It was becoming increasingly difficult for her to balance these disparate elements, as well as to manage to heed the *Digest's* government line.

This loss of objectivity had begun to bother Hobart Lewis, who in April 1963, when discussing a proposed military piece, cautioned, "We hope you will write it as a military reporter and correspondent, reporting on the outfit. In this case, we do not want you to participate. We want complete unanimity, top objective reporting and not first person 'I was there' material." They wouldn't send her back to the now-beleaguered village of Binh Hung.

RIGHT BEFORE DICKEY LEFT for Miami, Stevie Blick recalled Dickey swore her to secrecy and had her write down the phone number of a man in Washington, with instructions that if she didn't come back to New York within a certain period of time, Stevie was to call the number and rip up the piece of paper. Years later, Stevie figured that Dickey had gone "underground" not only because she loved the intrigue, but because she was doing something for the CIA. She thought the number might have been General Lansdale's. Bill Garrett scoffed at the idea. "Dickey, CIA? I doubt it. The woman was too voluble; you couldn't shut her up."

By 1963 Lansdale's baby, Operation Mongoose, had met with little success, and he had slipped into a more distant area of operations.

However, there is no reason to doubt that he was still very much involved, and that Dickey's latest assignment was of interest to him and to other members of the intelligence community. In her expense breakdown for that period, which included a lot of running back and forth from Miami to New York to Washington, as well as trips to Fort Bragg, North Carolina, to cover U.S. Special Forces (another doomed piece for the *Digest*), she visited intelligence sources who also happened to be personal friends, and who, like Dickey, had a sense of holy mission about current events—the only difference being that they knew a lot they weren't telling her. She visited Arleigh Burke, who was then director of the Center for Strategic Studies at Georgetown University; Ed Lansdale's associate, Bernard Yoh; the Pentagon; and the Citizen's Committee for a Free Cuba, a CIA-funded organization "of which I was naively a founding mother," she'd note ruefully a year later. In fact, if ever Dickey's naive patriotism and desperation were being manipulated by the government, which she unwittingly assisted, it was in the paranoid miasma of Florida with the Commandos L. A year later a more enlightened Dickey told Joseph Carter, Sunday editor for the *New York Herald Tribune*, "I *speculate* with considerable backup from government sources in the State Department, CIA, and Department of Defense that in setting up their relations with the clandestine Cuban freedom fighters, they do not have matching objectives. I speculate further that the real objectives of each agency are a function of its sensitivity to the party in power. (Such a situation has a precedent in Laos, where in 1961 I saw that the State and Defense departments' objectives were mutually contradictory)."

Stevie said that Dickey was always nervous about her relationship with *Reader's Digest,* never knowing whether what she wrote would please them. Hobart Lewis, now editor-in-chief, was aware of Dickey's growing frustration, but he believed all of that was behind her with her new proposal, one that he was personally excited about. He called it "Two Men and a Girl, Against the Governments of the U.S., Cuba, and Russia." Although Lewis, writing on June 5, 1963, did not believe she and her middle-aged "freedom fighters" had a chance to succeed, "it is bound to be unsuccessful; even if it is, in the minds of all who participate, highly successful, it is really a pitiful and minute and nearly futile gesture." But he felt that it was a brave act, "a little candle of freedom flickering," not only a "great action story," but potentially a novel of desperate people who had no other choice but "hopeless action." If Dickey pulled off the story, it would be "a small classic in the annals of the fight for freedom." He believed that it was critical for the American people to be constantly reminded that their own freedom was in danger. He also hoped she would be able to work into it some of the facts about guerrilla fighting that the magazine had so long wanted to publish, since the Commandos L viewed themselves as guerrilla fighters.

Sparked by Lewis's enthusiasm, Dickey supplied him with information he requested, including the locations where 9,300 communist agents were purportedly being "trained in Cuba for Red subversion of other countries." The information came from an associate of hers, a former officer at one or more of the bases and a "source well thought of by the U.S. authorities."

Besides paying Commandos L's rent, the *Reader's Digest* also funded the purchase of two Power Hawk engines for Cuesta's speedboat. Now the Commandos L could concentrate on enlarging its war chest in the form of bonds sold to the Cuban community. Tony Cuesta henceforth referred to Dickey as "the angel of Hialeah."

The house Dickey rented to serve as a barracks for the Commandos L was in a working-class Cuban neighborhood in Hialeah, Florida. Like the others in the neighborhood, it was a box-shaped, two-bedroom cinderblock house, painted pale yellow, with a backyard and garage. But unlike the others, its front lawn boasted no religious statuary. It was at the end of a paved county road.

A sunroom in the southwest corner of the house, called the "Florida room," together with the living room and kitchen had been converted into a weapons factory by the previous renter, a Mr. Villaverde, whom thirty-one-year-old Ramón Font described as "a CIA man." It was here that the balding Ramón had learned to make bombs, including the mine that put the hole in the side of the Russian freighter *Baku*.

"I was pleased to end up owning the command post after I'd only been assigned, so to speak, to penetrate it," Dickey wrote on August 16, 1963, the night she moved from a borrowed apartment in Miami into the barracks. "But I didn't know till today that what I really 'own' is an arms factory. But I do—the Florida room of the house is just that by tonight. . . ."

Cuesta believed the onetime CIA safe house in Hialeah was secure enough to train troops and store a portion of the arsenal needed for

Operation Mangrove, the name given to their next raid on Cuba—to be launched from a deserted Bahamian island.

Every morning Dickey would wake at five and join the twenty-odd commandos in an icy dive into the Atlantic Ocean. She also joined their classes in survival and demolition. Cuesta remarked that her endurance was tougher than that of some of the boys. "With Dickey's ovaries we have enough balls to outfit the whole platoon," he boasted.

The barracks had very little furniture, a few mattresses, a refrigerator for keeping the nitroglycerine cool, work benches for cleaning ancient crud-covered bullets, and tables for assembling napalm bombs. "No Smoking" signs in English and Spanish were tacked to the walls. Under Ramón Font's instructions, Dickey and the other commandos spent their afternoons making napalm bombs. Dickey copied down the instructions for making the bombs as though it were a recipe for Aunt Lutie's meatloaf. One ingredient, flour, came from the U.S. Department of Agriculture and was marked "For Needy Families." The finished bombs were stashed under a heap of dirty clothes inside the clothes closet. When Dickey called her brother, Robert (an old hand at working with explosives), to ask him a technical question about the bombs she was helping to manufacture, Robert voiced his disapproval, but he ended up sending her two Du Pont handbooks on high explosives. "I thought if she was going to be fooling with the stuff, she should know what she was doing," he later commented.

"I think anyone who prepares a napalm bomb is already guilty of first-degree murder," she wrote. "I remember my righteousness in 1958 when I made the picture in Mayarí, Cuba, to prove that two lousy bombs of it had in fact been airdropped on dwellings in Batistiano B-26s. And here we've made dozens of bombs. What else can I say?" When she wasn't typing up her notes or packing napalm, she would help polish bullets.

One night after finishing the usual dinner of rice and beans, Dickey and two of the commandos were in the kitchen washing dishes. "Are you ready to die?" one the commandos asked the other as they dried the dishes.

"Ready as I'll ever be," came the answer.

If anything, the odds comforted Dickey, as did the single-mindedness of purpose. It was David against Goliath, men of will against weapons, a concept in which she had tremendous faith precisely because she had seen it work before—in Cuba, in the hands of some of these very same men. When she wrote in her journal, "These men are the little handful of people in any society who are not just willing but anxious to gamble for immortality by doing. Something. Anything," she was writing about herself.

When Dickey stood under the grapefruit tree in the Hialeah backyard, she thought of her grandparents. Their house in the swank Miami suburb of Coral Gables, a few miles south, where she had been sent by her parents a lifetime ago to keep her out of trouble, also had a grapefruit tree. Her grandmother would shout at her not to eat the unripe fruit because she would get sick. Now, standing in her orange pedal pushers and rubber thongs—the same ones in which she had traipsed around Laos and South Vietnam—she would suck in the citrus, wipe its burning tang from the edges of her mouth, then light a cigarette, since smoking was not allowed inside the house. *"Vea en un libre Cuba,"* she would say, practicing her Spanish. "See you in a free Cuba."

A month after Dickey moved into the Hialeah barracks, the calm of the shabby street was shattered by sirens. Without a warrant, officers of the Miami and Hialeah police forces and U.S. customs agents entered the house and hauled away the weapons. There were no arrests.

In a *Miami News* article dated September 22, 1963, the police described the Hialeah barracks at 1261 SE 8th Court as "bulging with bombs and raw explosive materials." Members of the metro bomb squad confiscated twelve gallon cans filled with cornmeal and explosive napalm for firebombs, sixteen sticks of dynamite, twenty bombs with inserted fuses, ten pounds of black powder, liquid fuel, and a quantity of dynamite "in a deteriorated and dangerous condition." Also confiscated were three rifles, a machine gun, and a 20-mm Lahti cannon.

Dickey, identified as Georgette Meyer, a Miami resident and renter of the house, was quoted in the news article as saying, "I have been fighting tyrannies for twenty years." As the officers crated out the volatile weapons cache, Tony was moved by Dickey, her hands on her hips, upbraiding the police and customs officials. "You should give these boys the weapons they need," she said. "Who are you working for, anyway, the United States or Fidel Castro?"

"We're fucked," said Tony Cuesta. "The route to Cuba will be long and hard."

On October 21, 1963, after replenishing their weapons with the reserve Tony Cuesta had cached elsewhere, the group moved blindly in four boats through the night waters of the Intercoastal Highway off Miami Beach. Like the others, Dickey wore military fatigues.

As the lead boat passed a sandy spit called Haulover Beach, the tiny fleet was flooded by lights from a Coast Guard cutter. The cutter came dangerously close to bisecting Dickey's fifty-foot boat as one of the officers shouted, "There they are! We've got them now." This time the Commandos L lost their entire arsenal: an estimated forty thousand dollars' worth of submachine guns, automatic rifles, explosives, incendiaries, hand grenades, antitank weapons, and ammunition. A news brief about the seizure in the *New York Herald Tribune* noted: "It was no surprise to find Dickey Chapelle aboard the mother boat."

The next day the despairing Commandos L held a press conference. They branded the action a "criminal act" and accused the United States of being "an ally of Castro communism." Since the Commandos L were subjected to "constant persecution," Cuesta announced that they were going to set up headquarters inside Cuban territory. Dickey and Cuesta were the last to leave the press conference.

"Bravo, Tony," she said. "You have the same fighting spirit as George Washington."

THE ASSASSINATION of President Kennedy in November 1963 ended U.S. interest in raids on Cuba; and by the spring of 1964 the White House would order a halt to all its sabotage raids on Cuba. Whether taking a cue from current events or simply losing interest in Dickey's overly emotional commitment to a doomed cause—"Free Cuba" now appeared on the bottom line of her correspondence with her editor—the *Digest* informed her they were not interested in funding any more underground work.

Dickey's articles written in the barracks, five in all, were lopsided depictions of the Commandos L as heroic freedom fighters when in fact they were often rabid fanatics who were not above extorting money from the community for their war chests. "I know they're not Eagle Scouts," a contrite Dickey wrote her editor when he rejected her romantic portrait, "but they're in the freedom-fighting business." By now, once again, Dickey was too emotionally involved to see the issue clearly.

On the more practical side, she needed to save face and to hang on to her vaunted position as the *Digest*'s "bayonet border specialist."

Assisted by a bequest of $10,500 from her aunt Lutie, Dickey asked her editor to let her remain in Florida. She would pay her own expenses while finding another group to attach herself to. She clearly had no memory of some long-ago advice offered by Tony when she had set off on the disastrous trip to Vienna: "If you stay long enough, you can make a life's career out of a story," he had written, "but how does it get published?"

Andy Jones, the editor in charge of Dickey's Florida beat, agreed to let her take one more crack, on spec. Though the CIA was now actively suppressing any more free-lance raid parties, there were still adventurers chomping at the bit. Dickey's desperation led her to Gerry Patrick Hemming, a media-savvy ex-marine and soldier of fortune. The brawny six-feet-six Hemming could often be seen swaggering on the streets of Miami in battle fatigues, parachuting in the Florida Keys and Everglades, and giving articulate interviews to television reporters as leader of the Intercontinental Penetration Force, code name Interpen.

According to an Interpen fund-raising letter found among Dickey's papers, Interpen's "Guerilla Warfare Instructors" organized training camps for dissatisfied Cuban exiles out of the Florida Everglades and the Florida Keys.

At some point even fellow romantic General Lansdale became alarmed, warning Dickey about "sticking her neck way out" with her choice of company. Dickey responded, he recalled, by "disappearing and hiding out for a time. The next I heard was when the U.S. Navy fished her out of the brine, badly hurt from the fire, explosion, and sinking of the boat of some Cuban adventurers en route to a raiding attack. She hadn't wanted me to stop her, thus the silence."

Dickey had met Hemming briefly in 1958, in Havana, when she was covering Fidel Castro for the *Reader's Digest* and he had been running guns for the rebel army. He had little use then for publicity by the *Reader's Digest*. Twenty-six years later, serving time in prison on a narcotics trafficking conviction, Hemming recalled the meeting. "The first thing I asked her was 'Dickey, don't you think you're getting a little too old for this stuff?'" He laughed. "She would get upset when I told her that." But Hemming, then in his twenties, relented; he could use the publicity and, more important, "she was airborne-qualified and tough." A few days later he introduced her to the Cuban exile Felipe Vidal Santiago, leader of commandos.

Santiago, a career military man, led the 1957 abortive navy uprising against Batista at Cienfuegos, escaping capture by fleeing to Panama. In 1958 he returned, joined the rebels, and, upon Castro's triumph, was named head of Havana Maritime Police. In mid-September 1959 he was upped to commandant and named naval attaché in Caracas, until he resigned in protest "over Dr. Castro's dictatorial policy" in Colombia, where he sought asylum on March 5, 1960, one day after a French munitions ship exploded in the Havana harbor. Four days later Santiago was accused by the Castro government of being a CIA agent, responsible for the sabotage. Santiago made a statement to the wire services in Bogotá that Castro's charges were "ridiculous," claiming he had gone to Cúcuta, Colombia, on a few days' leave and sent in his letter of resignation and defected there.

An undated Teletype concerning Santiago found among Dickey's collection states that he served as contact between freedom fighters and the nucleus of naval personnel still in Cuba but against Castro, read Camus, and was well known for smuggling people out of Cuba. In the mountains of Cuba Dickey had heard of Santiago, who was now planning his sixteenth clandestine trip to pick up Soviet soldier defectors and drop off weapons to members of the anti-Castro underground. He invited her to accompany him. "This is a headline story if I ever heard of one," Dickey excitedly wrote Andy Jones in November. She believed her bad luck was finally taking a turn.

According to Hemming, who would be involved with some of his non-Cuban protégés, the operation was to "get Raúl Castro" and "to identify supposed caves in Cuba where Russian nuclear weapons were hidden." Telling Dickey she'd have to defend herself when they landed, he got her a shotgun, "in case we would run into a couple of pigs."

The ex-marine described Dickey as "well connected in the government." He believed somebody in Washington was telling her what to do and who to do it with. "She would always be with groups that never got anything done. Now, why was that? Because somebody wanted her to monitor those groups." Despite Hemming's belief in Dickey's CIA connections—she also had reservations about him, later referring to him as "the imaginative ex-marine with literary ambitions"—Dickey was moved into Santiago's safe house, described as four rooms on the Miami River with a dock in the backyard. Because the group was under "rigid surveillance," Dickey did not leave the house during the day. At night, her face blackened, she helped load weapons, food, and gear into the twenty-two-foot boat. Word had been received by this time that the escapees, including children, were waiting at the rendezvous point in Cuba, "sealing their fate if the rescue boat didn't show up," as Dickey wrote Andy Jones. On December 30, at about one o'clock in the morning, their boat was sunk. Dickey wrote her wary editor that she believed it "could have been done by a double agent within Commandos X—there was a suspect American among them" or by any of the U.S. agents slinking around the Miami River, a hotbed of skullduggery. Dickey spent the night trying to pump out the boat with the assistance of a Miami police officer.

For the next five nights they worked on the boat. During the daylight hours, the thirty-seven-year-old Felipe Santiago stood in front of the commandos, teaching them the Cuban firing commands: *"¡Preparán, spuntán, fuego!"* ("Ready, aim, fire!") In the event of capture, they would be executed, and Cuban custom demanded they give their own firing commands.

On Sunday, January 5, 1964, the boat, loaded with 230 gallons of gasoline, set out with Dickey, Santiago, and two non-Cuban members of Commandos X aboard. By sunrise Miami was little more than a distant skyline. For eight months Dickey had been waiting for this moment. The sky overhead was cloudless, the sea choppy but open. The commandos soon discovered that the gasoline drums were fouling the rudder controls, but as long as someone sat on the stern and bailed, they would stay afloat.

Dickey broke out her cameras and began shooting, admitting that "no matter the angle, the pathos of the mission was obvious." But, like the slender Santiago, she remained optimistic. When he admitted he never expected to have an American woman as a crew member, Dickey replied by splashing him with the bailing bucket. The idea of messing up a naval commander thrilled her. "I'm only an observer," she shouted gaily.

At that instant there was a *whroom!* The boat was on fire. Dickey felt a hand pushing her backward, overboard.

Twenty-five miles southeast of Miami gas spilled into the boat's bilge, ignited by a spark from the engine. All the passengers were burned, Dickey badly on the face and hands. They swam wildly away from the burning craft, its gasoline fire following them across the water. Within minutes, from the safety of a fishing boat, Dickey watched Felipe's craft explode, finding the cherry-red column of flame with its curling black edges reaching for the noon sky the most beautiful picture she had ever failed to get on film. Her uninsured cameras had been left on the boat.

An Associated Press article in the January 6 issue of the *Milwaukee Journal* reported the incident, quoting Dickey as saying, "It was a real blast." Tony's son, Conrad "Ron" Chapelle, then in the air force in Tehran, heard about his onetime stepmother's latest adventure and wrote, "It's impolite as hell to say so, but aren't you a bit old for this sort of thing??? . . . There's not a darn thing I can do about it and I'll stop lecturing and sounding like Tony. . . . In the meantime, for God's sake don't forget to duck."

Hemming, who was not aboard, nevertheless felt that Dickey, outfitted in a World War II "Mae West kind of life belt that I told her wasn't worth a shit," caused the fire. "She had pushed a thirty-five-gallon drum of gasoline against the exhaust line and the boat exploded. We obviously had a security problem."

Dickey wrote Andy Jones that she had covered the story "from the only place I could have—at sea aboard the little boat." She contended she "did not know how the explosion had come about. I've since heard that one of the other folks aboard saw a blue flash behind the instrument panel just before the *whroom!* . . . I now conclude the insulation of the wiring had been damaged by salt water during the boat's immersion. If that's the case, the group's misadventure again must be laid at the doorstep of whoever sabotaged the boat." She added that she had been "raided, ambushed, blown up at sea, and shot over, 'not at,' by a .38."

The *Digest* ordered Dickey back to New York, where she hammered out more drafts, including a piece on U.S. Special Forces training she'd covered for the magazine at Fort Bragg, North Carolina. Her last try at the underground was a portrait of Felipe Vidal Santiago, who had been executed on May 27, 1964, in Cuba, after being tried as a CIA agent. Somewhat unflattering to U.S. policy, her article contradicted an Associated Press story, which the *Digest* preferred over her eyewitness coverage. Dickey was beginning to acknowledge a "communications problem" with the *Digest* because she "didn't have the guts to do as many drafts . . . as I've done . . . without understanding how they seem to misfire. . . ." According to Nancy Palmer, "when the *Reader's Digest* questioned her integrity, she was heartbroken."

That spring Dickey's lecture bureau booked her on another series of talks throughout the heartland. Dickey told "ten-thousand-odd people" about her adventures with the Commandos L and Commandos X, telling them, "I've seen U.S. government agents systematically break the hearts of Cuban exile freedom fighters." She wondered what had happened to the Cuban families they had set out to rescue.

19

A Moth to a Flame

DICKEY may not have been a great photographer or a brilliant writer, but she had no equal as an eyewitness, and the *Digest*'s rejection caused her great pain. Her honor was at stake.

"Next time I go out for you—if there is a next time—and it becomes obvious that it will be uncomfortable for me to *see* what happens, I doubt if I'll choose to try. I'll just alibi to myself that the reader won't know or care how it really was anyhow," she wrote bitterly to Andy Jones on June 16, 1964, "so there's no point to feeling it myself before I report it. I can always get some guy I've judged trustworthy to tell me about it later. Comfortably. But for some future story, I still want to know I'm able to force myself to see-or-get-hurt-trying."

"Dickey liked to play cowboys and Indians," said the editor years later. "She liked to put on those berets and hats. Sometimes she'd come up with something real good. I never questioned her credibility. I questioned her judgment. I liked her."

By this time it was apparent to Dickey and her editors that her passion for adventure—what she called "daring" or "the certainty of uncertainty"—was no longer voluntary. She was addicted to it, always chasing the high. She wrote Andy Jones that she wanted to trace narcotics from Red China to New York City's Harlem. "Time-consuming, expensive, and risky, but God! What a story!" She wanted to live among the anti-Red guerrillas in Latin America and to be positioned "under full wartime security control so as to make it possible for me to cover for you any commitment of U.S. forces to destroy Castro's missile sites."

During one of Dickey's trips to New York while living "underground" in Florida, she met a woman researcher at ABC news. Pat Powell, in her thirties, had recently returned from six weeks in Vietnam. Her experience over there had been so emotionally devastating that she had to find somebody to share it with, and she'd heard about the "legendary" Dickey Chapelle in Vietnam. They made a date to meet in the bar at the Overseas Press Club.

Dickey was sitting at one of the leather-covered booths when Pat arrived. "I didn't know whether she was Captain Marvel or one of those World War Two heroines. She was wearing a dress with shoulder pads, stiletto heels, lots of makeup, false eyelashes, and red lipstick. It was so World War Two, and this was the 1960s." But despite the bizarre attire, Pat Powell liked Dickey Chapelle. "I remember that the two of us went on a night patrol on the Appalachian Trail. We took the train from Grand Central Station. It reminded me of being a teenager sneaking out on some wild adventure. That's what I liked about her, the feeling we were doing something that stuffy adults never did. While we sat around waiting for it to get dark, she showed me wallet photos of young marines. I had a feeling that she'd slept with them, but nothing serious, what we would call 'a roll in the hay.' She was very excited because she had never led a night patrol before. I had the feeling she knew she was getting old and she was looking for somebody to pass the mantle on to."

BY 1964 AMERICA'S COMMITMENT to Vietnam's defense was deepening, the quagmire, as historians would refer to it, widening. Fifteen thousand American "military advisers" were now in South Vietnam, and by August, after an unsubstantiated attack on U.S. destroyers in the Gulf of Tonkin, Congress passed the Gulf of Tonkin resolution, which would give President Johnson the equivalent of a declaration of war. With more than 60 percent of Americans unconcerned about Vietnam, a country the president referred to as "pissant," the bill passed with "barely a murmur of dissent."

No longer strictly a heartland crowd pleaser, Dickey was now talking in Kentucky, Ohio, Pennsylvania, Texas, and New York. The closest thing to a foreign desk her audiences would encounter, she told them that the war could be won with advisers leading South Vietnamese troops. She wanted to see thirty thousand additional Green Berets, one leading every South Vietnamese patrol, which would keep American troops from fighting an Asian war, as President Johnson had promised. At the same time America would not be withdrawing its commitment to South Vietnam.

It wasn't an easy pitch, but it wouldn't have appealed to an increasingly strident Dickey if there hadn't been a challenge. At the time, the Green Berets were getting so much flak in the press that Dickey received a letter written in Special Forces "speak" asking for help from their commanding general, William P. Yarborough, at the John F. Kennedy Center for Special Warfare at Ft. Bragg, North Carolina. "Special Forces under fire in press here at home as result of serious misunderstanding in part of certain members of Fourth Estate. . . . Since you most knowledgeable of Special Forces in action, actually being a trooper yourself, all Green Berets would appreciate any lift you may give with a clear conscience."

Dickey did her spiel for them in auditoriums and faculty clubs. "The South Vietnamese are good soldiers," she told her high school audiences, "but they lack leadership." Then she would launch into her lecture, called "The Great Adventure," advising the young, attentive faces before her to look into a challenging career with the military as an adviser, leading "the anguished overseas so as to avoid nuclear holocaust." When she wasn't recruiting, she was assaulting the U.S. government's news censorship with her talk entitled "The Vanishing Correspondent" and what she viewed as "the greatest loss of freedom to my generation." And if this wasn't enough, she was now accusing the women in her audience for the shameful decline in military training. The *Wisconsin Daily Cardinal,* the University of Wisconsin's daily paper, heralded her as a speaker of "wit, passion, dynamism," whose experiences "on the front lines of battle are as impressive as any five-star general's row of ribbons," while the women in Falls River, Virginia, found her "alarming."

Dickey's friend at the Pentagon, Ed Lansdale, tried to help her get to Vietnam on April 1. He wrote to United States Air Force General Chief of Staff Curtis E. LeMay, whose "air commandos" were operating in Vietnam with the Vietnamese air force. LeMay's "Air Gorillas," as some army advisers referred to them, were a specially trained tactical force. They dressed in unusual nonregulation outfits, favoring French bush hats with red pom-poms, and had recently picked up some negative press when the Vietnamese air force bombed a Cambodian border village.

"[Chapelle is] the one reporter I know who understands guerilla warfare from having seen so much of it," Lansdale wrote. "She is an outspoken gal who is the darling of the Marine Corps, but she does get in close and knows counterinsurgency the way Ernie Pyle knew the ground war in World War II. The real good paramilitary forces hold her in high esteem and affection."

General LeMay, famous for his comment that the North Vietnamese should be bombed "back to the Stone Age," responded on April 16 that his air commandos' activities were drawing to an end. A short time later Lansdale told Dickey that "LeMay was told to bring his B-26s home."

The following month Dickey was subpoenaed to speak before the House Un-American Activities Committee in Washington, where a cold war bill was being discussed. The proposed "Freedom Academy," a central clearinghouse for information about the workings of foreign governments, was to be yet another tool in offsetting communist propaganda. To Dickey the academy was a welcome alternative to the inefficient, official government briefings, which, she told the committee, "have misled and misadvised . . . reporters . . . by intent and design."

When the committee asked if she knew of any instances where the U.S. press had been manipulated by "the Reds," Dickey nodded. Ears pricked up in expectation of a list of names. Dickey replied that the commies were manipulating the news simply by "making sure the press doesn't get in the act." Since Americans were so "tremendously disinterested" in what was going on in Laos and South Vietnam, since 90 percent of the Vietnamese people lived beyond reach of the jeep and the telegraph, since no reporters were there to bear witness, those people would easily be conquered and controlled.

"We can be manipulated," she explained to the bewildered politicians, "by gaps in our coverage." She went on to describe the combat in Binh Hung, which she had been "privileged" to experience. As they stared dumbly, she emphasized that improved communication meant the willingness "to share their danger. I made six jumps with the Vietnamese airborne; that was the one year when I really felt that I had earned my right to carry that wonderful passport . . . because it was my country saying, 'We are backing you in the fighting,' and nothing in the world had convinced the paratroops that we meant it. Not their equipment, which was marked 'Made in the U.S.A.,' but the fact that there were five of us who were jumping with them . . . and that should be the objective of the Freedom Academy. . . ."

By August Dickey once again had an assignment from *National Geographic.* The danger would begin on September 15, when she would fly over the Ho Chi Minh Trail, the network of dirt roads through Laos and Cambodia carrying men and supplies from North Vietnam to communist forces in South Vietnam. If time permitted, she would also cover the activities of the U.S. naval advisers on the Mekong River.

She needed the time to get off her crutches. In July, paranoid that the army might discover her problem and strip her of her precious parachute wings, she had arranged through a doctor friend of Nancy Palmer's for "secret" surgery on her kneecaps. She had spent weeks recuperating in New York's Roosevelt Hospital from the surgery that U.S. Marine Commandant Wallace Greene pointed out to the chairman of the board of *National Geographic* magazine "was caused by injuries received during a parachute jump with the army airborne troops!"—inferring that such a disaster would never befall Dickey with the marines.

Hobbling around the Overseas Press Club, Dickey was once again chipper and expectant. Her career, so long stalled in Florida, was moving forward. Even her story on Felipe Vidal Santiago, "Requiem for a Hero," had been scheduled (although the *Digest* would shelve it again). She wrote Andy Jones, "Your treasured letter brings me much the same ungentle satisfaction as when I first heard that 'Nobody Owes Me a Christmas' was on its way to print." Sometimes, at one of the OPC's popular exotic cooking nights, or when entertaining guests in her apartment with a pot of spaghetti, she'd suddenly say, "If you don't mind, I'd just like to get back to my people." She meant the U.S. military advisers who were dying unheralded and the embattled village of Binh Hung.

In the fall, at the U.S. Army Civil Affairs School in Fort Gordon, Georgia, Dickey gave a talk with Ed Lansdale on counterinsurgency to fifty-three advisers ordered to South Vietnam. Afterward she tossed away her crutches and began a workout regimen. She ran two miles a day, past the United Nations building and along the East River, and pressed the weights she kept under her bed. Sometimes Stevie would watch her, shaking her head and muttering, "I just don't believe you're the age you say you are."

National Geographic gave her a monthly guarantee of $1,200, a $2,000 advance for expenses, and a purchase price of $2,500 for her manuscript with a color page rate of $200, less the monthly guarantee. Although one of her editors suggested she spend a few days in the comfort of the Hotel Majestic in Saigon before heading for the bush, and to be sure and "not get shot" (*National Geographic* assumed no responsibility for personal injury or death), she couldn't wait to get started.

When Dickey arrived in Laos on October 2, 1964, it was a far more slippery Emerald City than it had been three years earlier. Officially there was no American presence. In fact, that past January American and Thai pilots had flown a series of commando raids into North Vietnam in propeller-driven fighter bombers with Royal Lao Air Force markings; while they'd bombed Pathet Lao troops in Laos and North Vietnam, regular U.S. aircraft had conducted photo reconnaissance missions alongside.

After two sweltering weeks, Dickey was firming up final details with the Royal Lao Air Force for her flight over the Ho Chi Minh Trail. She wanted to illustrate the character of the trail and the air-to-ground actions aimed at cutting off its northern, Laotian end. She wrote her photo editor, Herbert Wilburn, on October 18 that "U.S. naval aircraft from the 7th Fleet carriers have been flying high-level jet, armed reconnaissance missions over all parts of Laos, including the Trail area, on request of Laotian rightists. . . . On the record, their military planes, those of the Royal Lao Air Force, under a very friendly general named Ma, operating from their headquarters at Savannakhet, fly many missions over the Laotian panhandle (the Trail area) with bombs and rockets under their wings." Dickey added, not for the record, "They come back two hours later with bomb racks empty."

She had already made some pictures of the air bombing, her pride restored as she spoke of flying the first "purely recon mission in the history of the Royal Lao Air Force." Eager to do more in-depth coverage and get more "exclusive" photographs for *National Geographic,* she wrote later, "I had no idea what I was up against." She excitedly wrote the *Geographic* that she also planned to cover the Trail in Vietnam, "so that the *Geographic* will have a record of the Southeast Asia communist supply lines and the efforts to cut them by air, sea, and land." She planned to begin on November 7, "for weather reasons." The U.S. ambassador to Laos, Leonard Unger, and Laotian General Ma endorsed her plan, as did the American High Command of the entire region, and General Westmoreland's chief of staff in Saigon, Major General Richard Stilwell. She even had permission to fly with Air America to any spots not accessible by the Royal Lao Air Force.

That same week Dickey wrote the nervous Lutie, who was distressed over reports in the *Milwaukee Sentinel* about stepped-up violence and Buddhist immolations in Vietnam. And Lutie feared for Dickey's safety. In a tone she'd once used on Edna, Dickey wrote soothingly, "I met the two men whose writing about the war out here is most often printed in the *Sentinel.* I told them how you . . . had been so disquieted . . . and asked them why they didn't make clear that most of the country at any given time was quiet, and most of the streets in Saigon had never heard a grenade explode or seen a Buddhist immolation. . . . They both laughed and reminded me that their editors considered good news no news and only the relatively sharp changes—political or violent—as news at all." Dickey added she was "well and busy" and "taking pretty pictures," because unlike the wire reporters, her editors at *National Geographic* were interested strictly in the "scholarly approach" to news, and the *Reader's Digest* had always liked "happy-ending stories." How she must have missed writing the kinds of letters she had to George, in which she could share every mad moment, knowing it all would be received with great spirited approval.

By October 20, as America stepped up its extensive bombing of North Vietnam, Dickey found herself close to the Thai border at Savannakhet, Laos, to schedule her flight with the Lao air force commander. General Ma greeted her enthusiastically and in Pidgin English invited her to ride in his tactical planes to photograph the Trail. "It is very, very dangerous—but very, very important for you to do it," the general told her. "The American people must understand the nature of the Trail. . . . You can see its true nature only from my airplane."

Dickey was to report back to his base in one week to begin the coverage. In the meantime, she went out with the Royal Lao Infantry to Thakhek, a village less than a hundred miles north of Savannakhet, to look over a Trail flank and spend the weekend climbing rocks in the rain.

Arriving as planned at the airport in Savannakhet a week later, she was directed to another building. She hesitated to proceed farther without an escort but was waved on by General Ma's adjutant and told to find her own way.

"As I stepped into the room," she wrote Herbert Wilburn at *National Geographic,* "I could see that a tactical briefing was going on. General Ma was listening, and the local U.S. Air Force attaché, Colonel Van Bibber, was talking as he held large black-and-white photographs, obviously . . . just the kind of pictures you might expect from the reconnaissance planes of the 7th Fleet (which the U.S. had publicly stated were serving the Lao government). Before I grasped what I was looking at, the colonel stopped and bodily removed me from the room, telling me in most unflattering language that I was an intruder. I replied that I had entered only on the direct orders of General Ma's adjutant, and certainly did not insist on being present. I did, however, want to know how in the colonel's judgment I could expect to keep my appointment with General Ma; the colonel replied that Ambassador Unger in Vientiane was the only person to whom I should appeal; otherwise he, the colonel, would continue to protect General Ma from my intrusion."

Dickey flew up to Vientiane that night, arriving late, but not too late for the marine guard at Ambassador Unger's residence to invite her in. Ambassador Unger saw her at once and appeared "delighted" by her plans. Speaking warmly of the *National Geographic,* he assured her of his support and said he would so instruct his senior air attaché, Colonel Tyrell, and Colonel Van Bibber—both of whom were his subordinates. She was treated to a briefing by Colonel Tyrell that seemed to bear out the ambassador's promise and then was flown by Tyrell back to Savannakhet in his personal plane so that General Ma would see she had the full backing of the United States ambassador.

Call it women's intuition, call it a rerun, but Dickey didn't quite trust Ambassador Unger. Could it be, she wondered, that Unger was unaware of the real military strategy in his area of responsibility? Actually, according to Christopher Robbins's *The Ravens,* a book about "the men who flew in America's secret war in Laos," Unger knew well what was going on.

After conferring with the command group in Saigon, and receiving General Stilwell's approval of the plan that she fly with General Ma, Dickey flew back to Savannakhet. In possession of written credentials to the Royal Lao Air Force, she waited excitedly in her hotel room, as instructed, for a visit from "some American officers." After three long days they showed up—"crew cuts, flat guts, sport shirts—introducing themselves as 'semiclandestine.'" To Dickey that seemed consistent with the covert nature of the United States in Laos, and she resisted the temptation to joke about being "semiclandestine."

The men offered to help Dickey with her assignment. After they left, she dashed off a note to the magazine to expect the photos after her delay. "I thought I had surmounted the last roadblock to getting the photos," she later wrote Wilburn, "the last but for being shot down." In fact, she was never to see General Ma again.

When the three men returned, it was to inform Dickey that General Ma now refused to allow her to accompany him because "he suddenly couldn't understand English and I was a woman and Buddhist warriors do not go into combat accompanied by women." After several attempts to correspond with Ma, and in possession of several invitations from his pilots to fly her, Dickey realized she would never get her story. She was feeling every bit the fool, done in once again by representatives of her own government, this time in the Land of a Million Elephants. Unaware of the extent and nature of American military involvement, Dickey was nevertheless aware intuitively of certain unsettling facts and implications. She knew that the Royal Lao Air Force was not guided by the expressed will of its own commander, nor even by the U.S. ambassador. She believed it was commanded by the clandestine types who had come to visit her. In November she left Laos for Saigon and the Mekong Delta, where she had set up an interview with a young American naval lieutenant, Harold Dale Meyerkord.

"It's going to happen on the Mekong in an ambush," the lean, blond Meyerkord told reporters, predicting his death in a sudden, blinding burst of fire. The twenty-seven-year-old naval lieutenant, already a legend in South Vietnam, was adviser to the Vietnamese commander of the Twenty-third River Assault Group, nineteen vulnerable gunboats used to carry Vietnamese troops to battle on the narrow, muddy tributaries of the Mekong Delta. The iron boats carried mortars, 40- and 20-mm guns, and .50- and .30-caliber machine guns and ranged from thirty-five to sixty-five feet in length.

Dickey joined up with Meyerkord in the rice-rich Mekong Delta province in Vinh Long, where the ugly little war was brutally real and such a hotbed of VC sniper fire that chopper pilots slowed their roters only long enough to let off passengers. The Delta, which was a forty-five-minute chopper ride from Saigon and, with thousands of miles of waterways, about as large as California, was historically one of the great outlaw haunts of Asia and now the perch of the Viet Cong.

Like Dickey, Meyerkord did not wear a flak jacket. He carried his carbine on automatic, loading it with a clip and tracers. "An adviser who is overly cautious and places needless stumbling blocks in an operation is a handicap" was Meyerkord's credo. He was famous for routing VC in the narrow canals and aiding Vietnamese sailors with no concern for his own safety. He amazed and inspired Dickey. With him she felt herself on the right track; all it took was finding a kindred spirit.

They were transporting troops along a canal, past jungles, fields, and houses, watching for Viet Cong. Dickey carried an automatic carbine and held the bullets in her right-hand pocket and her film in the left-hand pocket. What would Father Hoa say about her carrying a weapon? she wondered. Would he still tell her she went too gently? A young reporter, Richard Boyle, later went on patrol with Meyerkord. Meyerkord told him Dickey had saved his life "when she fired a warning shot with her carbine, springing a VC ambush."

Dickey wrote of her trip with Meyerkord in her most rapturous tone, thankful for deliverance from Looking-Glass Laos into something she understood. "Here and now, the sum total of virtue . . . is . . . the ability to shoot back fast." Blessed reality. The way she now dealt with her fear, besides the usual fussing with her cameras, was by forcing herself to "think about somebody other than yourself—you won't be so scared." After several weeks with the lieutenant, on patrols and running through villages under enemy barrage, Dickey spent Christmas 1964 riding out of the Delta on a sampan with three inches of freeboard towed by another sampan. "The motion required to just raise my camera would have capsized us," and the best gift was "the . . . joy at simple survival."

The assignment earned her the Vietnamese navy's silver twin-sail insignia, which she placed on the black navy beret alongside her Vietnamese parachute wings.

Dickey returned to Saigon's Hotel Majestic, where she could now watch VC-attacked tankers burning downriver as she sipped a Pernod on the terrace. A letter from Lutie was waiting, telling her she hoped she was spending Christmas "with somebody you like."

A few weeks later Dickey learned of a competitor on the Meyerkord story: Boyle, the green but resourceful twenty-two-year-old from San Francisco. She knew public information officers were on hand at JUS-POA (Joint United States Public Affairs Office) to advise reporters about the war; she herself avoided the government press office like the plague, but her hunch that Boyle could be found there was correct.

Dickey had been seeing more and more of Boyle's sort of reporter lately and believed them to be a danger to themselves because of their lack of combat experience, ignorance about the country, and foolhardy behavior at diplomatic conferences. They were also a menace to her. They were young, tough, and filled with energy. Boyle may never have seen combat, but he had already stepped on her story.

Boyle was honored and flattered to meet the famous Dickey Chapelle. "I kept asking her questions about Fidel Castro," he said years later, "but she didn't want to talk about him. She talked about Meyerkord. I think she was in love with the guy, not sexually, but worshipped him."

Dickey invited Boyle to lunch at the Majestic, a hotel the young, broke free-lancer thought lovely despite the beggars on the floor waiting to be thrown bits of food. To the blue-eyed Boyle, this was just another sign of what he termed "the overwhelming corruption of the South Vietnamese government." He thought it sad, since Saigon was such a beautiful city, with its wide, tree-lined boulevards, French opera house, and beautiful women in their flowing *ao dais*.

At the rooftop terrace restaurant, from which guests could watch firefights, Boyle ordered steak and drank Pernod. Everyone in the restaurant treated Dickey like an old friend. Press people continually stopped by the table; waiters knew her by name. As she drank coffee and Pernod, the randy Boyle looked her over. He thought she was "real gutsy" and far older than forty-five. "Women are still beautiful at that age," he commented, "but she was lined and leathery and not well groomed." But he greatly admired her "tiger-stripe" fatigues, like those worn by Vietnamese officers. Hers were precisely tailored, not the standard, ill-fitting American issue. She gave him the address of a tailor in Saigon. "We talked about the nitty-gritty kinds of things," he remembered, "like where to go to get your film developed, things like that." Her helpfulness surprised him, "because usually photographers don't help other photographers."

He told her that he hated being in choppers, open boats, and tanks, because he didn't feel he was in charge of his own destiny but subject to the luck of its commanders. "Dickey didn't feel that way at all. She told me that what scared her were foot patrols, because of the mines, and that she was always very careful on patrols, making sure to pick seasoned people to go with." Dickey struck him as being "disillusioned about America, like she wasn't happy about where it was going."

Right before they finished lunch, Dickey asked him to hold off printing his article on Meyerkord until she'd published hers. She thought it was her story. She'd done a lot of work on it, and if he filed before she did, she'd be "up the creek with *National Geographic.*" Boyle figured, "So that's why she took me to lunch, just to butter me up." But despite the feeling, he liked her and agreed to hold off for a reasonable time.

Three months after Dickey's patrol, Meyerkord was killed in an ambush. By then the young man who'd answered to the call "Hornblower" had been lauded as a hero by the press and by Dickey as "audacious, ebullient Lieutenant Meyerkord . . . husband, father, leader, and teacher of men, dead of a bullet in the brain on a muddy canal. . . ." He was awarded the Navy Cross. Her letter of condolence to Mrs. Meyerkord was her fourteenth to the widow of an American adviser in Vietnam. The *National Geographic* paid her for her story "of derring-do" and put it in their inventory.

Dickey came home to Milwaukee in January. She spent two weeks with her aunt Lutie, who was then living in Dickey's old house on Shorewood Boulevard. She was invited to speak at Shorewood High and did so, refusing a fee. Lutie thought she looked tired and too thin, but Dickey had a ninety-day, forty-speech lecture tour to begin. In Dayton, Ohio, draping the captured Viet Cong flag around her shoulders, a helmet with mosquito netting on her head, she looked like a wiry apparition from warrior hell. Once again campaigning for military advisers and reporting that "we are losing the war," she addressed the College Women's Club, where somebody had drawn a mustache across one of her publicity photos. "It means I'm truly famous," she told Stevie Blick cheerily.

In April 1965, one month after America committed its first ground troops, two marine battalions, to Vietnam, Dickey arrived at the University of Wisconsin at Madison, where her brother taught geophysics. The placid, affluent lakeside college had become a hotbed of student opposition to America's presence in Vietnam. The University of Wisconsin was among the first colleges to hold "teach-ins"—combined faculty and student discussions examining America's position in Vietnam. Dickey had been invited to participate in one on April 2. She had accepted the invitation with a feeling of "honor." But for the first time she felt as though she were fighting the war all by herself. More than one thousand protesters carried placards decrying American policy, tactics, and deployment. The rally lasted ten hours. Faculty members argued that the United States was losing in Vietnam and had no clear objective. There was no border to restore, no permanent government to support. During a question-and-answer period, Dickey's gravelly voice crackled over the dense crowd. She asked how the protesters could stand the "intolerable" weight of their cardboard signs. "Hanoi just loves that kind of thing, you know," she said, hurt and confused. "They love to point at our people back home who are undermining everything we're trying to do. I looked up the word *treason* . . . and I guess it's not that . . . maybe 'sedition' would describe it. I don't believe you quit because you are losing, and I don't believe you have to lose."

To prove her point, she sparked the idea for a group of students to form the Committee to Support the People of South Vietnam. It would eventually bring speakers with opposing views to the campus, an opportunity to debate the growing dissident movement.

While in Madison, she stayed at her brother's house. His four children liked watching her put on makeup, hypnotized by all the tubes and colors. The children enjoyed their aunt's visits, during which they learned how to play dice and jump down the front stairs and fall into a paratrooper's roll. But, looking at Dickey, Bob thought that all those patrols and hardships had exacted their price. When she returned from the "teach-in" she was strangely quiet, sitting on the couch in the Victorian house and smoking one cigarette after another. "I could turn those demonstrators around," she rasped. "Just give me a couple of weeks with them."

Later that week Dickey addressed a group in Wilmington, Delaware. Positioned on the lectern like miniature rockets were Russian and Chinese artillery shells, which she had collected. Many of the women at the spring luncheon of the American Association of University Women had voted for President Johnson because he had promised not to send American boys to fight a war that Asian boys should be fighting. Now these same women were worried.

Well, she had something to tell them. She'd been concerned about it since World War II, and now she saw it as the answer to why the Soviets loomed so strong. Except for the U.S. Special Forces training, she believed the American military was inefficiently trained—and the culprit was Mom. Since the Second World War she'd watched the decline of military forces. At the Richmond Women's Club, she reminded her audience that it was women who exerted pressure in the years following the war "to bring the boys home and water down the training, which resulted in the degeneration of our forces from strong to ridiculous." They had to improve their tapioca training "if we want to win the war."

On April 20 she debated the former U.S. ambassador to Southeast Asia, Donald R. Heath, at Denison University in Granville, Ohio. Heath's position was that the United States should negotiate the crisis in Vietnam. Dickey's unwavering opinion, that the United States should take a firm stand, found favor with at least one listener—a coed from Adrian, Michigan. The young lady and her girlfriends, inspired by Dickey's tough talk, wanted to do something positive. "We are sick of apathy," she wrote. "We want to write to our American advisers and tell them we are proud of them." She thanked Dickey for "stirring the minds of many." The letter was like a tonic.

THE *National Observer,* the Dow Jones–owned weekly that Dickey described as "right of center," sent her to Santo Domingo, the capital of the Dominican Republic, in the middle of June. Fourteen thousand marines had landed there two months earlier to support a junta of guards once loyal to the former dictator Rafael Trujillo.

President Lyndon Johnson had stated that the U.S. government possessed hard evidence of communist leadership in the Dominican rebel forces. Dickey had met Ramón Pichirilo Mejia, the Dominican rebel commandant, eight years before, in the makeshift rebel hospital in the Cuban mountains. He was the man who'd not been expected to survive his wounds. This landed her the job with the *National Observer,* which wanted her to do an article on him. She parachuted into Santo Domingo with the paratroopers of the Eighty-first Airborne, eagerly and "like a girl with my eyes wide open."

After one night patrolling with the paratroops, Dickey located the rebel commandant. The two went on night patrol through the same streets she had patrolled with the airborne. After speaking to Mejia and the young rebels—who reminded her so much of the idealistic Castro fighters—Dickey could not in good conscience dismiss them as communists. At that point she experienced "a moment of truth that comes uniquely to most professional observers of human conflict." She had taken the assignment, she wrote, "to find a villain." But when she sat down to write, she realized to her amazement that she had found an ally.

"My life had at different times and places been protected by two groups of armed human beings now committed to mortal combat against each other. The U.S. paratroops defending the freedom they knew; the rebels as best they could resisting an oppression they knew. How had these forces come face to face with loaded weapons?" With the lines blurring around her, she now had only one desire—to be back in a foxhole or a mud hut, where nothing was relative.

DICKEY ASKED *National Geographic* for one more crack at covering the Ho Chi Minh Trail in Laos. The magazine refused.

"You couldn't go to a war where she didn't show up," commented Bill Garrett. (After Dickey's death, on the one occasion that he spoke with Tony Chapelle, Tony explained, "I just couldn't keep up with her.") As far as Garrett was concerned, Dickey had never been the world's greatest photographer; now, burdened by an increasing lack of objectivity and continuing insecurity in her professional life, she was even less so. "She wasn't that good, and she really had to hustle to keep the work coming. But she would stick with a story two or three months while another reporter would stay two days. And she would bring back the facts, no matter how long it would take."

In the magazine's farewell tribute to her in February 1966, the issue that carried Dickey's story on Lieutenant Meyerkord's River Assault Group 23, Garrett claimed that she was drawn to violence like a "moth to a flame. . . ."

Later he said "her rationalization was that she was so appalled by war that she felt she should show how horrible it is," he said. "That way she could help. But I don't really think that was the truth. It wasn't patriotism, either. She had this fascination for the military.

"The truth was that she was drawn to the excitement and thrived on it. She wasn't any kind of sex maniac or anything like that, hanging around military men. She played down sex totally, although she wasn't sexless. But she didn't want to attract attention in the field. She was so good at it that when we were in Calcutta in 1962, she got kicked out of a ladies' room. She'd go and run several miles a day just to keep in shape so that she could go into combat and not hold up a military patrol. Like a frustrated marine sergeant." In Garrett's opinion she was the old rough-and-ready World War II journalist. "And by Vietnam," he said, "it was all getting a bit rusty."

The *Reader's Digest,* Dickey's longtime supporter if not of late, also turned down her request to be sent to Binh Hung, which she'd been unable to visit on her previous trip. After the CIA-assisted murder of President Diem in 1963, the village had lost its patronage, and Father Hoa was under constant siege from the enemy and also from jealous Vietnamese army officers (and would be replaced by one of them). Dickey appealed without success to Hobart Lewis. "Since I am the only person of non-yellow skin to wear their fighting patch," she wrote, "I feel I belong with them to see whatever happens and to report on it."

That September Dickey introduced Ed Lansdale, Kennedy's golden boy of covert activities, to her editor at the *National Observer.* He helped to convince the paper to send her back to Vietnam, where she would cover, among other things, the long-abandoned disastrous forced resettlement of the country's peasants known as the Strategic Hamlet Program. She signed a twelve-week contract with the publication. Her first assignment was close to her heart: following a group of marine recruits from boot camp to Vietnam.

This time Dickey had a lot of trouble getting a visa to South Vietnam. Much of the problem might have been her highly visible opposition to press censorship, as well the move in American policy from small covert activities to a bureaucratic military setup. She went to Washington to try to speed up the process, stopping in at marine headquarters to see General Wallace "Wally" M. Greene, Jr., the commandant of the U.S. Marine Corps, and Sergeant Robert Morrisey, Greene's aide.

Morrisey had been friends with Dickey for ten years, first meeting her in San Diego when she'd come to do her "spec" story on the marines. He liked to say he knew her "before she was the famous Dickey Chapelle." He had seen her through a lot, but he'd never seen her as emotional as on that particular fall day in 1965. Dickey's loud, gravelly voice plowed down the hall like a steamroller. As always when she came to visit the commandant, she was wearing her "best bib and tucker" and carried her well-traveled, emblem-patched Australian bush hat.

The commandant was sitting behind his huge desk when Morrisey ushered Dickey inside. The feisty Wally Greene looked at Dickey's hat and shook his grizzled head.

"What is it, sir?" she asked.

"I don't see any marine insignia there," he commented in a voice as ragged as Dickey's. "What's the matter, aren't they tough enough for you?"

Dickey shook her head. "Oh, no, sir," she answered.

Morrisey watched the commandant pull his worn, brass anchor-and-globe marine insignia from the lapel of his jacket and hand it to Dickey.

For one of the few times in her life, Dickey was speechless. "Wha...?" she asked, confused.

"Go on, take it," said the commandant.

"You—you're giving this to me?" She was dumbstruck.

"Wally" Greene, a deliberate man, nodded. "I don't think anybody will mind."

Dickey fumbled with the insignia as she set it on her hat. She shook her head, mumbling something unintelligible.

The commandant asked why she was going back to Vietnam for a fifth time.

"Well, sir," she explained, fingering her hat, "except for multiplication of my figures and the depth of my conviction by a factor of ten, my report in 1965 is almost word-for-word identical with the one I so presumptuously drafted at your suggestion in 1962. Not quite, of course, because then there weren't any marines ashore in South Vietnam and thank heaven there are some now. I'm looking forward to covering them."

Morrisey recalled that his boss shook his head, then looked at her. By this time she was grinning. "Don't worry, sir," she said, smiling, "I'll march in the back of the patrol. It's too easy to get shot up front."

As she and Morrisey moved out of the commandant's office and down the hall, she continually stopped to show people the commandant's insignia. Now she walked more slowly than Morrisey; her big, loping strides no longer seemed natural as much as willed. Despite her surgery, years of grueling patrols and parachuting had taken their toll. As usual, she held a Pall Mall cigarette between her nicotine-stained fingers, pausing now and then to indulge in a smoker's cough.

Morrisey didn't see her often over the years. "Sometimes she would call from some airport or dock," needing his help to get military transport, or else she would drop by for a quick visit. Nevertheless he and his wife felt close to her. Dickey gave Mary Jane Morrisey a family heirloom, a sapphire-and-diamond bracelet.

"She said she never wore it," recalled Mary Jane, who liked Dickey also, despite her penchant for acting "dramatic for the effect." Sergeant Morrisey did not have a good feeling about Dickey's trip to Vietnam, and "neither did she."

When Dickey finally received her visa to Vietnam, she made an arrangement with Barry Farber at WOR radio to do taped interviews and feature pieces for his show. The "bayonet border specialist," as he called her, had been a guest on Barry's show many times. He supplied Dickey with a tape recorder, but no salary. "It was to give her experience," he said later. "It was going to be Dickey Chapelle in the jungle with the marines."

DICKEY FLEW TO MILWAUKEE to say good-bye to Aunt Lutie. While there she arranged for the State Historical Society of Wisconsin at the Madison campus of the University of Wisconsin to archive the contents of the half-dozen black metal file cabinets in her spartan apartment. She wrote Nancy Palmer a note, asking her to send the eighteen cartons of her material on to the University if they got to be "too much." (Fourteen years later, Palmer did.)

Lutie, as usual, hand-washed Dickey's underthings. "How do you get them so sparkling white?" Dickey exclaimed in delight. When she hugged her aunt good-bye, Lutie later admitted to an inexplicable feeling that she would not see her niece again.

Although Dickey knew a lot of people and was a celebrity of sorts, there were few other than Stevie and Tony that she spent time with when she was in New York. She stopped over to see Tony and Kay, still living in the apartment on West End. Kay baked Dickey her favorite pineapple upside-down cake, took a look at Dickey's severe hairdo, and said, "You know, it wouldn't hurt you if you got some tail now and then." And then, like Helga before her, Kay left Dickey and Tony to talk privately.

The night before Dickey left for Chicago to begin her assignment, she called Stevie Blick in the middle of the night, waking her to cancel their lunch date for the next day. Stevie told Dickey to be sure to write her from Vietnam, because Stevie's nephew was still collecting foreign stamps. Stevie would not dare tell her she was getting too old to go chasing after patrols, and her advice to stay in New York and earn some real money had also fallen on deaf ears. What Stevie said was "I don't know why you have to go back there. You already said we weren't winning."

Dickey flew out of Chicago for San Diego on September 25, 1965, with a planeload of raw marine recruits. Most of them had never been in a plane. One told her, "Well, I guess when the marines say you'll see the world, this is what they mean." During the flight Dickey kept her tape recorder on, interviewing all the recruits. Most of them were drowsy now, but she was filled with energy and found herself looking out the window of the plane and remembering that first trip out to California twenty years earlier with the navy flight nurses.

"Bobby pins," she muttered into the tape cassette. "We were talking about the availability of bobby pins in the Pacific." Her voice was uncharacteristically slow and wistful. "We were also judging the looks of the officers. I do not think I have ever felt so precious and so special as I did then, as we all did then." She recalled the names of the nurses and noted that she should try to find them.

Marine Corps Air Station, El Toro, California. October 11, 1965. Looking out the window of the air terminal snack bar, Dickey watched the sandstorm being kicked up by the Santa Ana winds. The hot, howling gusts came swooping down from the inland southern California mountains. Typhoon strong, they had been known to pull up telephone poles and send cars sliding down ravines; often they were blamed for an increase in homicides.

She had arrived early that morning to see her recruits off for Vietnam and planned to follow within a few days. She had seen wartime good-byes for the battles of Iwo Jima and the Chosen reservoir from this same place, but this good-bye was "curiously different. . . . It is hard to realize how inexorably sentimentality has drained out of American manners—until you remember the open tears as troop ships pulled out past the Golden Gate Bridge during World War Two," she wrote in the *National Observer*, October 11, 1965.

She recalled how she thought the wartime tissue factories would go into overtime with all those tears. But not this time. "I did not see a young woman weep unashamedly. It was the men's mothers and mothers-in-law," she wrote. "The clinging embraces at dock or planeside, so vivid in my memory from other wars, just did not seem to happen." She had the sense that "their mutual emotion missed a deep note somewhere. . . .

"If you judged the 1965 fighting man by his words," she noted, "he had a job, not a mission." The woman searched the faces for signs, portents, clues. There were no songs or slogans. Would it be different when the men got to Vietnam and into their foxholes? Would the feeling of being part of something bigger than each of them fill their souls? She was depending on it. The C-130 Hercules transport plane squatted on the concrete apron of the El Toro air station, its side and fuselage doors open.

Inside the snack bar, marines were drinking coffee and banging the vending machines like cynical Las Vegas slot machine players. Cans of half-warm soup, their last stateside meals, came banging out of the metal slots. At one of the long rows of picnic tables, Dickey recorded a marine trying to auction off a small red phone book, bragging about the "action" it contained. There were no takers. Phone numbers of local girls didn't seem valuable en route to Vietnam. Another marine was bent over the barrel of his M-16, cleaning off the grit from the wind. Some of his buddies dozed, leaning against their rifles.

"If I could wrap you up and put you in my seabag, you know I would, honey," one of the marines said to his wife.

"You got a cigarette?" she asked. He handed her one from his pack. "I mean I need a pack," she said with sudden nervous irritation.

"Sure, honey." He handed over his pack.

The woman wore a summer dress with a green-and-blue pattern and red tennis shoes. Her friend, another marine wife, was wearing white spike high-heel shoes, a silk scarf around her head, and a red dress with an elasticized waistband. She wasn't saying much; mostly she just looked at her husband and bounced their sixteen-month-old baby daughter on her lap.

The baby, in a yellow knitted cap and yellow plastic panties, was restless and crying. "There, there," said the young mother.

The young father comforted the baby, then turned his head away. "She's going to be big when I get back," he said. He turned to his daughter. "Won't you, honey?"

Suddenly the PA system blared: the plane was ready for boarding. The men moved out, rifles slung over their shoulders. Dickey's gaze was drawn to the two women seeing off their men. The woman in the red tennis shoes stood up and brushed at her dress, put out her cigarette, and pursed her lips. She moved to the door of the snack bar, patting her hips and pulling down her dress. The woman with the baby followed. Dickey followed the women outside. She noticed a bright orange Huey helicopter parked at the end of the runway, the word *RESCUE* printed in big white letters across its nose. She smiled. "Deliverer of mercy," she muttered. "Whenever I see you where we're fighting, you give me so much comfort."

The last of the men boarded. The two women stood close together watching the plane, the wind lifting their skirts above their knees. The sound of the wind and engines grew deafening. The woman with the baby placed her hands over her daughter's ears. The side doors closed, then the door to the fuselage—reluctantly, it seemed to Dickey.

The two women stood, immobile, as the plane began its taxi. They were caught in the plane's jet stream, their figures shimmering and waving in the wind. Dickey thought the two women a much heartier breed than her generation. After the plane was airborne, they remained where they were, their faces riveted to the now blank spot in the concrete apron. The woman in the red tennis shoes was fighting tears. A tall marine sergeant approached, his twill khaki uniform starched for a dress parade. Placing a hand under her elbow, he escorted her and the other woman to a white 1963 Volkswagen parked outside the airfield's chain-link fence.

Dickey stood alone on the tarmac. The wind and grit scratched her face and crawled around her mouth.

When she arrived in Saigon in October 1965, the city was already bulging with two million inhabitants; the atmosphere was tense, set on edge with a brink-of-catastrophe feeling. Saigon was sinking under the weight of endless coups, a steady influx of peasants fleeing the warring countryside, and the loud American presence with its matériel, tanks, and bombers. One writer called it the "tinderbox of the world." If Dickey felt as though the curtain were finally rising, she said nothing of it to her dinner companion, Bernie Yoh, onetime adviser to President Diem and press contact for the village of Binh Hung. Bernie couldn't understand why she'd returned, why any of them had returned.

Bernie, who had left the country in 1962, had returned recently to work again on Ed Lansdale's team. Lansdale's theories of counterinsurgency—that the key lay in winning the hearts and minds of the Vietnamese people through examples of democracy—had been carried out using a small, dedicated staff of Americans who understood Asians and simultaneously backed up by CIA-sponsored covert operations, paramilitary raids, and psychological operations against the North Vietnamese and Vietminh; the program was supported enthusiastically by the Kennedy cold warriors. But by 1965 America's war no longer favored Lansdale's freewheeling missionary zeal, narrowing his command with bureaucrats from its military machine. When the Shanghai-born Yoh, a self-described "freedom fighter" and "old guerrilla businessperson," returned to Saigon, he took a quick look around and told his friend Lansdale, "There's no place here anymore for our kind of operation."

Bernie had last seen Dickey in New York, madly packing up her papers for Wisconsin. Now, in Saigon, he couldn't think of anything to say to her, which was unusual. But now he felt uneasy. "I had been a big shot there," he said years later. With Diem gone and many of his associates now in prison, Yoh took to sleeping with a loaded M-16 and kept his trousers, filled with grenades, next to his bed. Everywhere he looked he saw VC's.

Over their dinner of steak and beer, Bernie thought Dickey looked awful. They'd gone back to her tiny, dark room at the Rex, the hotel favored by American military officers. While he tried painfully to make conversation, she was preoccupied with her equipment, her cameras and lenses, and kept fussing with the recorder. Bernie wondered how she was going to move around with her three Leicas and the bulky four-pound tape recorder. Who was going to protect her on the patrols?

"The marines won't be able to protect you the way the Sea Swallows did," he pointed out. She left some of her luggage and her typewriter with Bernie, telling him she'd pick it up after she got off her marine patrols. Bernie recalled Dickey called him from Da Nang. "Usually she'd say, 'I can't wait to get to Saigon and some good food, these rations are terrible.' She didn't say it. I really don't know why she called."

Dickey arrived in the port city of Da Nang on October 19. The marines had made over a former French brothel—broken-down motel rooms set off from a muddy riverbank by concertina wire—into a press center. It was raining when Dickey walked into the correspondents' bar. Sam Stinson, a reporter from California, recalled she looked like a small, drowned rat. "She grabbed me and said, 'Sonny, would you get me a couple of beers?' "

Sam and Dickey spent the night talking and were later joined by two wire-service reporters, UPI's Joe Galloway and Bob Poos, working for AP. Galloway, then a cocky twenty-three-year-old, figured Dickey for fifty and wondered who would carry her pack and take responsibility for her on an operation. At first Sam was put off by her language, she sounded so much like a marine. But after a while he relaxed, realizing it was her way of putting him at ease. Much to Galloway's surprise, she explained she didn't want anyone fussing over her because she was a woman. The following day the chopper Sam and Dickey were in came under fire.

"Dickey just kept fiddling with her cameras and seemed very calm; she said, 'This might turn into something interesting yet.' " But the next day on ground operations, with artillery ringing all around them, he remembered her turning to him and asking "Oh, Sam, when is this all going to end?"

On October 23 Dickey set off for her first marine and ARVN (Army of the Republic of Vietnam) search-and-clear mission, Operation Red Snapper, twenty miles north of Da Nang, which lasted two days. In a dispatch she filed for the *National Observer* from Red Snapper, she wrote, "Like most Americans, I had often read that casual phrase *search and clear* with the mention that a few VC had been killed or captured and that U.S. casualties were light. Now I wanted to see what the words meant."

As far as she knew, Operation Red Snapper would be the first among mountains known to shelter Viet Cong. The outfit she chose, First Platoon of F (for Foxtrot) Company of the Second Battalion of the Third Marine Regiment, differed from several hundred such platoons in Vietnam only in its immediate assignment. It was farthest from the center of the line and would see the most action. And, she noted proudly, "They had never had a member of the press with them before, man or woman. . . .

"It was the flank outfit, the most exposed, the bait in the trap," she wrote. "I . . . wanted badly to understand just how the men on offensive patrols were doing their jobs . . . in suspected, if not outright, VC territory.

"So that night just after the sun went down . . . in faint starlight, with the final sunrise glow a purple stain beside rain clouds . . . as the sixteenth person in the line of fifty-one, I began the first combat patrol I had seen in Vietnam with American troops. We rise to our feet, slip packs on our shoulders, check our belts to be sure we have left nothing behind. I start to study intently the silhouettes of the man beside me and behind me, and of course the shadow of Sergeant Benz's helmeted head and laden shoulders. . . . I try to start to listen hard. For it is sound, not sight, that will reassure me in the darkness.

"We are on our way down through the elephant grass of the hill to a saddle from which the next hill—neither grass nor jungle, but balding black rock—looms over us.

"A minute before we were still separate individuals. Now as a night patrol on suspect earth, we are something more. It is an entity committed to steady movement across space. We cannot go quickly, and yet we have become inexorable as an organism on one course with one will. . . . As long as I can half see, half sense the sergeant in front of me, I walk in faith: if there are bogey men, they cannot frighten me in this company or in this place."

Although she'd come closer than ever to recapturing the feeling that had so long eluded her, Red Snapper was otherwise a disappointment, turning up only meager results. But she felt she was onto the elusive scent and was also hoping she'd see some action from the Viet Cong during the next mission, Black Ferret, scheduled for November 2. She was killed two days into that operation, one described in the official marine history as "disappointing." Its most noteworthy incident was the death of Dickey Chapelle, "who had covered marine operations since World War II." As a further result of that operation, one marine was killed and thirteen were wounded. Two Viet Cong were killed, six were captured, and seventy-nine suspects were taken into custody.

Epilogue

THE OFFICIAL marine intelligence on the death of Dickey Chapelle states in part, "She was evacuated to B Med at Chu Lai, where she died on or shortly after arrival without having spoken a word." From there her body was flown to Da Nang, where the press waited.

The dramatic death of Dickey Chapelle was made even more newsworthy by the fact that she was the first American woman reporter ever killed in action, as pointed out by her friend S. L. A. "Slam" Marshall in his obit in the *Los Angeles Times* on November 21, 1965. It hit the front page of *The New York Times* and papers across the world. The television news footage, shot seconds after the explosion, was flown back in time to make the local late news in the States. For a brief moment, television viewers all over America saw the intimate, brutal end of a woman many had never heard of.

That same evening in New York, the telephone rang in Tony Chapelle's battleship-gray apartment. Kay Chapelle answered. Somebody from the Overseas Press Club wanted to talk to Tony about a memorial service they were planning for Dickey. When Kay asked what they were talking about, a stranger told her Dickey had been killed earlier that day in Vietnam. Kay, who liked Dickey, hung up the phone and began to cry. She had read her autobiography, *What's a Woman Doing Here?*, at least three times.

Tony Chapelle and his night nurse at the New York University Hospital heard the news on Barry Farber's radio show. The nurse told him that as a little girl she'd wanted to be a daring war correspondent. When Kay telephoned, Tony said, "I know," and hung up. Kay recalled that Tony couldn't stand to lose things. "He was never the same after Dickey died. I feel like a part of him died, too."

Clancy Stone was shooting a Boy Scout Jamboree in northern Idaho when he heard Dickey was killed. He wasn't surprised at how it had happened. "You expect that," he said. "I think people who keep exposing themselves to danger and constant combat do have a death wish, whether they know it or not." He said he had never met a woman like Dickey, "of whom I can honestly say she thrived under fire." And he credited her as well for "turning me on to older women."

Malcolm Browne, the Pulitzer Prize–winning *New York Times* reporter, knew Dickey briefly in Cuba and in Saigon and raised some questions that others who knew Dickey certainly wondered about, particularly those who sensed she wouldn't be coming back. "I think that she . . . must have been getting sloppy, because generally speaking, you know, she'd been in combat enough to know, as we all know, that there are things that you do. . . . Never be the first person in line. Keep your eyes on the ground. Don't look at the next fellow's back."

It is doubtful that Dickey was getting sloppy or looking back. She was so aware of what she had to do on a patrol that it was by then an automatic reflex. It takes only a second, however, the split second of unrepentant fate—a fly buzzes close to the face, the hand and eye follow; a second for a feeling arriving, the one that envelops and blesses, the one that Dickey was hunting—when the nylon wire was tripped.

Dickey was cremated and brought back to Milwaukee on November 12 by an honor guard of six marines, one of whom, Staff Sergeant Albert P. Milville, had been tossed flat by the explosion and would be returning immediately to Vietnam. The honor guard was an extraordinary tribute for a civilian and a woman.

After a marine service ceremony at the First Unitarian Church in Milwaukee, Dickey was buried next to her parents at the Forest Home Cemetery. About ninety people were in attendance on that rainy day, including Lutie and Dickey's brother. Sergeant Robert Morrisey and a representative from *National Geographic* magazine had flown up on the same "white knuckle" flight from Washington, D.C. Decorating the gravesite were a bouquet of roses in the name of the Hungarian Freedom

Fighters and a single red rose wrapped in a white ribbon with one word: "Tony." Taps were sounded.

One month later paratroopers of the U.S. Army's Eighty-second Airborne Division staged a mass jump in honor of Dickey from helicopters over a drop zone about fifteen miles east of Santo Domingo in the Dominican Republic. She had jumped with them there earlier that year. The paratroopers named the drop zone "Dickey Chapelle." The *National Observer* announced that as a result of the "large volume" of letters received upon Dickey's death, they were preparing a booklet of her articles and photographs to be offered free to the public.

In tribute to her, students at the University of Wisconsin's Committee to Support the People of South Vietnam began collecting for CARE packages to be distributed by marines in Vietnam. West Coast contributors gave two thousand dollars in her name for CARE's school-building program in Vietnam. The project was endorsed by the governor of Wisconsin, seven out of ten members of the university's Board of Regents, the army, navy, air force, coast guard, and six thousand University of Wisconsin students who signed a petition supporting the drive. The petition was later presented to McGeorge Bundy, the head of President Johnson's National Security Council staff.

On December 12 the *Washington Post* reported that two boxcars loaded with Christmas gifts from local schoolchildren along with a dozen more from outlying areas would form the start of the Dickey Chapelle train, named for the woman correspondent killed recently in Vietnam. The train would travel across the country, picking up other boxcars along the way to San Francisco, where the gifts would be transported to Vietnam on Christmas Day. The honored guests at the departure of the Washington train were Vice President Hubert H. Humphrey; Vu Van Thai, ambassador of the Republic of Vietnam; and actor Raymond Burr.

ON NOVEMBER 4, 1966, Lewis Walt was an embattled lieutenant general facing what was fast becoming the army's war. The broadshouldered marine stood under a bright sun in a tiny South Vietnamese village near Chu Lai, to dedicate the Dickey Chapelle Memorial Dispensary. The H-shaped building of rough, unfinished lumber, built by the Ninth Marine Engineers, would contain forty-four beds. The funds had been donated by the relief agency CARE and Dickey's friends to benefit the Vietnamese in that area.

While the Third Marine Division Band played "Faith of Our Fathers" and "The Navy Hymn," Vietnamese children sang. The Vietnamese and American military stood quietly as the veteran World War II combat correspondent Jim Lucas of the Scripps-Howard News Syndicate remembered Dickey as "one hell of a girl" who refused to trade on her femininity to get her stories—and didn't need to. "She beat us to death. We couldn't keep up with her. We ceased to try."

Afterward, as a bugler played taps, General Walt and the Vietnamese province chief lifted a bedsheet covering a marble plaque set in a concrete flagpole base in front of the dispensary. The inscription read, "To the memory of Dickey Chapelle, war correspondent, killed in action near here on 4 November 1965. She was one of us and we will miss her." It was signed by the marine commandant, General Wallace M. Greene.

Walt said he did not know when the love affair between the Milwaukee-born woman and the marines had begun, or why. He recalled dinner with Dickey the year before. "When she left that night she told me she was going out on patrol the next day," Walt said. "I told her to be careful and to keep her head down."

Dickey had looked at Walt and said, "When my time comes, I want it to be on a patrol with the marines."

BIBLIOGRAPHY

Bailey, R. H. *The Home Front WW2*. New York: Time-Life Books, 1977.

Bernstein, Carl. "The C.I.A. & the Media." *Rolling Stone* (October 20, 1977).

Berry, Henry. *Semper Fi, Mac*. New York: Arbor House, 1982.

Bilstein, Roger E. *Flight in America 1900–1983*. Baltimore: Johns Hopkins University Press, 1984.

Bourne, Peter G. *Fidel, A Biography of Fidel Castro*. New York: Dodd, Mead & Company, 1986.

Boyle, Richard. *Flower of the Dragon*. San Francisco: Ramparts Press, 1972.

Boyne, Walter J. *Smithsonian Book of Flight*. Washington, D.C.: Smithsonian Books/Orion Books, 1987.

Brown, Anthony Cave. *Wild Bill Donovan/The Last Hero*. New York: Times Books, 1982.

Brown, David, and Richard W. Bruner. *How I Got That Story, Members of the Overseas Press Club*. New York: E. P. Dutton, 1967.

Browne, Malcolm. *The New Face of War*. Indianapolis: Bobbs-Merrill Co., 1965.

Casey, William. *The Secret War Against Hitler*. Chicago: Regency Gateway, 1968.

Chapelle, Dickey. "Bond of Remembrance." *Cosmopolitan* (December 1945).

———. "Borrowed Easter." *Reader's Digest* (April 1954).

———. "Cat Brown, Master of the Med." *Reader's Digest* (March 1958).

———. "Cuba—One Year After." *Reader's Digest* (January 1960).

———. "The Executioners." *Argosy* (October 1958).

———. *The Face of War, Vietnam*. North Hollywood: Milton Luros, 1965 (a one-shot magazine).

———. "The Fighting Priest of Vietnam." *Reader's Digest* (July 1963).

———. "Helicopter War in South Vietnam." *National Geographic* (November 1962).

———. "How Castro Won." *Marine Corps Gazette* (February 1960).

———. "How the Marine Boot Shapes Up Today." *National Observer* (October 4, 1965).

———. "I Roam the Edge of Freedom." *Coronet* (February 1961).

———. "Is News Controlled?" *National Photo Journalist* (1963).

———. "It's Mostly the Pros Who Say Farewell." *National Observer* (October 11, 1965).

———. "Leading Lady." *Life Story* (July 1945).

———. "Nobody Owes Me a Christmas." *Reader's Digest* (December 1957).

———. "Now I Know Why the Algerians Fight." *Pageant* (April 1958).

———. "On Okinawa, A Rehearsal for War." *National Observer* (November 1, 1965).

———. "The Quality of Mercy." *Reader's Digest* (October 1957).

———. "Remember the 16th of July." *Reader's Digest* (April 1959).

———. "Searching Vietnam for Victor Charlie." *National Observer* (November 8, 1965).

———. "There'll Be No Christmas for Them." *Saturday Evening Post* (December 26, 1953).

———. "Turkey: The Land Where Russia Stops." *Reader's Digest* (June 1958).

———. "The Untold Story of the Marines in Lebanon, Part One." *Argosy* (November 1958).

———. "War of Nerves: The Marines in Lebanon." *Argosy* (December 1958).

———. "Water War in Viet Nam." *National Geographic* (February 1966).

———. *What's a Woman Doing Here? (A Reporter's Report on Herself).* New York: William R. Morrow & Company, 1962.

———. "What's a Woman Doing Here?" (condensed from the book). *Reader's Digest* (February 1962).

———. "You Must Know You Have Become a Legend." *National Observer* (June 28, 1965).

———, and Richard D. Adler. "The Marine Who Fought for Castro." *Argosy* (November 1960).

———, and Tony Chapelle. "Locust Wars." *National Geographic* (April 1953).

———, and Tony Chapelle. "Village Life in India." *National Geographic* (April 1956).

Edwards, Julia. *Women of the World, The Great Foreign Correspondents.* Boston: Houghton Mifflin, 1988.

Ellis, Frederick, R. Master's thesis, "Dickey Chapelle: A Reporter & Her Work." University of Wisconsin, 1968.

Fall, Bernard B. *Street Without Joy.* Harrisburg, Pa.: Stackpole Books, 1961.

Federal Writers Project. *New York Panorama.* New York: Random House, 1938.

Field, Michael. *The Prevailing Wind: Witness in Indo-China.* Portsmouth, N.H.: Methuen, 1965.

FitzGerald, Frances. *Fire in the Lake.* New York: Vintage Books, 1973.

Hart, B.H. Liddell. *History of the Second World War.* New York: Putnam, 1971.

Hinckle, Warren, and William Turner. *The Fish Is Red, The Story of the Secret War Against Castro.* New York: Harper & Row, 1981.

Ienaga, Saburo. *The Pacific War: WWII & the Japanese 1931–1945.* New York: Pantheon, 1978.

Karnow, Stanley. *Vietnam: A History.* New York: Viking Press, 1983.

Knightley, Philip. *The First Casualty.* New York: Harcourt Brace Jovanovich, 1975.

Landis, Fred. "The CIA and *Reader's Digest.*" Covert Action Bulletin, no. 29 (Winter 1988).

Levenstein, Aaron. *Escape to Freedom (The Story of the International Rescue Committee).* Westport, Conn.: Greenwood Press, 1983.

Martin, Lionel. *The Early Fidel.* Sacancus, N.J.: Lyle Stuart, 1978.

Marton, Endre. *The Forbidden Sky, Inside the Hungarian Revolution.* Boston: Little, Brown, 1971.

McClintock, Robert. "The American Landing in Lebanon." *U.S. Naval Institute Proceedings* (October 1962).

Meyer, Dickey. *Girls at Work in Aviation.* New York: Doubleday, 1943.

———. *Needed: Women in Aviation.* New York: Robert McBride Company, 1942.

———. *Needed: Women in Government Service.* New York: Robert McBride Company, 1943.

Meyer, G. L. "Why We Want to Fly." *United States Air Service Magazine* (September 1933).

Michener, James A. *The Bridge at Andau.* New York: Fawcett Crest, 1957.

Moeller, Susan D. *Shooting War, Photography and the American Experience in Combat.* New York: Basic Books, 1989.

Morison, Samuel Eliot. *History of U.S. Naval Operations in WW II.* Vol. 14. Boston: Little, Brown, 1950.

Nevin, David. *The Pathfinders.* New York: Time-Life Books, 1980.

Nichols, David. *Ernie's War, Best of Ernie Pyle's WWII Dispatches.* New York: Random House, 1986.

O'Neel, Paul. *Barnstormers & Speed Kings.* New York: Time-Life Books, 1981.

Page, Tim. *Page After Page, Memoirs of a War-Torn Photographer.* New York: Atheneum, 1989.

Persico, Joseph E. *Casey.* New York: Viking, 1990.

Powers, Thomas. *The Man Who Kept the Secrets (Richard Helms & the CIA).* New York: Alfred A. Knopf, 1987.

Ranelagh, John. *The Agency, The Rise & Decline of the CIA.* New York: Simon & Schuster, 1986.

Reader's Digest Illustrated History of World War II. Pleasantville, N.Y.: Reader's Digest Association, 1978.

Ritchin, Fred. "The Photography of Conflict." *Aperture* (Winter 1984).

Robbins, Christopher. *The Ravens, The Men Who Flew in America's Secret War in Laos.* New York: Crown Publishers, 1987.

Schreiner, Samuel A. *The Condensed World of the Reader's Digest.* New York: Stein and Day, 1977.

Sheehan, Neil. *A Bright Shining Lie.* New York: Random House, 1988.

Shulimson, Jack, and Major Charles M. Johnson. *U.S. Marines in Vietnam, the Landing and the Buildup, 1965.* Washington: USMC History and Museums Division, U.S. Marine Corps, 1978.

Simpson, Christopher. *Blowback.* New York: Weidenfeld & Nicolson, 1988.

Smith, General Holland M., USMC (ret.), and Percy Finch. *Coral & Brass, "Howlin' Mad" Smith's Own Story of the Marines in the Pacific.* New York: Charles Scribner's Sons, 1949.

Sulzberger, C. L. *American Heritage Picture History of WWII.* New York: Simon & Schuster, 1966.

Szulc, Tad. *Fidel: A Critical Portrait.* New York: William Morrow & Company, 1986.

Tallman, Frank. *Flying the Old Planes.* New York: Doubleday & Company, 1973.

Time-Life Books. *This Fabulous Century, 1930–1940.* New York: Time-Life Books, 1969.

———. *World War II.* New York: Time-Life Books, 1989.

Tuchman, Barbara W. *The March of Folly: From Troy to Vietnam.* New York: Alfred A. Knopf, 1984.

Weisberger, Bernard A. *Cold War, Cold Peace, The United States and Russia Since 1945.* Boston: Houghton Mifflin, 1984.

Wheeler, Keith. *The Road to Tokyo, WWII.* New York: Time-Life Books, 1979.

Wood, James Playsted. *Of Lasting Interest (The Story of the Reader's Digest)*. New York: Doubleday, 1958.
Yergin, Daniel. *Shattered Peace*. Boston: Houghton Mifflin, 1977.

PERIODICALS

Aperture
Life
National Geographic
Newsweek
Time
U.S. News & World Report
The New York Times
New Yorker
Milwaukee Journal
The National Observer
The Overseas Press Bulletin
Reader's Digest

INDEX

About the Author

Roberta Ostroff is an award-winning journalist and screenwriter who has written for *USA Today, US News & World Report, Rolling Stone, Geo,* and the *Los Angeles Times.* She lives in Altadena, California.